# Human Resource Management for the Hospitality and Tourism Industries

*Human Resource Management for the Hospitality and Tourism Industries, Second Edition*, takes an integrated look at human resource management (HRM) policies and practices in the tourism and hospitality industries. Utilizing existing HRM theory and practice, it contextualizes it to the tourism and hospitality industries by looking at the specific employment practices of these industries, such as how to manage tour reps or working in the airline industry.

It initially sets the scene with a broad review of the evidence of HRM practice within the tourism and hospitality industries. Having identified the broader picture, the text then begins to focus much more explicitly on a variety of HR policies and practices such as: recruitment and selection, legislation and equal opportunities, staff health and welfare, and remuneration strategies in the industry.

This second edition has been fully updated with:

- new legal information, data, statistics and examples;
- a new chapter looking at HRM policies and practices in events;
- new international examples of best practice for prescriptive teaching and discussion, and international case studies to exercise problem-solving techniques and contextualize learning;
- an enhanced Companion Website for students and lecturers, including: PowerPoint slides, a student test bank, additional case studies and links to additional resources.

Written in a user-friendly style, each chapter includes: a chapter outline and objectives, HRM in practice, boxed examples, reflective review questions, web links, discussion questions and further reading to aid understanding and test knowledge.

**Dennis Nickson** is Head of the Department of Human Resource Management, University of Strathclyde, UK.

## Companion website

A companion website accompanies this book at www.routledge.com/cw/nickson and includes additional resources for both students and lecturers.

**Student Resources**

- Chapter commentaries.

- A test bank of multiple choice questions for each chapter for students to test their understanding.

**Lecturer Resources**

- PowerPoint slides with chapter outlines and tables, line figures and photographs from the book.

- Additional case studies to provide further examples of theory in practice.

# Human Resource Management for the Hospitality and Tourism Industries

## Second edition

## Dennis Nickson

Lanchester Library

WITHDRAWN

Routledge
Taylor & Francis Group

LONDON AND NEW YORK

First published 2007
by Elsevier

This edition published 2013
by Routledge
2 Park Square, Milton Park, Abingdon, Oxon OX14 4RN

Simultaneously published in the USA and Canada
by Routledge
711 Third Avenue, New York, NY 10017

*Routledge is an imprint of the Taylor & Francis Group, an informa business*

© 2007, 2013 Dennis Nickson

The right of Dennis Nickson to be identified as author of this work has
been asserted by him in accordance with sections 77 and 78 of the
Copyright, Designs and Patents Act 1988.

All rights reserved. No part of this book may be reprinted or
reproduced or utilized in any form or by any electronic, mechanical,
or other means, now known or hereafter invented, including photocopying
and recording, or in any information storage or retrieval system,
without permission in writing from the publishers.

*Trademark notice*: Product or corporate names may be trademarks
or registered trademarks, and are used only for identification
and explanation without intent to infringe.

*British Library Cataloguing in Publication Data*
A catalogue record for this book is available from the British Library

*Library of Congress Cataloging in Publication Data*
Nickson, Dennis.
   Human resource management for the hospitality and tourism
   industries/Dennis Nickson. – 2nd ed.
   p. cm.
   Includes bibliographical references and index.
   1. Hospitality industry – Personnel management.   2. Tourism –
   Personnel management.   I. Title.
   TX911.3.P4N53 2012
   647.94068'3 – dc23
   2012019466


ISBN: 978-0-415-64211-8 (hbk)
ISBN: 978-0-08-096648-9 (pbk)
ISBN: 978-0-08-096649-6 (ebk)


Typeset in Helvetica
by Florence Production Ltd, Stoodleigh, Devon

MIX
Paper from
responsible sources
FSC® C004839

Printed and bound in Great Britain by Bell & Bain Ltd., Glasgow

# Contents

# Illustrations

## Figures

## Tables

# Preface

This book stems from a longstanding interest in how tourism and hospitality organizations and managers seek to manage their employees. As a highly labour-intensive industry, tourism and hospitality organizations are often heard to talk of how their people are 'their greatest asset'. However, even a cursory understanding of the nature of work, employment and people management in tourism and hospitality points to the many paradoxes and contradictions that are apparent in studying human resource management (HRM) in the sector. This book seeks to explore some of these paradoxes and contradictions in seeking to submit the cliché of 'our people are our greatest asset' to critical scrutiny. That said, the book is in many respects a standard HRM text for the tourism and hospitality sector, recognizably following the traditional concerns of organizations as to how they best attract, maintain and develop an effective workforce.

In talking about tourism and hospitality the book is also aware of the many debates about how the sector is best conceptualized. There are many common attributes that are associated with both hospitality and tourism activities, which could encourage them to be seen synonymously. Equally, though, some would argue for distinctiveness between the two. Like most colleagues writing in this area the book acknowledges these debates, while also at times rather fudging the distinction between tourism and hospitality. That said, for this edition of the book there is greater consideration of the events industry as a related, but distinct, area of tourism and hospitality. The rationale for including the events industry is in part a pragmatic one; increasingly others are making the distinction between events and other allied tourism and hospitality activities so there is a need to consider this issue in further detail in this edition of the book. Additionally, the chapter on events allows for a consideration of the particular challenges of managing volunteers – something that is distinct about the events industry. Thus the new chapter, while considering some aspects of paid employment in events, is predominantly focused on the management of volunteers and I think brings forward lots of new and interesting issues.

Ultimately, debates are set to continue among the academic community about how best to situate events, tourism, hospitality, leisure, travel and, increasingly, passenger transport in discussing employment in these areas. However, regardless of how boundaries or overlaps between these activities are portrayed, it is important not to lose sight of the one thing that is clearly paramount in all organizations operating in these areas: the need to deliver service to customers and the need to manage people in such a way that they offer a quality service. The manner in which organizations in different countries, cultures and market niches address this issue may vary enormously, and this difference sustains many of the concerns outlined in the book.

In attempting to understand the importance of context to explain HRM practices, the book also aims to be international in its focus and its use of sources and examples. Thus, while the primary focus of the book is the UK, there are numerous examples from a variety of other countries across the world. The same point is also true in terms of examples of organizational practice. A number of examples are drawn from what is usually described as the commercial hospitality sector, which is well served by research. Many of those activities which are more oriented towards travel and tourism are also represented, though material of this nature is not quite so voluminous. A further aspect of context is the need to understand the dynamic and changing environment in which tourism and hospitality organizations operate. Political, economic, social and technological changes significantly affect tourism and hospitality organizations and the experience of work for those people who are employed in the sector; and the book is cognizant of this point throughout. This dynamism is also apparent with regard to emergent debates about new concepts which allow for an appreciation of the changing nature of the employment experience of the tourism and hospitality workforce. For example, work I have done with colleagues on aesthetic labour – how employees embody the tourism and hospitality product by 'looking good' or 'sounding right' – points to the manner in which organizations increasingly take an interest in their employees' appearance as a source of competitive advantage. This book is designed to provoke thought and debate about aesthetic labour and a myriad of other issues and encourage the readership to challenge its conclusions and stimulate further reading and research.

As has already been stated, this book is the culmination of a longstanding interest in the area of tourism and hospitality employment, both as a teacher and researcher. In that sense it is also an opportunity to draw on many of the ideas and writings of innumerable students and colleagues who have influenced my thinking. In particular, I have enjoyed sharing debates and running ideas on a regular basis past Tom Baum, who is now a colleague in the Department of Human Resource Management at Strathclyde. As I acknowledged in the first edition, once again I would very much like to recognize a huge debt to the work of Yvonne Guerrier, Rosemary Lucas and Roy Wood. Over the years they have given freely of their time, advice and ideas and shaped many of the ideas

expressed in this book. I hope this updated version of the book can continue to take its place alongside the work of my illustrious colleagues in encouraging students and practitioners to think about how to improve the working lives of the many who rely on tourism and hospitality for their employment.

# Acknowledgements

First and foremost, I would like to thank my wife, Susan, for always being there for me and for making sure that I never lose sight of what's important in life. I'd also like to thank Carol Barber at Taylor & Francis for her encouragement in completing this revised edition.

# Abbreviations

| | |
|---|---|
| ACAS | Advisory, Conciliation and Arbitration Service |
| AIDS | acquired immune deficiency syndrome |
| BA | British Airways |
| BALPA | British Airline Pilots Association |
| BAME | black, Asian and minority ethnic |
| BARS | behaviourally anchored rating scales |
| BHA | British Hospitality Association |
| CBI | Confederation of British Industry |
| CIPD | Chartered Institute of Personnel and Development |
| CRE | Commission for Racial Equality |
| DMTI | diversity management training initiative |
| DRC | Disability Rights Commission |
| EAP | employee assistance programme |
| EAPA | Employee Assistance Professionals Association |
| ECJ | European Court of Justice |
| EFILWC | European Foundation for the Improvement of Living and Working Conditions |
| EHRC | Equality and Human Rights Commission |
| EIRO | European Industrial Relations Observatory |
| EOC | Equal Opportunities Commission |
| EPWN | European Professional Women's Network |
| ERA | Employment Relations Act |
| ET | employment tribunal |
| EU | European Union |
| EWC | European works council |
| FDI | foreign direct investment |
| GOR | Genuine Occupational Requirement |
| HASWA | Health and Safety at Work Act |
| HCIMA | Hotel and Catering International Management Association |
| HCN | host-country national |

| | |
|---|---|
| HCTS | hotel, catering and tourism sector |
| HIV | human immunodeficiency virus |
| HR | human resource |
| HRD | human resource development |
| HRM | human resource management |
| HSE | Health and Safety Executive |
| ICE | Information and Consultation of Employees Regulations 2004 (ICE Regulations) |
| IDS | Income Data Services |
| IHRM | international human resource management |
| IiP | Investors in People |
| ILO | International Labour Organization |
| IMD | international management development |
| IRS | Industrial Relations Services |
| JCC | joint consultative committee |
| JRF | Joseph Rowntree Foundation |
| LEP | local employment partnership |
| LPC | Low Pay Commission |
| LRD | Labour Research Department |
| MAC | Migration Advisory Committee |
| MBA | Master in Business Administration |
| MBO | management by objective |
| MNC | multinational company |
| NMW | national minimum wage |
| N/SVQ | National/Scottish Vocational Qualification |
| NTO | national training organization |
| NWDA | North West Development Agency |
| PCN | parent-country national |
| PGVP | Post Games Volunteer Project |
| PMS | performance management systems |
| QC | quality circle |
| RfO | Race for Opportunity |
| RTC | Red Tape Challenge |
| SHRM | Society for Human Resource Management |
| SME | small- and medium-sized enterprise |
| SSC | sector skills council |
| TCN | third-country national |
| TFA | Tourism for All UK |
| TGWU | Transport and General Workers Union |
| TQM | total quality management |
| TUC | Trades Union Congress |
| UKCES | UK Commission for Employment and Skills |
| UN | United Nations |
| VET | vocational education and training |

| WERS | Workplace Employment Relations Survey |
| WTR | Working Time Regulations |
| WTTC | World Travel and Tourism Council |

# Human resource management and the tourism and hospitality industry: an introduction

COMPANION @ WEBSITE

## CHAPTER OBJECTIVES

**This chapter sets the scene for the book. It considers the nature of the tourism and hospitality industry and some of the approaches to managing people adopted by organizations and how these approaches can vary. Therefore the aims of this chapter are:**

- To recognize the importance of tourism and hospitality as an employment sector.

- To outline the diverse range of sub-sectors and occupations under the broad heading of tourism and hospitality.

- To consider the nature of the workforce.

- To review the range of models/theories concerned with human resource management and how these might be applied to the tourism and hospitality sector.

## Introduction

The importance of tourism and hospitality employment in both developed and developing countries is attested to by the World Travel and Tourism Council (WTTC), who suggest that travel- and tourism-related activities account for 8.7 per cent of world employment, sustaining directly or indirectly over 255 million jobs, which equates to one in 12 jobs worldwide (World Travel and Tourism Council, 2012). However, while the quantity of jobs is unquestionable, the *quality* of many of these jobs is of great concern to academics and policy-makers alike. Despite the rhetoric of policy-makers and business leaders that people are the industry's most important asset, many remain unconvinced that such a view is borne out by empirical evidence. For example, Douglas Coupland, the notable cultural commentator, has for many captured the *zeitgeist* when he talks pejoratively of 'McJob', which he describes as 'A low-pay, low-prestige, low-dignity, low-benefit, no-future job in the service sector. Frequently considered a satisfying career choice by people who have never held one' (Coupland, 1993: 5; see also Lindsay and McQuaid, 2004). MacDonald and Sirianni (1996) recognize the challenges of living and working in a service society which, according to them, is characterized by two kinds of service jobs: large numbers of low-skill, low-pay jobs, and a smaller number of high-skill, high-income jobs, with few jobs being in the middle of these two extremes. Such a situation leads labour analysts to ask what kinds of jobs are being produced and who is filling them. This point is also true for the tourism and hospitality industry and it is important at the outset of this book to add a caveat about the generalizability (or otherwise) of the conditions of tourism and hospitality employment worldwide. Hence Baum (1995: 151; see also Baum, 2007), reflecting the diversity of employment within the sector, notes that:

> In some geographical and sub-sector areas, tourism and hospitality provides an attractive, high-status working environment with competitive pay and conditions, which is in high demand in the labour force and benefits from low staff turnover. . . . The other side of the coin is one of poor conditions, low pay, high staff turnover, problems in recruiting skills in a number of key areas, a high level of labour drawn from socially disadvantaged groups, poor status and the virtual absence of professionalism.

Organizations and managers in the tourism and hospitality industry face real challenges in recruiting, developing and maintaining a committed, competent, well-managed and well-motivated workforce which is focused on offering a high-quality 'product' to the increasingly demanding and discerning customer. This book seeks to address some of the key human resource issues that have to be tackled in order that organizations can maintain such an environment. To do so it will critically review some of the problems which lead many to characterize tourism and hospitality employment as generally unrewarding and unappealing, while also considering examples of good practice, important policy responses and models of human resource management (HRM) which may offer cause for greater optimism in the way people are managed within the tourism and hospitality industries.

## What are the tourism and hospitality industries?

Many academics, industrialists and policy-makers have attempted to define the nature of the tourism industry – and the place of the hospitality sub-sector within this broader conceptualization – yet there is still no single commonly

accepted definition. Hence, there are inherent problems seeking to define what is a large and diverse sector, which means many of the activities may overlap, and could be described as encompassing tourism and hospitality. For example, Lucas (2004), in her work on employment relations in the hospitality and tourism industries, chose to talk in broad terms about the hotel, catering and tourism sector (HCTS). This characterization of the HCTS recognizes that, in reality, many jobs in hospitality and tourism 'share common attributes and are associated with both hospitality and tourism activities' (p. 4). Clearly, then, we should recognize the potential for a lack of precision in describing the tourism and hospitality industries.

In an attempt to avoid too much imprecision and, at the same time, capture the diversity of the sector, this book uses the framework offered by People 1st, which is the sector skills council (SSC) for the hospitality, leisure, travel and tourism sector, to exemplify the broad range of activities that may be seen in the HCTS. The reason for using People 1st is that SSCs are government-licensed bodies in the UK responsible for improving skills within the industry. SSCs are employer-led and, among other things, aim to engage employers in raising the skills of a defined industry sector, supporting efficiency and productivity improvements and helping to ensure that the sectors remain globally competitive (see Chapter 7 for the role of People 1st in improving skills and training in hospitality, leisure, travel and tourism). Therefore, People 1st suggest that the sector as a whole is made up of 14 sub-sectors (People 1st, 2010a):

- hotels
- restaurants
- pubs, bars and night-clubs
- contract food service providers
- membership clubs
- events
- gambling
- travel services
- tourist services
- visitor attractions
- youth hostels
- holiday parks
- self-catering accommodation
- hospitality services.

That said, it should also be noted that at the time of writing, People 1st are currently in the process of integrating the passenger transport industries following their merger in July 2011 with GoSkills, the SSC for the passenger transport industries. The merger with GoSkills will create a unified body for hospitality, passenger transport, travel and tourism (People 1st, 2011a).

The key point remains that in the broad classification of travel, tourism and hospitality there is massive diversity in the types of jobs generated, in relation to their technical and skill demands, educational requirements, terms and conditions and the type of person that is likely to be attracted to employment in them. To illustrate this point we can consider Baum's (1997: 97–8) description of the range of people a person buying a package holiday is likely to interact with:

- the retail travel agent;
- insurance companies;
- ground transport to and from the airport;
- at least two sets of airport handling agents (outbound and return);
- airport services (shops, food and beverage outlets, bureaux de change) (outbound and return);
- the airline on all legs of the journey;
- immigration and customs services;
- local ground transportation;
- the hotel or apartment;
- tour services at the destination;
- companies and individuals selling a diversity of goods and services at the destination (retail, food and beverage, entertainment, cultural and heritage, financial, etc.);
- emergency services at the destination (medical, police, legal); and
- service providers on return (photography processing, medical).

Baum characterizes all of these possible intermediaries, and the interactions they will have with the holiday maker, as crucial in 'making or breaking the tourist experience'. Thus while the physical product is important, for most tourists the quality of their experience is likely to be also reliant to a large degree on the interactions they will have with the variety of front-line staff in the travel, tourism and hospitality industry. These so-called 'moments of truth' (Carlzon, 1987) are therefore crucial for organizational effectiveness, success, competitiveness and profitability. Indeed, within an industry that is characterized by diversity and heterogeneity in terms of the purpose, size, ownership and demands of the enterprise, the only real point of homogeneity is delivering service to customers and the need to manage people in such a way that they offer a quality service. The corollary of this point would be the belief that such front-line staff would therefore be sufficiently well paid, trained and motivated to offer outstanding service. The reality, however, is that often such staff have the lowest status in the organization, are the least trained and are the most poorly paid employees of the company.

In recognizing the diversity both of the range of sub-sectors and types of jobs they are likely to generate, this book cannot consider all of these aspects in detail. Indeed, more is known about employment in certain sub-sectors than others. For example, the commercial hospitality industry encompassing hotels, restaurants and pubs, bars and night-clubs is the largest sub-sector, with around 70 per cent of employees in the UK (People 1st, 2010a). Unsurprisingly,

then, the commercial hospitality industry is well served, with extensive research on the nature of employment and HRM practices in the UK, Europe and elsewhere in the world (see, for example, Chand and Katou, 2007; D'Annunzio-Green et al., 2002; European Foundation for the Improvement of Living and Working Conditions, 2012; Knox and Walsh, 2005; Lucas, 2004; Poulston, 2009). As a consequence, many of the examples drawn on in this book are from the commercial hospitality industry. However, the book also draws on the wider array of travel- and tourism-related organizations. In addition, Chapter 13 is given over to considering the events sub-sector and, in particular, the challenges of managing a large volunteer workforce who work alongside paid employees in the events sub-sector. The greater concentration on the events sub-sector in this edition of the book reflects the growing importance of events as an increasingly discrete though related sector to tourism and hospitality (see, for example, Baum et al., 2009a; Bowdin et al., 2010; Van der Wagen, 2007). Ultimately, the main aim of the book is to attempt to understand the potentially diverse employment experiences of those working in what we will broadly think of as the tourism and hospitality industries. Thus, how does the experience of an airline flight attendant differ from that of a pot washer in the kitchen in a small restaurant to a receptionist at the front desk of an international hotel or to a tour rep working on an 18–30-type holiday?

A further issue to consider is the manner in which the sector is heterogeneous in terms of the predominance of small- and medium-sized enterprises (SMEs). People 1st (2010a) note that within the UK hospitality, leisure, travel and tourism sector 73.5 per cent of establishments are SMEs, while also noting that 26.2 per cent are owner-operated with no staff. Heterogeneity is also seen in relation to the way that organizations adopt differing routes to competitive advantage, depending on which type of market they operate in. For example, full service carriers in the airline industry are likely to have very different approaches to HRM compared to low-cost airlines (Eaton, 2001; Spiess and Waring, 2005; however, see 'HRM in Practice 1.1'). The same is true for the hospitality sector, which may range from first-class and luxury hotels providing extravagant, full 24-hour service to the more homely comforts of a bed and breakfast establishment; from fast-food restaurants to Michelin-starred restaurants. In turn, the jobs provided by these various organizations demand a variety of skills and attributes from those employees interacting with customers, which again will impact on human resource (HR) strategies such as recruitment and selection and training.

## Who makes up the tourism and hospitality workforce? A brief snapshot

The International Labour Organization (ILO) (2001), in their wide-ranging report on the global tourism and hospitality industry, provide evidence that suggests that the industry globally is largely reliant on what Wood (1997a) has described as so-called 'marginal workers', such as women, young workers, casual employees, students, relatively high numbers of part-timers and migrant workers. For example, within the UK women make up 58 per cent of the broader hospitality, leisure, travel and tourism workforce (People 1st, 2010a). Significantly, though, there is often gender segregation within occupations, with 63 per cent of chefs being men and 79 per cent of travel agents being women, for example. Of the overall hospitality, leisure, travel and tourism workforce nearly half are employed on a part-time basis, and again there are significant gender differences, with 72 per cent of women working on a part-time basis compared to 28 per cent of men. Young people are also prominent within the hospitality, leisure, travel and tourism sector. For example, 15 per cent of the workforce is aged between 16 and 19, over one-third (34 per cent) between 20 and 29; in total 45 per cent of the workforce are under 30. Only 13 per cent of the workforce are aged between 50 and 59 and only 6 per cent are over the age of 60 (People 1st, 2010a). Related to this last point, a significant part of the tourism and hospitality workforce consists of students, who are an increasingly important segment of the labour market for hospitality and tourism organizations (International Labour Organization, 2001). They are prepared to work for low wages and be flexible in their working patterns (Canny, 2002), creating what Curtis and Lucas (2001) describe as a 'coincidence of needs' between employers and students. Thus, nearly three-quarters of all students who are working are employed in the retail and hospitality industries and the vast majority of students who are working do so in front-line jobs such as sales assistants, waiters/waitresses and check-out operators (Canny, 2002; Curtis and Lucas, 2001). The number of ethnic minority workers in the sector is 14 per cent, which is higher than the economy as a whole (9 per cent) (People 1st, 2010a). A further and increasingly important segment of the labour market is migrant labour. One-fifth of the workforce were born overseas, and in recent years the expansion of the European Union (EU) in 2004, in particular, has led to an influx of Eastern European workers into the sector (particularly the hospitality industry) (Lucas and Mansfield, 2010; also see Chapter 4).

## Review and reflect

If you are currently working in the tourism and hospitality industry while completing your studies, list what you consider to be good and bad aspects of your job and your reasons for this.

Having briefly considered the nature of the hospitality and tourism industry and the characteristics of its workforce, attention now turns to understanding HRM and the increasingly important role it is considered to play in organizational success.

## What is HRM?

## Definitions of HRM

There have been many attempts to define what exactly HRM might be, and indeed Heery and Noon (2008) recognize that it is a subject of considerable academic analysis and that, ultimately, 'there is no common agreement on what HRM means' (p. 214). Resultantly, they offer ten definitions, which they feel capture the complexity and dynamism of HRM as a subject of academic study:

1  *A label* – HRM is seen as simply being another name for personnel management and there is nothing distinct or special about HRM.
2  *A convenient shorthand term* that allows for the grouping together of a whole series of sub-disciplines that are broadly concerned with people management, such as employee relations, industrial/labour relations, personnel management and organizational behaviour.
3  *A map* to help guide students and practitioners to understand the concept and ideas associated with the management of people.
4  *A set of professional practices* – this view suggests that there is a range of personnel practices that can be integrated to ensure a professional approach to managing people. In this view a potentially key role is likely to be played by the Chartered Institute of Personnel and Development (CIPD), which is the professional association for those entering the HR and personnel profession.
5  *A method of ensuring internal fit* – again, this view sees the need to coordinate approaches to people management, but here the coordination needs to be with other areas of the organization. This view of HRM also envisages a greater involvement from all managers, from corporate executives through to line managers in dealing with HR issues.
6  *A method of ensuring external fit*, where HRM activities have to be fully integrated with the demands of the external environment. Consequently there has to be a fit between the external environment and the business strategy of the organization, of which HRM is considered a vital aspect.
7  *A competitive advantage*, where HRM is the means by which an organization can gain competitive advantage – this is a view best captured by the cliché of 'our people are our greatest asset'.
8  *A market-driven approach* – the main point of such an approach is that decisions will often be market-driven and the needs of the business determine the manner in which employees are treated: some may be treated well, others less well.
9  *A manipulative device* – this critical view of HRM sees it as an inherently exploitative and manipulative practice and merely a tool of the exploitative nature of capitalism.

10 *A hologram* – this view of HRM captures much of the above discussion in recognizing the fluid identity of HRM and the way it has multiple meanings, thus defying precise definition.

Clearly, what the above discussion points to is that HRM means many things to many people, depending on whether you are a manager, an employee or an academic, and there is no single definition that will adequately capture the potential complexity of the topic.

## Review and reflect

Which definition do you find most persuasive and why?

That said, for the purposes of this book we will recognize HRM as being broadly about how organizations seek to manage their employees in the pursuit of organizational success. Reflecting this point the book utilizes the concise definition offered by Storey (1995: 5). Thus, HRM 'is a distinctive approach to employment management which seeks to achieve competitive advantage through the strategic deployment of a highly committed and capable workforce, using an integrated array of cultural, structural and personnel techniques'. The challenge of HRM, then, would seem to be how to recruit, deploy, develop, reward and motivate staff, leading to them being a source of competitive advantage. As the above discussion suggests, however, there is more than one route to seeking competitive advantage and this point is further considered in examining the notion of 'hard' and 'soft' HRM.

## Hard and soft HRM

As well as providing the concise definition utilized above, Storey (1987) also provided one of the earliest and most enduring attempts to recognize different approaches to HRM. These different approaches are captured by the idea of hard and soft HRM, each of which is now briefly described. The *hard* version is seen to be an instrumental and economically rational approach to HRM. In this view people-management strategies are driven by strategic considerations to gain competitive advantage, maximizing control while achieving the lowest possible labour cost. This approach is quantitative and calculative, and labour is a commodity/resource, the same as any other. The focus is on the *resource management* aspects of HRM. On the other hand, the *soft* version is seen to be much more about adopting a humanistic and developmental approach to HRM. As a result, an organization's people-management approach is likely to be more consensual and based on a high level of managerial commitment to employees, which is intended to lead to mutual high commitment from

employees, high trust, high productivity and so on. Employees are seen as being proactive, capable of being developed and worthy of trust and collaboration. This approach focuses on the *human* aspects of HRM.

---

### Review and reflect

Reflecting on your answers from the first review and reflect question, to what extent do the good and bad aspects you listed equate to hard or soft aspects of HRM?

---

What hard and soft approaches to HRM point to is that employers will vary their people-management strategies. Of course, critics may also suggest that the hard/soft dichotomy remains too blunt and does not take into account the manner in which organizations may be engaging in both hard and soft HRM approaches simultaneously for different groups of employees. HRM in Practice 1.1 offers an example of how there can also be differences in approach in broadly similar market segments where it might be imagined that approaches are likely to be similar.

---

**HRM IN PRACTICE 1.1:**
## Contrasting approaches for pursuing a low-cost business strategy in the airline industry

Companies have choices in the approaches they develop in competing on the basis of low cost. Within the airline industry, recent years have seen a number of businesses competing on the basis of cost. Two contrasting models have been identified, which offer different approaches to competing on cost. In the 'Southwest model' the approach is characterized by enhancing employee commitment and working in partnership with trade unions. On the other hand, the 'Ryanair model' is much more about controlling employees and avoiding trade unions. Each of these approaches creates a distinctive set of HRM practices.

Southwest Airlines aim to build shared goals, knowledge and mutual respect based on the idea of relational competence, which allows employees to work with colleagues and customers in a positive manner. Recruitment and selection, training and development and job design are all geared to first identifying and then further developing these attributes. Other notable features of their approach include a strong commitment to work–family balance and a clear commitment to job security for employees. As part of this approach to employment security, Southwest Airlines work in partnership with the trade unions and, despite the major economic challenges facing the airline industry engendered by the Gulf War crisis in the early 1990s, 9/11 and a huge rise in fuel costs in 2008, the company has been able to avoid layoffs. The Southwest approach sees employees as partners in reducing costs and producing value and not as a cost to be minimized.

Ryanair, on the other hand, has developed a much more adversarial approach based on controlling employees. The company has an active approach to resisting trade unions, facing challenges from its employees that it engages in victimization and harassment, which led to a court ruling that the company had acted in an intimidating manner in refusing to work with the trade unions. Ultimately, the company is characterized as following a low-road model with little attention to HRM concepts.

Derived from Gittell and Bamber (2010)

Clearly, there are likely to be a number of external influences that impact on HRM policies and practices. These external influences will reflect a variety of political, economic, social and technological aspects. Consequently, in response to the changing environment in which organizations are operating, they may in turn vary their approaches to HRM to take account of external influences. Consequently, these variations in hard and soft approaches are likely to have differing impacts on employees, as HRM in Practice 1.2 outlines.

## HRM IN PRACTICE 1.2:
## Hard and soft approaches to HRM in the airline industry

The tourism and hospitality industry is particularly sensitive to economic cycles and political trouble and can be badly affected in times of uncertainty. For example, the global nature of the industry means that it is vulnerable to external events that cause fluctuations in tourist visits and spending. The global 2001–4 economic downturn, 9/11, the Iraq War and the outbreak of SARS in the Far East all led to a drop in revenue in the industry. These factors reduced the number of travellers internationally and left uncertainty and fragility in the tourism market. Many of these aspects are particularly pronounced in the airline industry, and trade unions have often railed against the manner in which employees are used as 'shock absorbers' to protect the industry from the cyclical nature of the market. These hard approaches to HRM led to major redundancy programmes in a number of airlines, especially after 9/11. On the other hand, a number of companies sought a softer approach to HRM, which aimed at increasing the customer responsiveness of their front-line staff. British Airways (BA), for example,

had a series of initiatives in the 1980s and 1990s, such as 'Putting People First' and 'Winning for Customers'. Among other things these initiatives sought to introduce team-working, extensive training programmes, enhance quality procedures and multi-skilled staff. As companies alternate between hard and soft approaches to HRM, employees may become confused as to what the company message is. Ultimately, employees may well be a company's 'greatest asset', but in times of uncertainty and downturn are equally expendable, as recent history shows.

Derived from Grugulis and Wilkinson (2002); International Transport Workers Federation (2004)

Indeed, more recently the economic crisis which began in 2008 had a particular impact on the tourism and hospitality sector, and as a consequence the decline of economic activity led to cuts in employment in a number of countries (see, for example, European Foundation for the Improvement of Living and Working Conditions, 2012; HRM in Practice 1.3).

## HRM IN PRACTICE 1.3:
## Job losses due to the global financial crisis

The tourism sector suffered a decline that began in the second half of 2008 and intensified in 2009 after a number of years of growth. A sharp reduction in tourist flows, length of stay, tourist spending and increased restrictions on business travel expenses led to a significant contraction of economic activity in the sector worldwide. Consequently, as the global financial crisis began to bite in 2009, tourism and hospitality organizations, along with other sectors of the economy, sought to cut jobs to reduce costs and remain competitive in a challenging economic environment. Aer Lingus developed a 'transformation plan', which meant that it would operate fewer flights, meaning that fewer cabin crew and backroom jobs would be needed. As well as the loss of over 670 jobs, remaining staff also faced changes in working practices, as well as pay reductions. BA also announced plans to cut over 1,700 jobs and pay freezes for remaining staff. Job losses were also seen in the hotel sector, with Accor and Hilton both shedding hundreds of jobs.

Derived from Allen (2009); International Labour Organization (2010a); Sharkey (2009); Wearden (2009)

A similar attempt to recognize that there may be different approaches to HRM is also seen in the debate over whether organizations should aim to achieve 'best fit' or 'best practice'.

# Best fit vs best practice HRM

Boxall and Purcell (2000) suggest that attempts to understand the way in which organizations approach the management of their human resources can be seen with regard to whether they aim for 'best fit' or 'best practice'. On the one hand, the best-fit school argues for an approach to HRM that is fully integrated with the specific organizational and environmental context in which they operate. On the other hand, best-practice advocates argue for a universalistic approach to HRM in which all firms who adopt a range of agreed HR policies and practices are more likely to create a high-performance/commitment workplace, as organizations aim to compete on the basis of high quality and productivity.

## Best fit

One of the earliest and most influential attempts to develop a model that recognized the need for a fit between the competitive strategy and HRM was that offered by Schuler and Jackson (1987). Schuler and Jackson developed a series of typologies of 'needed role behaviours' that enabled the link between competitive strategy and HRM practices to be made. The type of needed role behaviours within Schuler and Jackson's model was contingent on the overall strategies that an organization could adopt to seek competitive advantage and the HRM approach adopted to sustain this.

First, there is an *innovation* strategy, where organizations seek to develop products or services that are different from competitors, such that the focus here is on companies offering something new and different. Organizations adopting this approach seek to develop an environment where innovation is allowed to flourish. As a result, the role behaviour needed from employees in such a scenario is characterized by things like a willingness to tolerate ambiguity and unpredictability, the need to be creative and risk-taking. Given these characteristics, the type of HRM strategy flowing from this approach is based on having a large number of highly skilled individuals who are likely to enjoy high levels of autonomy.

Second is the *quality enhancement* strategy, wherein firms seek to gain competitive advantage by enhancing the product and/or service quality. The approach once again points to certain HRM practices to support a total quality approach. These practices include the encouragement of feedback systems, teamwork, decision-making and responsibility being an integral part of an employee's job description and flexible job classifications. The intent of these practices is to create needed employee behaviour such as cooperative, interdependent behaviour, and commitment to the goals of the organization.

Lastly, the *cost reduction strategy* sees firms attempting to gain competitive advantage by aiming to be the lowest-cost producer within a particular market segment. The characteristics of firms seeking to pursue this strategy are tight controls, minimization of overheads and pursuit of economies of scale, in the pursuit of increased productivity. In following such a strategy, organizations

may use higher number of part-timers, seek to simplify and measure work via narrowly defined jobs that encourage specialization and efficiency, and offer short-term results-oriented appraisals. Needed employee behaviours include: repetitive and predictable behaviour, low levels of risk-taking activity and a high degree of comfort with stability.

This support for the importance of HRM practices 'fitting' the organization's own strategically defined market segment to create a fit between the functional areas of marketing, operations and HRM is also seen in the work of Lashley and Taylor (1998). Lashley and Taylor describe four basic archetypes within which tourism and hospitality organizations can be potentially located. These archetypes are the *service factory*, the *service shop*, *mass service* and *professional services*. These characterizations are based on the degree of customization and labour intensity involved in the service on offer, in terms of the degree of customer contact required between employees and customers.

The service factory has relatively low labour intensity and low customization, i.e. high standardization. The service factory is most obviously exemplified by fast-food operators, especially McDonald's. The service shop involves more customization, but relatively low labour intensity. The defining difference to the service factory lies in the degree of standardization within the process. Lashley and Taylor draw upon the example of TGI Friday's to argue that although there are high levels of standardization in the tangible aspects of the organization, such as the menus, layouts, décor and staff uniform, there is also some scope to customize the customers' eating and drinking experiences. This customization is by virtue of their more extensive menu, and more importantly, greater spontaneity and authenticity in the intangible aspects of the service provided by front-line staff. The next classification is mass service, where service processes involve a relatively high degree of labour intensity, though a limited amount of customization. Lashley and Taylor assert that the Marriott hotel brand typifies a mass service organization, as their four-star offering is similar to others in relation to the tangibles, reflecting the highly competitive nature of the mid to upper segment of the hotel market. As a result of this convergence of the tangibles, the key lies in the intangibles and the scope available to organizations to differentiate themselves on the basis of service quality. Within this process of differentiation a key role is played by the staff via the relatively high level of contact with customers. The final grouping is professional services, where there is a high level of service to individual customers and a high degree of labour intensity, as exemplified by hospitality management consultants.

The key point which emerges from the work of Lashley and Taylor is the likely relationship between the service operation type adopted by the organization and the style of HRM which best fits it. For example, it is apparent that in the four-star hotel sector a broadly soft approach to HRM, as exemplified by high discretion in relation to the intangibles, moral involvement and a moderate trust culture, is suggested as being important to sustain a high-quality, total quality management (TQM)-based approach to the service offering. At the other end of the spectrum, McDonald's are suggested as exemplifying a command-and-control style characterized by things such as low discretion for employees, limited responsibility and autonomy and scripted service encounters. Importantly, Lashley and Taylor (1998: 161) see the command-and-control approach as being right for what McDonald's are aiming to offer their customers (see also HRM in Practice 1.6):

> the historic success of the McDonald's organization in delivering their market offer . . . is partly due to the ability to develop and maintain a close fit between the key characteristics of the strategic drivers and actual service delivery through utilization of an appropriate HRM style.

The key point remains that organizations, in developing a certain product market strategy, ensure that their HR policies and practices are congruent and cost-effective with this strategy.

## Best practice

While arguments for best fit advocate a close fit between competitive strategies and HRM, those in favour of best-practice approaches to HRM suggest that there is a universal 'one best way' to manage people. By adopting a best-practice approach it is argued that organizations will see enhanced commitment from employees, leading to improved organizational performance, higher levels of service quality and ultimately increases in productivity and profitability. Usually couched in terms of 'bundles', the HRM practices that are offered in support of a high commitment and performance model are generally fairly consistent. For example, Redman and Matthews (1998) outline a range of HR practices which are suggested as being important to organizational strategies aimed at securing high-quality service:

- *Recruitment and selection* – recruiting and selecting staff with the correct attitudinal and behavioural characteristics. A range of assessments in the selection process should be utilized to evaluate the work values, personality, interpersonal skills and problem-solving abilities of potential employees to assess their 'service orientation'.
- *Retention* – this includes the need to avoid the development of a 'turnover culture', which may of course be particularly prevalent in tourism and hospitality. For example, the use of 'retention bonuses' to influence employees to stay.
- *Teamwork* – the use of semi-autonomous, cross-process and multi-functional teams.
- *Training and development* – the need to equip operative-level staff with team-working and interpersonal skills to develop their 'service orientation' and managers with a new leadership style which encourages a move to a more facilitative and coaching style of managing.

- *Appraisal* – moving away from traditional top-down approaches to appraisal and supporting things such as customer evaluation, peer review, team-based performance and the appraisal of managers by subordinates. Generally, all of these performance appraisal systems should focus on the quality goals of the organization and the behaviours of employees needed to sustain these.
- *Rewarding quality* – a need for a much more creative system of rewards and, in particular, the need for payment systems that reward employees for attaining quality goals.
- *Job security* – promises of job security are seen as an essential component of any overall quality approach.
- *Employee involvement and employee relations* – by seeking greater involvement from employees, the emphasis is on offering autonomy, creativity, cooperation and self-control in work processes. The use of educative and participative mechanisms, such as team briefings and quality circles (QCs), are allied to changes in the organization of work that support an 'empowered' environment.

In simple terms, best practice is likely to entail attempts to enhance the skill base of employees through HR activities such as selective staffing, comprehensive training and broad developmental efforts like job rotation. Additionally, it also encourages empowerment, participative problem-solving, teamwork and performance-based incentives.

---

### Review and reflect

Think of an organization that you are familiar with – for example, where you are currently working or one where you have spent time on placement. To what extent do their HR practices evidence either a best-fit or best-practice approach? Why would you characterize it this way?

---

## Models or reality?

Of course, ideal types and academic models may not always reflect the complex reality of what really goes on in tourism and hospitality organizations. Schuler and Jackson, for instance, freely admit the description of their three competitive strategies as pure types often does not reflect the reality of, for example, organizations pursuing two or more competitive strategies simultaneously. The same point can also be made with regard to hard and soft HRM; it is not uncommon for organizations to vary their approaches to employees depending on any given practice. For example, with regard to labour flexibility, the use of numerical flexibility may well reflect fairly hard approaches to HRM, while functional flexibility and multi-skilling exemplifies a much softer approach (also see Chapter 4). A further issue is the predominance of SMEs in tourism and hospitality. It is often suggested that their small scale means that they are unlikely to have the necessary means to employ the kind of HRM expertise needed to develop sophisticated soft approaches, for example. Nevertheless, they are still likely to require HR policies that require at least some thought with regard to their business circumstances.

While some understanding of debate about soft and hard and best fit and best practice are important to place HR practices within a broader theoretical context, in reality, regardless of these various ideal types, all organizations have to manage employees on a day-to-day basis. We can illustrate this in Figure 1.1, which outlines the notion of an HRM cycle.

Figure 1.1 is useful in allowing us to appreciate that these broad aspects of attracting, maintaining and developing a workforce are constant and that organizations and managers, both specialist HR and line managers, are wrestling with HR issues on a day-to-day basis. However, while a number of the functional aspects of HRM are unlikely to differ, the manner in which

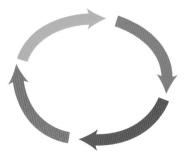

**Attract an effective workforce**

- HR planning/labour markets
- recruitment and selection

**Maintain an effective workforce**

- rewards and welfare
- labour relations, e.g. the role of trade unions
- grievance and disciplinary procedures

**Develop an effective workforce**

- training and development
- performance appraisal

**FIGURE 1.1** The HRM Cycle

organizations actually develop their overall strategy will. In these circumstances models that allow for recognition of differing strategic intent in HRM are still useful in allowing us to appreciate why and how companies differ in their approaches to HRM in tourism and hospitality. It would be naïve to imagine we could talk in very broad terms about HRM in tourism and hospitality. The reality is far too complex, and as we have already noted, the employment experience for employees can vary enormously depending on the type of organization they work in and the job or role they have within their organizations. With this recognition we should consider the key question: so what does HRM in hospitality and tourism look like? Reflecting some of our earlier discussion of hard and soft and best fit and best practice, we can also crudely distinguish between those who argue for a pessimistic view of HRM in the sector and those who suggest that increasingly organizations are seeking a much more progressive approach to managing their employees.

## The bad news ... pessimistic views of HRM in tourism and hospitality

Generally tourism and hospitality has often struggled with negative perceptions about employment practices and conditions. This perception has often been matched by the reality, with the management of human resources remaining a challenging problem for tourism and hospitality organizations worldwide (see HRM in Practice 1.4).

### HRM IN PRACTICE 1.4:
### HRM in tourism and hospitality: a worldwide concern

A recent survey of 243 managers from 60 different countries – encompassing North America, Europe, Asia, the Middle East, South America and Africa – identified HRM issues as the most troubling for general managers and corporate executives in the global hotel industry. The identification of HR issues as the most troubling concern was despite economic issues, which currently cast a long shadow across the industry. Although the survey found that there were challenges around economic and environmental issues, the primary concern for managers was HRM. In particular, there was concern about attracting talent and retaining people. Concerns were also expressed about the quality and consistency of training and employee morale. The survey also found that unmotivated staff and lack of experience were common hurdles to providing good-quality service. When the results are broken down by region they remain the same, so attraction, retention, training and morale are the top four concerns of managers, regardless of where they are in the world.

Derived from Enz (2009)

Keep and Mayhew (1999) and Kusluvan *et al.* (2010) suggest the industry has a number of personnel problems, including:

- generally low wages, unless skill shortages act to counter this, such as for chefs;
- unsocial hours and shift patterns that are not family-friendly;
- the pool of low-skilled and easily replaceable employees;
- over-representation of women and ethnic minorities in low-level operative positions, with better paid, higher status and more-skilled jobs filled by men, pointing to undeveloped equal opportunity policies in the sector;
- unprofessional managers and owners;
- poor or non-existent career structures and use of casualized seasonal employment;
- over-reliance on informal recruitment methods;
- lack of evidence of good-practice personnel/HRM practices;
- little or no trade union presence;
- high levels of labour turnover;
- difficulties in recruitment and retention of employees;
- competitive pressures which drive a cost-cutting and short-term approach to HRM.

Recognizing this reality of poor employment practices, Riley *et al.* (2000) and Riley and Szivas (2009) recognize the importance of economics and judgements about the relative value of skill as key determining factors for HRM policies and practices in tourism and hospitality. Of course, this point is likely to be true of any industry, but as Riley *et al.* and Riley and Szivas point out, these issues have a particular resonance in tourism and hospitality due to the nature of the sector. That is not to say that organizations and managers in the industry are not well aware of new managerial thinking on HRM. However, they also find themselves wrestling with 'traditional problems', which are underpinned by 'fundamental labour economic imperatives' (Riley *et al.*, 2000: 120). Importantly, these problems limit managerial actions and this leads Riley *et al.* (2000) to argue that the behaviour of managers is determined 'by the structures and forms under which they live' (p. 119). This economic imperative creates a short-term perspective on managerial decision-making and strategy in relation to HRM, and also means that management are more likely to deploy a weak internal labour market. An obvious impact of this is that HRM concerns of tourism and hospitality organizations are constantly directed to short-term responses to issues such as recruitment, selection and basic training, rather than more long-term areas which could conceivably offer more development and career progression for existing employees. Equally, as tourism and hospitality organizations draw on skills that are not especially unique and are readily available in the external labour market, this means that firms often deploy a weak internal labour market. Consequently, within this context, HRM practices are configured in a relatively unsophisticated manner (Riley and Szivas, 2009).

Another reason for continuing pessimism is the general attitude of employers, and particularly the extent to which they are willing to recognize the extent of the HRM problem in the sector. The DfEE (2000) registers with some incredulity the awareness of low pay, for example, existing alongside the naïve view of employers of tourism and hospitality as a 'good' employment sector. Thus, although in a number of locations labour shortages were clearly reflective of an unwillingness of employers to offer competitive pay and terms of conditions of employment, the DfEE (2000: 35) notes how 'We were struck by the extent to which employers described pay and working conditions as "reasonable" or even "good" while at the same time reporting extensive recruitment problems, skills gaps and labour turnover.' This disjuncture between the views of employers and employees is also noted by the ILO in a recent report on the international tourism industry. They recognize how:

> Employers' representatives generally consider that the turnover in the industry should be attributed to the essentially transient nature of part of the workforce, namely students, young mothers and young people as a whole, as well as the general difficulty in retaining staff. Employees, on the other hand, frequently cite low pay as a reason for changing employment, though a lack of career structure and benefits would appear to be of even greater importance.
> (International Labour Organization, 2001: 6)

This inability by industry to recognize the most glaring of issues is longstanding and can also be seen in relation to things like a degree of hostility and opposition from the employers associations in the industry, such as the British Hospitality Association (BHA), to governmental initiatives such as the minimum wage and Working Time Directive (see Chapter 4). The BHA still remains unsure of the benefits of such initiatives, despite support from others who argue these initiatives are likely to have a potentially positive impact on the industry (see, for example, Lucas, 2004).

Given the above discussion it is unsurprising to see a long history of support for the proposition that tourism and hospitality remains a poor employment sector. From Orwell's *Down and Out in Paris and London* in the 1930s to recent work by the likes of Chand and Katou (2007), the European Foundation for the Improvement of Living and Working Conditions (2012), Kelliher and Johnson (1997), Kelliher and Perrett (2001), Lucas (2004), McGunnigle and Jameson (2000), Poulston (2009) and Price (1994), the dominant paradigm has tended to stress the negative aspects of working in the sector. For example, McGunnigle and Jameson surveyed a selected number of hotels from the top 50 hotel groups ranked by ownership of bedroom stock, which were considered to be most likely to exhibit good-practice HRM. Despite this, they concluded that 'This study suggests that there is little adoption of HRM philosophy in corporately owned hotels in the UK sample . . . [and hospitality] . . . has a long way to go before it can claim that it is encouraging a "culture of commitment"' (McGunnigle and Jameson, 2000: 416). Similarly, Kelliher and Perrett (2001), drawing explicitly on Schuler and Jackson's typology, develop a case study analysis of a 'designer restaurant'. Such a restaurant might be thought of as potentially developing a more sophisticated approach to HRM as they sought to differentiate themselves from chain establishments such as Hard Rock Café and TGI Friday's. However, although the restaurant had moved to a more sophisticated approach to HRM in areas like planning, training and development and appraisal, and ostensibly sought an 'innovation' strategy, 'there was little real evidence that human resources were seen as a source of competitive advantage' (p. 434). Instead, the HRM approaches adopted by the restaurant were much more reflective of immediate environmental constraints, such as the difficulties in recruiting and retaining staff.

In short, following their wide-ranging and exhaustive review of the extant research that has examined HRM practices within tourism and hospitality, Kusluvan *et al.* (2010: 177) note that most of this research has 'concluded that individual or bundles of HRM practices in the tourism and hospitality industry are unprofessional, underdeveloped, and inferior when compared to other industries and are not practiced in a way that generates employee commitment, satisfaction and motivation'. In sum, any number of reasons may account for poor personnel practice in the tourism and hospitality industry. Economic determinism, the predominance of SMEs, a low skill base, employer antipathy to a more progressive approach to HRM, labour market characteristics, organizations ensuring best-fit HRM practices to support a high-volume, low-cost strategy; all are plausible reasons for a view of HRM which is not necessarily premised on high skills, high wages and a high-quality route to competitive advantage. That said, it would be equally wrong to paint a wholly pessimistic picture. It was recognized earlier in the chapter that there are also examples of good practice HRM, particularly in certain sub-sectors of the industry and in market segments where organizations are likely to seek differentiation on the basis of offering high-quality services.

## The good news . . . best-practice HRM in tourism and hospitality

In recent years there has been the emergence in the UK and elsewhere of a number of awards which have sought to identify organizations who offer 'best places to work'. Some of these – such as the *Sunday Times* Best Companies to Work For awards; the globally oriented Great Places to Work Institute's Great Places to Work; and, within the US context, *Fortune* magazine's list of the top 100 best workplaces – draw examples from across the economy. In that sense there have been a relatively small number of hospitality and tourism companies that have appeared in these various lists over the years. However, companies that have appeared consistently in the various lists include Marriott International, Four Seasons, Starbucks, Hilton International, Kimpton Hotels and Restaurants and McDonalds (see also HRM in Practice 1.5).

## HRM IN PRACTICE 1.5:
## *Fortune*'s Best companies to work for

A recent analysis by Hinkin and Tracey (2010) of some of the practices of service-oriented companies appearing within *Fortune*'s top 100 companies points to a number of key HR practices which have led to their designation as being a great place to work.

First was the existence of a strong organizational culture that emphasizes the value of people. For example, within Marriott there is clear and consistent communication from the top of the organization from the CEO, Bill Marriott, so employees are aware of his views on a wide array of issues that impact the company.

Second was a high level of flexibility in their scheduling of employees, through things such as job shares, a compressed working week and flexitime, with Starbucks offering flexible schedules to their employees.

Third, companies also had a number of innovative staffing practices to create and maintain a pool of appropriate, high-quality labour. In this sense companies would often publicize awards that they had won in order to attract the best talent, and also have dynamic media aimed at recruiting potential applicants. Awards would also be given to employees who refer others to the organization, though such new employees have to work for a minimum period of time before such awards are given to the existing employees. There are also rigorous recruitment and selection procedures, with Starbucks, for example, involving both managers and employees in the selection process.

Fourth, the importance of training and development was recognized, especially in the first few weeks of the job. Four Seasons, for example, have an initial 12-week training programme, which includes 30 hours of classroom training, cross-functional exposure, formal testing and an opportunity to stay for 24 hours in the hotel to give employees a direct means to learn about how guests should be treated. There was also significant ongoing training and a culture of promoting from within to encourage a strong internal labour market.

Fifth was performance management, particularly in terms of making clear the performance expectations employees are expected to fulfil. Attempts to assess performance are also strongly linked to other key HR practices, such as development initiatives.

Lastly, compensation and benefits are seen as being key in attracting, retaining and motivating employees to perform at a high level. Aspects such as profit sharing and having a comprehensive range of benefits were considered important in this regard.

In addition to these more general awards, there are also more sectorally focused awards. Started by *Caterer and Hotelkeeper* in 2006 and running until 2009, the Best Places to Work in Hospitality awards celebrated outstanding employment practice in the hospitality sector, recognizing companies who were doing the most to attract, train, retain and motivate staff to ensure they were well-equipped to offer world-class standards of customer service. Winners were consistently expected to go above and beyond the basic HR requirements and be committed to staff development and creating a positive working environment in becoming an employer of choice. Initially, the past Best Places winners were selected by a panel of hospitality and HR experts. However, in 2009 the process went a step further by introducing a more scientific, web-based judging mechanism, which allowed employers to provide details about the environment, training and benefits they offer. Additionally, in 2009 employees were given a chance to provide first-hand feedback on what it is really like to work in a Best Places to Work organization (see HRM in Practice 1.6). Although the award was discontinued in 2009, a new award was started in 2011 (see details at http://www.bestemployersinhospitality.com).

Hoque (2000) has also taken issue with arguments which portray the hospitality industry as backward and unstrategic, particularly with regard to larger hotel establishments. He suggests that 'it is perhaps time researchers

## HRM IN PRACTICE 1.6:
## McDonald's a great place to work?

One company that enjoyed consistent success in *Caterer and Hotelkeeper*'s Best Places to Work in Hospitality awards is McDonald's, who won awards in 2007, 2008 and 2009. In addition, the company has also been recognized in the *Sunday Times* Best Places to Work and by the Great Places to Work Institute, appearing in their top 10 World's Best Multinational Workplaces. For an organization long-plagued with the epithet of McJob it is suggested that the awards are a sign that such a characterization is outdated, with 79 per cent of employees recently suggesting that they feel 'very proud' to work at McDonald's. This statistic is reflected in the average length of stay in the company, with crew members staying on average for three years and managers for 15 years. The company has been praised for its progressive HR practices, especially in areas like flexible working, rapid career progression and providing significant development opportunities. For example, McDonald's is the largest provider of apprenticeships in the UK, and along with other development initiatives this allows employees to gain nationally recognized qualifications. These and other initiatives are part of the annual £30 million invested by the company every year for training and development.

Derived from Paton (2010) and Thomas (2010)

stopped highlighting the example of "bad management" and branding the industry as under-developed or backward, and started identifying approaches to hotel management capable of generating high performance' (p. 154; also see HRM in Practice 1.7).

## HRM IN PRACTICE 1.7:
## The HRM quality enhancer hotel

The hotel in Hoque's (2000) research, which is termed the 'HRM quality enhancer hotel', employed 140 staff and was part of a large international chain. In relation to their approach to HRM, a number of practices were prominent in the hotel. Recruitment and selection emphasized the need for employees to have an aptitude for customer care, although this tended to be 'spotted' at interview rather than through psychometric or behavioural tests. The hotel used extensive induction programmes to lessen the potential of employee turnover. The use of cross-functional teams aimed to generate cooperation and team-building and staff were encouraged to view the hotel as a unit rather than a collection of discrete functions. Allied to this, extensive multi-skilling and cross-functional flexibility was encouraged; this 'cross exposure' allowed staff to see a number of the other parts of the hotel. There was extensive decentralization, which sought to encourage responsible autonomy, for example through a well-understood empowerment scheme operating in the hotel. Consultation via a representative consultative committee allowed employees to voice their views on the running of the hotel. Further to this consultation, the hotel also operated an annual attitude survey. Employees were appraised on a yearly basis. The appraisal system was used for succession planning and the hotel was also working towards linking appraisal with a merit-based remuneration system. Employees were also encouraged by a strong internal labour market which promoted from within, whenever possible. Finally, throughout the hotel there was an overriding emphasis on quality and the need to offer 'outstanding customer service'.

The key point emerging from the above discussion is what good-practice HRM is likely to look like in the tourism and hospitality industry, often encompassing a sophisticated range of practices. It is also, of course, noteworthy that much of the evidence above would suggest that good practice is more likely to be found in larger organizations, particularly in multinational companies (MNCs). In that sense, although the discussion above is useful in offering a description of organizational practices that support a professional, high-quality approach to service, there might be concerns at the extent to which these practices are representative of the industry as a whole (Nickson and Wood, 2000).

## Where this books stands

While Boxall and Purcell (2003: 61) suggest that 'there is quite a lot of agreement on what constitutes "bad" or "stupid" practice' in relation to HRM, this does not stop organizations often developing rather bad or stupid HR practices. As we have already noted, tourism and hospitality is likely to offer huge diversity with regard to HRM policies and practices and it would be nice to think that these are rarely bad or stupid. Experience equally tells us, though, that this is not always the case. In recognizing this point, this book aims to develop a realistic account of how employers in tourism and hospitality develop and implement their HRM policies and practices and what this will mean for employees. It will certainly celebrate good practice, but equally will not be afraid to point to bad practice. This sentiment points to the fact that while best practice is something to which organizations should aspire, the reality is that there may be a number of constraints in achieving best practice, a point which Boxall and Purcell (2000: 199) recognize:

> While all employers will benefit from avoiding the real 'howlers' of HRM practices that are well known for their dysfunctional or perverse consequences – they are often constrained by industry and organizational economics from implementing a deluxe version of best practice.

In sum, while all tourism and hospitality employers are, for a variety of reasons, unlikely to aspire to the deluxe version of best practice, they should at least aim to avoid the real howlers, as suggested by Boxall and Purcell. The remainder of the book considers how they might do this in considering policies and practices in a variety of organizational and occupational settings.

## Conclusion

This chapter recognized the importance of tourism and hospitality as an employment sector. The sector provides a large and diverse number of jobs and will be important for future job creation throughout the developed and developing world. While the number of jobs produced by the tourism and hospitality industry is impressive, there are some concerns about the type of employment experience within the sector. The nature of the labour market and the reliance on 'marginal' workers has led to a number of pessimistic views of HRM practice. More upbeat accounts point to the manner in which concerns with providing good-quality service are improving HR practices. Underlying this debate are a number of models of HRM which provide a framework in which to locate the strategies adopted by tourism and hospitality organizations. Ultimately, though, we have to be cautious to not over-generalize the nature

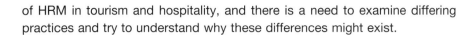

of HRM in tourism and hospitality, and there is a need to examine differing practices and try to understand why these differences might exist.

## Discussion questions

1  What are some of the key HR challenges in tourism and hospitality?
2  Discuss the view that the reliance in tourism and hospitality on 'marginal workers' means that developing sophisticated HR practices is not necessary?
3  What are the differences between hard and soft variants of HRM?
4  Why is it important for all tourism and hospitality managers to have some awareness of HRM?
5  What are the likely future people-management challenges for tourism and hospitality organizations?

## Further reading

Baum, T. (2007) 'Human resources in tourism: still waiting for change', *Tourism Management*, 28, 6, 1383–99.

Hoque, K. (2000) *Human Resource Management in the Hotel Industry*, London: Routledge.

Kusluvan, S., Kusluvan, Z., Ilhan, I. and Buyruk, L. (2010) 'The human dimension: a review of human resource management issues in the tourism and hospitality industry', *Cornell Hospitality Quarterly*, 51, 2, 171–214.

Lashley, C. and Taylor, S. (1998) 'Hospitality retail operations types and styles in the management of human resources', *Journal of Retailing and Consumer Services*, 5, 3, 153–65.

Lucas, R. (2004) *Employment Relations in the Hospitality and Tourism Industries*, London: Routledge.

Marchington, M. and Grugulis, I. (2000) '"Best practice" human resource management: perfect opportunity or dangerous illusion?', *International Journal of Human Resource Management*, 11, 6, 1104–24.

Riley, M. and Szivas, E. (2009) 'The valuation of skill and the configuration of HRM', *Tourism Economics*, 15, 1, 105–20.

## Recommended websites

The Chartered Institute of Personnel and Development (CIPD) is the main professional body for HRM practitioners in the UK. Their website can be found at http://www.cipd.co.uk/default.cipd and includes a number of downloadable items once you have registered for the site, which is free.

The Society for Human Resource Management (SHRM) is the world's largest association devoted to human resource management; its website can be found at http://www.shrm.org/about/Pages/default.aspx

The *Sunday Times* 100 Best Companies to Work For annual lists of award winners can be found at http://www.bestcompanies.co.uk/list_intro.aspx. There is also a short commentary on what makes the company such a good place to work. For example, if you click through to the list of 2012 Big Best Companies you will find more details on why McDonald's, Marriott, Intercontinental Hotels and Hilton were considered to be among the 25 top companies in the UK.

The Great Places to Work Institute produces lists for over 40 countries, showing great places to work; further details can be found at http://www.greatplacetowork.net. Click on the global tab on the front page and this brings up the sites for the various countries.

http://www.hrmguide.co.uk is a very good general guide to HRM issues in the UK. Within the site there are also links to HRM issues and practices in a range of other countries, including Australia and the United States.

The ILO and the United Nations World Tourism Organization collaborated on a project across 2007–2009 to address the issue of how to sustain 'decent work' in tourism. Details can be found at: http://statistics.unwto.org/sites/all/files/pdf/ilo_unwto.pdf; http://statistics.unwto.org/sites/all/files/pdf/ilo_eng.pdf; http://statistics.unwto.org/sites/all/files/pdf/ilo_pres.pdf

In 2011 the ILO produced an excellent toolkit, which has a very good chapter on HR issues, decent work and tourism; see http://www.ilo.org/wcmsp5/groups/public/---ed_dialogue/---sector/documents/instructionalmaterial/wcms_162289.pdf

The Work Foundation (formerly the Industrial Society) has some interesting material on their site, including a number of downloadable reports on aspects of work and employment: http://www.theworkfoundation.com/Reports

*Caterer and Hotelkeeper* is the trade magazine of the hospitality industry and has a search engine at http://www.caterersearch.com/Home/Default.aspx. The archive has numerous stories on aspects of HRM in the sector.

There is lots of useful advice about pursuing a graduate career in hospitality and tourism at http://www.prospects.ac.uk/hospitality_tourism_sport_sector.htm

## Additional material

Go to www.routledge.com/cw/nickson to find PowerPoint slides, chapter commentaries, test banks and additional case studies for each chapter.

# International human resource management

COMPANION @ WEBSITE

## CHAPTER OBJECTIVES

**As tourism and hospitality organizations increasingly internationalize, they face a number of challenges in managing their human resources. This chapter considers these challenges; specifically, the aims of the chapter are:**

- To consider the nature of international human resource management.

- To outline and discuss different strategic dispositions to internationalization.

- To appreciate the importance of a multinational company's country-of-origin and the effects of host countries on HRM policy and practice.

- To assess challenges facing multinational companies operating in the tourism and hospitality industry in attempting to transfer HRM practices across national boundaries.

## Introduction

The continuing growth of world markets, increased availability of management and technological know-how in different countries, advances in telecommunications and greater regional political and economic integration are just some of the factors that are increasingly leading to the globalization of many tourism and hospitality multinational companies (MNCs). Resultantly, the contemporary tourism and hospitality industry is increasingly global and this is important in a number of ways. As more and more tourism and hospitality MNCs are now selling their products outside their home countries, they face a number of issues in terms of how they approach a range of human resource management (HRM) issues. For example, to what extent will they try to transfer policies and practices that are successful in the home country to host countries? In thinking about the mix between parent country and local managers, how will they staff their units overseas? The globalization of business is making it increasingly important to understand how multinational enterprises can operate more effectively in seeking to answer these types of questions. As they cross national boundaries, tourism and hospitality MNCs face many challenges related to issues like: language, culture, economic and political systems, legislative frameworks, management styles and conventions. To assess some of these issues the chapter will consider the emergence of international human resource management (IHRM); and relatedly the issue of comparative HRM. In many respects the former aspect is largely focused on issues associated with how MNCs manage their employees across national boundaries. The latter aspect is more about why and in what ways human resource (HR) policies and practices may differ in a variety of different countries. Of course, these two aspects are very much intertwined (Ferner, 2010). For example, MNCs may attempt to transfer certain HRM practices, and this process may be successfully achieved in certain countries and be much more problematic in others – the chapter will seek to assess why this might be the case.

## The emergence of IHRM

We should begin by defining what IHRM is. Torrington (1994: 6) suggests that, 'In many ways international HRM is simply HRM on a larger scale; the strategic considerations are more complex and the operational units more varied, needing co-ordination across more barriers.' A slightly different view is offered by Schuler et al. (1993: 720), who define IHRM as 'human resource management issues, functions and policies and practices that result from the strategic activities of multinational enterprises and that impact on the international concerns and goals of those enterprises'. In a similar vein, Boxall (1995: 5) also locates the locus of IHRM primarily within the choices faced by MNCs, and sees it as being 'concerned with the human resource problems of multinational firms in foreign subsidiaries (such as expatriate management) or, more broadly, with the unfolding HR issues that are associated with the various stages of the internationalization process'. Thus, on the basis of these definitions it can be seen that, compared to domestic HRM, IHRM is likely to involve the MNC in more diverse activities, greater involvement in employees' private lives (for example, the impact of the expatriation cycle), greater risk exposure, more external influences and generally greater complexity than would be found managing domestically. Most obviously these issues can be seen in terms of how MNCs seek to coordinate and integrate a range of units throughout the world, leading Schuler et al. (1993: 719) to ask a crucial question: 'Can MNCs link their globally dispersed units through human resource policies and practices, and if so, how?' In many respects, any attempt to answer this question can be found in the seminal work of Howard Perlmutter.

# Perlmutter: the 'father' of IHRM

Harzing (2004a) is representative of much of the IHRM literature that suggests that the typology outlined by Perlmutter (1969) is crucial in attempts to characterize the approach adopted by MNCs not only to HRM, but also finance and accounting, marketing and production. Indeed, Mayrhofer and Brewster (1996) recognize how Perlmutter's typology has become a virtual synonym of analytical approaches to understanding IHRM, such that they talk of his role as the originator and 'father' of the discipline.

Perlmutter's (1969) work attempts to delineate differing orientations, or strategic dispositions, adopted by multinational organizations with his starting point being that claims to multinationality should be based on more than simply generating sales overseas. Consequently, Perlmutter outlines an ethnocentric approach which is home-country oriented, a polycentric approach which is host-country oriented and a geocentric approach which is world oriented (a further orientation of regiocentric – i.e. regionally oriented – was added in 1979 by Heenan and Perlmutter). In general, the ethnocentric strategy suggests that companies should maximize their parent company control to integrate subsidiaries, at the cost of local responsiveness. Resultantly, the ethnocentrically oriented MNC believes in the superiority of the way of doing things in the home country, and this informs their strategies for staffing and managing overseas units. This approach implies centralized systems with authority high at headquarters, with much communication in the form of orders, commands and advice. Managers of the home country of the parent company are, therefore, recruited, trained and developed for key positions anywhere in the world to ensure that the home-country approach is easily transferred and that host-country nationals (HCNs) fully understand headquarters' culture.

The polycentric approach allows for more local responsiveness and is premised on the view that the MNC should respond to prevailing local conditions where practicable. Hence, in this orientation local people know best and organizations thus seek to pursue an approach of localizing operations as quickly as possible. Local staff are employed in core positions in the host country and enjoy high levels of autonomy and local opportunities for further promotion.

The final orientation, geocentrism, is, as Caligiuri and Stroh (1995: 497) note, 'When MNCs desire an integration of all of their foreign subsidiaries and the melding of a worldwide corporate culture.' Consequently, organizations seek 'the best man [sic], regardless of nationality, to solve the problems anywhere in the world' (Perlmutter, 1969: 13). The geocentric approach envisages competitive advantage emanating from the organization's ability to draw on a rich array of national and cultural perspectives, allowing for a global strategy which is also respectful of local circumstances – the notion of 'think global, act local'.

Which of these approaches an international organization could be characterized by is dependent on attitudes inferred from 'the assumptions upon which key product, functional and geographical decisions were made' (ibid.: 11). Importantly, though, Perlmutter feels that 'There is some degree of ethnocentricity, polycentricity or geocentricity in all firms' (ibid.: 11), and it is thus unlikely that any of these orientations are ever found in pure form. Nonetheless, Perlmutter argues strongly that one predominant disposition can usually be discerned, with Paauwe and Dewe (1995: 84) suggesting that any dominant attitude or state of mind of the corporation is likely to be 'determined by the phase of internationalization in which the company finds itself and by its history'. The implicit sense of an evolutionary approach to internationalization is a clear and important theme of Perlmutter's work, and equally clear is his recognition of the difficulties and complexity of attaining the most advanced form of the 'ideal' geocentric approach, such that 'The route to pervasive geocentric thinking is long and torturous' (Perlmutter, 1969: 16). This view that the most developed form for the MNC is the geocentric 'ideal' is something now routinely supported in much of the international business and management literature, as exemplified by Caligiuri and Stroh (1995: 495), who suggest that the geocentric strategy is:

> the 'ideal', as it attempts to balance both global integration and local responsiveness. In a hierarchy, the geocentric strategy would be the best because it incorporates both of the theoretical ideals. Polycentric and regiocentric strategies would be second because they satisfy the local responsiveness ideal (usually at the cost of global integration). Ethnocentric strategies, focusing on headquarters control, are neither globally integrated nor locally responsive.

A shift to a global orientation is likely to be dependent on the organization having the wherewithal to create and appoint a pool of genuinely 'global' managers, assuming this is in fact possible. This approach requires a sophisticated HR planning system and training infrastructure to enable an organization to enact such a strategy. Some of the issues engendered by this discussion are identified in Table 2.1, which suggests some of the implications for organizations which wish to pursue a geocentric HRM strategy.

## The impact of centricity in the tourism and hospitality industry

Roper et al. (1997, 1998) examine the factors that influence and determine success for international hotel groups in the global market place. They argue that centricity – defined by them as an approach to international management – is one of the key factors that influence all business decisions and their subsequent successful implementation. Consequently they examine the possible causal relationship between centricity and organizational success, and particularly whether organizations should be seeking to move to the geocentric 'ideal'. Interestingly, they disaggregate centricity at a number of levels, both in terms of orientation and functional areas of management. First, they suggest

| TABLE 2.1 A geocentric human resource profile | |
|---|---|
| Organization | Key decision makers from diverse backgrounds operating on a global basis. |
| Company culture | Integrated and draws on experiences, attitudes and beliefs held by people from different countries. |
| Recruitment | Based on ability rather than nationality. Recruits drawn from a range of different countries to core positions. |
| Training and development | Managers from all countries treated as equal. People developed through a range of overseas assignments and drawn together in cross-cultural teams to learn from each other. |
| Terms and conditions | General principles adopted which draw on practice from around the globe, yet also allow for a response to local circumstances. |
| Employee relations | General principles adopted which draw on best practice from different countries. European Works Council, international committees/task groups, etc., may be established. |
| Source: Roper *et al.* (1997: 381) Reprinted by permission of the authors. | |

that centricity can be viewed from three interrelated perspectives: management's mind-set and the attitudes and beliefs of key senior managers in the organization; corporate strategic predisposition and the way this will shape the company's mission, governance structure, strategy, organization structure and organizational culture; and finally, subsidiary-level predilection. Of these, Roper *et al.* suggest that the first two have the most influence, particularly in the way that management attitudes and beliefs will inform and dictate strategic and operating decisions.

Nickson (1999) reports research from three pseudonymous tourism and hospitality companies, Americo, Frenco and Swedco. Using Perlmutter's framework, the three companies evidenced differing orientations, as outlined in HRM in Practice 2.1.

## HRM IN PRACTICE 2.1:
## Mapping Perlmutter's orientations in the global hotel industry

Americo was an American company who had internationalized relatively recently. The company was now undergoing a fairly rapid process of internationalization and seeking a more global orientation. Americo seemed to have a control-oriented ethnocentric approach to internationalization, with use of American expatriates or longstanding

'Americanized' Americo people in key positions, such as general manager. Control was further enhanced by the use of 'task forces' to transfer the corporate message. There was some evidence of the beginnings of attempts to aspire to a more global outlook, such as by the use of well-known consultants and academics who were working with the company to encourage a less Amerocentric view.

Frenco was a major travel and tourism multinational who was seeking a more global orientation. The Frenco corporate culture was used as a unifying mechanism across the company, as the organization attempted to sustain a broadly geocentric approach. Nonetheless, there was some evidence of post- or neo-colonialism in the use of French expatriates in certain parts of the world. Attempts to sustain a 'global' approach were facilitated by the movement of a cadre of 'global' managers across brands/countries. Many of these managers also attended Frenco's corporate university, which attempted – with some success – to encourage a more global outlook.

Swedco was a relatively small MNC with a small presence outside of Scandinavia. Generally, Swedco was seeking a control-oriented ethnocentric approach facilitated by Swedish or Danish expatriate managers in pivotal positions in overseas units. The company seemed largely successful in their attempts to transfer the 'Swedco Way', the company's core corporate culture, though there was some scepticism in the only unit in the UK with a non-Scandinavian/Swedish manager.

## Review and reflect

What are some of the likely advantages and disadvantages of companies pursuing an ethnocentric, polycentric or geocentric approach to internationalization?

## International staffing

A further key issue in IHRM is the way in which MNCs seek to staff their overseas units. Contingent upon the predominant headquarters orientation – as based on Perlmutter's typology – MNCs are likely to use a mix of parent-country nationals (PCNs), third-country nationals (TCNs) and host-country nationals (HCNs). For example, MNCs may utilize PCNs in the early days of an overseas unit's existence, but over time it is likely that TCNs and particularly HCNs will play an ever greater role. Consequently, organizations are likely to see a range of advantages and disadvantages to the utilization of PCNs, HCNs or TCNs; some of these are considered in Table 2.2.

| TABLE 2.2 Advantages and disadvantages of using PCNs, TCNs and HCNs | | |
|---|---|---|
| | Advantage | Disadvantage |
| PCNs | Familiarity with the home office's goals, objectives, policies and practices, allowing for direct control over the subsidiary. | Difficulties in adapting to the foreign language and the socio-economic, political, cultural and legal environment. |
| | Allows for career development for high-performing HQ employees. | Can be expensive; for example, the excessive cost of selecting, training and maintaining expatriate managers and their families abroad. |
| | Easier exercise of control over the subsidiary operation by transferring and establishing organizational culture. | May create tensions in the host country; for example, the host country may insist on localizing operations and promoting local nationals. |
| | | Potential for expatriate failure' for example, family adjustment problems. |
| HCNs | Knowledge of the local environment, legislation, market and business practices. | Difficulties in exercising effective control over the subsidiaries operation. |
| | Provides career path for high-performing HCNs, thereby increasing motivation and commitment. | Communication difficulties in dealing with home-office personnel. |
| | Lower costs incurred in hiring HCNs. | Lack of opportunities for HCNs to gain international and cross-cultural experience. |
| | Responsive to demands for localization of subsidiary operation, and so is perceived well by the local government and employees. | |
| TCNs | Perhaps the best compromise between securing needed technical and managerial expertise and adapting to a foreign socio-economic and cultural environment. | Host countries' sensitivity with respect to nationals of specific countries; for example, Greece and Turkey. |
| | Although potentially as socialized into the company as a PCN, may be seen as less threatening and a neutral alternative. | Local nationals are impeded in their efforts to upgrade their own ranks and assume responsible positions in the multinational subsidiaries. |
| | Expands the talent pool within the MNC. | Overuse of TCNs may lead to the MNC 'losing control' of subsidiaries. |
| Source: Adapted from Collings and Scullion (2006) and Harzing (2004b). | | |

International organizations would usually have three broad motives for sending managers abroad. The first one of those is to fill positions when HCNs are unavailable or difficult to train. In a more control-oriented ethnocentric approach, PCNs or suitably socialized TCNs may be sent to maintain control due to them knowing the organizational 'rules' and culture better, thus allowing them to make the 'right' kind of decisions. Second, organizations may seek to develop managers with long-term potential by giving them valuable international experience, which is likely to enhance their standing in the organization. Such transfers may occur even when suitably qualified HCNs exist. Lastly, there may be attempts to develop a more geocentric approach, whereby control is achieved by acculturation, socialization and interaction among managers of different nationalities, with the intent of creating a 'global' corporate culture, which de-emphasizes national cultures, and a cadre of managers able to disseminate such an approach. The idea would be that managers would become less ethnocentric if they were to come into contact with a variety of cultures and different cultural perspectives.

## The role of international managers in tourism and hospitality

Gliatis and Guerrier (1994) report on research conducted with a small sample of several expatriate managers. The research was based on interviews conducted in four large international hotel companies with seven personnel specialists and eight hotel managers (all from different countries and, interestingly, all male), on assignments outside their home country. The research was carried out in the UK and in Greece and sought to answer several key questions (Gliatis and Guerrier, 1994: 230):

- Why and how do hotel chains use international assignments for managers?
- When would they seek to fill a post with an expatriate manager and when with a local manager?
- How is the use of expatriates changing?
- What problems do they perceive in their use of international transfers?
- What type of person is attracted to an international career?
- What do managers who follow international career paths perceive they gain from this type of career path?
- What do they perceive as their main problems?

The main focus of this research was why expatriate managers fail, although Gliatis and Guerrier do tangentially address wider questions on organizational strategy towards crossing national boundaries. They suggest that companies would ordinarily see the rationale for expatriation as comprising three main reasons. The first of these is to solve specific staffing problems in a particular location – for example, a lack of suitably qualified personnel. The second is as

part of a management development process in which managers benefit from the exposure to a range of countries, cultures and international issues. The final reason would be as a process of organizational development, whereby transfers are seen as encouraging global coordination, integration and commitment to the company. A further element to this may also be more control-oriented, in the sense that organizations will seek to integrate via the use of (usually home-country) expatriate managers to spread the coordinating 'glue' of corporate culture to ensure that organizational practices and policies are 'correctly' followed. As a result of the research, Gliatis and Guerrier also added a fourth reason as suggested by the personnel specialists – the use of expatriation as a tool for motivating and retaining managers within a company. Gliatis and Guerrier found evidence of all of these strategies in their research and also found that expatriation tended to be more appropriate for operational roles, such as general manager, resident manager, food and beverage manager and rooms division manager, while locals would ordinarily fill the positions of personnel managers, financial managers and chief engineers on account of their local expertise.

D'Annunzio-Green (1997), reporting on research within five international tourism and hospitality organizations – representing the airline, fast-food and hotel sectors – suggests that her case study organizations were largely pursuing a geocentric or polycentric approach. Her work is useful in its reporting of the research, but also in terms of its contextual discussion of how organizations approach international management development (IMD). An organization which aspires to a more global outlook faces a number of issues in terms of approaches adopted to things such as: international career pathing, organizations developing international managers, adaptability of employees to new cultures and language and the effect of training and adaptation. MNCs intending to pursue a geocentric approach must address a number of questions:

- Is there a constant supply of mobile staff?
- Can they be released on time from existing positions?
- Is there a database advanced enough to manage a geocentric approach to training and development?
- Is the company willing to invest the time and money required to ensure such a system will operate effectively?

As D'Annunzio-Green (1997: 200) suggests,

> For organizations wishing to develop a truly international manager, there needs to be a major transformation in managerial careers and develop-ment opportunities to enable the acquisition of the skills, knowledge and experience needed to work in a global market place.

Based on findings from a self-completed postal questionnaire sent to the senior HR specialist within the organizations, D'Annunzio-Green found that three of the organizations in her research were pursuing a geocentric approach, with the other two being characterized respectively as polycentric/geocentric and geocentric to regiocentric. The questionnaire was followed up with in-depth interviews with the HR director in three of the organizations, and this allowed D'Annunzio-Green to add more detail as to why the organizations are characterized in such a way. For example, in a British-owned airline company, which is conceptualized as shifting from an ethnocentric to a geocentric approach, a key role is increasingly played by HCNs and TCNs, and all of the 30–40 graduates taken on to the company's management training scheme had to undertake a number of international postings during their training period. Allied to this approach, the company also had a sophisticated database to track career moves and mechanisms to ensure all vacancies worldwide were notified to company personnel.

Similarly, an American-owned hotel MNC communicated all international postings via a computerized personnel database. This company, also considered geocentric and committed, in the words of the company, to 'developing truly international managers' (ibid.: 204), selected international managers on the basis of good performance appraisals, a minimum of five years with the company and language proficiency in at least two languages. Additionally, the selection criteria was also based on adaptability, international background and a high level of mobility. The common strand of a sophisticated computerized global transfer system was also found in the final organization, a Japanese-owned hotel MNC. Again, this company was considered geocentric, and as part of their IMD had a ten-year training and development plan which culminated in a general-manager position. During this time the candidates, who theoretically could come from any country, would undertake a part-time MBA and placements in at least three countries to encourage mobility, cultural empathy and global business awareness.

## Review and reflect

What are some of the key skills needed to be a successful expatriate manager in the international tourism and hospitality industry?

In sum, Gliatis and Guerrier's and D'Annunzio-Green's work is useful in pointing to the likelihood of organizations within the tourism and hospitality sector adopting different approaches to internationalization and their utilization of international managers. In particular, the attempt by D'Annunzio-Green to add greater detail to what may denote a geocentric approach is useful in

suggesting a range of organizational practices and policies which appear crucial in facilitating such an approach.

Much of what we have been discussing to-date has largely been about the manner in which MNC companies seek to develop their overall orientation and the implications of such an approach with regard to international staffing. Beyond this focus, there is also a need to consider the broader aspect of comparative HRM, which is more concerned as to why certain HRM practices may differ from country to country. To begin to discuss this issue we should recognize the importance of the country-of-origin of MNCs.

## Country-of-origin

Ferner (1997) provides a review of the country-of-origin literature and some of the substantive issues engendered by this work. From the relatively small body of research examining the country-of-origin effect, Ferner believes that two important generalizations can be extrapolated.

The first generalization is that the literature provides support for the notion that the nationality of ownership is a significant determinant of MNC behaviour and thus any examination of MNCs' strategies should take cognizance of the national economic and business cultures out of which they emerged. An example of this would be the proposition that American and Japanese MNCs have in the past tended to be more ethnocentric and reliant on expatriate managers to ensure organizational practices and policies are 'correctly' followed. Therefore, this 'imperial' approach was concerned with close control over foreign subsidiaries and led to greater formalization and centralization and a reliance on formal systems, policies and standards to manage human resources globally.

A further interesting aspect identified by Ferner (1997) is whether it is sensible to characterize, as an example, differences between Japanese and British MNCs as being due to some inherent quality of 'Japaneseness' or 'Britishness', or whether such differences stem from other factors, such as stage of internationalization, corporate structure and proportion of units represented overseas. Furthermore, the implications of national specificity would seem to preclude any real possibility of either a literal or even figurative 'stateless' organization, reflecting Van Maanen and Laurent's (1993: 283) view that 'All MNCs bear something of a cultural stamp that originates in the society where the organization was first designed' (see also Hu, 1992). Therefore, as Ferner (1997) cogently agues, even if the home country does not provide the bulk of sales, operations and employment, in reality it is likely to play a highly significant role in relation to locus of ownership and control, staffing of board and senior positions, strategic decisions emanating from the home country and also in the location of innovative activities such as research and development. Given Ferner's support for the notion of an MNC's entrenched rootedness to a national economic and business culture it is unsurprising to find him asking the question of 'what features do they "absorb" from the national background?' (ibid.: 24).

In answer to that question the second generalization is that the extent of the possible national influence on MNC behaviour is contingent upon the issues under consideration. Consequently, nationality manifests itself more in relation to some issues than others. For example, industrial relations practices are more likely to resemble the practices of the local environment. These considerations are also closely related to the convergence/divergence debate, and the extent to which the forces of convergence may be subverting national differences. At its broadest macro-social level, convergence theory is a recognition of the influence of over-arching trajectories and logic of capitalist development. This socio-structural argument suggests that societies and organizations will increasingly come to resemble each other as they accept the inevitability of universalistic tendencies in relation to technology, economic development, industrial policies, management style and HR practices. Consequently, over time a universal type of business organization will emerge and management practices and organizational performance will be shaped by the 'logic of industrialization' and technological change, rather than cultural or environmental variables. Within this process a key role will be played by MNCs, who act as carriers of 'best practice' across national boundaries.

Clearly, a key role in this process is ascribed to MNCs, and this raises the interesting spectre of MNCs acting as forces for convergence around the practices of the most 'successful' national business regimes. In essence this means that nationally specific versions of capitalism emerge to be disseminated by the hegemonic country's multinationals (Smith and Meiksins, 1995). There is still much support for the notion that the United States continues to be the predominant source of what are considered 'good-practice' approaches to both general business management and, more particularly, HRM (and see HRM in Practice 2.2).

## HRM IN PRACTICE 2.2:
## American dominance of global economy and the international hotel industry

Many writers argue that there are three key dimensions underpinning the process of globalization: economic, political and cultural. It is also often argued that globalization is, in reality, better conceptualized as Americanization. With regard to economics, a key aspect is the rise of the multinational firm. By the early twentieth century, US firms were becoming more important players in the international economy, beginning to eclipse their established European competitors.

During the Second World War and into the post-war period, US firms were in a position to exploit, by trade and with foreign direct investment (FDI), first the inadequacies and then the decline in European manufacturing capacity, aided of course by Marshall Aid and US government desires to create bulwarks against communism in Europe and Asia – *Pax Americana*. During this time American management methods were vigorously exported through FDI, and education and training institutions in Europe. With regard to politics, and particularly global governance, many argue that it is the United States particularly and, to a lesser extent, the industrialized countries of the European Union which drive the operations and policies of institutions such as the World Bank, International Monetary Fund and the World Trade Organization. Finally, there appears to be a growing passion around the world for all things American, and few things reflect American culture better than the likes of Coca-Cola, Disney and McDonald's, who seem to embody Americana. A number of these aspects are seen in the history of hotel internationalization, which was initially attributed to Conrad Hilton. He sought to place his 'little Americas' across the globe, leading many to talk of Hilton in venerable terms as the 'founder' of internationalization in the hotel industry. As well as explicitly offering a challenge to communism, many of the operating standards and procedures established by Hilton and other pioneering American hotel chains are still apparent today. This dominance can be seen with regard to aspects of the 'hardware' – that is, the physical product – but importantly also the 'software' – that is, the management of people. This software increasingly aims to support high-quality approaches to service via aspects such as empowerment.

Derived from Nickson and Warhurst (2001)

Brewster (1995: 207), for example, argues that 'the analyses and prescriptions laid out in the standard management textbooks are, fundamentally, drawn from one particular culture: that of the USA'. Guest (1990: 377) also makes a clear connection between HRM and the 'American Dream':

> The growth of HRM in the UK clearly owes something to the political, economic and business climate of the 1980s and the tendency during the decade to look to the United States as a model of good practice in all these fields. American multinationals have been to the forefront of HRM innovation in the UK and the leading advocates are all American.

Branine (1994) makes the cogent point that it is much more likely that non-American managers would adopt American management styles or techniques, while at the same time suggesting it is difficult to envisage American managers adopting policies that were originally from, for example, Mexico, Fiji or Peru. The important point, then, is the applicability and transferability of the putatively

American approach to management and whether there may be an enduring American influence on any convergent tendencies if HRM is to be the new model for managing organizations throughout the world.

### Review and reflect

Does the American dominance of the globalization process mean that we are all increasingly 'Americanized'?

However, more recently there has been an increasing interest in the growth of FDI from developing and transition economies, in particular China and India. As Thite *et al.* (2012: 252) note, 'it is anticipated that in the new world economy, the balance of power will shift to the East as China and India continue to evolve as two of the most attractive inward and outward FDI countries'. Consequently, there is also the potential for a move away from the dominant paradigm of seeing international HRM through Western thinking and concepts. Indeed, Thite *et al.* (2012: 256) argue that (also see HRM in Practice 2.3):

> It is clear that the universal or US model does not have applicability to the emerging MNCs. If the East becomes, in popular jargon, the new West, we need to develop newer models to aid the understanding of how Asian MNCs, particularly from China and India, are going to exercise control in an increasingly multi-polar world.

### HRM IN PRACTICE 2.3:
### From the American century to the Asian century?

While many would characterize the twentieth century as the American century, there is increasingly talk of the twenty-first century being an Asian century. More particularly, the economic rise to prominence of China and India (or as some have described it, 'Chindia') has led many to proclaim a shift in the balance of economic power from the West to the East. Some of this debate is characterized by hyperbole, and more level-headed analysis would point out that despite being powerful emerging economies, China and India are still developing economies. Nevertheless, it is clear that at the beginning of the twenty-first century a key trend that is significant for IHRM is the rise of the Chinese and Indian economies. China and India have become 'hotspots' for FDI and present unique challenges to Western MNCs taking advantage of these opportunities. For example, a recent CIPD report on talent management in the so-called BRIC countries (Brazil, Russia,

India and China) identified a number of key HR challenges in India and China, including skill shortages. Although India is often portrayed as being dominated by high-level IT skills, in reality its talent pool is much patchier and there are major issues in developing the skills that expanding businesses require. Similarly, while China – like India – has a high number of graduates, the number who are 'industry-ready' is small. More generally, in some sectors of the economy the country is a long way from having the number of skilled, capable people required by both domestic organizations and the ever-increasing number of Western MNCs locating in China.

Derived from CIPD (2010a); Scullion *et al.* (2007); Sheth (2011); Sommer (2006)

## Country-of-operation

However strong the country-of-origin effect, it is likely that units of MNCs in overseas locations will be influenced, to a greater or lesser extent, by what Ferner (1994: 92) has termed 'the host country effect'. This effect is likely to be manifested in one of two ways: the 'culturalist' perspective and the 'institutionalist' perspective (Olie, 1995).

## The importance of culture in IHRM

The 'softer' culturalist perspective draws attention to cultural distinctiveness in terms of the differing values, ideas and beliefs shared by people within any given society. These aspects will then be taken into the organizational setting and uniquely influence individuals' workplace behaviour. Tayeb (1994) suggests that the culturalist perspective is important primarily due to three reasons. First, it recognizes the differences of cultural norms, values and attitudes from one society to another, such that people's thinking is likely to be shaped by what is considered appropriate behaviour within that society. Second, different cultural groups will behave differently under similar circumstances because of the differences in their underlying values and attitudes. Lastly, culture will play a major part in shaping social institutions, work organizations, managerial behaviour and personnel policies. In short, national culture, at least in part, will have an impact in shaping the values, attitudes and behaviour of managers and employees in organizations.

It is important to recognize that culture remains an essentially vague and contested concept, with literally hundreds of definitions. Equally, though, many have attempted to research the impact between culture and workplace behaviour, with one of the most famous writers in this area being Geert Hofstede. Hofstede (1980, 2001) studied 117,000 IBM staff across more than 50 countries and identified the following four basic dimensions which describe the differences of national culture:

1　*Power distance.* This is the extent to which inequalities among people are seen as normal. This dimension stretches from equal relations being seen as normal to wide inequalities being viewed as normal. Where high power distance exists there may well be a very clear hierarchy, and managers would be expected to manage and direct subordinates. Cultures with low power distance are likely to be more consensual, with employees expecting to be consulted in decision-making.

2　*Uncertainty avoidance.* This refers to a preference for structured situations versus unstructured situations. This dimension runs from being comfortable with flexibility and ambiguity to a need for extremely rigid and certain situations. Cultures with high uncertainty avoidance would prefer clear rules, while low uncertainty avoidance cultures would be more comfortable working with few rules.

3　*Individualism.* This examines whether individuals are used to acting as individuals or as part of cohesive groups. This dimension ranges from collectivism to individualism. In individualistic cultures there is likely to be a desire to work independently. In contrast, in collectivist cultures there is likely to be a greater preference to work with others or in groups.

4　*Masculinity.* Hofstede distinguishes between 'hard' or 'masculine' values, such as assertiveness and competition and 'soft' or 'feminine' values of personal relations, quality of life and caring for others. In masculine cultures, work is valued as a central life interest. By comparison, feminine cultures are more likely to stress the value of social rewards.

Based on these dimensions, and a later dimension of time and whether cultures have a long-term versus a short-term orientation, Hofstede categorized countries into clusters, based on the relative similarities between cultures. If we accept the idea of stereotyping as a common way of perceiving different nationalities, Hofstede's work may be open to criticisms (indeed, see the recent debate between Hofstede (2002), McSweeney (2002a; 2002b) and Smith (2002) on the recent publication of an updated version of *Culture's Consequences*). For example, critics question the representativeness of his work as it was based solely on IBM employees. Equally, there is much argument as to whether cultures can really be thought of as homogenous, as Hofstede's work does not allow for the existence of subcultures within a country based, for example, on social class, gender and region. Critics would also question whether cultures remain unchanging over time. However, most writers view the work of Hofstede as important, and as somewhere between a stereotypical description of a national culture and a useful tool for discovering an alien culture. So in that way it can be used as a practical framework for managers to understand potential cross-cultural differences in managing different individuals or in different cultures. To conclude on Hofstede's work, most people would agree that the framework is helpful as a heuristic device to assist the process of learning about a new culture. Hofstede's findings are

useful when applied as a general model that requires interpretation of specific circumstances. It is important that culture assessment focuses on the general make up of a nation or culture. This can be thought of as a curve, where most people will be near the 'norm', but there will be people in every society who exhibit characteristics that are distinctly different. Therefore these 'mainstream' cultural traits are best considered as a tendency, or a description of the behaviour of the average individual, but clearly there is the potential for other individuals to behave differently. Lastly, Hofstede's work is important in suggesting that true convergence in management and organizational practices will never occur due to the varying cultural differences outlined above.

## The institutional perspective

The difficulty in operationalizing and making concrete such amorphous notions as tradition and culture has led a variety of writers to shift the analysis more towards social institutions, such as education, vocational training patterns and employment/industrial relations. Ferner (1994: 93) suggests that 'there is more to national variation than some nebulous notion of "cultural difference"', and as a result, attention should also be paid to more concrete institutional factors. This point is also noted by Tayeb (1994: 431), who recognizes that 'The term "nation" refers not only to culture, but also to other social, economic and political institutions which have a significant bearing on the management style of organizations located in particular countries.' The recognition that culture should not be seen as a synonym for nation and an omnibus variable representing a range of social, historical, political and economic factors lies at the heart of the institutionalist perspective. The 'harder' institutionalist argument is primarily concerned with structural aspects within society and organizations, such as the division of labour and career, status and reward structures. These features are generated by the institutions of the host country which, as previously noted, will affect elements such as education, training and employment/industrial relations systems. Indeed, it is often the employment/industrial relations system which is most often cited as the least permeable aspect of a host-country environment, as this may often be based on a state-regulated legislative framework. Hence, there is likely to be tension between activities carried out by an MNC and the national system of employment/industrial relations in any given host country. This is particularly apparent within countries which have strong regulatory frameworks, which are likely to be a source of rules with which the MNC must comply. For example, an American MNC may ordinarily work without trade unions, but in locating in Germany may be forced to recognize and negotiate with trade unions due to the regulatory framework (though see Royle (2002) and Royle and Towers (2002) for an interesting discussion on how McDonald's have sought to override regulatory mechanisms in Europe by aggressively deterring employee interest in trade unions, avoiding compliance with collective bargaining agreements and evading, creating or manoeuvring to dominate local and national works councils). In sum, the impact of both the culture and institutions means that an MNC has to consider carefully what HRM policies and practices they can transfer because, as Ferner notes (1997: 33):

> not all elements [of an MNC's human resource policies] are 'exportable' being too rooted in native cultural assumptions; and second because to varying degrees host countries present obstacles to the 'import' of elements of foreign business systems, and colour the operation of those which are transferred.

MNCs have to consider the extent to which the differences between the home and host country's cultural and institutional environment are likely to support or undermine specific approaches to HR issues such as recruitment and selection, reward or performance appraisal. Thus, recognition of all of the above variables allows for an assessment of the impact of specific national institutional, legal and cultural frameworks, so as to be able to answer questions about the balance between *exportive*, *adaptive* and *integrative* approaches to corporate HR policies (Taylor *et al.*, 1996). Taylor *et al.* use these terms in a similar manner to our earlier identification of Perlmutter's ethnocentric/polycentric/geocentric profile. Thus the exportive approach sees central HR policies being exported to subsidiaries and is similar to the ethnocentric mind-set. The adaptive approach is similar to Perlmutter's polycentric approach and sees HR policies at subsidiaries reflecting local conditions. Lastly, the integrative approach mirrors Perlmutter's geocentrism and draws on best-practice HR policies and practices from around the globe in an integrated manner, while still recognizing the need for a degree of local variation in different markets.

## MNCs and HRM policies and practices in the tourism and hospitality industry

We have recognized that MNCs face choices in both the manner in which they develop their overall approach to IHRM and then how this will determine their approach to international staffing and what HR policies and practices they seek to transfer and how this might be mediated by a range of factors in the country-of-operation. Of course, MNCs are likely to want to maintain and develop a degree of consistency in their ways of managing people on a world-wide basis. Equally, though, in order to be effective locally, they may also need to adapt those ways to the specific cultural and institutional requirements of different societies. We can now briefly assess some of the evidence of how tourism and hospitality MNCs may be seeking to address these issues.

Nankevis and Debrah (1995) report on management practices in a selection of hotels in Singapore and Australia to discuss common and disparate themes within diverse national, cultural, social and labour market environments. The basic premise of Nankevis and Debrah is that the hospitality industry is increasingly looking to HRM to enhance organizational success and competitive advantage. To test this proposition they used a questionnaire with 35 multiple-choice questions, which were occasionally supplemented by open-ended follow-up comments for clarification or enlargement. The questionnaire was divided into four major categories: type of hotel; employee details; personnel management/HRM practices; and guest feedback. There were 109 responses (89 from Australia and 20 from Singapore) from 201 questionnaires. In relation to a range of HR issues, Nankevis and Debrah found considerable differences in approaches in Singapore and Australia and such differences were attributable to elements such as national, cultural, social, labour market phenomenon and management styles. Nonetheless, their findings did 'also appear to confirm the increasing globalism of guest market requirements and hotel management responses' (ibid.: 512). This was particularly so in relation to the MNC hotel companies surveyed, leading Nankevis and Debrah (ibid.: 511) to suggest that 'A potential consequence of [the high proportion of hotels owned by multinationals] is the standardization of service along with increased efficiency, productivity and thence profitability.'

Similarly, Jansen-Verbeke (1996) reports on research undertaken in hotels (including international hotels such as Hilton International) in Belgium and the Netherlands which suggested a high level of uniformity in managerial practices. Jansen-Verbeke utilized Hofstede's seminal framework to assess the extent to which cultural differences may exist between Belgian and Dutch managers. The research consisted of a written questionnaire, comprising 45 questions asking managers about their everyday practices in hotel management, and the sample consisted of 64 respondents. As Jensen-Verbeke (ibid.: 547) notes, 'The analysis shows that there are only a few differences in the practices of hotel managers in Belgium and the Netherlands.' To explain this convergence Jansen-Verbeke points to a range of factors, such as: the two countries belonging to the same cultural region; the homogenizing effect of organizational culture, reflecting the fact that most MNCs have a strong organizational culture; and the culture of the hotel industry in general, particularly in terms of uniform procedures in guest contact and an emphasis on quality of service. Of these, it is particularly noteworthy that organizational culture and the culture of the industry seem to play such a key role in the process of homogenization and convergence.

## Review and reflect

What are some of the potential challenges facing tourism and hospitality MNCs in attempting to transfer their HRM practices across national boundaries?

The above discussion seems to suggest that the continued growth of MNCs is likely to lead in the future to greater standardization of services, as organizations seek greater efficiency, productivity and profitability by utilizing the full range of 'soft' techniques, leading to a burgeoning sector-wide 'best-practice' approach to HRM and quality service (and see also Nickson, 1999). A counter argument is offered by Mwaura *et al.* (1998). In their research on the ITT Sheraton Hotel China they found significant evidence of Sheraton's corporate culture being in conflict with several aspects of Chinese culture. For example, Chinese managers and subordinates were not prepared to accept responsibility to ensure responsiveness to the hotel guests. A similar issue was also apparent in attempts to engender a commitment to customer satisfaction via training. Many of the local employees were reluctant to contribute to discussions in training sessions in case they 'lost face' (see also HRM in Practice 2.4)

## HRM IN PRACTICE 2.4:
## A failure to prepare for challenges in China

As we noted earlier in the chapter, China is becoming an ever more important part of the business world. Locating in China as an expatriate manager brings a number of challenges. Research reported by Dewald and Self (2008) which examines three internationally operating hotel chains – one American, one Asian and one Hong Kong Chinese – found very limited cross-cultural training for expatriate managers. In the Asian chain the pre-departure training consisted of a book, *Welcome to China*. Upon arrival in China the expatriates had a brief meeting with the locally based HR manager to explore 'dos and don'ts' in China. Similarly, in the Hong Kong Chinese-owned company expatriates received a welcome file which contained the 'rules' for China. Also similarly, the director of training and development of the American company noted the company offered insufficient training, describing it as 'disastrous'. This lack of pre-departure and on-site training within these internationally operating hotels seems rather puzzling, with expatriate failure rates being as high as 40 per cent. Moreover, as well as getting to grips with the challenges of adapting to the Chinese culture, expatriate managers face a range of challenging HR issues in China. Miao *et al.* (2011), reporting the findings from interviews with 11 general managers who had been working in China 1.5–21 years, found the main cultural challenges in dealing with employees were: getting staff to take initiative and responsibility; dealing with the desire of Chinese employees to be promoted quickly; losing staff through staff poaching and turnover; and recruitment and retention difficulties. As one general manager noted in talking about an unwillingness of Chinese employees to take responsibility, 'I would say they don't take initiative to make changes and bring in effort. They are also less flexible when it comes to changing.' Another, in

recognizing the difficulties with employees in China wanting fast promotions, said, 'My God, it's very strong. They just want to be general manager after six months. The problem is that they want to be managers very soon and if I don't give them promotion, they get another higher position and they are gone.' To address retention issues managers would look to be creative in reward structures, such as conducting quarterly review of people's salaries and offering extensive training and development opportunities. It seems, then, that multinational tourism and hospitality companies should be more strategic in seeking to develop training programmes that prepare managers for the particular challenges they are likely to face in China.

Similar results were also found by D'Annunzio-Green (2002) in her research on the experience of expatriate managers in Russia. Here, the attempts by expatriate managers to engender and maintain high service standards were often thwarted by the different attitudes to service of the Russian staff. Many of the staff, particularly those over 30, still exhibited behaviours that were developed during the communist-era Soviet system. Under this system Russians would never complain about service, no matter how bad it was. Resultantly, the lack of a customer orientation is still apparent in a large number of the staff. What the work of Mwaura *et al.* and D'Annunzio-Green exemplifies is that Western management practices cannot always be transferred in the tourism and hospitality industry on account of differing cultural and organizational working environments (see also Lucas *et al.*, 2004; Zhang and Wu, 2004).

## Conclusion

We noted how, increasingly, tourism and hospitality organizations may be operating on an international or even global basis. It was recognized that, in internationalizing, organizations face choices in their strategic disposition – for example, whether they adopt a broadly ethnocentric or polycentric approach. The overall strategic disposition of an MNC will also impact on how they develop their international staffing. In addressing issues of this nature, MNCs may seek to utilize practices only from their home countries, imitate practices typical of other countries or increasingly utilize an amalgam of HRM practices drawn from many other companies and countries, especially in pursuit of notions of 'best practice'. We noted how this has led many to talk in terms of whether there is increasing convergence in the manner in which HRM policies and practices are developed. In this view HRM practices are 'culture free' and universalistic, and so the transfer of managerial practice is straightforward, particularly if that practice is considered as 'best practice'. On the other hand we also noted the enduring influence of host-country culture and institutions leading many to argue for divergence. In the latter view HRM practices are 'culture bound' and difficult to transfer because of the primacy of differentiating effects of national culture or the need for MNCs to respond to differing legal and regulatory framework in a number of countries.

## Discussion questions

- What is the difference between international and comparative HRM?
- Is Hofstede's work still useful to understand variations in management practice?
- How did America come to dominate the global economy and what has been the impact on HRM?
- What are the likely consequences of the rise of China and India for IHRM?
- How might there be tension between home- and host-country cultures when a tourism and hospitality organization internationalizes?
- How is the institutional framework in a nation likely to impact on an MNC's HR practices?

## Further reading

D'Annunzio-Green, N., Maxwell, G. and Watson, S. (2002) *Human Resource Management: International Perspectives in Hospitality and Tourism*, London: Continuum.

Ferner, A. (1994) 'Multinational companies and human resource management: an overview of research issues', *Human Resource Management Journal*, 4, 2, 79–102.

Ferner, A. (1997) 'Country-of-origin effect and HRM in multinational companies', *Human Resource Management Journal*, 7, 1, 19–37.

Hofstede, G. (2001) *Culture's Consequences: International Differences in Work Related Values*, 2nd edn, London: Sage.

Nickson, D. and Warhurst, C. (2001) 'From globalization to internationalization to Americanization: the example of "Little Americas" in the hotel sector', in M. Hughes and J. Taggart (eds), *Multinationals in a New Era: International Strategy and Management*, Basingstoke: Palgrave.

Perlmutter, H. (1969) 'The torturous evolution of the multinational corporation', *Columbia Journal of World Business*, 4, 1, 9–18.

Thite, M., Wilkinson, A. and Shah, D. (2012) 'Internationalization and HRM strategies across subsidiaries in multinational corporations from emerging economies: a conceptual framework', *Journal of World Business*, 47, 2, 251–8.

## Recommended websites

You can find further details of Hofstede's work, including how different countries 'score' on his dimensions, at http://www.geert-hofstede.com

The Asia-Pacific Federation of Human Resource Management (APFHRM) is the network of HR and people-management associations' representative countries in the Asia-Pacific region. Their website can be found at http://www.apfhrm.com/index.php, and contains lots of interesting information on HR challenges in the Asia-Pacific region.

The European Industrial Relations Observatory (EIRO) website can be found at http://www.eurofound.europa.eu/eiro. The site offers news, analysis and up-to-date information on key developments in industrial relations in Europe.

The International Labour Organization (ILO) is a specialized agency of the United Nations responsible for labour issues globally. Their website can be found at http://www.ilo.org

## Additional material

Go to www.routledge.com/cw/nickson to find PowerPoint slides, chapter commentaries, test banks and additional case studies for each chapter.

C H A P T E R **3**

# Organizational culture

## CHAPTER OBJECTIVES

**This chapter considers the increasing importance of organizational culture to tourism and hospitality organizations. The objectives of this chapter are:**

- To assess debates about the manageability of culture.

- To consider the various aspects of organizational culture.

- To recognize the role of organizational culture in a broader HRM strategy.

## Introduction

We recognized in the previous chapter the importance of national culture and particularly the manner in which it is likely to have an impact on workplace behaviour. The same is also true within organizations. All organizations will have a culture which will have an impact on the way employees behave within the organization. As we have already recognized in Chapter 1, within human resource management (HRM) employees are seen as a key resource. Our core definition of HRM from Storey talked about cultural aspects of HRM, so part of the way in which employees, as a key resource, can be managed is through the use of organizational culture to generate commitment to the organization and its values. Thus, as Ogbonna (1992: 80) notes, 'the achievement of HRM objectives requires the management of the organizational value system (culture) and this requires skilful implementation'.

Often, within tourism and hospitality such values will be concerned with encouraging employee buy-in to customer care and service quality initiatives, which organizations see as a form of competitive advantage in the crowded marketplace. This process of seeking buy-in from employees is likely to have a significant impact on a range of human resource (HR) practices, such as recruitment and selection, training and remuneration. For example, as we discuss in Chapter 5, tourism and hospitality organizations may look to recruit and select those who are considered to 'fit in' with the culture. However, while many organizations and managers within the tourism and hospitality industry now see the management of organizational culture as a potential source of competitive advantage, there are others who caution against the overly optimistic claims made for organizational culture. Recognizing these competing views on organizational culture, this chapter will aim to offer a balanced assessment of the place of organizational culture within a broader HR strategy. Specifically, in examining organizational culture there are three key questions that need to be addressed.

1   What is organizational culture?
2   How can we study it?
3   What role does organizational culture play in organizational success?

## In search of a definition

Before we begin to move towards a definition it is important initially to recognize debates about the terminology employed to describe the manner in which organizations attempt to use culture as a device to create integration and cohesion across the organization. Central to this debate is the key question of the manageability or otherwise of culture (Legge, 1994). Commonly in books or articles the terms 'organizational' and 'corporate' culture may be used interchangeably. Legge (1994) cautions against this uncritical use of the two terms. For example, she argues that 'in using the term "corporate" culture, many writers seem to be imputing a culture created by senior management for the lower orders to swallow' (p. 407). In this view 'corporate' culture is something an organization *has*. Consequently, it can clearly be managed for the benefit of the organization and its members. On the other hand the use of the term 'organizational culture' reflects the manner in which culture emerges from social interaction among organizational members; something that an organization *is*. In the latter view culture may be difficult to manipulate, change or manage. Given some of the claims that are made about the link between organizational or corporate culture and organizational success this is an important caveat from Legge and one that should be borne in mind throughout the chapter.

Notwithstanding debates about whether the preferred terminology should be organizational or corporate culture, we should attempt to define the concept. Brown (1998) recognizes the multiplicity of definitions of organizational culture and the differing intellectual traditions that they come from. Based on these various definitions, Brown (1998: 9) offers his own:

Organizational culture refers to the pattern of beliefs, values, and learned ways of coping with experience that have developed during the course of an organization's history, and which tend to be manifested in its material arrangements and in the behaviour of its members.

For many this can be succinctly summarized as 'The way we do things around here' (Deal and Kennedy, 1988: 4). As we noted earlier, all organizations have their own unique culture, and in recent years attention has focused on the manner in which organizations can potentially use culture to unlock the commitment and enthusiasm of employees. This process of unlocking commitment and enthusiasm is by no means straightforward or uncontested (Thompson and McHugh, 2001). For example, we should be aware of the notions of subcultures, such that all organizational members might not subscribe to the organizational vision. Recognition of the potentially contested nature of organizational culture is important because it points to the manner in which there may be a disjuncture between the rhetoric and reality of organizational culture. Brown (1998) expresses this point as the espoused culture and the culture in practice. The former may be the positive view that is presented for public consumption, while the latter may allow for a more critical reading of any given organizational culture; to further appreciate this point the chapter now considers competing views of organizational culture.

## Competing views of organizational culture

The discussion above points to the debate about whether culture is, in fact, manageable; to recognize some of the competing claims made about culture we should acknowledge the useful work of Ogbonna and Harris (2002a). In reviewing organizational culture they attempt to categorize the range of work into three broad labels: the optimists, the pessimists and the realists.

## Optimists

A key aspect of the optimist's position is that culture can be used as a mechanism to facilitate organizational unity and cohesion. Thus, 'the key works of key "cultural optimists" show that this perspective not only assumes the existence of unitary cultures in organizations but it also implies that cultural control by top management is possible and desirable' (Ogbonna and Harris, 2002a, p. 35). Indeed, Ogbonna and Harris suggest that in recognizing the manageability of culture, optimists 'generally argue that those organizations that fail to control their cultures will be missing an opportunity to harness their human resources' (p. 35). The optimist's view relies on a lot of assumptions, not least that the interests of senior managers are shared by others in the organizational hierarchy. This type of thinking was particularly prevalent in much of the research and writing about organizational culture in the 1970s and 1980s, most obviously exemplified by the excellence genre, or what Thompson and McHugh (2001) refer to as the 'corporate culture merchants', such as Peters and Waterman (1982). Optimists also argue that there is a potentially positive relationship between organizational culture and business performance (and see HRM in Practice 3.1).

## HRM IN PRACTICE 3.1:
## Strong culture at the Regent Hotel

Kemp and Dwyer (2001) reflect an optimistic view of organizational culture in their research undertaken in the Regent Hotel, Sydney. The starting point of Kemp and Dwyer's research is that culture is viewed as an integrating, unifying phenomenon, shared by all organizational members. In this manner culture can be used to integrate and bind organizational members; it becomes a normative 'glue'. The authors believe that a 'strong' culture is an important enabling force in strategy formulation and ultimately is a major aspect of enhancing organizational performance. Drawing on interviews with 45 managers and employees of the hotel, Kemp and Dwyer recognize a variety of ways in which cultural aspects are integral to the development of HRM practices. For example, they suggest that within the hotel control is primarily through attempts to ensure that the employees offer quality service and exceed guests' expectations. Thus,

> Behavioural control is exerted through hotel training. Staff are taught how to enjoy their job and that they should greet guests at all times with a smile. In the attitude workshop staff are told that 'smiles are what count'. These smiles need to be as crisp as their daily dry-cleaned uniforms.
>
> (p. 87)

Even before the extensive attitudinal and behavioural training, control is exerted through recruiting the 'right' kind of people, who identify with the corporate objectives. It is also suggested that control is not too tight, but rather the Regent Way corporate culture encourages the 'right' kind of behaviour. If employees exhibit the right kind of behaviour this is recognized in formal celebrations of cultural values, often in the form of ceremonies which celebrate an aspect of the organizational culture. To illustrate this point Kemp and Dwyer recognize how the Regent Hotel rewards staff who exceed expectations in some way with a formal presentation in front of their peers, arguing that 'These ceremonies are extremely motivating and serve to ensure a repeat of the superior performance by the staff member' (p. 84). Culture, it is suggested, permeates every aspect of operations at the Regent Hotel, shaping the employees' responses to guests and also management's responses to their most important asset, their human resources. According to Kemp and Dwyer, the Regent Hotel exemplifies a strong culture in

which top management set the game plan and then individuals throughout the organizational hierarchy have responsibility for operationalizing the plan. The cultural approach of the Regent Hotel has resulted in breaking down the barriers between the thinker and doers. It is suggested that staff at the hotel share a strong awareness of the corporate mission and philosophy. They all know that the 'Regent Way' encourages 'Regent People' to be innovative and creative.

## Pessimists

Ogbonna and Harris (2002a) note that academics tend to predominate in this group and often approach the issue from largely theoretical perspectives. In that sense pessimists seek to develop the 'explanatory power of the culture concept rather than in identifying its practical utility for managers of organizations' (p. 36). Thus, and arguably in response to the excellence genre, much of the research and theorizing from the 1980s onwards has frequently questioned the extent to which organizations can manage culture successfully. The main thrust of the pessimist's critique is that such a complex issue as culture has been overly simplified by the optimists: 'it is argued that culture is located at the deepest level of human consciousness, of which neither researchers nor managers have sufficient knowledge to influence' (p. 36). A second strand to the critique is the unitary assumptions that underpin the optimist's position on culture. Pessimists would point to the potential for conflict and contradiction in organizations, which may be at odds with what the leaders and managers in an organization think (see HRM in Practice 3.2).

**HRM IN PRACTICE 3.2:**
**Culture as an Orwellian mechanism**

One of the more pejorative critiques of 'corporate culturalism' is that offered by Wilmott (1993). Wilmott talks about the Orwellian nature of corporate culture, with its nascent totalitarianism and *Nineteen Eighty-Four*-style doublethink, which attempts to create 'governance of the employee's soul'. He suggests that corporate culture is largely interested in creating a monoculture where alternative views or competing cultures are not tolerated. By excluding those considered as inappropriate in the recruitment and selection process and eliminating any alternative values by training, corporate culture aims to strengthen core organizational values. Any attempt to challenge the prevailing culture is considered a 'crime against the culture'. Consequently, corporate culture is *a totalitarian remedy for the resolution of indeterminacy and ambiguity: thought control through uniform definition of meaning.* . . . In Orwell's Oceania, 'freedom is slavery' and 'ignorance is strength'. In the world of corporate culture, 'slavery is freedom' and 'strength is ignorance'.

(p. 527, emphasis in original)

## Realists

The last category suggested by Ogbonna and Harris (2002a) are the realists. Increasingly, many researchers and writers are seeking a middle-way between the optimists and pessimists, and this has led to the emergence of a realist research agenda. Realists recognize that, potentially, culture can be changed. Equally, though, they eschew the idea that this process will always be controlled by top management. Consequently, 'realists are neither in support nor against the management of organizational culture. Rather, they advocate fuller explorations of the application of the concept, in order to develop greater understanding of the dynamics of cultural change' (p. 37). For example, Ogbonna and Harris note how culture change is more likely to occur during the formation of the organization, periods of crisis or during leadership turnover. In sum, the realist position, which is advocated by Ogbonna and Harris, is one which aims to merge theoretical rigour with contributions to the practicality of how organizational culture may be usefully used within a specific organizational context.

### Review and reflect

Using an organization with which you are familiar, consider the extent to which you would adopt either the optimistic, pessimistic or realist perspective to describe its culture.

## How can we study organizational culture?

Brown (1998) suggests that a number of different aspects or elements of culture have been identified and all of these various aspects are useful in attempts to study organizational culture:

- material objects;
- corporate architecture and corporate identity;

- symbols;
- language;
- metaphors;
- stories;
- myths;
- heroes;
- ceremonies, rites and rituals;
- norms of behaviour;
- values, beliefs and attitudes;
- basic assumptions;
- ethical codes; and
- history.

As Brown recognizes, there may be a degree of overlap between the above elements, a point we shall return to. Another key theme running through these various aspects of an organization's culture is the extent to which they may be manifest or visible. Schein (1985), for example, offers a well-known model which describes three levels of cultural phenomenon in organizations: visible manifestations, values and the deepest level of basic underlying assumptions. The first level consists of artefacts and creations that construct the physical and social environment of the organization. This level is the most superficial manifestation of culture and includes things like corporate logos, dress codes and written and spoken language used in the organization. The second level is concerned with values, beliefs and attitudes, which become prominent in the manner in which individual organizational members justify their actions and behaviour. As Lashley and Lee-Ross (2003: 154) note, 'The extent to which members hold these core values and norms as unquestionable determines whether the organizational culture is "strong" or "weak".' The last level is the most fundamental and relates to basic and tacit assumptions which impact on how organizational members perceive, think and feel. Schein (1985: 18) suggests that:

> Basic assumptions . . . have become so taken for granted that one finds little variation within a cultural unit. In fact, if a basic assumption is strongly held in a group, members would find behaviour based on any other premise inconceivable.

To further consider the manifest and not so manifest levels of culture, the chapter now returns to some of Brown's elements of culture.

## Material objects, corporate architecture and corporate identity and symbols

These aspects of an organization's culture provide a visible and manifest way in which it can be assessed. For example, mission statements are an obvious manifestation of material objects within organizations. Sufi and Lyons (2003) note how mission statements are now considered an important part of any company's strategic planning processes. The same authors note how mission statements can act as an important tool for tourism and hospitality organizations to communicate with organizational members and those outside the organization, such as customers and suppliers. A good mission statement should have some of the following components (Sufi and Lyons, 2003: 258): concern for the customer; purpose; identity/image; differentiation factors; corporate values; products; markets; concern for survival; growth; profitability; company philosophy; and employee and social concern.

Beyond mission statements, service organizations are also increasingly aware of how they portray their corporate image, both in terms of attempts to offer aesthetically pleasing 'hardware' and 'software' (Nickson *et al.*, 2001). Aesthetics are a sensory experience through which objects appeal in a distinctive way. This appeal does not necessarily have to be beautiful, but rather and more simply expressive. Materializing the concept of a company requires the transformation of an abstractly defined identity into the adoption of a style; in practice, the production of an aesthetic experience. Aesthetics have always been important to companies. Companies past and present use aesthetics to express corporate identity. These expressive forms are most obvious in the 'hardware' of organizations, such as marketing material (internal and external), product design and the physical environment of workspaces/offices (Witz *et al.*, 2003). Three points are worth noting with regard to the expression of corporate identity.

First, as symbols and artefacts, these aesthetics are intended to influence the perception of people as either customers or clients; organizations 'use these symbols in a vivid, dramatic and exciting way, because they know that symbols have power to affect the way people feel' (Olins, 1991: 71). Second, they are intended to add value to the company: 'Generally speaking, when companies use identity expressed through design, they use it as a commercial tool; their purpose is to make greater profit out of what they do in the short term' (ibid.: 53) Third, in highly competitive markets with little to differentiate most goods and services, aesthetics contribute to organizational distinctiveness: 'intangible, emotional. The name and visual style of an organization are sometimes the most important factors in making it appear unique' (ibid.: 75). Here we could think of McDonald's Golden Arches, for example (see also Bryman (2004) for a more general discussion of theming in other tourism and hospitality settings).

With regard to 'software' services, organizations are becoming increasingly concerned to regulate the appearance of their staff, through the use of uniforms, dress codes and appearance standards. Rafaeli (1993), for example, considers how the dress and behaviour of customer-contact employees shapes customer perceptions of service quality. As she suggests:

the thrust of organizational management of employees' dress is that the appearance of employees communicates something about the organization. The assumption is that what employees wear while at work, and how they appear when interacting with customers, can influence customers' feelings about the organization and the service that it provides.

(p. 182)

Disney, for example, has a 36-page cast members' appearance guide detailing length and style of hair and the colour and quantity of cosmetics (Henkoff, 1994; see also Bryman, 2004; van Maanen, 1991). Some of the implications arising from how organizations are increasingly seeking competitive advantage via employees' appearance or their 'aesthetic labour' (Nickson *et al.*, 2001) are further considered in Chapter 5.

## Language and metaphors

Bryman (2004) recognizes that, increasingly, service organizations aim to create performativity in the service encounter through the use of performative labour. Such labour is described as 'the rendering of work by managements and employees alike as akin to a theatrical performance in which the workplace is construed as similar to a stage' (p. 103). The use of a dramaturgical or theatrical metaphor is one that has often been used with regard to the manner in which service employees perform emotional labour (Hochschild, 1983). As Burns (1997: 240) notes, the emotional demands made of front-line tourism and hospitality employees is that they should 'constantly be in a positive, joyful and even playful mood'. Brown (1998) recognizes how language and metaphors aim to construct a common understanding in organizations so that abstractions such as 'good service', 'high quality' and 'excellence' are made meaningful. HRM in Practice 3.3 and 3.4 offer examples of how two organizations use language and metaphor, explicitly drawing on notions of performativity to create the right type of behaviour in their front-line employees.

### HRM IN PRACTICE 3.3:
### The use of language in Disney

| Everyday terms | Disney-speak |
| --- | --- |
| HR department | casting office |
| HR manager | casting rep |
| theme park visitor customer | guest |
| employee | cast member |
| front-line employee | host or hostess |

*continued overleaf . . .*

| public areas | onstage |
| restricted areas | backstage |
| theme park ride or show | attraction |
| hiring for a job | casting |
| job | role |
| foreman | lead |
| uniform | costume |
| job interview | audition |
| accident | incident |
| queue/line | pre-entertainment area |
| attraction designer | imagineer |
| talking robot | audio-animatronic figure |

Derived from Bryman (2004); IRS (2003a)

## HRM IN PRACTICE 3.4:
## Warm fuzzies and cold pricklies: the use of metaphor in Pizza Hut

Bate (1995: 44–45) notes that during the 1980s and early 1990s, Pizza Hut's employee induction programme made use of a booklet called *Feelings*. The booklet attempted to set out what employees should feel and particularly how they should display warm feelings, or what were termed 'warm fuzzies', during their work. Negative feelings were characterized as 'cold pricklies'. These two feelings were anthropomorphized into two cartoon characters: a malevolent, spiky-haired, spiky-bearded dwarf (cold prickly) and an appealing, round-eyed, cuddly powder-puff creature (warm fuzzy). Warm fuzzies were shown helping old ladies and giving out 'positive strokes' to everybody. In contrast, cold pricklies were seen getting wet and angry under black storm clouds and showing hostility to customers. The coldest of cold pricklies was the Big Fat Zero, who kept customers waiting, refused to smile and ignored people altogether. Warm fuzzies were represented in the booklet booting out cold pricklies and smiling no matter how hectic things became. In attempting to create the right kind of emotional labour the company aimed to ensure Pizza Hut employees saw themselves as warm fuzzies and acted accordingly by demonstrating the right kind of positive feelings towards customers, even when they did not necessarily feel like doing so.

> ## Review and reflect
>
> To what extent should tourism and hospitality organizations be able to use aesthetic and emotional labour to exert control over the manner in which employees behave? What are the likely challenges of using these types of cultural controls?

## Stories, myths, heroes and history

Deal and Kennedy (1999) note how stories are an important part of an organization's culture due to their ability to transmit cultural values. Corporate stories will often focus on exemplifying core values in the organization, often with recourse to the achievements and daring-do of cultural heroes, such as the founder of an organization. In an earlier work, Deal and Kennedy (1988) suggested that these heroes personify the organizational values and epitomize the strength of the organization. In becoming a 'John Wayne in pinstripes' heroic figures in organizations become role models for employees to follow. For example, Herb Kelleher, co-founder and long-time chief executive officer (CEO) of Southwest Airlines, is well known for his attempts to generate a sense of fun in the workplace. Known as the 'High Priest of Ha-Ha', Kelleher, who founded the company in 1971 and stepped down as Chairman in 2008, was integral in creating a corporate culture premised on fun. He believed in encouraging Southwest's flight attendants to joke and kid with passengers. Sunoo (1995) suggests that this strategy to hire the best people, treat them with respect and give them the freedom to make decisions and to have fun just being themselves has created some of the most loyal employees in the airline industry. Indeed, Bearden (2001) notes that in the immediate aftermath of 9/11 each of Southwest's 32,000 employees agreed to give back some of their pay to ensure company stability in a turbulent business environment (see also HRM in Practice 3.5).

### HRM IN PRACTICE 3.5:
### Stories and myths from some of the great hospitality entrepreneurs

Nickson (1997) argues for the importance of appreciating the need for an understanding of history in reviewing the autobiographies and biographies of Charles Forte, Conrad Hilton, Kemmons Wilson (the founder of Holiday Inn) and Bill Marriott (senior). Nickson notes the manner in which the stories and myths surrounding these famous hospitality entrepreneurs play an integral part in creating a corporate aura and set of values. For example, the three American 'giants' – Hilton, Wilson and Marriott – are suggested to exemplify the American Dream, which sees America as a land of opportunity, where individuals, by hard work and self-improvement, can achieve great success. A key element of this is respect for 'rugged individualism' (Guest, 1990: 390) and a willingness of individuals to grasp their opportunities by pushing back the frontiers, both literally and metaphorically. In a literal sense, Hilton was brought up in the 'half-civilized country' of New Mexico, where his father nearly became a victim of his own pioneering spirit as he was one of only two men to survive an attack by Apache Indians, an attack that left five others dead. The young Bill Marriott also demonstrated his frontier spirit on a camping trip in killing a deadly snake – naturally 'the biggest rattler anyone could remember' (O'Brien, 1977: 52–3) – and two menacing brown bears. In a metaphorical sense some of this frontier spirit is evidenced in the notion of the self-reliant small businessman who sets up his own business and makes it successful. A common theme in the accounts is the humble beginnings of the subjects' organizations. Hilton, for example, famously described his first hotel, the Mobley, purchased in Cisco, Texas in 1919, as 'a cross between a flop house and a gold mine' (Hilton, 1957: 109). Bill Marriott's early business career began with an 'A & W' root beer franchise which he acquired in 1927, while Charles Forte's move into business came with the opening of a milk bar in 1934. From such beginnings the nascent organizations quickly flourished and many of the operating procedures and management styles described in those early years can to some extent still be observed in the contemporary hospitality industry. For example, Hilton is credited with being the 'founder' of internationalization in the hotel sector and many aspects of the present Marriott philosophy, such as empowerment, can trace their history to Bill Marriott senior's way of doing business.

## Norms of behaviour, values, beliefs and attitudes and basic assumptions

Our earlier discussion of aspects such as performative labour and the mechanisms utilized by tourism and hospitality organizations to engender the right kind of emotional labour points to the manner in which they strive to achieve appropriate behaviour. Many tourism and hospitality organizations may well recognize that attempting to connect with their employees to generate a more fundamental level of engagement in the appropriate values, beliefs and attitudes or even basic assumptions in the organizations, may be doomed to failure. In this sense the ability of tourism and hospitality organizations to achieve cultural change at the deepest levels of basic assumptions may well be impossible. Of course, employers will use a variety of mechanisms to create the right kind of behaviour. Some of these may be cultural mechanisms, as

described above; others may simply be about the use of other means of control. For example, while some might claim that the 'strong' culture at McDonald's is largely created by the prevailing organizational culture, more critical authors would point to aspects such as de-skilling and the use of non-human technology (Ritzer, 2004). Even cultural mechanisms may be underpinned by more rigid control mechanisms. Ogbonna and Wilkinson (1990) report the example of one supermarket that, as part of a culture-change programme, encouraged employees to smile more when engaging with customers. However, the company went one step further in introducing 'smile supervisors' who were tasked with assessing whether employee smiles were genuine. If smiles were felt not to be genuine, employees were reprimanded by the smile supervisors. Needless to say, this approach created a good deal of employee resentment. In reality, most organizations will simply settle for the right kind of outward behaviour being manifested by their employees, without recourse to smile supervisors, even if such a performance is simply a manifestation of resigned behavioural compliance.

Clearly, then, there are a number of functions that organizational culture will play. In this normative view of corporate culture, it attempts to foster social cohesion, so that it becomes the 'cement' or 'glue' that binds an organization together so it may offer coordination and control, reduction of uncertainty, a means to motivate staff and ultimately competitive advantage. Throughout this chapter, though, we have alluded to some of the potential difficulties in sustaining this normative view of culture. Beyond this point there is also a need to recognize the debate about whether there really is any evidence to support a relationship between organizational culture and performance, particularly whether culture can enhance the effectiveness of an organization's performance (also see HRM in Practice 3.6).

## HRM IN PRACTICE 3.6:
## Managers' belief in the value of corporate culture improving organizational performance

A survey of 340 senior Canadian executives across a range of organizations found significant support for the impact that corporate culture can have in enhancing organizational performance. For example, on the question of corporate culture's impact on organizational performance:

- 82 per cent of executives surveyed said that culture has a strong or very strong impact on their organization's performance;

- 61 per cent of executives said their organization's corporate culture drives sales and increases revenue;

- 53 per cent said it lowers labour turnover;

- 57 per cent said it gives a sense of belonging to organizational members.

It was also noteworthy that 62 per cent of the respondents suggested that cultural fit is more important than necessary skills in the hiring of new talent.

Derived from http://www.waterstonehc.com/cmac/archives/2008

Alvesson (2002: 53–54) suggests that there are four views on the relationship between organizational culture and performance:

1    The so-called strong-culture thesis. In this view employees are assumed to be inculcated into a strong organizational culture and resultantly demonstrate a high level of commitment to the organization and its values. Within the strong culture thesis it is assumed that the strength of the culture will be directly correlated with the level of profits in a company.

2    A reverse relationship between culture and performance. In this view it is suggested that high performance leads to the creation of a strong corporate culture. Organizational success creates common orientations, beliefs and values and an acceptance of the 'way of doing things'.

3    A contingent view of culture. In particular circumstances or conditions a particular type of culture is appropriate or even necessary and is likely to contribute to efficiency.

4    The need for adaptive cultures. Cultures that are able to respond to changing circumstances or a change in the business environment are the key to good performance (see HRM in Practice 3.7).

## HRM IN PRACTICE 3.7:
## A failure to adapt?

The failure of a culture to adapt may arguably partially explain the inability of Forte to resist the hostile takeover mounted by the Granada organization. Nickson (1997) notes the important role played by Lord Forte, the founder of the company, and how his influence was pervasive in the culture. In time, Lord Forte was succeeded by his son, Rocco Forte, though many foresaw the difficulties of succeeding Lord Forte. Lashley and Lee-Ross (2003) note how the strong power/role culture created in the Forte group was anachronistic and uncompetitive and left the company vulnerable to the takeover. Several pieces written during the height of the takeover battle seemed to question the extent to which Rocco Forte could carry on his father's legacy, especially if the previously strong culture was creating rigidity and group-think in the organization.

Ultimately, in considering the relationship between culture and performance Alvesson (2002: 54) notes that 'the relatively few systematic studies on the culture–performance link lead us to conclude that none of these four ideas have received much empirical support'. For example, much of the earlier work on culture, as exemplified by Peters and Waterman (1982), was often underpinned by support for the strong-culture thesis. Thompson and McHugh (2001), among others, question the evidence offered by Peters and Waterman and others supporting the strong-culture-enhanced performance thesis. As they suggest, 'The tenuous link between cultures, excellence and performance turned out to be highly fragile' (ibid.: 199). Generally, then – and despite the often upbeat view that managers have of organizational culture, as exemplified in HRM in Practice 3.6 – the case for whether a 'strong' organizational or corporate culture is integral to the success of an organization remains unclear. More broadly, while it might seem intuitively true that, for example, adaptive cultures are self-evidently superior, again the evidence seems sparse, as far as Alvesson is concerned.

## Organizational culture and HRM: a reprise

Throughout this chapter we have considered the relationship between cultural mechanisms and HRM strategies. Equally, we have also recognized debates about the manageability of culture or whether organizational culture can be causally related to enhanced effectiveness or performance in organizations. Ultimately, as we have already recognized, there are no easy answers to these issues and there is a need to recognize the many competing claims or views about the nature of organizational culture. That said, Ogbonna and Harris' espousal of the realist position is one that attempts to reconcile some of these debates. If we accept the realist position, then there may be instances in which culture may be managed or changed in support of organizational aims. As a corollary, attempts to manage culture in support of organizational aims will mean the adoption of certain HRM practices. Specifically, we should recognize that attempts to sustain a degree of cohesion through cultural mechanisms is likely to mean that organizations will look to recruit those individuals who are deemed to 'fit in' with the prevailing culture. Once recruited, employees will then undergo an intense period of induction and socialization to be fully inculcated into the organizational culture. This process of inculcation is further reinforced through training and development activities, which as we noted within hospitality and tourism, will often be directed towards enhancing quality service. Lastly, organizations may choose to reward those who are seen to have internalized the values of the organization through enhanced financial rewards, such as those described in Kemp and Dwyer's case study of the Regent Hotel.

## Review and reflect

What are some of the likely challenges facing tourism and hospitality organizations who are seeking to use organizational culture as a unifying device as part of their broader HRM strategy?

That said, there is a need to consider some of the potential contradictions and dilemmas in managing culture. Some of the contradictions and dilemmas may well be posed by the sectoral context in which an organization operates. For example, with regard to tourism and hospitality, Ogbonna and Harris (2002a: 39–40) note how:

> the tensions between the key employment features of the industry – such as labour flexibility, low pay, poor terms and conditions, casualization and feminization – and the traditional 'high commitment' objectives of culture management programmes make this an important industry for the study of organizational culture.

Recognizing this point, they go on to indicate some of the limitations in the extent and manner of cultural intervention in the case study companies reported in their study. For example, Ogbonna and Harris remain sceptical of the ability of tourism and hospitality organizations to achieve cultural change at the deepest levels of basic assumptions across the organizational hierarchy. The ability to achieve deeper levels of cultural transformation may be problematic due to working conditions and terms of employment, such as unsocial working hours and low pay. Equally, the managers interviewed in Ogbonna and Harris' (2002a) case study organizations recognized the difficulties of gaining significant commitment from peripheral workers (Table 3.1).

**TABLE 3.1 HRM and culture: contradictions and dilemmas**

| Ideal HRM goals | Contradictions and dilemmas |
| --- | --- |
| Tight 'fit' between organization and individual | Labour shortages, competition for labour, ad-hoc recruitment and selection |
| Quality and service | Difficult customers |
| High trust and commitment | Surveillance, tight control, low pay |
| Strong internal labour market | High labour turnover, high percentage of part-time employees |
| Source: adapted from Ogbonna (1992). | |

Ultimately, in considering the implications for practitioners, Ogbonna and Harris (2002a) suggest that their findings point to how culture can best be managed. Crucial to this point is the need to recognize that a differentiated approach is likely to work best, reflecting the core and peripheral workforce in the tourism and hospitality industry. In that sense, core staff, who are long-serving and exposed to extensive and intensive culture programmes, may well be inculcated to a large degree into the organization's culture. However, for peripheral workers, 'practitioners may well focus their attention on ensuring behavioural compliance and appropriate emotional displays' (p. 50). Clearly, then, this points to the need for organizations to consider differentiated, complex and sensitive change programmes as these are more likely to be successful in gaining culture buy-in from organizational members.

## Conclusion

Alvesson (2002) suggests that too much organizational culture thinking has been grounded in assumptions about the potentially positive consequences of culture, a trend which arguably emerged with the panacean nature of the excellence genre, which captured the managerial imagination when it first emerged in the early 1980s. Over time more reflective and critical accounts have sought to temper some of this initial enthusiasm for the role that culture can play within the organization. Ogbonna and Harris' characterization of optimists, pessimists and realists neatly captures the evolving nature of the debate about organizational culture and its ability to enhance commitment among organizational members. In adopting a realist position Ogbonna and Harris attempt to recognize that culture can be managed, though the extent to which this process may be successful remains contingent. The nature of the industry, organization, occupation, employment status within the organization and many other things beside are all likely to impact on the extent to which organizational members ultimately immerse themselves in the basic assumptions of the organization, or simply manifest resigned behavioural compliance.

## Discussion questions

- In what ways might organizational and corporate culture be considered different?
- How can tourism and hospitality organizations use organizational culture to improve service quality?
- Suggest arguments for and against the proposition that only by having a strong corporate culture can organizations be successful.

# Further reading

Brown, A. (1998) *Organizational Culture*, 2nd edn, London: Pitman.

Kemp, S. and Dwyer, L. (2001) 'An examination of organizational culture: the Regent Hotel, Sydney', *International Journal of Hospitality Management*, 20, 77–93.

Legge, K. (1994) 'Managing culture: fact or fiction', in K. Sisson (ed.), *Personnel Management: A Comprehensive Guide to Theory and Practice in Britain*, Oxford: Blackwell.

Ogbonna, E. (1992) 'Organizational culture and human resource management', in P. Blyton and P. Turnbull (eds), *Reassessing Human Resource Management*, London: Sage.

Ogbonna, E. and Harris, L. (2002a) 'Managing organizational culture: insights from the hospitality industry', *Human Resource Management Journal*, 12, 1, 33–53.

van Maanen, J. (1991) 'The smile factory: work at Disneyland', in P. Frost, L. Moore, M. Louis, C. Lundberg and J. Martin (eds), *Reframing Organizational Culture*, London: Sage.

Wilmott, H. (1993) 'Strength is ignorance; slavery is freedom: managing culture in modern organizations', *Journal of Management Studies*, 30, 4, 515–52.

# Recommended websites

There are a number of useful weblinks and case studies, which can be found at http://www.new-paradigm.co.uk/Culture.htm

You can find lots of interesting case studies of how corporate culture works in organizations at http://www.waterstonehc.com/cmac/canadas-10. Among other things the site lists Canada's ten Most Admired Corporate Cultures.

Southwest Airlines has a unique culture which stresses the fun nature of the business; details can be found at http://www.southwest.com/html/about-southwest/index.html

Edward de Bono and Robert Heller are well-known management gurus and they have some interesting thoughts on organizational culture, which can be found at http://www.thinkingmanagers.com/business-management/corporate-culture.php

# Additional material

Go to www.routledge.com/cw/nickson to find PowerPoint slides, chapter commentaries, test banks and additional case studies for each chapter.

CHAPTER

# 4

# Labour markets

## CHAPTER OBJECTIVES

**This chapter considers the nature of labour markets in the tourism and hospitality industry. Specifically, the objectives are:**

- To appreciate the different levels of analysis in understanding labour markets.

- To understand the particular sectoral characteristics that determine the tourism and hospitality labour market.

- To consider debates about the use of flexible labour strategies within tourism and hospitality organizations.

COMPANION @ WEBSITE

## Introduction

We should start by asking a key question: what do we mean when we talk about labour markets? At any one time people will be trying to either change their job or acquire a job and employers will be looking for employees, and this means that, in principle, in the external labour market all workers are assumed to be competing for all the jobs all the time. In reality, of course, this may not be the case and we can appreciate this by disaggregating different types of labour markets. Within this process there is also a need to have some awareness of a range of macro-economic issues, political and social factors and their impact on the external and internal labour markets, which will change and affect the work of human resource practitioners directly and visibly in terms of issues like employee/industrial relations, recruitment, training and development and pay. It should also be recognized that the nature of labour supply is equally important and demographic changes are having a significant impact on labour supply. In that sense it is generally acknowledged that a number of countries are experiencing, to a greater or lesser extent, a number of challenges with regard to labour supply. For example, as we noted in Chapter 2, China and India face significant skill shortages at both managerial level and lower down the occupational ladder. Within a European context, the Boston Consulting Group (2011) recognizes that by 2030 an additional 45 million employees will be required in Western Europe to sustain economic growth, while also recognizing that present birth rates suggest this figure will be difficult to reach. Similar issues are also seen within a UK context, along with a number of other trends that are impacting on labour supply:

- Declining birth rates mean that young people make up an increasingly smaller part of the population.
- Increases in longevity, plus more young people entering higher education, means that the 'greying' of the workforce is likely to become more apparent.
- The workforce is becoming increasingly feminized, with more women entering the labour market.
- The role of people from ethnic minorities is likely to become increasingly significant.
- Migrant workers, especially those from the so-called A8 Accession states in Eastern Europe, have in recent years made up much of the labour shortfall.

## Levels of analysis in the labour market

To further appreciate some of the points discussed above we can develop an understanding of labour markets by recognizing several different levels of analysis, encompassing both the external and internal labour market. We begin with understanding the external labour market – that is, the labour market outside of the organization – and initially consider the idea of a transnational labour market.

### Transnational labour market

Throughout time, economic migration has meant that people have been willing to move to find work or better-paying jobs. Indeed, one of the key drivers of an increasingly transnational and international labour market is the role of multinational companies (MNCs). We have already noted in Chapter 2 how the continuing growth of world markets, increased availability of management and technological know-how in different countries, global competition and international customers, advances in telecommunications and greater regional political and economic integration have all increasingly pushed MNCs down the road to seeking a more global orientation. We also noted how MNCs face

choices in how they staff their overseas units, including the use of expatriate managers and how the use of such managers is commonplace in the tourism and hospitality industry. Expatriate managers can be seen as denoting a rather more strategic use of human resources by MNCs.

In addition to this more strategic movement of individual managers, individuals may also choose to move internationally in their search for work or enhanced career development. For example, Joppe (2012) notes figures from the United Nations (UN) Population Division, which estimates that around 214 million people are currently resident outside of their country of origin. Of that number, the International Labour Organization (ILO) estimates that there are around 105 million migrant workers worldwide, with nearly 60 per cent of this number either in Europe or North America, around one-third in Asia/the Middle East and the remainder in Africa, Latin America/the Caribbean and Oceania. Joppe also recognizes that within this overall figure of 105 million the share within the tourism industry, and particularly hotels and restaurants, is growing rapidly. Indeed, in a recent major review of migration in the international hotel industry it was found, among other things, that:

- migrants are a vital source of skills and labour for the hotel industry in countries, developed and less developed, across the world;
- the experience of migrant workers and their employers in the hotel industry varies greatly according to country, culture and context;
- migrant labour, at varied levels, will continue to play a significant and often major role in the workforce of the hotel industry in most countries;
- there is a clear North–South divide in the roles and responsibilities of migrant employees in the hotel industry, with those from poorer countries working at the less skilled end of the workforce spectrum and those from developed countries taking senior managerial and technical positions.
- there is a strong consensus in the hotel industry that migrant workers are vital to the operational viability of the sector and will remain so for the foreseeable future;
- migrant workers are seen to benefit the industry in terms of the skills and commitment they bring to the organizational culture of hotel businesses;
- migrant workers are recognized to bring a skills profile into the industry which is frequently unavailable in the local labour market;
- hotel businesses benefit from the culturally diverse skills which migrant workers bring to their employment.
- migrant workers in some developed countries are significantly over-qualified for the working roles that they play in the hotel industry.

(Baum, 2012: v–vi)

A further aspect which is encouraging migration is the creation of regional trading blocs. It is widely recognized that the European Union (EU) is the most developed trading bloc and already evidences a high degree of economic and social integration. With regard to employment, a key issue has been the commitment to sustain the free movement of labour between member states. A good example of this free movement can be seen in the movement of workers that took place as a result of the expansion of the EU in 2004 and, to a much lesser extent, 2007. In May 2004 the EU saw the accession of ten new member states (Poland, Czech Republic, Hungary, Slovakia, Lithuania, Latvia, Slovenia, Estonia, Cyprus (Greece) and Malta), with the addition of a two further states, Bulgaria and Romania, in 2007. Some of the employment implications of the increase from 15 to 27 countries within the EU are considered in HRM in Practice 4.1.

## HRM IN PRACTICE 4.1:
## EU expansion: a solution to labour and skill shortages in tourism and hospitality?

The accession of the ten new states from Central and Eastern Europe in 2004 meant another 74 million people joined the world's largest single market. While there was some concern at the notion of large numbers of people seeking to move from Central and Eastern to Western Europe, with the new immigrants proving a strain on existing member states, in reality the movement across Europe was relatively small. In part, this is explicable by the fact that initially only the UK, Irish and Swedish governments allowed people from the new accession states to work, as long as they registered. The other EU countries agreed to impose restrictions on immigration from Eastern Europe until 2011. Similarly, within the UK there still remain limitations on the areas in which nationals from Bulgaria and Romania (the so-called A2 countries) can work, with only a very small number of temporary jobs in food manufacturing (around 3,500) and agriculture (21,500 jobs) open to them. The decision of the British government to open up the labour market in 2004 to the ten new member states was largely driven by the recognition of significant labour and skill shortages in a number of industries, including hospitality and tourism. In the period of May 2004–June 2010 over one million applicants from the so-called A8 countries (the new accession countries minus Cyprus [Greece] and Malta) applied to register for the Worker Registration Scheme in order to work in the UK. The vast majority (66 per cent) of these applicants were from Poland. Employers in tourism and hospitality were quick to recognize this new source of labour, with close to 200,000 migrants working in the sector. Many of those moving from the A8 member states were young, well educated and highly motivated, and research has pointed to the manner in which migrant workers have been viewed very positively by British employers. It is suggested that employers have employed migrant workers ahead of British workers due to perceptions that they have a superior work ethic compared to indigenous workers. A number of research reports have reported employers using terms such as 'motivated', 'reliable',

'committed', 'excellent attitude', 'hardworking' and 'flexible' to describe migrant workers. They are also often prepared to work longer hours and ask for more shifts. As well as these positive reasons, Lucas and Mansfield (2010: 172) also note that 'the availability of a migrant labour force means that the labour market becomes even more segmented, as an additional group of marginal workers are employed at rates of pay that do not reflect their skills or qualifications'.

Derived from Clark and Hardy (2011); Janta *et al.* (2011); McCollum and Findlay (2011)

While the accession of a number of new member states proved a useful source of labour for a number of tourism and hospitality employers in the UK and Ireland in particular, it remains to be seen in the future with the opening up of the other EU countries whether this supply of labour will continue to be available to the same extent (Lucas and Mansfield, 2010). Indeed, as the expansion of the EU opened up opportunities for some workers to move to the UK, the UK government has also at the same time sought to restrict labour migration from non-EU countries (see HRM in Practice 4.2).

## HRM IN PRACTICE 4.2:
## The points-based system and its effect on Britain's ethnic restaurant sector

In February 2008 the UK introduced a points-based system for non-EU nationals who are seeking to come to work in the UK. The new system is based on five tiers: Tier 1 covers highly skilled migrants; Tier 2 skilled workers; Tier 3 low-skilled workers; Tier 4 students; and Tier 5 temporary or exchange workers. With the accession of the A8 countries and the influx of people to work in relatively low-skilled jobs it was decided that the Tier 3 route would be closed to anyone other than EU nationals.

What has particularly concerned some in the hospitality sector in the UK is the tightening up of opportunities for Tier 2 skilled workers, which includes chefs. As of April 2011 there will only be 20,700 people from outside the EU able to work in skilled professions under Tier 2, and these measures will be in place till at least April 2014. This situation has created significant concerns for restaurants in the speciality ethnic sector, which is estimated to be worth approximately £3 billion to the UK economy. In particular it is suggested that this sector will face increasing recruitment difficulties as in the past it has relied on recruiting chefs from outside the EU, particularly from Bangladesh, Pakistan and Sri Lanka. Chefs from outside the EU will now only be allowed to be recruited if an organization can demonstrate that an unfilled post is skilled to degree level, appropriate for a chef with at least five years' experience, paying at least £28,260, and not in either a fast-food or standard fare outlet. These criteria are outlined by the Migration Advisory Committee (MAC), which is the non-departmental public body of economists and migration experts who aim to provide transparent and evidence-based advice to the government on migration issues.

Part of the reason for the MAC further tightening the criteria for recruiting chefs from outside the EU is to encourage employers to invest more in up-skilling the native workforce. Thus, some are supportive of the idea of making it more difficult to recruit from outside the EU, suggesting that there is a need to get British people back to work. Indeed, in August 2010 People 1st launched a work-based professional chef qualification covering Indian, Bangladeshi, Chinese and Thai cuisines, including units on dim sum, noodles, spices and herbs, and using a tandoor. The government has also taken on board the comments from the industry and has funded the creation of a new body, the Hospitality Guild, to help ethnic restaurants recruit skilled staff from within the UK. In April 2012 the Hospitality Guild, in partnership with People 1st, launched a trial of five Asian and Oriental Centres of Excellence in England to train chefs; they will, in particular, target the young unemployed to encourage them to consider an apprenticeship in an Indian, Bangladeshi, Chinese or Thai restaurant.

Derived from Churchard (2012a); Harmer (2010a); Migration Advisory Committee (2011); Smedley (2011)

## Review and reflect

To what extent do you support recent UK government policy on immigration? Outline arguments for and against the use of migrant labour from both an organizational and societal point of view.

## National labour market

At the national level the government has a major influence on the labour market, and the manner in which policy is developed with regard to employment and economic issues will clearly impact on the nature of the national labour market. Generally speaking, when governments come to develop their labour market policy they face a choice in terms of the extent to which they will seek to regulate employment policies and practices. For example, it is often argued that there is a distinct difference between a European approach to labour markets, which is often described as the European social model, or in its more recent guise the European Commission's idea of 'flexicurity' (Heyes, 2011), and the so-called Anglo-Saxon approach, which is represented by the United

States, and to an extent the UK. In simple terms it is suggested that the European approach has tended to offer much greater regulation to achieve a balance in interests between capital and labour. Thus there is an element of flexibility, but this is also offset by the idea of security, including a number of employment rights. On the other hand, with the Anglo-Saxon approach to labour markets, and especially in the United States, the approach has relied much less on regulation and instead has operated on a free-market basis, wherein employers have few constraints on the way they choose to employ people. Of course, this description of a European and Anglo-Saxon approach is something of an oversimplification, though it is useful to delineate broadly differing approaches to the labour market. In considering these archetypes within the UK context in recent years, the UK has sought a balance between these two approaches with the so-called 'third way', which sought both a degree of regulation and flexibility. To appreciate why this is the case it is worthwhile briefly considering recent labour market developments in the UK, within the context of the discussion above.

In recent years there has been something of a change in policy within the UK. In the period 1979–97, the Conservative governments of Margaret Thatcher and John Major felt that there was too much regulation and the key thrust of much of their policy towards the labour market was to remove what they viewed as rigidities in the labour market. By espousing a free market with little regulation, the Conservative governments argued that employers had greater freedom in developing their employment policies and practices and that this was important for wealth creation. The shift towards much less regulation in the labour market was felt to be especially important for small businesses, who often complain about the deleterious impact of too much regulation on their business. As part of a whole series of legislation such as the Wages Act 1986, Trade Union and Labour Relations Consolidation Act 1992 and the Trade Union Reform and Employment Rights Act 1993, the Conservative governments sought to limit and restrict the autonomy and influence of trade unions, as well as allowing employers much greater latitude in areas such as hiring and dismissing workers and pay-setting.

With the election in 1997 of the 'New' Labour government, Tony Blair attempted to keep many elements of the flexible approach advocated by the previous Conservative governments, though at the same time the Blair government did introduce some measures to regulate employment. First, they signed up to the enlarged EU Social Chapter in 1997. Although the Social Chapter is not a legislative programme, it does provide mechanisms for harmonizing minimum standards of employment and social provision across the EU. The previous Conservative government (1992–7) had negotiated an opt-out, but with the Labour government signing up to the Social Chapter a number of HRM policies were affected.

From a labour market point of view the most important impact was the introduction of directives on parental leave, working time, part-time employees and, most recently, temporary agency workers. The Parental Leave Directive allows parents to take up to three months of unpaid leave after the birth of a child, up to their eighth birthday (see HRM in Practice 4.3).

## HRM IN PRACTICE 4.3:
## Female-friendly? How do countries compare?

There is much debate about how best to respond to greater feminization in the labour market and how best to balance work and family. A key issue within this broader debate is the support from the state to women in providing maternity leave and pay and facilitating a return to work. The vast majority of developed countries have a paid parental leave scheme, though practices do vary significantly between countries, which is a good indicator of the extent to which governments are willing to intervene in a key labour market issue. For example, in the UK women are entitled to 52 weeks of maternity leave regardless of their length of service and also have the right to return to work to the same job after 26 weeks paid maternity leave. Employers also have to 'seriously consider' requests from parents for more flexible working. The UK government is also looking to further extend paid paternity leave as well as making maternity and paternity arrangements more flexible. With this initiative the aim is to encourage both parents to share responsibility at the birth of a child, with new regulations likely to be in place by 2015. This situation in the UK is in contrast to the United States, where there is no nationwide policy on parental rights and no national provision for maternity leave, paid or otherwise. The same was also true until recently for Australia, where a scheme introduced in 2011 provides paid parental leave for 18 weeks for parents, usually mothers, who have been on the payroll for at least ten of the 13 months prior to the birth. The most family-friendly countries are arguably Sweden and Norway. For example, in Sweden both parents are entitled to 18 months off work and in Norway one year's leave is paid at 80 per cent of salary.

Derived from Australian Government (2009); Groskop (2006); Income Data Services (2011a)

The Working Time Regulations are considered more fully in Chapter 11. The regulations on part-time employees requires employers to treat them no less favourably than full-time employees. For example, part-time staff should receive the same pay and benefits, on a pro-rata basis, as full-time employees. Most recently the Agency Worker Regulations came into force on 1 October 2011. Prior to the regulations coming into force, temporary agency workers had some employment protection in areas such as discrimination, victimization, trade union membership, a minimum wage and working time. The new regulations give agency workers a series of additional rights from day one of their

employment – for example, access to facilities such as the canteen, childcare and access to any job vacancies within the organization. After they have been in the same job for 12 weeks with the same hirer, they are entitled to equal treatment for pay and other basic working conditions, such as annual leave and rest breaks. Weeks are accumulated for the agency worker regardless of how many hours per week they work (Labour Research Department, 2011a).

As we have already noted in Chapter 1, hospitality and tourism is particularly reliant on part-time workers, and it was felt that this and the other directives, particularly the Agency Worker Directive, would be potentially harmful to the viability of many businesses, particularly small business. In reality, though, the impact has been less than feared, in part because employers have been able to water down the regulations to lessen their impact. For example, there is already evidence of employers taking advantage of legal exclusions to lessen the impact of the agency workers legislation (Brockett, 2012; see also Hurrell, 2005). In addition to signing up to the idea of implementing regulatory EU employment directives, the Blair government also introduced a range of employment-related legislation. Most noteworthy were the National Minimum Wage Act 1998, Employment Relations Act 1999 and Employment Act 2002. These acts established minimum employment standards in areas such as pay, dismissal and trade union recognition.

While all of these aspects have certainly added some regulation to the labour market and impacted on tourism and hospitality employers' HRM policies, in reality the UK is felt to still have a relatively unregulated labour market compared to most other EU countries. In a recent review of arguments for and against employment regulation in the labour market, the CIPD (2011: 2) noted that 'the UK labour market is . . . one of the least regulated and most flexible in the developed world' (see also Coats, 2010). Moreover, the UK Conservative/ Liberal Democrat coalition government that was elected in 2010 have sought to reinforce the notion of flexibility within the labour market. In support of this process they have expressed a desire to revise what they consider to be 'burdensome' EU directives. In addition, they have also instigated an Employment Law Review, which is to run from 2010 to 2015 (see Department for Business, Innovation and Skills, 2012a). The coalition government has indicated that it sees too much 'red tape' and regulation in the labour market and consequently the review will consider employment laws with the aim of making it easier for businesses to employ people. Indeed, the government's belief that doing away with employment-related regulation will result in more employment has led to the creation of the 'Red Tape Challenge' (RTC), which encourages people to comment on areas where they would like to see regulation lessened (Department for Business, Innovation and Skills, 2011). There has been much debate about the likely consequences of this review. On the one hand, employer organizations such as the Confederation of British Industry (CBI) (2011) and the Recruitment and Employment Confederation (2010) have applauded the reassertion of the importance of full flexibility in the

UK labour market, with the latter organization suggesting that 'the UK employment model is world-class . . . [and] it is the flexibility of the employment market that has driven UK plc. success' (ibid.: 33). On the other hand, the trade union movement has expressed significant concerns at what they see as an attack on employment rights. Plans, for example, to cut workers' access to employment tribunals and increase the service qualification for unfair dismissal from one to two years have been characterized by Unite, the UK's largest union, as 'a charter for bullies and rogue employers' (cited in Labour Research Department, 2012a: 16; also see Chapter 12). What is clear is that the UK remains closer to an Anglo-Saxon view of the labour market, with relatively low levels of intervention compared to a number of other European countries, and the emphasis is more on the 'flexi' rather than 'security' element of the notion of 'flexicurity' (Heyes, 2011).

What much of the above discussion points to is the recognition of the impact of government policy on employment policy and HRM practices in organizations. Thus, it is important to understand that this is an important environmental and contextual feature in terms of how firms will plan their labour market policies.

## Sectoral labour market

To consider the nature of the sectoral labour market in tourism and hospitality, we should remind ourselves again what kind of industry tourism and hospitality is. As we noted in Chapter 1, the tourism and hospitality industry can be taken to include a wide variety of organizations encompassing areas like hotels, guesthouses, bed and breakfast, farm houses, holiday parks, restaurants, pubs and cafes, airlines, cruise ships, travel agencies, tour companies, and so on. Equally, we also recognized that it would be wrong to imagine that the industry can be thought of as homogenous (an obvious example is the spread of different types of organizations in the industry, from the local chip shop to huge multinationals with a presence all over the world). Despite this growth in larger chains, most sectors of the industry are still dominated by small, usually owner-managed units consisting of family labour and a small number of helpers. Clearly, then, the sector is better conceptualized as heterogeneous. However, while there is great heterogeneity in the types and size of organizations, there may be certain recurring features in large parts of the tourism and hospitality industry, which are outlined below:

- Large numbers of individual units of varying size and many different types are located throughout the whole of the country and internationally.
- Many units operate 24 hours a day, seven days a week, 365 days a year.
- There are high fixed costs, a fixed rate of supply, but a fluctuating, seasonal and often unpredictable demand.
- It is both a production and service industry.

- There is a wide variety of customers seeking to satisfy a variety of needs and expectations. For example, leisure, business, conference and so on.
- Services are supplied direct to the customer on the premises and the customer usually leaves with no tangible product.
- Managers are expected to demonstrate proficiency in technical and craft skills as well as in management areas.
- Many different skills are required but there are relatively large numbers of semi-skilled and unskilled staff.
- The majority of staff are relatively low paid.
- Staff are often expected to work long and unsociable hours.
- There is a large proportion of female, part-time, casual, student and migrant labour.
- Generally trade union membership is low.
- There is high labour mobility within the industry, and a high turnover of staff joining and leaving the industry.
- The industry is labour intensive.

Perhaps the single biggest influence on the nature of labour markets in the tourism and hospitality industry is the recognition that there are often wide fluctuations in short-term demand for the product, which has major and obvious implications for the staffing of an organization (see Table 4.1).

Allied to this demand unpredictability is the fact that the industry is labour intensive, which means labour is a high cost in the total costs of tourism and hospitality businesses. Therefore many employers have tried to minimize labour costs. This has meant, as we noted in Chapter 1, that traditionally the industry has been staffed with what Wood (1997a) calls 'marginal workers', namely women, young people, students, migrant workers and ethnic minorities. Resultantly, it is argued by many that these workers form the basis of a casualized, part-time workforce. This workforce find itself in a low-skill job

| TABLE 4.1 Hotel demand variability | |
|---|---|
| | Examples of hotel demand variability |
| Daily | Morning rush hour, guest check-out and evening check-in; peak demands for restaurant services during meal time: breakfast (7–10 a.m.), lunch (12–2 p.m.) and dinner (7–10 p.m.). |
| Weekly | High occupancy during mid-week for business hotels, but low in weekends. More restaurant reservations at the weekend. |
| Seasonal | Winter closure of beach resorts. High occupancy rate in ski chalets during the winter. |
| Ad hoc | Flight cancellation leading to unpredictable demand for hotel rooms and meal services. 'Chance' guest bookings. |
| Source: Lai and Baum (2005). Reprinted by permission of Emerald Group Publishing Ltd. | |

characterized by relatively low pay, which leads to a lack of motivation and commitment on the part of employees, who may perceive they are in a job which is often stereotyped as being about servility. Of course, as we noted in Chapter 1, this description may be over-generalizing the employment experience of many working in tourism and hospitality, and this characterization is unlikely to be true for all organizations, or reflect the circumstances for all workers. For example, for many women, working part-time will allow them to match domestic and employment responsibilities. Equally, there may well be skilled craft jobs which require some formal training or education, as opposed to unskilled work which is just learnt on the job (see HRM in Practice 4.4).

## HRM IN PRACTICE 4.4:
## Working in paradise

Patricia and Peter Adler (2004) offer an interesting example of how within luxury hotels in Hawaii different types of employees are likely to have very different employment experiences. Based on a nearly ten-year ethnographic study, *Paradise Laborers* is an attempt to understand what goes on behind the scenes in five luxury hotels in Hawaii. Specifically, Adler and Adler offer an in-depth analysis of the complex organizational and social systems of the hotels and how this impacts on the experiences of those working there; and why, for many, working in the hospitality industry in Hawaii is akin to paradise. At the heart of the book lies Adler and Adler's typology of four different types of worker: new immigrants, locals, seekers and managers. New immigrants are those who fill the most menial, physically demanding jobs in areas such as housekeeping and stewarding, positions which are considered undesirable by indigenous Americans. This characterization of the new immigrants might suggest a life of hardship, drudgery and exploitation for this group of workers. However, Adler and Adler note how the new immigrants were:

> highly valued, even crucial, workers in the hospitality and other local industries. While others have depicted globalized workers as transient, our new immigrants became heavily tied to and invested in their new country by opportunity, family, community, work, and fierce loyalty.

(p. 217)

Locals are equally tied to Hawaii – indeed Adler and Adler characterize new immigrants and locals as being 'trapped', by choice, by the vicissitudes of the local labour market. For many locals, though, work in the resorts in regarded as being desirable, unsurprising perhaps when travel and tourism provides over 20 per cent of employment within Hawaii. Locals tended to occupy those jobs immediately above the entry jobs taken by new immigrants in positions such as valets and bellmen and tended to approach work with a 'work to live' attitude as

'they did not want to live in paradise if the cost was they could not enjoy it' (p. 60). The latter two groups of seekers and managers are characterized as being transient and primarily are affluent, middle-class, male, mainland Americans who are usually just passing through Hawaii. Unlike new immigrants and locals, seekers and managers are able to draw on their inherent cultural capital, such as their education, which allows them greater occupational choice. However, while managers are aiming to make a career in hospitality management, and often work long hours for relatively low rewards, seekers, or 'drifter workers' (p. 81), are attracted to Hawaii to experience a much more hedonistic lifestyle, where leisure is foregrounded over work, and work becomes a means to a recreationally focused end.

With regard to skill, Riley (1996) estimated that the skill composition in a typical unit in the hospitality industry would consist of 6 per cent managerial, 8 per cent supervisory, 22 per cent skilled craft workers and 64 per cent semi-skilled or unskilled operative staff, though see also HRM in Practice 4.5.

## HRM IN PRACTICE 4.5:
## Re-considering skill

Baum (2002) considers the nature of skill in the tourism and hospitality industry and argues the need for more expansive thinking about the issue. While broadly accepting Riley's characterization, Baum also points to the need to consider the changing nature of skills in tourism and hospitality, with the emergence of aspects such as emotional and aesthetic labour. These 'softer' skills are harder to classify and locate within traditional debates about the meaning of skill, dominated as they often are by the understanding of skills being 'hard', technical skills, often accredited by qualifications or an apprenticeship. Resultantly, the tendency towards describing much tourism and hospitality work as unskilled may be increasingly oversimplified. Relatedly, Baum also questions the overwhelmingly Western-centric view of skills, something that is inappropriate in a developing-country context. Here, many of the softer skills coming under the rubric of emotional or aesthetic labour may be highly valued.

In sum, then, the tourism and hospitality labour market is characterized by:

- a relatively large proportion of unskilled occupations;
- transferability of skills at any level between a broad range of establishments;

- often, but not inevitably, high levels of labour turnover;
- relatively low levels of pay, particularly for unskilled workers.

All of the above points mean that many organizations compete in what is often described as the secondary labour market.

## The internal labour market and the utilization of flexible labour

While the description of the broader context, as represented by the transnational, national and sectoral labour markets, is important, we should also consider some of the choices that organizations themselves will make in developing their internal labour market. Riley (1996: 12) describes the internal labour market in the following manner:

> The concept of the internal labour market is based on the idea that sets of rules and conventions form within an organization which act as allocative mechanisms governing the movement of people and the pricing of jobs. Such rules are about promotion criteria, training opportunities, pay differentials and the evaluation of jobs, but most importantly, they are about which jobs are 'open' to the external labour market.

Traditionally, many tourism and hospitality organizations have failed to develop strong internal labour markets, where skills are developed maximally via internal promotion and upgrading; managers have relied instead on the external labour market, which is cheaper because labour is plentiful (though see HRM in Practice 4.6).

## HRM IN PRACTICE 4.6:
## Who progresses in the UK café sector?

A recent study by Lloyd and Payne (2012) of the UK café sector found that branded organizations were more likely to offer career progression compared to independent cafes. Three of the 11 organizations studied by Lloyd and Payne had highly structured systems of training and development, which existed alongside clear pathways for progression. Where this was most developed in a branded coffee chain and sandwich shop the company encouraged progression with a clear pay and career structure that began at customer service assistant and provided steps to becoming a unit manager and beyond. From the wide range of people working as café assistants, including students, women with young children,

migrant workers and those employees actively seeking a career in the sector, Lloyd and Payne found that ten of the 25 assistants they interviewed wanted to progress either within their own organization or a similar type of organization. Interestingly, 11 of the 15 supervisors and assistant managers interviewed for the study had entered their job through internal promotion from café assistant. It is noteworthy that the findings from Lloyd and Payne support the idea that progression does take place internally, although qualifications seemed to play little part in the process. They concluded that internal labour markets in the café sector do offer a useful motivational tool for some workers who are looking to progress. However, they also recognize that while the job can be a stepping stone, it can be a long journey with the steps up within the café environment being characterized as incremental with limited changes to job tasks and small additions to pay.

Another aspect of the internal labour market is the choices that organizations may face in their use of various forms of flexibility. As we noted above, the aim of much of the legislation of UK governments in recent years has been to increase flexibility in the labour market. As Kelliher and Riley (2003: 99) note, 'Flexibility was seen as a means of enhancing competitiveness and adapting to changes in the business environment.' Much of the debate generated about the nature of flexibility in organizations was developed with recourse to the highly influential work of Atkinson (1984), which proposed the 'flexible firm' model. Although subsequently heavily criticized, the model does usefully distinguish between 'core' and 'peripheral' employees. The former group are characterized as being permanent, usually full-time, staff who are viewed as a valuable resource, likely to be multi-skilled and enjoying employment security and career progression. By contrast, the latter group are likely to be part-time or casual, enjoy little employment security, have fewer skills and be easily disposable, reflecting Wood's (1997a) view of marginal workers described earlier. In reality, as with other ideal types described in this book, these descriptions tend to oversimplify the nature of core and peripheral staff in hospitality and tourism (Deery and Jago, 2002). For example, Walsh (1990) has described how staff that would be thought of as 'peripheral' will often be integral to the running of a hotel and may be equally committed to the organization as core staff. Nevertheless, the notion of core and peripheral workers is useful in pointing to the types of labour flexibility utilized by tourism and hospitality organizations, two of the most prominent being functional and numerical flexibility.

## Functional flexibility

Functional flexibility is seen as the employer's ability to deploy employees, and more specifically core employees drawn from the primary labour market, between activities and tasks. In increasing the range of tasks that an employee can undertake, employers will expect employees to be capable of working in different functions within the same department, or even work between departments. Such an approach can lead to increased skills, job satisfaction, more meaningful work and enhanced career prospects for employees. Many descriptions of functional flexibility in the tourism and hospitality sector, though, have pointed to a rather ad-hoc approach, which may be more about covering short-term problems than creating a genuinely multi-skilled employee. This point has led Riley (1992) to describe true functional flexibility within tourism and hospitality as being a 'Cinderella idea'. However, Kelliher and Riley (2003) report research from four case study organizations in the hospitality industry who had enjoyed benefits to both employers and employees in introducing functional flexibility. Employers reported more efficient use of labour, lower labour costs, better operational functioning, improved customer service, reduced levels of labour turnover and an improvement of their position in the local labour market. Employees also reported increased job satisfaction, greater job security and enhanced remuneration (see also HRM in Practice 4.7).

## HRM IN PRACTICE 4.7:
## Marriott Marble Arch: aiming to multi-task and multi-skill

Lowe (2002) recognizes that, as with every other tourism and hospitality organization, the London Marriott Marble Arch hotel has to cope constantly with staff recruitment, retention and motivation to maintain high standards of customer service. The four-star hotel introduced a cross-training scheme to improve the skills of its employees to help them cope with the requirements of their job roles. To improve their staff recruitment and retention, the hotel set up its cross-training Discovery scheme. The programme was designed to increase staff skills and to ease career promotions into higher or sideways positions through developing employee skills in other areas. It also endeavoured to base labour scheduling on a flexible, multi-skilled workforce, allowing the hotel to use its employees in the most cost-effective manner. The scheme was targeted at every employee and was completed during normal working hours. Overall, it took more than 320 hours, spread over 40 one-day sessions, for the hotel to complete their Discovery cross-training. At the end of the formal training each participant received individual feedback and a certificate of achievement. The HR department was involved in coordinating the scheme, liaising with heads of departments and getting constructive feedback from participants in order to control and modify the scheme. Parallel to this, further developments were introduced, such as a two-week critical cross-training session, which was added to new associates' 90-day induction plan

in order to make them develop skills within their critical departments. For instance, new restaurant employees were supposed to spend time in the kitchen, bar and banqueting areas. In addition, the programme was made available all year round, and HR ensured employees had completed their cross-training before letting them move within departments.

The Discovery scheme led to substantial improvements. It impacted positively on two performance measures. First, the programme improved the Balanced Score Card, a tool used for measuring and communicating hotel performance at Marriott hotels. Second, the results of an annual employee survey significantly improved. Employees felt that training to carry out daily tasks improved, raising its score from 21 per cent to 87 per cent. They also believed their opportunities to develop their career had increased by 4 per cent, and 84 per cent felt that they had accessible job opportunities compared to only 9 per cent before the introduction of the scheme. As Lowe (2002), the HR manager at the hotel, commented, 'The initiative has proved invaluable to the London Marriott Marble Arch hotel. It is a concept that could easily be adapted to other businesses to help meet the constant challenge of staff recruitment and retention' (p. 14).

## Numerical flexibility

Numerical flexibility refers to the capacity of employers to adjust labour supply to fluctuations in business demand, which may equal less job security, low pay, lack of opportunities for training and career advancement for employees. Unsurprisingly, given this description, the peripheral workforce is most often associated with numerical flexibility. In pursuing numerical flexibility employers can look to either internal or external means (Lai and Baum, 2005). Internal means are largely concerned with the use of 'non-standard employment contracts', such as part-time and shift working and the use of temporary and casual workers. External means include aspects such as contracting out services – for example, a hotel contracting out its leisure facilities, and the use of agency staff (see HRM in Practice 4.8)

### HRM IN PRACTICE 4.8:
### Just-in-time labour supply in the hotel sector

Many four- and five-star hotels will often rely on agency staff recruited from employment agencies, particularly in areas such as housekeeping. Research by Lai and Baum (2005) suggests that hotels can reduce labour costs by utilizing agency staff and thus avoiding having to pay fringe benefits such as sickness cover, pension contributions, maternity leave payments and holiday entitlements, all of which are covered by the employment agency. Additionally, HR activities such as recruitment and selection, induction and training are often undertaken by the agencies. Lai and Baum suggest that one hotel in their research saved up to £500,000 each year in housekeeping payroll costs. In addition to cost savings, Lai and Baum also found that agency staff had often worked for the same hotel for a number of years with the consequence that quality and performance were improved.

In addition to functional and numerical flexibility, tourism and hospitality organizations can also use temporal flexibility, such as annual hours contracts and job sharing; and pay flexibility, such as enhanced payments in return for being functionally flexible.

It is interesting to briefly think about the descriptions of flexibility within our earlier discussion of hard and soft HRM. As we noted in Chapter 1, hard and soft HRM allow us to appreciate that the reason for organizations adopting certain HR practices may vary. Based on our description of the two approaches we could, rather crudely, characterize numerical flexibility as being largely about hard HRM. This hard approach emphasizes the use of labour that is aimed at reducing labour costs, either by the most efficient use of labour or, alternatively, its most effective exploitation. In this view, approaches to flexibility will be concerned with minimizing labour costs and ensuring the size and mix of labour inputs is adjusted to changes in product demand. On the other hand, the soft approach is more concerned with broadening employees' skills through training to create workforces which are flexible. Such a description is more concerned with functional flexibility.

As we have seen, the most frequently utilized method of flexibility in the tourism and hospitality industry is numerical flexibility, which is often characterized by low-paid, low-skilled, casual and part-time operative-level work. An example of such an approach would be a pool of available staff that could be called in at short notice to work in the organization – for example, in the banqueting department of a hotel. Indeed, many have argued that talk of flexibility and core and peripheral workers induces nothing more than an ominous sense of déjà vu within the tourism and hospitality industry. Due to the nature of the industry, patterns of employment within tourism and hospitality have largely been arranged in a way that promotes a high degree of employment flexibility, through the use of employment practices that have often left individual workers with limited opportunities for advancement and low job security. Wood (1997a: 168), for example, argues that

Flexible working practices in the commercial hotel and catering sector are not new to the industry, the use of part-time casual and part-time workers and multi-skilled staff being a common and arguable defining feature of labour organization in some sectors, most notably small hotel business.

## Conclusions

We have outlined a fairly bleak scenario of what traditionally the organizational characteristics of the tourism and hospitality industry have meant for those working in the industry. The tendency to short termism and ad hocism is the key feature of labour markets in the industry. Management responses to these issues are also similarly short term and ad hoc, with their role often being one of responding to situations and unanticipated crises, or trying to cope with varying demand. This, of course, leaves us with an obvious paradox: how can the tourism and hospitality industry compromise between the need for staffing flexibility and the attainment and maintenance of a quality service and product for the customer? There are no easy answers to this conundrum and even a cursory understanding of the nature of labour markets in tourism and hospitality allows us to appreciate this point.

## Discussion questions

- Should the tourism and hospitality industry rely on migrant labour?
- Outline arguments for and against regulation in the labour market.
- What are the characteristics of a strong internal labour market?
- What approaches can tourism and hospitality organizations use to increase the flexibility of their workforce?

## Further reading

Adler, P. and Adler, P. (2004) *Paradise Laborers: Hotel Work in the Global Economy*, Ithaca, NY: Cornell University Press.

Baum, T. (2012) *Migrant Workers in the International Hotel Industry*. Online, available at http://www.ilo.org/public/english/protection/migrant/download/imp/imp112.pdf

Deery, M. and Jago, L. (2002) 'The core and periphery: an examination of the flexible workforce model in the hotel industry', *International Journal of Hospitality Management*, 21, 4, 339–51.

Janta, H., Ladkin, A., Brown, L. and Lugosi, P. (2011) 'Employment experiences of Polish migrant workers in the UK hospitality sector', *Tourism Management*, 32, 1006–19.

Joppe, M. (2012) 'Migrant workers: challenges and opportunities in addressing tourism labour shortages', *Tourism Management*, 33, 3, 662–71.

Kelliher, C. and Riley, M. (2003) 'Beyond flexibility: some by-products of functional flexibility', *Service Industries Journal*, 23, 4, 98–113.

Lucas, R. and Mansfield, S. (2010) 'The use of migrant labour in the hospitality sector: current and future implications', in M. Ruhs and B. Anderson (eds), *Who Needs Migrant Workers?: Labour Shortages, Immigration and Public Policy*, Oxford: Oxford University Press.

## Recommended websites

The International Labour Office has a range of material on international and national labour laws which can be found at http://www.ilo.org/global/topics/labour-law/lang–en/index.htm

The European Foundation for the Improvement of Living and Working Conditions has some interesting material and other links at http://www.eurofound.europa.eu/areas/labourmarket/index.htm

The Migration Advisory Committee's website contains a number of interesting reports, including the latest Shortage Occupations list, and can be found at http://www.ukba.homeoffice.gov.uk/aboutus/workingwithus/indbodies/mac

## Additional material

Go to www.routledge.com/cw/nickson to find PowerPoint slides, chapter commentaries, test banks and additional case studies for each chapter.

# Recruitment and selection

COMPANION @ WEBSITE

## CHAPTER OBJECTIVES

**This chapter addresses recruitment and selection in the tourism and hospitality industry. In particular, the chapter aims:**

- To understand the differences between, yet complementary nature of, recruitment and selection.

- To appreciate the importance of job descriptions and person specifications/competency profiles in recruitment and selection.

- To recognize the type of people and skills that tourism and hospitality organizations are seeking.

- To consider the range of selection techniques available to tourism and hospitality organizations.

## Introduction

Generally, recruiting and selecting people to fill new or existing positions is a crucial element of human resource (HR) activity in all tourism and hospitality organizations, irrespective of size, structure or activity (see, for example, Baum, 2008). Although, as we noted in Chapter 3, the importance of service quality has increased the pressure on organizations to select the 'right' kind of individual, it is often widely suggested that too often decisions are made in an informal, ad hoc and reactive manner. This point may be especially true in smaller organizations that may not have well-developed human resource management (HRM) functions or recruitment and selection systems and may recruit irregularly, with heavy reliance on informal systems and methods (Jameson, 2000). Indeed, within the context of the hospitality sector, Price

(1994) found that of 241 hotels sampled in her research, one-third never used job descriptions or person specifications. More recently, Lockyer and Scholarios (2004) surveyed over 80 hotels and again found a general lack of systematic procedures for recruitment and selection. This lack of systemization may seem strange when many writers would point to the cost of poor recruitment and selection being manifested in such things as:

- expensive use of management time;
- retraining performers;
- recruiting replacements for individuals who leave very quickly;
- high labour turnover;
- absenteeism;
- low morale;
- ineffective management and supervision;
- disciplinary problems; and
- dismissals.

Clearly, then, it is important for organizations to consider how they can approach recruitment and selection to increase the likelihood of a successful appointment/decision and in a cost-effective manner. Reflecting this latter idea of cost-effectiveness, it is important to recognize the contingent nature of recruitment and selection. Thus, although there may be good-practice approaches to recruitment and selection, these are not going to be appropriate for all positions available in an organization. For example, for a management traineeship in a major hotel the company may use a variety of sophisticated and costly mechanisms culminating in an assessment centre. On the other hand, for a part-time seasonal position in a fairground the company may recruit an employee based on word-of-mouth. Indeed, in considering why it may be difficult for tourism and hospitality companies to aim for best practice in recruitment and selection, Lockyer and Scholarios (2004) recognize that the lack of formality can often be overcome by effective use of local networks in recruiting employees. For example, they suggest that the person responsible for selection should have a good knowledge of the local labour market and be able to make the best use of informal networks to find suitable employees.

A further point to consider by way of introduction is the notion of 'fit' between the individual and the organization that is seeking to attract and admit those who are considered 'right' for the organization, in terms of issues like commitment, flexibility, quality, ability to work in a team and so on. Thus, the match between the individual and organization may be 'loose' – that is, applicants having the ability to do the job – or 'tight', where the individual has to demonstrate not only technical competence but whether they have a specific personality profile to 'fit' the organizational culture, as discussed in Chapter 3.

In such circumstances there is clearly the possibility to see the notion of 'tight fit' between organization and individual in a slightly sinister way; we will consider this point throughout the chapter. Relatedly, there is the idea of discrimination being a key issue within the recruitment and selection process. Of course, at one level recruitment and selection is inherently discriminatory as, at times, organizations will have to choose between two or more applicants for a job, particularly for managerial positions. Crucially, though, such discrimination should be based on the applicant's ability to do the job. Thus, companies are discriminating all the time on the basis of whether or not candidates have the attributes and skills to do the job, but this should not contravene statutes in areas such as race, sex and disability (see Chapter 6). One final point by way of introduction is to recognize the range of skills which managers need in the recruitment and selection process. As many line managers in tourism and hospitality, as well as HR specialists, are increasingly involved in recruitment and selection it is important that they should recognize the skills required in such a process (see HRM in Practice 5.1).

## HRM IN PRACTICE 5.1:
## Skills involved in the recruitment and selection process

| *The recruitment and selection process* | *The skills required* |
|---|---|
| Job description | Evaluation of the vacancy |
| Person specification | Drafting the criteria |
| Advertisement | Summarizing |
| Shortlist | Fair discrimination |
| Interview | Questioning skills |
| Selection tests | Listening skills |
| References | Assessment skills |
| Decision | Evaluation |

## Recruitment

Recruitment is defined by Heery and Noon (2008: 381) as 'the process of generating a pool of candidates from which to select the appropriate person to fill a job vacancy'. In essence, in the recruitment process organizations are seeking to attract and retain the interest of suitable candidates, while at the same time also seeking to portray a positive image to potential applicants. Of course, recruitment is a dynamic process, as within organizations people are constantly retiring, resigning, being promoted or, at times, being dismissed. Equally, changes in technology, procedures or markets may all mean that jobs are re-configured and become available to the external labour pool and thereby trigger the recruitment and selection process. Having decided to recruit, organizations will ordinarily consider a range of questions to determine how they might approach filling the vacancy. Specifically, they might ask themselves the following questions (Torrington *et al.*, 2011: 159):

- What does the job consist of?
- In what way is it to be different from the job done by the previous incumbent?
- What are the aspects of the job that specify the type of candidate?
- What are the key aspects of the job that the ideal candidate wants to know before applying?

Conventionally, the answers to these questions will be provided by job analysis, the job description and person specification, which allow the candidates to gauge their chances of being appointed.

## Job analysis

Armstrong (2009: 444) defines job analysis as:

> the process of collecting, analysing and setting out information about the contents of jobs in order to provide the basis for a job description and data for recruitment, training, job evaluation and performance management. Job analysis concentrates on what job holders are expected to do.

Marchington and Wilkinson (2008) suggest that undertaking a job analysis may not be necessary for every time a vacancy arises, especially in organizations that have high levels of labour turnover. However, they do recognize that job analysis does allow for an examination of whether existing job descriptions and person specifications/competency profiles are appropriate for future needs. The same authors also recognize that there is likely to be variation in terms of the sophistication, cost, convenience and acceptability of job analysis, and this will also determine the methods utilized to analyse a job. Organizations may use one or more of the following methods: observation of the job, work diaries, interviews with job holders and questionnaires and checklists. The output from such job analysis is the job description and person specification.

## Job description

Heery and Noon (2008: 246) describe the job description as:

> A document that outlines the purposes of the job, the task involved, the duties and responsibilities, the performance of objectives, and the reporting relationships. It will give details of the terms and conditions, including the remuneration package and hours of work.

In many respects the job description can be thought of as a functional document which outlines the 'what' elements of a job. It should aim to provide clear information to candidates about the organization and the job itself, such that it acts as a realistic preview of the job. Importantly, as well as offering a realistic description of the nature of the job, the job description should also act as a marketing document that seeks to make the job look attractive to potential applicants.

## Person specification/competency profile in the recruitment context

While the job description considers the 'what' aspects of the job, the person specification is concerned with the 'who'. In this way the person specification should aim to provide a profile of the 'ideal' person for the job. In reality, the ideal person may not exist, but the person specification provides a framework to assess how close candidates come to being the ideal. Conventionally, the person specification is a document which describes the personal skills and characteristics required to fill the position, usually listed under 'essential' and 'desirable' headings. In that sense essential criteria form the minimum standard expected for any given job and will form the basis for potentially rejecting applicants. For example, if an advert for a tour company manager stipulates that the applicant must have a degree in a travel and tourism-related area with at least a 2:1 grade, then applicants without this qualification would be automatically excluded. On the other hand, the desirable criteria are those things which are considered over and above the minimum and should provide the basis for selection. For example, an organization may stipulate that for the same managerial job we have just outlined that, in addition to a 2:1 degree, use of a foreign language is desirable. If a candidate could use a foreign language they may be at an advantage to other candidates who do not, though ultimately the company may appoint somebody who does not have any foreign-language skills.

The two most important person specification models are those provided by Alec Rodger in 1952 and John Munro Fraser in 1966. As Marchington and

Wilkinson (2008: 238) note, 'although both methods are very old, they are still widely used, albeit in an adapted form'.

---

## Rodger's seven-point plan

1    Physical characteristics: the ability to lift heavy loads; appearance, speech and manner.
2    Attainments: educational/professional qualifications; work experience considered necessary for the job.
3    General intelligence: the ability to define and solve problems.
4    Special aptitudes: skills, attributes or competencies relevant to the job.
5    Interests: work-related or leisure pursuits that may have a bearing on the job.
6    Disposition: job-related behaviours, such as demonstrating friendliness.
7    Circumstances: domestic commitments or ability to work unsocial hours.

---

## Munro Fraser's five-fold grading system

1    Impact on other people: similar to Rodger's physical make up.
2    Qualifications and experience: similar to Rodger's attainments.
3    Innate abilities and aptitude: similar to Rodger's general intelligence.
4    Motivation: a person's desire to succeed in the workplace.
5    Adjustment: personality factors that may impact on things like ability to cope with difficult customers.

---

More recently, Marchington and Wilkinson (2008) note how many companies now use competency frameworks to outline the type of person that they are seeking. The focus of competency frameworks is on the behaviours of job applicants, and they are useful as they can also set a framework for other subsequent HR practices, such as performance management and pay. Marchington and Wilkinson (2008: 238) also note how 'the competencies can be related to specific performance outcomes rather than being concerned with potentially vague processes, such as disposition or interests outside of work'. The use of competencies tends to focus on areas such as team orientation, communication, people management, customer focus, results orientation and problem-solving.

Regardless of whether organizations are using person specifications or competency frameworks, tourism and hospitality organizations are now seeking employees, especially those who will interact with customers, with certain types of skills.

---

### Review and reflect

What are the types of skills that tourism and hospitality organizations are likely to seek in their front-line staff? How can these skills be discerned in the recruitment and selection process?

---

## The 'ideal' front-line tourism and hospitality employee

With the shift to a service economy, the type of skills demanded by employers has also shifted. Employers in hospitality and tourism in both the UK and elsewhere increasingly desire employees with the 'right' attitude and appearance (Chan and Coleman, 2004; Nickson *et al.*, 2005). The right attitude encompasses aspects such as social and interpersonal skills, which are largely concerned with ensuring employees are responsive, courteous and understanding with customers, or in simple terms, that they can demonstrate emotional labour. However, it is not only the right attitude that employers seek. Nickson *et al.* (2001) have developed the term 'aesthetic labour' – the ability to either 'look good' or 'sound right' (Warhurst and Nickson, 2001) – which points to the increasing importance of the way in which employees are expected to physically embody the company image in tourism and hospitality.

In an analysis of 5,000 job advertisements across a number of different occupations and sectors in the UK, Jackson *et al.* (2005) found that the skills stated as necessary by employers are 'social skills' and 'personal characteristics'; only 26 per cent of organizations mentioned the need for educational achievements. Within personal services this figure was less than 10 per cent. Furthermore, Jackson *et al.* found numerous instances of front-line service jobs asking for attributes that referred less to what individuals could *do* than to what they were *like*, such as being 'well-turned out' or 'well-spoken', or having 'good appearance', 'good manners', 'character' or 'presence'.

Nickson *et al.* (2005) also report evidence from a survey of nearly 150 employers in the retail and hospitality industry. On the question of what employers are looking for in customer-facing staff during the selection process, Nickson *et al.* found that 65 per cent suggested that the right personality was critical, with the remainder of respondents suggesting this aspect was important. Equally, 33 per cent of the employers surveyed felt that the right appearance was critical and 57 per cent felt it was important; only 2 per cent of respondents felt it was not important. These figures can be compared to qualifications, with only one respondent seeing qualifications as critical, 19 per cent of employers feeling it was important and 40 per cent suggesting it was not important at all for selecting their customer-facing staff.

In terms of the skills deemed necessary to do the required work, employers placed a far greater emphasis on 'soft' skills for customer-facing staff. Ninety-nine per cent of respondents felt that social or interpersonal skills were felt to be of at least significant importance, and 98 per cent felt likewise about self-presentation – or aesthetic – skills. Conversely, 48 per cent of employers felt that technical skills were important in their customer-facing staff and 16 per cent stated they were not important at all. The skills that matter to employers in customer-facing staff in tourism and hospitality are therefore generally 'soft', including aesthetic skills, rather than 'hard' technical skills, which will often be trained in when people join the organization (see HRM in Practice 5.2).

## HRM IN PRACTICE 5.2:
## 'Scotland with Style': aesthetic labour and employees who look good and sound right

Glasgow was once an industrial city. Now, over 85 per cent of the city's jobs are in services. Aiming for the city break tourist market, the city promotes its retail, cultural and hospitality attractions. By 2011 the city had more than 12,000 hotels rooms, comparable with many UK and European competitor cities. Glasgow has over 1,000 bars and restaurants and is second only to London as Britain's culinary capital. Glasgow is also acknowledged as the second largest retail centre in the UK outside London by both Experian and CACI in their rankings of the UK's top retail outlets. The city also now has a well-developed niche of designer retailers, boutique hotels and style bars, cafes and restaurants. Not surprisingly, the city has been described by US magazine *Travel and Leisure* as 'The UK's hippest and most happening city'. Three million tourists visit the city each year, generating £670 million annually in the local economy. In recognition of this new economic success, the city re-branded itself as 'Scotland with Style' in 2004.

To take advantage of this booming tourist market and reflecting the city's new image, tourism and hospitality employers want staff with the right customer-service skills. Job adverts specify that applicants be 'well spoken and of smart appearance' or 'very well presented'. One Scottish-based boutique hotel company, Hotel Elba, created a sophisticated recruitment, selection and training programme for its new staff. Opening a new hotel in Glasgow, the company deliberately placed job advertisements in the *Sunday Times* rather than local evening newspapers. As a consequence, the typical front-of-house employee taken on was in their twenties, a graduate and well travelled. Recruitment literature featured a person description not a job description, asking applicants to assess themselves by the 13 words that characterized that company's image, such as 'stylish' and 'tasty'. After a telephone interview, application with CV and then a face-to-face interview, there was a ten-day induction in which extensive grooming

and deportment training was given to the staff by external consultants. Sessions included individual 'make-overs' for staff, teaching them about haircuts/styling, teaching female staff about make-up, male staff how to shave and, for all, the expected appearance standards. The sessions were intended to relay 'This is what we want you to actually look like . . . you have to understand what "successful" looks like . . . what "confident" looks like.' The hotel wanted staff that were confident, with a good attitude and appearance. 'There is an Elba look', said the hotel manager, 'neat and stylish . . . young, very friendly . . . people that fit in with the whole concept of the hotel' (Nickson *et al.*, 2001: 180). The hotel wanted staff able to project the company's image and help it differentiate itself in a crowded and competitive market. It is a policy that seems to pay: the hotel claimed above-average occupancy rates for the city.

Derived from Glasgow City Council (2011); Nickson *et al.* (2001, 2005)

Of course, we should recognize that the use of person specifications and competency frameworks may still involve a degree of subjectivity, especially in judging which potential employees have the 'right' kind of attitude or appearance. Evidence suggests that employers will often make judgements which penalize people for not having the 'right' appearance or attitude (Nickson *et al.*, 2003). Clearly, then, there is the potential for overt and not so overt forms of discrimination in how person specifications and competency frameworks may be used by those making the final decision about who is to be employed by the organization, a point considered in further detail in Chapter 6.

Ultimately, in considering the person specification or competency profile it would seem sensible for organizations to consider several points.

- Are all the items on your person specification/competency profile relevant to the job?
- Are you reasonably sure that none of your criteria would discriminate unfairly against a group of potential candidates?
- Would your person specification/competency profile enable a shortlisting and interviewing panel to distinguish clearly between candidates?

Having reviewed the importance of the job description and person specification/competency requirements we can now move on to consider how organizations can attract the interest of appropriate potential employees. Initially, there may be a choice as to whether the organization looks to somebody internally or looks to the external labour market. For example, for a promotable position organizations that are seeking to sustain a strong internal labour market may have a policy of offering this position in-house to existing staff first. Equally, though, the organization may feel that offering such positions to the external labour market is important to bring in new ideas and new blood. In deciding on their target group, organizations may also wish to address issues such an under-representation of a particular group, such as ethnic minority employees or women managers, a point that is further considered in the following chapter.

Generally speaking, organizations have a number of methods which they can consider in seeking to engage with their target market for new employees. First, as we have already noted, they may use existing employees. For example, this can be in relation to promotable positions or also in terms of word-of-mouth approaches, which are commonplace in tourism and hospitality, especially for front-line positions (see HRM in Practice 5.3).

## HRM IN PRACTICE 5.3:
## Fancy a job in easyJet?

It was reported in 2006 that easyJet responded to chronic staff shortages by asking passengers on a number of its flights whether they wanted a job. Cabin crew, as well as highlighting the emergency exits and demonstrating the lifebelts, were also told by the company to tell passengers about job vacancies in the company. Consequently, on a number of flights cabin crew announced to passengers that if they were 'up for the challenge' they could visit the company's website to fill in an online application. As a company spokesman noted, 'It's just a new way of recruiting staff. We are a low-cost airline – it saves money on advertising. It also gives passengers the opportunity to go up and ask the crew what it's like to work for easyJet.'

Derived from Jones and Vasager (2006)

Alternatively the organization may choose to use external contacts, such as job centres. Indeed, this may well be something that organizations see as important in their attempts to be good corporate citizens (see HRM in Practice 5.4).

## HRM IN PRACTICE 5.4:
## Offering a helping hand to the unemployed

A number of tourism and hospitality companies have made a commitment to helping long-term unemployed people back into work by signing local employment partnerships (LEPs) with Jobcentre Plus. Under this initiative employers pledge to give job interviews and work placements to unemployed people specially

trained by Jobcentre Plus, with a view to ensuring they go on to attain a permanent job. Marriott agreed to commit to offering a number of job opportunities across the UK in a range of positions, including room attendants, food and beverage and cleaning positions. Travelodge have also had great success in using the initiative and in the period January–September 2008 they filled 130 of 192 vacancies with staff through LEPs. Chrissie Herbert, HR director for Travelodge, was full of praise for the initiative: 'I can't recommend LEPs highly enough. If you consider the cost of advertising versus the cost of using LEPs you can see why. We are saving thousands of pounds on the cost of recruiting in a time when every company is reviewing its spending.'

Derived from Gilbert (2008); Thomas (2008)

A further key aspect of looking externally for new employees is the import-ance of advertising and media. An obvious starting point here is print media, specifically the press. The use of print media to advertise jobs is one of the most popular formal methods of recruitment. When thinking about where adverts are best placed, organizations need to be cognizant of the labour market on which they are hoping to draw for a particular job. In recognizing the most appropriate labour markets, organizations could conceivably place adverts in either the local/national press or in trade and professional journals. For example, for a front-line position it is likely that the local press will be used, while for a managerial or specialist position the use of the national press or trade press may be more appropriate. In using print media it is important to consider the manner in which organizations can portray the desired image; here we will consider how this issue can be addressed.

When organizations advertise vacancies it is important that they convey the right message in order to attract suitable applicants and discourage those who do not have the necessary attributes. Equally important is that advertisements project a positive image of the company and in that sense adverts can be considered a selling document. Initially, organizations have the choice to go it alone and contact the media directly, or alternatively they can deal with an advertising agency, which can help in drafting and placing an advert. Advertising agencies can be thought of as experts who can offer advice on the choice of advertising copy and the choice of media. They may also have better contacts to ensure advertising space at short notice. The only drawback is that agencies may also be rather costly. Regardless of whether an agency is used or not, there are certain key points which should be borne in mind in devising an advert, and at the very least the following aspects should be apparent (Torrington *et al.*, 2011: 165):

- name and brief details of the employing organization;
- job role and duties;

- training to be provided;
- key points of the person specification or competency framework;
- salary;
- instructions about how to apply.

Moreover, organizations should also consider the image they are portraying; the Chartered Institute of Personnel and Development (CIPD) and the Institute of Professional Advertisers (IPA) outline the following criteria for judging excellence in recruitment advertising (Chartered Institute of Personnel and Development, 2006):

- visual impact;
- typography and balance;
- clarity of message to the target audience;
- promotion of job vacancy;
- projection of a professional organizational image;
- focus on workplace diversity.

With regard to the final bullet point, it is important to reiterate that adverts must not discriminate on grounds of age, sex, race, sexuality, religious orientation or disability.

---

### Review and reflect

Using the above criteria, attempt to find a job advertisement for a tourism and hospitality organization which exemplifies at least some of these aspects, and briefly describe why these aspects make a job look attractive.

---

In addition there are other areas which can potentially be used, including TV, radio, cinema, careers exhibitions, conferences and open days and posters. While TV, radio and cinema adverts have been utilized to recruit in areas like the military or teaching, they are much less likely to be used by tourism and hospitality organizations. The other options could all be conceivably used. For example, TGI Friday's, the American restaurant chain, have successfully used open days to recruit staff in the UK. As a company with a very distinctive service style, open days are felt to be useful to expose potential employees to the nature of the work they will be undertaking. As the company is looking for very outgoing individuals who can do things like juggle or sing while serving customers, the open day is designed to assess such aspects. Team tasks and tricks and dances are just some of the things that potential employees will be expected to demonstrate in their 'audition' during the open day (Baker, 1999; see HRM in Practice 5.5).

**HRM IN PRACTICE 5.5:**
**Who would you most like to be stuck in a lift with?**

Hills (2004) reports on the recruitment process in Tiger Tiger, one of the UK's most popular night-club groups. As part of their recruitment process they host open days to allow potential employees to sample the Tiger Tiger atmosphere. A general manager, Beverley Harley, is quoted as saying that 'the leisure sector is a particularly social and competitive one and we're on the hunt for hardworking team players'. As part of assessing whether applicants have these attributes, during the open day potential employees take part in various 'fun' activities, including being asked who they would most like to be stuck in a lift with and which type of animal they would choose to be.

An increasingly used source of recruitment is the internet. Parry and Tyson (2008), in a recent analysis of the use and success of online recruitment methods, note that in the United States in particular online recruitment has begun to displace more traditional methods. Similarly, within the UK in the annual survey of recruitment and retention undertaken by the CIPD (2010b) it was found that the use of corporate websites was the most effective method for attracting applications. Sixty-three per cent of respondents, covering the economy as a whole, suggested that this was the most effective method. Other popular methods included the use of recruitment agencies (60 per cent), local newspaper advertisements (36 per cent), employee referral schemes (35 per cent) and word-of-mouth (24 per cent). The internet is playing a growing role in organizations' recruitment strategies. For most companies the use of the internet tends to be in terms of sections on their websites that allow job seekers to check for current vacancies. Beyond this facility there may be more strategic approaches to using the web, particularly with regard to the ability to receive and process job applications online. For example, Chynoweth (2009) notes how McDonald's has recently moved to using an online application system for all hourly paid positions. Within this process the company incorporates a psychometric assessment which is used to sift initial applicants, a process that has replaced the first face-to-face interview which the company used to use. As the company receives over 2,000 applications per day for hourly jobs, by removing the need for a face-to-face interview the company has estimated that it saved around £1 million. The company does use face-to-face interviews later in the recruitment process, so potential employees can spend time in the restaurant (also see HRM in Practice 5.6).

## HRM IN PRACTICE 5.6:
## Hilton International: spreading the web

Beal (2004) notes how Hilton International wanted to improve its fast-track Elevator programme – a selection tool introduced in 1998 and designed to recruit highly talented graduates as future hotel general managers. As new graduates had to learn the role of a manager in a short period of time, the tool had to be extremely reliable to pick up the right candidates. As such, the Elevator scheme, which involved hand-processing and scoring an application form, conducting a face-to-face meeting, psychometric testing and conducting a final 24-hour assessment centre, proved costly and time-consuming, especially in terms of senior management involvement. To streamline its selection tool, Hilton International commissioned the business-psychology consultancy Human Factor International to introduce a web-based screening system – a so-called 'virtual psychologist' – running in five European languages. This online tool would not have been possible without a technological breakthrough which allows for a time limit on the intellectual-reasoning part of the test. The system was successfully implemented in 15 working days, from Christmas 2003 to 20 January 2004.

Since the running of the programme, Hilton has invited applicants through presentations at the main European hotel schools and universities to apply through the website (http://www.hilton-elevator.com/home.htm) and complete the standard application form. Those who pass the initial sifting are then asked to fill in online 'personality' and 'workplace values' questionnaires. At this stage all candidates receive an electronic report analysing their results and providing tailored career advice. Successful candidates are then invited to complete three ability and skill tests of 15 minutes each before being selected to the assessment centre. At the end of the assessment centre, unsuccessful candidates receive detailed e-mailed feedback outlining the reasons why they have not been chosen and inviting them to phone in if they want to have further explanations. As Christine Jones, director of the consultancy Human Factor International, adds, 'Even unsuccessful candidates have told us they have been pleased with the feedback they have been given, and are comfortable with it' (p. 31). By introducing the online system, Hilton International has been able to reduce the number of assessment days without damaging the quality of its new recruits. Indeed, the 14 graduates who first joined Hilton International through this tool had to pass only two final assessment centres rather than the five or six previously needed. As John Guthrie, head of international management at Hilton International, comments,

> While unlikely to save significant costs in pure cash terms, getting rid of manual processes has freed up managers' time to concentrate on more value-adding work. Additionally, it helps to portray the organization as more contemporary and technologically oriented and strengthens our appeal in a competitive search for talent.
>
> (p. 32)

The Chartered Institute of Personnel and Development (2009a) notes other reasons for employers using online recruitment, including:

- reducing cost per hire;
- increasing speed to hire;
- strengthening the employer brand;
- greater flexibility and ease for candidates;
- broadening the applicant pool.

It is also important to recognize potential disadvantages of using online recruitment, including (ibid.):

- It may limit the applicant audience as the internet is not the first choice for all job seekers.
- Use of online recruitment could give rise to allegations of discrimination.
- It can make the recruitment process impersonal.
- Websites which are badly designed or have technical difficulties can put applicants off.

Beyond individual company websites there are other commercial websites, such as http://www.tourism-jobs.org, which aims to allow job seekers to access jobs in a wide variety of travel and hospitality areas, including airlines, hotels, cruise liners, restaurants and other travel companies. Lastly, the Chartered Institute of Personnel and Development (2009a) also notes the growing importance of the range of Web 2.0 technologies to connect with potential employees, such as blogs, web-based communities and hosted services including social networking sites such as Linked-In, Twitter and Facebook, which alone has over 150 million global users. For example, Marriott International launched its own Facebook game in 2011, My Marriott Hotel. The game was launched largely due to the company's need to fill 50,000 jobs worldwide by the end of 2011. Although not designed to be part of the company's recruitment process, the game does give players a virtual taste of jobs and opportunities in the company and Marriott hope the game will make them more competitive in regions such as Asia where there is, as we noted in Chapter 2, a war for talent (Siedsma, 2011). Indeed, there are also emerging trends with companies using Web 3D to allow potential employees to interact with existing employees through programmes such as Second Life. It seems clear that, as the internet continues to evolve, e-recruiting will continue to grow in importance and sophistication.

We noted earlier in the chapter how a key aspect of recruitment and selection was cost-effectiveness. As a result it is not necessarily sensible to use certain recruitment methods for certain jobs, and in reality the aim should be to ensure the best method to hit the particular target group for a particular job, and in a cost-effective manner. The recognition of the need for a contingent approach to recruitment is apparent from the research outlined in Table 5.1 (see also HRM in Practice 5.7).

**TABLE 5.1  Main sources of recruitment in the hospitality industry**

|  | Operative (%) | Management (%) |
| --- | --- | --- |
| Job centre | 87 | 13 |
| Local press | 80 | 30 |
| Word-of-mouth | 70 | 35 |
| Employment agencies | 32 | 57 |
| Trade press | 26 | 66 |
| National press | 8 | 24 |
| Personnel consultants | 2 | 42 |

Source: Adapted from Kelliher and Johnson (1997).

## HRM IN PRACTICE 5.7:
## 'Realistic' recruitment in the cruise industry

Raub and Streit (2006) recognize that, as within other tourism and hospitality settings, human resources are crucial to success in the cruise industry as guests are in constant contact with service staff and, unlike conventional hotels, cannot usually wander 'off site'. Regardless of the pressure this is likely to create for front-line service staff, many people might think that working in the cruise industry is likely to be exciting and fun. In reality, life on board a cruise ship can be difficult for staff – for example, they are likely to face cramped and difficult living conditions. The unique work context in the cruise ship industry means that many organizations attempt to offer a 'realistic' and 'honest and objective' view of working life in the industry, which means that staff do not have an unrealistic view of it. Key to this approach is the use of several types of recruitment media such as interviews, company-specific videos, company presentations, written information (such as fact sheets) and web-based information. This realistic job preview is placed alongside the positive aspects of the job – for example, the manner in which working on cruise ships can significantly broaden the professional and individual horizons of young employees. By balancing both positive and negative aspects of working in the industry in this realistic manner companies seem to be able to lessen high levels of labour turnover, thus increasing retention and potentially enhancing job satisfaction.

At this juncture in the recruitment process the organization will hopefully have generated sufficient interest from suitable applicants. In that sense it is important for organizations to periodically review the recruitment process and evaluate its effectiveness against this kind of criterion. Additionally, the organization may also want to consider the issues of costs and equal opportunities issues. Ultimately, in evaluating the process of recruitment, organizations can ask themselves several key questions:

- Do recruitment practices yield sufficient numbers of suitable candidates to enable the organization to select sufficient numbers of high-quality employees?
- Could a sufficient pool of suitable candidates be attracted using less expensive methods?
- Are recruitment methods fulfilling equal opportunity responsibilities?

Depending on the type of job, and presuming that there is more than one candidate, the final part of the recruitment procedure is the notion of shortlisting. The outcome of the recruitment process is to produce a shortlist of candidates whose background and potential are in accordance with the profile contained in the person specification/competency framework. This is a way of making good use of the information gathered to-date about the candidate. We can also appreciate the need to ensure that things have gone smoothly so far. In this sense, if there has been a problem – say, with the advert – shortlisting can conceivably be a problem (if, for example, there are insufficient numbers of candidates who are appointable or indeed if there are too many candidates). Presuming that there are sufficient numbers of suitably qualified people for the position, the conventional method is to shortlist by comparison with the person specification/competency framework. However, Torrington *et al.* (2011) note that if there are a large number of applicants for a job, there may be fairly arbitrary criteria, such as people being excluded because of their handwriting style or because of unconventional work histories. As Torrington *et al.* recognize, such shortlisting techniques are wholly unsatisfactory, being potentially both unlawful and certainly unfair. A fairer approach is likely to be based on a rigorous and systematic view of each candidate via five stages (Torrington *et al.*, 2011: 174):

1 Essential criteria for shortlisting.
2 Individual selectors produce their own list of a given number of candidates.
3 Selectors reveal their lists and try to reach a consensus, if an outcome is still not clear.
4 Selectors discuss why certain candidates are preferred and others not.
5 Selectors produce a final shortlist after negotiation and compromise.

We have now reached the stage where the organization is ready to move on to selection.

## Selection

So far in this chapter we have essentially been examining the notion of recruitment and how organizations attempt to attract the interest of potential employees. We can now go on and examine the idea of how organizations match potential employees to jobs via the processes of selection, when organizations will decide who is the most appropriate person for the job. We will do this by contextualizing the process, and then go on and look at some of the techniques utilized by organizations in selecting new employees. We will then assess some of the possible problems within this process and finally examine the way most organizations approach the idea of selection.

As Heery and Noon (2008: 409) note, selection is 'the process of assessing job applicants using one or a variety of methods with the purpose of finding the most suitable person for the organization'. Increasingly, many writers argue that the selection of staff may well be the most important aspect of HRM, as staff are increasingly expected to become effective immediately. Allied to this point is the cost of various selection techniques, which means organizations will want to get it right first time. However, despite this recognition there is no one best way which is universally recognized as the best method of selecting the right person for the job. Torrington *et al.* (2011: 179) argue that 'while the search for the perfect method of selection continues, in its absence HR and line managers continue to use a variety of imperfect methods'. What this quote points to is that no single selection method can guarantee success in terms of choosing the right person for the job, especially given the level of human involvement in the process. As organizations recognize this conundrum, they are adopting a variety of techniques to address questions of selection. Thus, the methods selected are influenced by the employer's view of what is required to provide a satisfactory basis for decision-making and awareness of the appropriateness of particular techniques to provide what is sought. Before we go on though and examine various selection techniques in detail, it is important to recognize two points which complete the context of the selection process.

The first idea is that the selection process is a two-way process. Often, the perception is that the organization has all the power in the process of selection. However, this is not strictly true, even though it may seem that way when you are going through the process. Selection is in fact a two-way process, because people have the option to pull out of the process or turn down a job. For example, a major international hotel company may advertise a graduate trainee scheme and get an initially good response, such that over 300 application packs are sent out to potential employees. Of those only 127 are returned. Following the selection process 23 are offered jobs, 19 accept the offer and only 15 actually start with the company. What this example illustrates is that selection may also be occurring from the potential employees' point of view, especially when the labour market is buoyant or their particular skills are in

demand. The second point is the selection criteria. Selection does not take place in a vacuum – there is also the context of whether the person will fit in with the job requirements, so the person–job interaction is important. As we have already noted, there is also the question of whether the person will fit in with the group or work team or department and whether they will be able to work with colleagues. Finally, there is the question of whether the person will fit in with the organizational culture and the way things are done in a particular organization. The ways organizations attempt to find this out are myriad, and we can examine some of the techniques that they utilize in the selection process. The first method, which is the most popular, is that of interviewing.

Although criticized – for example, many argue interviewing is not very good in predicting actual performance in the job – the interview remains a key part of, and is usually the central element of, the selection process in many tourism and hospitality organizations. Indeed, the interview is often characterized as being the third part of the 'classic trio': application form/CV, references and interview. In that sense, for many people their experience of the selection process will be filling in an application form, including supplying two references and then going along to an interview. As far as selection methods are concerned, the interview is seen as the most straightforward and least expensive approach, and what most candidates would expect. Employers in the UK often express concern about the fairness of psychometric testing, and yet continue to use and seem relatively happy about interviews, despite the potential for bias and discrimination. The interview remains popular, then, despite poor evidence of validity and the fact that other methods have more predictive power in terms of job performance. Regardless of the latter points, the interview remains enduringly popular as a selection tool. The Chartered Institute of Personnel and Development (2010b) annual survey of recruitment and retention found that interviewing remained the most common form of selection method. Seventy-eight per cent of organizations use competency-based interviews and over 60 per cent of respondents in the survey also used interviews that followed the contents of a CV/application form or a structured interview. Although increasingly more sophisticated techniques are emerging, such as psychometric testing and assessment centres, they are in addition to, rather than replacing the interview.

## Review and reflect

Think about an employment interview that you have attended and whether you felt it was a 'good' or 'bad' interview and what influenced your judgement, either positively or negatively.

Riley (1996) feels that the interview is sometimes unfairly criticized because too much is expected of it, and it is also done badly. He also makes the point that it is quick, convenient and, when done well, an effective selection method. Riley (1996) describes the interview as 'A conversation with a purpose', and that purpose is to meet four objectives:

1   To decide if an applicant is suitable for a job.
2   To decide if the person will fit into the existing work group or organization as a whole.
3   To attract applicants to the job.
4   To communicate essential expectations and requirements of the job.

Essentially, then, the interview process is about gathering information which allows for an evaluation of the appropriateness of the individual for a particular job. Interviews can either be one-to-one, sequential or phone-based; again, it is likely that for the majority of positions in tourism and hospitality the first type will predominate. To have a good interview regardless of which type it is, it is also suggested that certain conditions should be met (Torrington *et al.*, 2011). These conditions are concerned with aspects such as attention being paid to noise levels, avoiding interruptions, lighting, dress and manner of the interviewer, positioning of furniture and attempts to create an informal atmosphere. These aspects are concerned with taking away as much of the anxiety of the situation as is possible to ensure interviewees perform to the best of their ability. There are several things which should be recognized in interviewing (Chartered Institute of Personnel and Development, 2010c; Industrial Relations Services, 2000a, 2006a; Torrington *et al.*, 2011):

*   Interviewers should only talk around 20 per cent of the time, the remaining time should be filled by interviewees.
*   Open questions are more useful, so questions starting with 'what', 'why', 'when', 'which' and 'how' can be very useful to elicit information from candidates. For example, instead of asking a question like 'Did you enjoy your last job?', the interviewer could ask 'What did you enjoy about your last job?' (also see HRM in Practice 5.8).
*   Interviewers recognize and like candidates from similar backgrounds to them in terms of things like social class and educational background.
*   It is estimated that interviewers often make their decision within the first 4–9 minutes of an interview, which would seem to exemplify the 'self-fulfilling prophecy' effect, wherein interviewers ask questions designed to confirm initial impressions of candidates gained before the interview or in the early stages.
*   Interviewers are susceptible to the contrast effect whereby they allow the experience of interviewing one candidate to affect the way they interview other candidates.

- Interviewers are vulnerable to prejudices with regard to aspects such as sex, race and age.
- Interviewers are affected by physical cues – for example, spectacles equals greater intelligence.
- Interviewers need to be aware of the 'halo' or 'horns' effect when, either in a positive or negative manner, some trait or personal characteristic influences or overwhelms all other thoughts.
- There is a need to recognize the importance of non-verbal communications, or what is commonly described as body language. For example, interviewers and interviewees should aim to be open in their stance and throughout the interview sustain animated yet controlled body language.

## HRM IN PRACTICE 5.8:
## Making interviews unnecessarily stressful or challenging

There are many ways to ask a question in an interview. Often there seems an unnecessary emphasis on creating an uncomfortable environment for interviewees. This could be by the use of 'stress questions', which are asked in a disparaging or aggressive manner to see how interviewees may react in uncomfortable or stressful situations, something that is unlikely to be appropriate for most jobs. Other examples might be interviews conducted in bizarre circumstances. For example, applicants for a new 'Dreamieland' theme ride in Manchester found themselves being interviewed by the Dreamie himself, an oversized figure made of rubber. Questions were asked by a real interviewer in the next room, who watched candidates via a hidden camera. Applicants were assessed on how they dealt with the shock of being interviewed by the Dreamie. As a spokesperson said, 'we wanted outgoing candidates who responded positively to the character'. One applicant said, 'This high-pitched voice spent 20 minutes asking me questions. It was quite unnerving.' Alternatively it could just be inappropriate questions asked by interviewers. For example, a survey by recruitment consultants, Accountemps, found that interviewers often asked questions designed to make interviewees squirm. Examples of such questions included 'What is the one question you don't want me to ask you?'. One interviewer even hid his face behind a large newspaper and instructed a candidate to 'Say something that is going to make me put this newspaper down.'

Derived from Anon (2001); Anon (2002); Chartered Institute of Personnel and Development (2010c)

Despite the many criticisms of the interview as a selection method, it remains extremely popular. It is worth remembering as well that often many of the criticisms are largely about the interviewers themselves and not the process.

As Watson (1994: 211) aphoristically notes, 'employment interviewing is like driving. Most people rate themselves highly; the consequences of mistakes can be serious and when something goes wrong there is a tendency to blame the other party.' Similarly, Taylor (1998: 130) has suggested that 'individuals will not tolerate criticisms of their performance as lovers, drivers or interviewers, since all such criticisms strike deep into the core of the human ego'. As Riley (1996) argues, although interviews are subjective and require judgement, so do other management activities and the real problem is not the interview but the way it is carried out. To conclude, it is worth noting the view of the Industrial Relations Services (2000a: 12), who suggest that, 'there are few more complex, intuitive, intelligent or sophisticated information processors than a competent and confident interviewer'. With the interview set to continue as an integral part of the selection process, it is important for individual managers to recognize the need to develop their interviewing skills as an essential part of their managerial skillset.

Beyond interviewing there are a number of other techniques which organizations can conceivably utilize in selecting employees. An obvious aspect to this is the use of tests and psychometric testing. In general, a test may refer to something like a dexterity test for a manually skilled employee or an attainment test – for example, typing skills. More specifically, psychological or psychometric tests are tests which can be systematically scored and administered. These tests are used to measure individual difference in aptitude, ability, intelligence or personality. Organizations are increasingly using these types of tests, particularly for managerial positions (Industrial Relations Services, 2002). That said, psychometric tests are a source of great debate, particularly the use of personality tests. Much of this debate is concerned with whether tests of this nature can genuinely predict future workplace behaviour. Aptitude tests may test specific abilities in relation to verbal, numerical, spatial or mechanical skills to provide an indication of how well applicants will cope with the job. General ability or intelligence tests are used to test how well individuals think on their feet, and will be about analytical reasoning and ability to think critically. The most controversial tests are personality tests, which are often described as Orwellian or biased, manipulative and intrusive as they attempt to assess how people will cope with demands, or how people will cope with stress, rigidity or attitudes to authority or creativity.

There are a number of issues which arise in the use of personality tests. For example, there are concerns about how comparable information is. Equally, there are major concerns about the gender and ethnic bias in tests (Industrial Relations Services, 2002; Labour Research Department, 2003a). Lastly, a number of occupational psychologists have expressed concerns at so-called off-the-shelf models, which may be used in organizations in an inappropriate manner and may be, in the words of one personnel specialist, 'no more reliable than a *Cosmopolitan*-style questionnaire' (cited in Sappal, 2005: 40). In sum, rather like many of the other selection methods described above, the proper

use of psychometric testing can help organizations make objective and more reliable selection decisions, as long as they are used in an appropriate manner and administered properly.

Other methods which could be used by tourism and hospitality organizations include things like presentations. For example, an applicant for a training manager's job is likely to be required to give numerous presentations, and the organization may want to assess their presentation skills. Organizations may also use various group methods, which often involve problem solving. These activities may involve some element of role playing. By undertaking such problem solving in small groups, applicants will have the opportunity to demonstrate things like ability to work within a group, creativity, interpersonal skills and so on. One final method is the so-called in-tray exercise which will simulate an in-tray of a manager and the applicant has to go through the tray and make decisions on the problems they find.

Finally we come to the last method of selection, the assessment centre, which ordinarily refers to a process rather than a physical centre. Assessment centres utilize a mix of all of the above techniques; due to the opportunity to use a variety of methods – all of which are potentially assessing different aspects of the candidates – they are often described as the 'Rolls Royce' of selection methods (Industrial Relations Services, 2005a). In this sense they are widely considered the most objective and best predictive selection tool for future performance. Equally, though, we should also recognize that assessment centres are also complex to design, time consuming and costly, meaning that they are often, though not exclusively, reserved for appointing managerial or graduate-level staff (see HRM in Practice 5.9).

## HRM IN PRACTICE 5.9:
## The use of assessment centres by easyJet

The Industrial Relations Services (2002) notes that as a major airline easyJet is concerned to get it right in recruiting staff, especially pilots, who are one of the company's most expensive resources in terms of salary, training and career development. The assessment centre for pilots was introduced in 1999 and has now been extended to the recruitment of cabin crew and call-centre employees. The assessment centre for pilots is particularly demanding, covering two days. Potential pilots face a range of challenges which aim to assess aspects such as team-working, ability to cope under pressure, ability to adhere to standards and technical knowledge. Additionally, captains who attend the assessment centre are also assessed against leadership and decision-making criteria. Day one of the assessment centre is largely concerned with a range of tests and activities such as group work, personality tests and interviews. If the applicants successfully get through day one, they progress to day two. The second day is a flight simulation exercise which assesses the candidate's basic handling skills, as well as broader aspects such as flight management and crew resource management skills. Cabin crew undertake a one-day assessment in which the company evaluates potential employees against a number of competencies, including conscientiousness, sense of urgency, initiative, empathy, self-confidence and enthusiasm. To assess these aspects candidates have an ice breaker and the 'easyJet test'. The test measures things like mathematical ability, knowledge of easyJet and other factors relevant to the job – for example, knowledge of foreign currencies.

In order for the overall process of recruitment and selection to be considered successful, it is important that it is: considered fair by candidates; cost-effective; user friendly; acceptable to both the organization and the candidates; and reliable and valid. The reliability of a selection process refers to the extent to which a selection technique achieves consistency in what it is measuring over repeated use. Validity can be seen in three different ways. First, face validity refers to the issue of whether the selection procedure was seen to be valid to candidate and tester. Face validity can be particularly important in terms of organizations being able to attract good candidates in the future. Second, predictive validity is concerned with whether the outcome of selection is able to predict the ability to perform effectively when in post. Lastly, content validity is about ensuring that the test or exercise used to assess certain skills is actually relevant to the job in question.

Once the selection procedure is over there is also a need for the organization to ensure that there is feedback to both the successful and unsuccessful candidates. Organizations should aim therefore to give feedback as soon as possible. It is also important to recognize that for the feedback to be meaningful it should be specific as opposed to being too vague to allow candidates to fully appreciate why they did not get the job. A benefit from giving constructive feedback is that at the end of the recruitment and selection process the organization is still maintaining a positive image. Rather like much of what we have previously discussed, the provision of feedback is an essential part of how organizations can portray themselves in a positive manner throughout the recruitment and selection process.

## Conclusion

Clearly, tourism and hospitality organizations are faced with a mass of possible methods and techniques by which to approach the question of recruitment and selection. As we described in the introduction, there is no single best way to recruit and select. Instead, organizations should be prepared to develop a contingent approach. On the one hand, this may simply mean employing

people on the basis of word of mouth or because they responded to an advert in the window of a restaurant, for example. On the other hand, it may be the culmination of a lengthy and expensive selection process, particularly for managerial and graduate-level positions.

In answer to the question of whether there has been significant change in recruitment and selection in the tourism and hospitality industry in recent years, the answer would be 'yes and no'. Yes in terms of a shift to organizations looking for the 'right' people in terms of attitudes and behaviour and adoption of more sophisticated techniques, such as psychometric testing. Equally, though, we could also answer no in terms of the widespread use of traditional forms of recruitment and selection, such as interviewing. Moreover, evidence continues to suggest that the recruitment and selection process in many tourism and hospitality organizations often remains ad hoc and informal, especially for operative and front-line positions.

## Discussion questions

- Is it ethically acceptable to recruit and select people on the basis of whether they have appropriate aesthetic skills?
- Is it right for hospitality and tourism organizations to rely on informal methods of recruitment?
- How can e-recruitment best be used by tourism and hospitality organizations?
- What are some of the problems associated with the use of (1) interviewing and (2) testing in selecting employees?

## Further reading

Baum, T. (2008) 'Implications of hospitality and tourism labour markets for talent management', *International Journal of Contemporary Hospitality Management*, 20, 7, 720–9 (also see the rest of the articles in this special edition on talent management).

Lockyer, C. and Scholarios, D. (2004) 'Selecting hotel staff: why best practice does not always work', *International Journal of Contemporary Hospitality Management*, 16, 2, 121–35.

Nickson, D., Warhurst, C. and Dutton, E. (2005) 'The importance of attitude and appearance in the service encounter in retail and hospitality', *Managing Service Quality*, 15, 2, 195–208.

Parry, E. and Tyson, S. (2008) 'An analysis of the use and success of online recruitment methods in the UK', *Human Resource Management Journal*, 18, 3, 257–24.

Raub, S. and Streit, E. (2006) 'Realistic recruitment: an empirical study of the cruise industry', *International Journal of Contemporary Hospitality Management*, 18, 4, 278–89.

## Recommended websites

The Advisory, Conciliation and Arbitration Service (ACAS) has a useful publication on recruitment, which is available at http://www.acas.org.uk/media/pdf/5/e/Recruitment_and_induction_(OCTOBER_2010).pdf

The Chartered Institute of Personnel and Development has a very informative factsheet on recruitment, which can be found at http://www.cipd.co.uk/subjects/recruitmen/general/recruitmt.htm?IsSrchRes=1

There are a variety of different links covering recruitment and selection at http://www.hrmguide.co.uk/employee_resourcing

There are a number of useful resources which are helpful in preparing for a selection interview; these can be accessed at http://career-advice.monster.co.uk/job-interview/careers.aspx

There are a number of really useful resources to help with preparing for employment interviews and tests (including psychometric/personality testing) at http://www.prospects.ac.uk/interview_tests.htm

## Additional material

Go to www.routledge.com/cw/nickson to find PowerPoint slides, chapter commentaries, test banks and additional case studies for each chapter.

# Equal opportunities and managing diversity

## CHAPTER OBJECTIVES

**This chapter reviews the nature of equal opportunities and managing diversity in the tourism and hospitality industry. The main objectives of this chapter are to:**

- Appreciate the differing aspects which drive approaches to equality and diversity.

- Consider the employment experience of socially defined minority groups.

- Discuss the role of legislation in attempting to create greater equality.

- Recognize the importance of managing diversity as a more business-oriented approach to equality.

## Introduction

Increasingly, when we look at adverts for positions in tourism and hospitality organizations, we will see the statement that the employing organization is 'an equal opportunities employer'. Does this mean we are likely to find equality of opportunities within organizations? Have we managed to get rid of discrimination? Have we got a just society where sex, race/ethnicity, disability, age, religion and sexuality are no more important than eye colour? Is there equality in relation to issues such as recruitment and selection, training and development, remuneration, career development and promotion? A recent report by the Equality and Human Rights Commission (EHRC) (2010) on fairness and equality in Britain, while recognizing that there had been significant strides in encouraging greater equality, also noted that real challenges remained. Thus, Trevor Phillips, chair of the EHRC, noted in his foreword to the report that:

> too many of us remain trapped by the accident of our births, our destinies far too likely to be determined by our sex or race; our opportunities far too often conditioned by the fact that our age, or disability, our sexual preferences, or deeply held religion or belief make us lesser beings in the eyes of others.
>
> (p. 7)

In a similar vein, in reviewing the global picture on employment discrimination, the International Labour Organization (ILO) (2011) highlights the fact that despite encouraging developments in the fight against long-recognized forms of discrimination in the workplace, significant problems still persist.

This chapter will discuss how certain social groups may experience disadvantage in the workplace, regardless of their qualities and abilities. The manner in which organizations are seeking to address the issue of equal opportunities may vary considerably, and here it is helpful to recognize the useful distinction offered by Goss (1994) with regard to the issue of equal opportunities. Goss makes a distinction between what he terms a 'short-term' compliance agenda, and a much more proactive 'long-term' agenda. The former agenda is driven largely by the idea of complying with legislation to avoid penalties. For example, there is no upper limit on compensation awarded by an employment tribunal in discrimination cases and whether an employer unintentionally discriminates is no defence. Clearly, this type of agenda is driven by organizational self-interest. In contrast, the long-term agenda is premised on notions of efficient management of human resources, creating a good organizational image, managing diversity and social justice, though some of these aspects may, in reality, also be in the organization's self-interest. In many respects we can think of equality and diversity in terms of:

- *Legal aspects*: failure to comply with legislation in this area can mean employers facing unwelcome publicity and potentially large payouts as a result of employment tribunal decisions.
- *Ethical aspects*: it is ethically and morally right for organizations to seek to offer equality of opportunity to all.
- *Business aspects*: it makes good business sense to encourage equality and diversity to ensure the organization draws on the widest possible labour market to make sure that they are maximizing the best use of all available resources. Equality also makes good business sense in terms of potentially widening the customer base and also portraying a positive company image.

Of course, in reality, the approach to equality and diversity adopted by organizations may well be informed by all of these aspects. Increasingly, though, within a more strategic HRM approach it is suggested that many organizations are recognizing the business case for equality and diversity.

Noon (2010a) outlines four main reasons for the business case. First is the better use of human resources, wherein if managers discriminate on the basis of sex, race/ethnicity, disability and so on, then they could be neglecting or overlooking talented employees. This situation could also create a sense of disgruntlement in existing organizational members and talented people may leave the organization. Second, a more diverse workforce, reflecting society as a whole, has the potential to widen the customer base of organizations, particularly in face-to-face service businesses, such as those found in hospitality and tourism. Third is the creation of a wider pool of labour for recruitment into the organization. By being an inclusive organization, there is the possibility to attract the most talented employees. Last is the creation of a positive company image. If an organization has a clear policy and commitment to fair treatment backed by its practices then this can portray a positive image to employees, potential employees, customers and suppliers. That said, despite these legal, ethical and business aspects, discrimination still remains a very real issue within society generally and workplaces specifically, so the chapter will now move on to consider steps that may be taken to eradicate discrimination in all its forms.

## The employment experience of socially defined minority groups

A good starting point to further consider the issue of equal opportunities is to recognize some of the barriers that may affect the employment of certain groups of workers. We will initially consider women, black, Asian and minority ethnic people, people with disabilities, older people and gay and lesbian employees.

## Women

Across the economy as a whole, women now make up 49.4 per cent of the workforce, though nearly half of all women work part-time (Labour Research Department, 2011b). Despite making up nearly half of the workforce, women still remain under-represented in senior- and middle-management positions. For example, across the economy as a whole, although there is now greater representation of women in the boardroom of Britain's leading companies, women still remain relatively under-represented, despite evidence which suggests that having a more gender-balanced board enhances business performance (Davies Report, 2011; Sealy and Vinnicombe, 2012). There is also continuing disparity in women's pay, relative to men, and although the gender pay gap has narrowed considerably in the last 30 years or so, women still earn only around 87p for every £1 earned by men (Equality and Human Rights Commission, 2010).

These disparities in the economy as a whole are also seen in the tourism and hospitality industry. Although 59 per cent of the workforce is female, only 6 per cent of company directors are women, a figure well below the national average, reflecting the fact that only five of the sector's FTSE 100 employers have female directors on their board (Eade, 2009). Across Europe the picture is more encouraging, and in recent years there has been a significant improvement in the number of women at board level. In 2006 travel and leisure had the lowest level of boardroom representation, with no representation at all compared to sectors like household goods and services, where 18.9 per cent of boards were made up by women (European Professional Women's Network, 2006). By 2010 the same survey found that leisure and hotels were now in the top five, with over 15 per cent of board members being women (European Professional Women's Network, 2010). For managerial positions below board level, although the number of women managers in the UK tourism and hospitality industry is significantly higher than many other industries, it still remains disproportionately low given the overall level of female representation within the workforce (Doherty, 2008; People 1st, 2010b). Women may also face particular barriers in the workplace in the tourism and hospitality industry, including (Hotel and Catering International Management Association, 1999; People 1st, 2010b):

- lack of childcare provision;
- difficulty of combining work at senior level with caring responsibilities;
- dominant masculine organizational culture;
- preconceptions and gender bias;
- lack of networking and exclusion from informal networks of communication;
- lack of visible women in senior positions to act as positive role models;
- lack of flexible, part-time opportunities at higher levels in the industry;
- the macho atmosphere in certain workplaces, such as the professional kitchen;
- sexism and sexist attitudes;
- poor career planning.

There are a number of ways in which organizations can begin to address some of these issues; HRM in Practice 6.1 presents an example of a proactive response to encouraging women's employment.

**HRM IN PRACTICE 6.1:**
**Opportunity Now: a proactive response to gender equality**

Opportunity Now was originally set up as Opportunity 2000 in October 1991. Its aim was to increase the quality and quantity of women's participation in the workforce. Membership is open to any organization, large or small, and currently stands at over 200 organizations, including British Airways and McDonald's. Those organizations joining Opportunity Now commit themselves to overcoming the barriers to recruitment, retention and development of women. Opportunity Now provides advice to employers and shares information on best practice in areas such as developing flexible working arrangements, improving childcare, career break options and training and education to increase women's opportunity at work. To further help organizations, Opportunity Now also runs a benchmarking exercise on gender equality, which helps employers to chart progress while at the same time providing a checklist for organizational change.

Derived from Income Data Services (2003); Opportunity Now (2005); Opportunity Now website (http://www. bitcdiversity.org.uk)

## Black, Asian and minority ethnic people

A recent report from Race for Opportunity (2010) notes the overall increase in the number of black, Asian and minority ethnic (BAME) people in the UK from around 5.5 per cent of the population in 1991 to over 10 per cent by 2010, with an expectation that by 2051 over one-fifth of the UK population will be from an ethnic minority. The same report, however, notes that despite BAME people making up more than 1 in 10 of the population, BAME workers make up just 8.5 per cent of employment. This employment gap means that people from ethnic minorities have much lower rates of employment than the white population and are twice as likely to be unemployed. When ethnic minority employees are employed it is noteworthy that they tend to be concentrated in terms of occupational segregation, with a large number employed in the hospitality sub-sector in particular. For example, the Labour Research Department (2005) notes that 52 per cent of Bangladeshi workers are employed in the restaurant industry compared with only 1 per cent of white males. In addition, the Labour Research Department (2005) also noted a disparity in pay, with this 'black pay gap' meaning in some instances that workers from some communities earned on average £7,000 less than white workers. Despite the relatively large number of ethnic minority employees in hospitality-related occupations, there is evidence that suggests, as with women, under-representation in management positions. Mirroring the under-representation of non-white workers in management and boardroom positions across the economy as a whole (Race for Opportunity, 2009a), research by the HR consultancy Chess Executive found that BAME employees in hospitality, leisure, travel and tourism were much more likely to be working at non-management levels, with only 6 per cent working in middle- or senior-level management and just 2 per cent at board level (cited in Gilbert, 2007).

As we have already noted, BAME people now make up over one-tenth of the UK population, but continue to experience lower employment rates and less career progression compared to white workers. Consequently, there is a need for organizations to be proactive in their attempts to promote racial equality. The Income Data Services (2001) suggest a number of practical steps which can be taken by organizations, including:

- Ensure fair recruitment practices, such as recruitment schemes targeted at ethnic minority employees and targeted advertising to encourage more applicants from under-represented groups.
- Use images of ethnic minority employees in publicity and advertising material.
- Develop links with ethnic minority communities (often as a way of attracting new employees).
- Undertake ethnic monitoring.
- Ensure HR policies are in place to help foster and protect a diverse work environment (for example, dignity at work and harassment policies).
- Accommodate different religious beliefs in the multi-cultural workforce.
- Introduce diversity awareness training (particularly for managers).
- Set up internal networks for ethnic minority employees.
- Take positive action on training and development.

There has also been a similar type of initiative for BAME employees as Opportunity Now. Launched in October 1995, Race for Opportunity (RfO) is a business-led initiative organized by Business in the Community and aims to put race and diversity issues higher up the business agenda by investing in the UK's ethnic communities. RfO publishes periodic benchmarking reports which assess organizations in four key 'impact' areas:

- *People and employees*: looking at employment, including attraction, recruitment, selection, development, progression and retention of talented ethnic minority people.
- *Customers, clients and service users*: how organizations market goods and services to ethnic minorities as profitable consumers.
- *Community involvement*: diversity-proofing community involvement activities and initiatives to ensure inclusion of ethnic minority individuals and communities.
- *Supplier diversity*: engaging ethnic minority businesses in the organization's supply chain and as business partners.

(Race for Opportunity, 2009b)

## People with disabilities

Often, our perception of disability is likely to be based on narrow and out-dated assumptions – for example, equating disability with a visible physical disability, such as wheelchair use (O'Hara, 2007). However, of the estimated 8–11 million adults who are registered disabled, only a very small percentage are in a wheelchair (Riddell *et al.*, 2010). Around 3.4 million people with disabilities are in work, though employment rates for disabled people are less than half those of non-disabled people, with median hourly wages 20 per cent lower for men and 12 per cent lower for women (Riddell *et al.*, 2010). It is also instructive to note that 70 per cent of disabled people who are economically active or looking for work became disabled while in work (Labour Research Department, 2000a). Thus there would seem a strong moral argument that employers should aim to help people with disabilities back into the labour market. In a similar vein to Opportunity Now and RfO, there is also an attempt to be positive about disabled workers with the 'two-ticks' scheme. Under this scheme any employers using the 'two-ticks' (disability symbol) must (Labour Research Department, 2007):

- interview all applicants with a disability who meet the minimum for a job vacancy;
- ask disabled employees at least twice a year what can be done to ensure they can develop and use their abilities at work;
- make every effort when employees become disabled to ensure they stay in employment;
- take action to ensure that key employees are aware of the needs of disabled people;
- perform annual reviews of achievements towards making the workplace welcoming and accessible for disabled people, plan ways to improve and let all employees and customers know about this progress and future plans.

While the two-ticks campaign is important to changing workplaces practices, campaigners for people with disabilities are also attempting to shift percep-tions about disability. For example, a letter to *People Management* from a representative of Capability Scotland noted how language used to describe disability often shapes attitudes and perceptions (Bald, 1997). Bald's letter notes how people with disabilities are often described as 'suffering' from the disability, which can lead to misconceptions such as the amount of time they are likely to take off work. The letter also suggests preferred terminology to ensure that people are aware of using pejorative terms like 'the disabled', 'normal', 'mentally retarded' and 'confined to a wheelchair'. The preferred terms are 'people with disabilities', 'able-bodied', 'learning difficulties' and 'wheelchair users' (see also O'Hara, 2007; HRM in Practice 6.2; and a discussion of 'ten good reasons to employ a disabled worker in the hospitality industry' at http://www.tourismforall.org.uk/10-good-reasons.html).

**HRM IN PRACTICE 6.2:**
**Challenging negative perceptions of disability**

Recent work in the United States and Canada found significant evidence of prejudice, stereotyping and limited choices for people with disabilities accessing work in the hospitality industry. For example, the Canadian research covered 42 hotels that employed 11,161 employees, though the research found that fewer than 60 people with disabilities were employed in the hotels. This is perhaps unsurprising as the research also found that none of the participating hotels had policies or company documents, such as mission statements, referring specifically to employees with disabilities. Instead, the focus of the hotels tended to be on addressing the needs of guests with disabilities, rather than employees. Although some of the hotels did awareness training as part of broader diversity training, managerial interviewees nevertheless suggested that people with disabilities were felt to have higher training costs and be less productive. Managers also suggested that employees with disabilities were more likely to be inflexible, lack high levels of mobility, need expensive accommodating tools and constant mentoring and controlling. A further concerning aspect was the extent to which the hotels had a strong preference for employees being young and fitting a high level of physical attractiveness, mirroring our earlier discussion of aesthetic labour in Chapter 5. Similarly, the survey of 320 hospitality companies in the United States found that companies had concerns that people with disabilities would not have the requisite skills or be as productive. Concerns were also expressed about the potential costs of accommodating people with disabilities, even though most of such accommodations under the Americans with Disabilities Act are not usually exceptionally costly. It is suggested that education lies at the heart of changing attitudes to enhance the employment opportunities available to people with disabilities, such as addressing misconceptions that people with disabilities lack the appropriate skills, are less productive and costly to accommodate.

Derived from Gröschl (2007); Houtenville and Kalargyrou (2012)

## Older workers

Hope (2005) reports that the National Audit Office estimated that the cost of stereotyping on the basis of age costs the UK economy £31 billion each year in lost contributions. Indeed, a recent report from the Chartered Institute of Personnel and Development (2012a) on managing a healthy ageing workforce recognized that 'stereotypical thinking – both conscious and unconscious – about age and what people can or can't do influences the way people at work are managed and the way people themselves behave' (p. 6). This point is important as the same report also notes that the UK is running out of workers,

and although there are likely to be around 13.5 million job vacancies in the next ten years, only seven million young people will leave school/college. Within this context older people will be the main source of untapped labour, especially as there is no longer a compulsory retirement age in the UK with the removal of 65 as the default retirement age. It seems there is still some way to go to change attitudes about older workers if this resource is going to be used.

It was recently reported that age is the most widely experienced form of discrimination in Europe, with people over 50 feeling that employers prefer to hire a person in their twenties rather than an older person (Labour Research Department, 2011c). Thus, for older workers it can be especially difficult to gain a new job, especially once they are over 45. In that sense it is perhaps no great surprise that people aged 50–64 are more likely to be long-term unemployed, with nearly half of those unemployed aged 50–64 having been unemployed for longer than one year, compared with 30.6 per cent of those under 50 (Metcalf and Meadows, 2010). Arkin (2005a: 32) notes how some of the 'ridiculous comments' about older workers have the ring of comments which were often made 30 years ago with regard to sex and race discrimination. For example, he notes that prior to the introduction of the Race Relations Act in the 1970s some people argued that employing someone from an ethnic minority in a shop would put customers off. Certainly such attitudes have been prevalent in the tourism and hospitality industry, with one well-known restaurateur once famously suggesting that:

> I fail to understand why employers ought not to be able to discriminate about potential employees on the basis of age, at least for those who are in contact with the public. We are in a business where image counts as much as content. Of course, it is unfair to turn down older people with the required technical skills to do the job, but so what? It is not a perfect world.
>
> (Gottlieb, 1992: 20)

## Review and reflect

To what extent do you either agree or disagree with Gottlieb's sentiments and why?

The attitudes expressed by Michael Gottlieb still seem to be prevalent in at least some areas of the tourism and hospitality industry. For example, a recent study by Metcalf and Meadows (2010) found that awareness of age discrimination was lowest within hotels and restaurants, with the same study also finding that equal opportunities policies covering age were least common in the sector. Consequently they suggest that organizations in hospitality may need targeting to improve their age-related policies and practices. More generally the same study also found continuing illegal practices within recruitment. For example, 2 per cent of establishments normally included a preferred age range in their advertisements – something that is now illegal with age discrimination legislation – while 42 per cent sought information on age in the recruitment process and 28 per cent made age information available to recruiters.

Work by Qu and Cheng (1996), who surveyed 26 hotels in Hong Kong, and Magd (2003), who interviewed 21 managing directors in small- and medium-sized hospitality enterprises in the UK, is useful to appreciate how older workers tend to be perceived within tourism and hospitality. From a positive point of view the research suggests that employers tend to see older workers as having: low absenteeism, fewer accidents, low turnover rate, being motivated, hard-working and diligent, having a sense of responsibility, good communication skills and credibility with customers (see also HRM in Practice 6.3).

## HRM IN PRACTICE 6.3:
## Hospitality: a young person's industry?

Although McDonald's tends to be associated with a younger workforce they also employ older workers, recognizing the manner in which their social skills are highly appropriate for service operations. The company examined their workforce and found a positive correlation between age and high performance, productivity and job satisfaction. The results of McDonald's analysis showed that the higher the mean age of the workforce, the higher the service quality, customer visits, sales, profits and job satisfaction.

JD Wetherspoons is another company that is actively seeking older workers and who stopped using a retirement age in 2006. The company's oldest employee is 75. In recruiting older workers Wetherspoons was seeking to retain valuable skills and experience and give staff the choice of working for longer. In recruiting older workers the company found no evidence of higher levels of sickness absence for employees over 65. The company also finds that older workers are able to empathize with customers due to their broad range of experiences, and often command greater respect from customers. Although the company is very positive about older workers and actively recruits workers in their fifties and sixties, currently just 5 per cent of their workforce is aged over 50, with just 2 per cent over 60 and 78 per cent aged under 30.

Derived from *Human Resource Management International Digest* (2007); Income Data Services (2011b); Stevens (2009); Walker (2011)

On the other hand, research on older workers has also revealed that they are often perceived as: not having relevant skills, inflexible and reluctant to change, having low productivity, experiencing difficulty adapting to new technology and in keeping up with the speed of work. Many of these perceptions the Chartered Institute of Personnel and Development (2012a) has recently suggested are 'myths', which are not substantiated by research evidence. While most age-related discrimination is directed towards older workers, younger workers can also be affected. Smethurst (2004a) reports research from the CIPD which notes that the optimum age in the workplace to be judged as neither too old or too young is 35–40. For those under 35, 8 per cent of people reported being discriminated against for being too young.

## Gay and lesbian employees

Discrimination based on sexual orientation was only recognized relatively recently with regulations emerging in 2003. There are approximately 1.3–1.9 million gay and lesbian workers in the UK (Labour Research Department, 2003b) and the perception is that there is a higher proportion of gay and lesbian employees within hospitality and tourism. That said, there has been little research that has explicitly addressed the opportunities and experiences of gay men and lesbians within tourism and hospitality organizations. More generally, research has pointed to the discrimination faced by gay and lesbian employees. For example, the Labour Research Department (2000b) reports a survey by the TUC which found that 44 per cent of gay or lesbian employees had suffered some form of discriminatory treatment, most commonly name calling and homophobic abuse, but in some cases dismissal. Even with the introduction of legislation in 2003 there still seems to be evidence of continuing discrimination. For example, recent research suggests that gay men and lesbian women still fear discrimination if they 'come out' at work (Cahalane, 2010). With regard to sexual orientation, the Labour Research Department (2008a) notes how research has highlighted the positive effects on motivation and job satisfaction for lesbian and gay employees who feel able to 'come out' in the workplace. To help gay and lesbian employees to 'come out', Ward (2003) outlines a series of appropriate policy responses:

- *Understand the effects of the closet*: being gay and lesbian and not feeling that the workplace is sufficiently supportive to allow one to come out will often have a negative impact on the individual and their standard of work.
- *Recognize the benefits of 'coming out'*: many gay and lesbian employees describe coming out as the most significant event of their working life, often leading to increased job satisfaction, motivation and enhanced commitment to the organization.
- *Know your own people*: action may be needed to ensure that the organization is one in which staff feel safe to come out. This may require

the organization to explore their employees' attitudes to sexual orientation to determine the appropriate policy responses.

- *Raise awareness*: as with other forms of discrimination, discriminatory behaviour can often be unwitting. There may be a need to raise awareness of the issues surrounding sexual orientation through things like discussion groups.
- *Support a lesbian and gay network*: 'invisibility' at work is often an issue for lesbians and gay men, and an employee network can be useful to provide support and also raise the profile of sexual minorities with colleagues.
- *Ensure support from top management*: it is important to have a senior manager, who is not necessarily gay themselves, to act as a diversity champion for sexual minorities in the workplace.
- *Create a culture where people can come out*: much of the above suggests means by which this can be done. There is also a need to train managers to make the right decisions in support of such a culture.

## The legislative response

The above discussion gives us a sense of some of the issues affecting certain groups of employees. We can now move on to consider how these have been addressed, beginning with the emergence of equal opportunities legislation. Since the emergence of legislation in the 1970s in the UK, which initially sought to address sex and race discrimination, further legislation has been developed which addresses a number of other characteristics. These laws have sought to address the problems of discrimination generally and specifically to reduce such discrimination in the labour market and the workplace.

### Review and reflect

How successful is legislation likely to be in addressing equality issues?

While legislation has now existed for over 40 years, we should recognize that there is much debate about whether the legislation has been successful, and whether it has simply been embraced as rhetoric but without much success in implementation. Many believe that legislation cannot by itself eradicate a whole range of attitudes, which may encourage discriminating behaviour. For example, as the Equality and Human Rights Commission (2010: 25) note:

As powerful as the law and regulation may be, they are only two aspects of the way a society changes its behaviour. When trying to achieve sustainable change, far more potent, in the end, are the attitudes of the majority of its people.

While recognizing that the law cannot change attitudes overnight, it can, and does, effect change slowly. Some people would argue that it has in fact been too slow and its effects have been patchy. In that sense the law requires an end to discrimination; it does not actually require that employers do anything to promote equality. Related to this point there is also the distinction made by many commentators about the differences between the letter and spirit of the law. The former encourages a narrow interpretation of law, which may not be in the best interests of encouraging a more proactive approach to equality and diversity. The latter is potentially more flexible in offering the scope for decisions which encourage greater equality.

Having briefly contextualized the emergence of the legislative agenda, we can now go on and examine the actual provisions and what they mean for organizations. Prior to 2010, anti-discrimination legislation had been developed in a piecemeal manner. The Sex Discrimination Act (1975) and Race Relations Act (1976) were particularly important in denoting the first systematic attempt to address discrimination. These acts were later followed by other acts such as the Disability Discrimination Act (1995), the Employment Equality (Sexual Orientation) Regulations 2003, the Employment Equality (Religion or Belief) Regulations 2003, and finally in October 2006 discrimination based on age was made unlawful. However, as the Labour Research Department (2010: 3) note, 'the different tests for, and defences to, various types of discrimination caused confusion and uncertainty . . . especially as more personal characteristics fell under the scope of anti-discrimination legislation and the case for simplification and harmonization became overwhelming'. As a consequence, on 1 October 2010, the Equality Act (2010) came into force. The Act consolidates most of the previous legislation into one Act, with harmonized definitions of discrimination for the 'protected characteristics' of: age, disability, gender reassignment, marital/civil partnership status, race, religion/belief, sex and sexual orientation. The Act applies to all employers regardless of size.

There are various types of discrimination covered by the Act, with the most important being direct and indirect discrimination. Direct discrimination is where employees with protected characteristics are treated less favourably than other employees. For example, a policy to only recruit men to management posts. Indirect discrimination is where a particular requirement apparently treats everyone equally but has a disproportionate effect on a particular group and the requirement cannot be shown to be justified. For example, requiring a kitchen porter to speak fluent English. This might be a justifiable requirement for those in customer-facing roles, but for workers based in back-of-house positions, the requirement could be indirectly discriminatory in relation to race or disability as it is less likely to be objectively justified.

In addition to direct and indirect discrimination the Act also has provisions covering discrimination by association and perceptive discrimination. The former relates to when an individual is discriminated against because of their association with another person who has a protected characteristic. The latter aspect is where an employee is treated less favourably because they are believed (incorrectly) to have a protected characteristic. The Act also covers aspects such as harassment, third-party harassment (both of which are more fully covered in Chapter 11) and victimization, when an employee is treated badly as a result of making or supporting a complaint under the Act.

The Advisory, Conciliation and Arbitration Service (ACAS) (2010a) provides a useful guide to how the Act consolidates, and in some cases extends, the protection for employees who fall within a protected characteristic. In most cases the new Act involves relatively minor change, but one area that is worthy of further discussion is that of disability. In further strengthening the rights of people with disabilities the Act covers a new offence, 'discrimination arising from disability', where a disabled person is treated unfavourably because of something arising in consequence of their disability. With regard to discrimination arising from a disability, the Equality and Human Rights Commission (2011) cites the example of an employer dismissing a worker because she has had three months' sick leave. The employer is aware that the worker has multiple sclerosis and most of her sick leave is disability-related. The employer's decision to dismiss is not because of the worker's disability itself, but the worker has been treated unfavourably because of something arising in consequence of her disability (namely, the need to take a period of disability-related sick leave). It is also important to note how the Act adopts a broad definition of disability, with Section 6(1) of the Act talking of any physical or mental impairment which has a substantial and long-term adverse effect on the ability of somebody to carry out normal day-to-day activities. Indeed, the Labour Research Department (2010), in reviewing a number of employment tribunal decisions, note that there is no definitive list of what amounts to physical or mental impairment and employment tribunals are left to decide what may be considered a disability (see HRM in Practice 6.4)

## HRM IN PRACTICE 6.4:
## Conditions amounting to physical or mental impairment

Employment tribunals have taken a wide view of disability and have made it clear that the following forms of physical or mental impairment are capable of amounting to a disability.

- asthma
- migraines
- photo-sensitive epilepsy
- visual impairment
- injuries affecting mobility
- abdominal pain
- depression
- multiple sclerosis
- post-traumatic stress disorder
- dyslexia

- bipolar affective disorder
- cerebral palsy
- ME (chronic fatigue syndrome)
- colitis
- congenital myotonic dystrophy
- deafness
- emphysema
- diabetes
- mobility impairment
- paranoid schizophrenia

Conditions such as HIV/AIDS, as well as progressive conditions such as cancer, are also included under the Equality Act (2010). This protection extends from the date of diagnosis.

Source: Labour Research Department (2010)

The Act also places a duty on the employer to be proactive in making 'reasonable adjustments' to help people with disabilities to overcome disadvantage resulting from an impairment. Within tourism and hospitality there are many instances where managers may have to consider their response to potentially sensitive situations under the aegis of the disability aspects of the Equality Act.

---

### Review and reflect

As a manager think about how you might respond to the following scenarios:

- An applicant for a waiting job, who otherwise impresses in the interview, is visually impaired. There may be some concerns about them tripping over furniture, reading blackboard menus to customers or dropping plates on laps and so on.
- An applicant for a front-line position in a travel agency is facially disfigured and you are concerned about whether their appearance may put off customers.
- An applicant for a position as chef who is a wheelchair user.

---

To a large extent the approach to the scenarios outlined in the review and reflect section will be dictated, as we have already noted, by the notion of reasonable adjustments. Once it is established that a person is disabled then the employer has to make reasonable adjustments which accommodate their disability. For example, the Industrial Relations Services (2003b) notes some of the common adjustments made by employers, including:

- allowing absence for rehabilitation and treatment;
- altering a person's working hours;
- acquiring or modifying equipment;
- adjusting premises;
- transferring a person to another job;
- assigning a person to other work;
- providing a reader and interpreter;
- providing support workers;
- modifying instruction manuals.

With regard to the scenarios above, it is crucial to recognize, as the Labour Research Department (2010: 51) note, 'an employer that does not consider making any adjustment is very vulnerable to a disability discrimination claim'. In the case of the chef, health and safety considerations might lead an employer to suggest that the use of a wheelchair within the kitchen is likely to be impractical and it would be considered unreasonable to make significant adjustments to the premises. However, it may be worth taking further advice in such a scenario. On the other hand, visual impairment is likely to require a much more proactive response from tourism and hospitality employers (see HRM in Practice 6.5).

## HRM IN PRACTICE 6.5:
## Responding to the needs of visually impaired employees

Wendy Kerner is visually impaired, being completely blind in one eye and having little vision in the other. She works as a purchase ledger clerk at the 37-bedroom Lauriston Hotel in Weston-Super-Mare. Her main responsibilities are inputting petty cash, cheques and invoices into the hotel account's system and doing the weekly cheque run for the hotel's suppliers. Additionally, she also maintains the database of suppliers' details and occasionally helps out in reception if the hotel is busy. In order to support her at work the hotel secured funding from the government's Access to Work programme to purchase a range of equipment. The equipment included technology to enable her to print her work in Braille and software that enlarges print and speaks while Kerner types. Working practices at reception were also altered slightly to move from a handwritten list of petty cash transactions to printing a Braille version which Kerner can read.

Derived from Guild (2002)

A further facet of disability legislation which is particularly apposite for tourism and hospitality organizations is the need to ensure that employees are aware of the needs of customers who have a disability. The Equality Act (2010) requires employees to be able, to some extent, anticipate the needs of disabled guests. Employers can get advice from organizations such as Tourism for All UK (TFA), a national registered charity which aims to provide advice and support to disabled people and tourism providers to enhance the accessibility of tourism provision to the disabled. Among other things, TFA provides a series of Access for All training courses, which have been developed with the help of disabled people and industry professionals from across Europe.

Previously there had been three government-sponsored bodies which were responsible for promoting equality. With regard to sex and race the commissions were the Equal Opportunities Commission (EOC) and the Commission for Racial Equality (CRE), which were established in 1975 and 1976, respectively. With regard to disability, the Disability Rights Commission (DRC) was established in 2000. The EOC, CRE and DRC were responsible for the broad areas of sex, race/ethnicity and disability and there were no bodies responsible for sexual orientation or religion. In response to this situation and the emergence of age legislation in October 2006, the UK government established a single equalities body. This new body was known as the Equality and Human Rights Commission (EHRC) and came into being in October 2007. The EHRC is responsible for working towards eliminating discrimination, promoting equality of opportunity and human rights and advising on and, if necessary, seeking to enforce the law. With regard to employment, the EHRC issued a comprehensive Statutory Code of Practice in 2011 (Equality and Human Rights Commission, 2011), which aims to provide an authoritative, comprehensive and technical guide to the detail of law as contained in the Equality Act (2010). The code of practice is invaluable to HR managers or managers generally who want to understand the importance of the legal aspects of equality in organizations. The EHRC can also undertake formal investigations where there are allegations of discrimination and can, in certain circumstances, support individual legal claims.

The EHRC is also concerned with prohibiting discrimination in all areas of employment. For example, during the recruitment and selection process organizations should ensure that the right message is conveyed in recruitment advertisements which, as we noted in Chapter 5, should be carefully worded so that there is no indication that people of some backgrounds are preferred to others. Equally, in the selection procedure organizations should be wary of drawing up person specifications that are unjustifiably demanding. As we noted, there is also a need to consider whether certain selection tests may discriminate against people from minority backgrounds. Only the EHRC can instigate proceedings in relation to advertising, but individuals can pursue claims via the employment tribunal system in all other aspects of employment. The legislative threat centres on possible adverse publicity to the organization, as well as the direct and indirect costs of tribunal claims or commission investigation. In reality, a relatively small number of cases actually end up being heard in an employment tribunal. For example, the Advisory, Conciliation and Arbitration Service (2010b) notes that in 2009–10 it received over 25,000 cases with regard to sex, race or disability discrimination, though only a minority of these cases actually reached the point of being heard in an employment tribunal. Nevertheless, cases that are concerned with discrimination do not, as we noted earlier, carry an upper limit for compensation, so organizations should aim to avoid such cases, which may prove to be very costly. For example, the largest award in 2010–11 following an employment tribunal was £289,167 in a sex discrimination case, followed by disability (£181,083), age (£144,100), race (£62,530), religion (£47,633) and sexual orientation (£20,221) (Ministry of Justice, 2011).

Two other points are also important to note with regard to the legislation. The first is positive action. Positive action may be confused with what is often termed positive or reverse discrimination, or what in the United States is known as affirmative action. Positive discrimination seeks to redress previous inequality by giving priority to certain groups in the labour market. For example, an organization appointing a female candidate to a managerial position primarily because of her gender, rather than her managerial skills. There is much debate about the efficacy of positive discrimination, with Noon (2010b) offering an interesting overview of the debate, which is framed by several key questions:

- Will the best candidate be overlooked in favour of the candidate that meets other requirements (sex, ethnicity, disability, etc.)?
- Is this approach based on meritocratic principles?
- Even when a minority candidate is the best person for the job, does this approach raise suspicions in the minds of other employees and managers that they were only appointed because they are from a particular social group?
- Does this really solve the problem of unfair discrimination?

While the use of positive discrimination is illegal in the UK, such approaches have been used in the United States and other countries (see HRM in Practice 6.6).

**HRM IN PRACTICE 6.6:**
**Jobs for the girls**

Legislation was introduced in Norway in 2002 to ensure at least 40 per cent of boardroom seats are reserved for women. The decree initially affected only state-owned firms, but by 2005 all public companies had to enforce the quota. While equality groups and trade unions were supportive of the move, employers feared

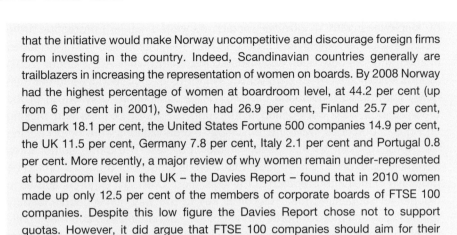

that the initiative would make Norway uncompetitive and discourage foreign firms from investing in the country. Indeed, Scandinavian countries generally are trailblazers in increasing the representation of women on boards. By 2008 Norway had the highest percentage of women at boardroom level, at 44.2 per cent (up from 6 per cent in 2001), Sweden had 26.9 per cent, Finland 25.7 per cent, Denmark 18.1 per cent, the United States Fortune 500 companies 14.9 per cent, the UK 11.5 per cent, Germany 7.8 per cent, Italy 2.1 per cent and Portugal 0.8 per cent. More recently, a major review of why women remain under-represented at boardroom level in the UK – the Davies Report – found that in 2010 women made up only 12.5 per cent of the members of corporate boards of FTSE 100 companies. Despite this low figure the Davies Report chose not to support quotas. However, it did argue that FTSE 100 companies should aim for their boards to be 25 per cent female by 2015 or face government sanction. Quotas have been introduced in a number of other European countries, and Norway, Austria, Belgium, France and the Netherlands, among others, are all seeking to have at least 30 per cent female representation on boards.

Derived from Davies Report (2011); European Parliament (2012); Fouche (2008)

---

## Review and reflect

Outline arguments for and against positive discrimination.

---

While positive discrimination is unlawful in the UK, positive action is not. Positive action may encompass a range of policy initiatives which aim to promote equality of opportunity through the provision of facilities, procedures or actions that redress disadvantage suffered by groups with protected characteristics in the labour market or organization. For example, under positive action it is lawful to encourage and provide training for members of one sex or racial group who have been under-represented in particular work in the previous 12 months. In addition, advertisements can explicitly encourage applications from under-represented groups within the organization, though there are no guarantees that they will get the job.

One final point when we are talking about discrimination legislation is that of genuine occupational grounds, where discrimination is permitted due to protected characteristics being specified as a Genuine Occupational Requirement (GOR), which is outlined in Part 1, Schedule 9 of the Equality Act. A GOR is likely to be based on things such as authenticity, decency, privacy and the delivery of personal welfare services.

Two further facets of discrimination that also need to be considered are with regard to discrimination based on religion and beliefs and the position of employees with a criminal record. As noted earlier, protection from discrimination for employees based on their religious beliefs was introduced in 2003 and has now been consolidated into the Equality Act. Cooper (2003) reports evidence from 20 organizations in terms of their response to the then newly introduced regulations on religious discrimination. Only seven of the organizations were conducting a thorough review of policies and making changes to practices, while the remaining 13 organizations were simply adding the word 'religion' to their discrimination policies. The same author cites several legal experts who suggest that there is a need for organizations to be proactive in their interpretation of the legislation. One legal expert is quoted in Cooper as suggesting that 'religion is key to the way some people identify themselves – it's more important than ethnicity or nationality – and they rightly expect companies to accommodate their religious needs and protect them from discrimination' (p. 27). This point is particularly important when it is recognized that more than two-thirds of the population identifies with a religion (Black, 2007). Advice from the Advisory, Conciliation and Arbitration Service (2010c) points to a number of areas that organizations should be considering with regard to religious discrimination. For example, employers may adapt their recruitment processes so that anyone who is suitably qualified can apply and attend for selection, which may require some flexibility around interview/selection times, allowing avoidance of significant religious times, such as Friday afternoons. The Chartered Institute of Personnel and Development (2009b) also notes a number of practical accommodations to enable religious observance, including (also see HRM in Practice 6.7):

- allowing employees to take different public holidays so they can observe their own religious festivals, where these are different from those in the Christian calendar;
- adapting existing flexible job rosters;
- providing quiet rooms for prayer, contemplation or meditation;
- providing dedicated faith rooms.

## HRM IN PRACTICE 6.7:
## British Airways responding to the legislation on religious discrimination

Race for Opportunity (2004) reports how, in response to the regulations prohibiting discrimination on religious grounds, British Airway (BA) consulted with their employees via a series of focus groups and meetings. The intent of the meetings was to ensure that the needs of different groups of employees were managed to conform to the legislation. In discussing the issues with employees, some

of the key issues raised were: availability of prayer rooms, uniform and dress code regulations, labelling of food and time off for praying and religious festivals. Consideration of these topics was then used to develop a frequently asked questions section on the BA staff website.

The final area that is worthy of consideration in terms of discrimination is that of people with a criminal record, which is covered by the Rehabilitation of Offenders Act 1974. The Chartered Institute of Personnel and Development (2007a) suggests that one-fifth of the working population has a criminal record, with this figure being higher again for men, where the figure is around one in three. Although some employers may be wary of employing somebody with a criminal record, it is important to recognize that recent research by the Chartered Institute of Personnel and Development (2007b) found that only 23 employers out of 474 respondents across all employing sectors had a negative experience in employing ex-offenders. Moreover, the Act enables offenders who received less than a custodial sentence of up to 2.5 years to be rehabilitated, and their convictions to be 'spent'. This means that after a certain amount of time potential employees are able to answer no to the question of whether they have a criminal record or not. The length of time is dependent on the sentence received. It is important to recognize that it is illegal for an employer to discriminate on the basis of a spent conviction. Gledhill (2002) suggests that the hospitality industry, in particular, should look seriously to employing ex-offenders to address labour shortages and recruitment problems. He reports a Prison Service chef-training scheme which aims to train inmates to National Vocational Qualification level 2 in food hygiene and food handling. Prisoners on the scheme cook for fellow inmates and so get used to the pressure of working to deadlines, and a number of ex-offenders were successful in gaining jobs on release (see also Allcock, 2008).

## Managing diversity

In reviewing the debate about equal opportunities, what we have been largely talking about to-date is the meeting of statutory requirements to offer equal opportunities to all in the organization, or those who will potentially join the organization. In many respects this can be considered the short-term agenda as outlined by Goss (1994), where the emphasis is on meeting legal obligations to ensure separate groups are not discriminated against in the workplace. A longer-term agenda that aims to move away from such a narrow approach is suggested by the notion of managing diversity (Kumra and Manfredi, 2012).

Managing diversity is also particularly important, given that it would be remiss to imagine women or ethnic minorities or people with disabilities as a homogenous group. For example, women are divided by class, ethnicity, age and occupational status. Similarly, ethnic minorities are far from homogenous – for example, there may be major differences in the opportunities and employment experience between Asian employees and black African employees. In that sense resistance to equal opportunities policies may not come simply from white, non-disadvantaged men. Opposition to equal opportunities may also be seen from particular groups in society due to the fear of backlash, or being seen to have achieved a position based on grounds other than merit. Of course, the legislative agenda does not necessarily seek to create such perceptions or stereotypes – for example, it does not support positive discrimination. Nevertheless, the perception that equal opportunities is primarily driven by a defensive legislative agenda has led to the emergence of managing diversity as a potentially more strategic and business-oriented approach to engendering equality of opportunity. To consider this point we should consider three questions in relation to managing diversity:

1   What is managing diversity?
2   How are equal opportunities moved on by managing diversity?
3   What action does managing diversity require?

In answer to the first question, Ellis and Sonnenfield (1994: 82) define managing diversity as 'the challenge of meeting the needs of a culturally diverse workforce and of sensitizing workers and managers to differences associated with gender, race, age and nationality in an attempt to maximize the potential productivity of all employees'. In a similar vein, Kandola and Fullerton (1998: 8) suggest that:

> The basic concept of managing diversity accepts that the workforce consists of a diverse population of people. The diversity consists of visible and non-visible differences which include factors, such as sex, age, background, race, disability, personality and workstyle. It is founded on the premise that harnessing these differences will create a productive environment in which everybody feels valued, where their talents are being fully utilized and in which organizational goals are met.

With regard to the second question, Table 6.1 illustrates the manner in which the managing of diversity and equal opportunities are suggested as being different.

So the question we can ask ourselves is: to what extent are organizations moving to become diverse and multicultural, and if not how can organizations address this issue? At one level many would argue that the tourism and hospitality industry is, in all respects, be it unit, locality, clientele or labour

| TABLE 6.1 Differences between managing diversity and equal opportunities | |
| --- | --- |
| Managing diversity | Equal opportunities |
| Focuses on ensuring all employees maximize their potential and their contribution to the organization | Concentration on issues of discrimination |
| Embraces the full range of people in the organization; no one is excluded | Perceived as an issue for certain groups in the labour market, such as women, ethnic minorities, older workers and people with disabilities |
| Concentration on issues of movement within an organization, the culture of the organization and meeting business objectives | Less of an emphasis on culture change and the meeting of business objectives, premised more on moral issues and legislative compliance |
| Is the concern of all employees, especially managers | Seen as an issue to do with HR practitioners |
| Does not rely on positive action/ affirmative action | Relies on positive action |
| Source: adapted from Kandola and Fullerton (1998) | |

market, possibly the most international of industries. Baum (1996: A77), for example, notes how:

> Tourism . . . is almost unique in providing multicultural interface at a variety of levels and in many situations, simultaneously. It is an everyday experience for a Japanese visitor to London to be checked into a hotel by an Australian receptionist, supervised by an English front office manager of Afro-Caribbean origin, in a hotel owned by Middle Eastern financial interests, managed by an American hotel multinational who have appointed an Italian as general manager to the property.

However, while Baum's quote is useful in pointing to the multicultural nature of tourism and hospitality, we should also recognize that multiculturalism of this nature does not axiomatically equate to genuine opportunity for all in tourism and hospitality organizations. For example, research that has been conducted in the United States points to some success in diversity programmes. Wilborn and Weaver (2002) investigated diversity management training initiatives (DMTIs) by surveying 139 managers in a range of lodging properties. The managers were questioned about a variety of DMTIs, including aspects such as diversity awareness training for managers, cross-race/gender training teams, networking groups and minority internships. Nearly half of the managers surveyed felt that their organization offered a good diversity management training programme. Significantly, managers who were exposed to DMTIs had more positive feelings towards such initiatives in terms of recognizing their importance towards organizational success. In a similar vein, Speizer (2004) notes the success of Denny's restaurant chain in moving from being seen as one of the most racist companies in America to being number one on *Fortune* magazine's list of 50 best companies in America for minorities. To address the problem of racism, Speizer reports how Denny's appointed the first diversity officer to report directly to the CEO. With a budget of over $1 million dollars per year, the diversity officer was able to develop a series of initiatives. For example, they hired over 100 diversity trainers and insisted that all employees – from senior executives to dishwashers – attend diversity awareness classes. Denny's also sought to encourage more customers from ethnic minority groups and also diversified their suppliers, going from having no minority suppliers or contractors to spending over $616 million with minority suppliers between 1995 and 2000.

On the other hand, research undertaken by Gröschl and Doherty (1999) on a number of hotels in San Francisco points to a much more reactive approach, what they term a 'reactive diversification strategy'. Such an approach is largely concerned with complying with legislation in areas like affirmative action and training in equal opportunities areas such as the American Disability Act. As they note, though, 'the hotels have not been able, so far, to make the next step from tolerating diversity to valuing it' (p. 266). Indeed, more recent research by Gröschl (2011) examined the corporate websites of 25 large internationally operating hotel chains (14 from North America, eight from Europe and three from Asia), finding a mixed picture with regard to diversity management. For example, more than half of the selected companies did not have a diversity or diversity-related statement on their website. For those companies that did have such a statement there were 27 different dimensions of diversity, though the three dimensions of gender, disability and ethnicity were most prominent. Gröschl also found that there was often a lack of detail about diversity support structures within the organization and a narrow focus on measuring the benefits of diversity management, with several of the corporate websites simply highlighting quotas and employment targets. As Gröschl recognizes, corporate websites are a crucial communication and public relations device and it seems surprising that diversity management does not feature more prominently in some of the largest companies operating in the contemporary tourism and hospitality industry, though this latter discussion does point to the manner in which organizations need to think about developing and communicating diversity management policies.

Clearly, then, managing diversity is something that organizations have to think about in a proactive manner. There are no easy prescriptions as to how this approach can be achieved, though Kandola and Fullerton (1998) offer what they consider to be an integrated and coherent model of the diversity-oriented organization. They also suggest this model can be used as a benchmark to drive organizational initiatives and strategy. The idea of such an organization

is underpinned by the notion of the creation of a *mosaic* to encourage diversity in organizations:

**M**issions and values
**O**bjectives and fair processes
**S**killed workforce: aware and fair
**A**ctive flexibility
**I**ndividual focus
**C**ulture that empowers

Diversity-oriented organizations will seek to develop a strong and positive mission and core values statement, which recognizes that managing diversity is an important long-term business objective for the organization. In support of the mission and vision, all processes and systems in organizations (for example, recruitment, selection, performance appraisals, promotion decisions and so on) need to be audited and re-audited to ensure that no single group predominates. With regard to the skilled workforce, Kandola and Fullerton note the importance of ensuring that the entire workforce is aware of and guided by the principles of managing diversity. By understanding why diversity is important, employees can act in a manner which ensures their biases and prejudices do not influence the way they make decisions and work with colleagues. Such an approach may also require a proactive approach to equipping managers, in particular, with the right kind of skills to ensure managing diversity is supported by the requisite managerial capability. Active flexibility is important in ensuring that working patterns, policies, practices and procedures support the approach to diversity. For example, in recognizing the diverse needs of all employees, Kandola and Fullerton note the importance of adopting a 'cafeteria' approach to issues surrounding work–life needs. In advocating an individual focus Kandola and Fullerton note how sometimes 'special events' that focus on a particular group can actually serve to reinforce stereotypes or increase hostility to particular groups. Resultantly, things such as cross-cultural training programmes should aim to foster respect for employees as individual actors, rather than treating employees as members of a particular group, which categorizes differences. Finally, underpinning much of the above is the need to sustain the right kind of organizational culture. We have already noted the importance of organizational culture in Chapter 2, and in terms of managing diversity there is a need to ensure the prevailing culture encourages participation and creativity from all organizational members.

## Conclusion

At the outset of this chapter we asked whether we are likely to find equality of opportunities within organizations. The simple answer is no. There was evidence within the chapter to suggest that certain groups in society still continue to face discrimination which has a deleterious effect on their employment experience. That said, the chapter also recognized the manner in which legislation aims to eradicate such discrimination and how managing diversity seeks to encourage organizations to adopt a more proactive response to ensuring opportunity for all. Although equal opportunities and managing diversity may be represented as being dichotomous in their approach, in reality many organizations will adopt an approach that has elements of both. Many would recognize that valuing and promoting diversity in the workforce probably relies on a delicate balance between legal requirements and a business-driven desire to be an employer of choice and to attract and retain the best employees, regardless of their backgrounds.

## Discussion questions

- What are some of the arguments for and against the use of legislation to create equal opportunities in the workplace?
- Does it still make sense to talk about a glass ceiling for women in the tourism and hospitality industry?
- To what extent do you agree with the view that tourism and hospitality will always be a young person's industry?
- What is the difference between positive action and positive discrimination?
- What are the main points of difference between equal opportunities and managing diversity?
- What are the key elements of a managing diversity programme?

## Further reading

Gröschl, S. (2011) 'Diversity management strategies of global hotel groups: a corporate web site based exploration', *International Journal of Contemporary Hospitality Management*, 23, 2, 224–40.

Gröschl, S. and Doherty, L. (1999) 'Diversity management in practice', *International Journal of Contemporary Hospitality Management*, 11, 6, 262–8.

Kumra, S. and Manfredi, S. (2012) *Managing Equality and Diversity: Theory and Practice*, Oxford: Oxford University Press.

Noon, M. (2010a) 'Managing equality and diversity', in J. Beardwell and T. Claydon (eds), *Human Resource Management: A Contemporary Approach*, 6th edn, Harlow: Financial Times/Prentice Hall.

Noon, M. (2010b) 'The shackled runner: time to rethink positive discrimination?', *Work, Employment and Society*, 24, 4, 728–39.

People 1st (2010b) *The Case for Change: Women Working in the Hospitality, Leisure, Travel and Tourism Sector*, London: People 1st.

## Recommended websites

The ILO has produced an excellent global overview of discrimination in the workplace and how it is being tackled, which can be found at http://www.ilo.org/wcmsp5/groups/public/---ed_norm/---relconf/documents/meetingdocument/wcms_154779.pdf

The EHRC can be found at http://www.equalityhumanrights.com, and there is also a very useful guide to employers on the new Equality Act at http://www.equalityhumanrights.com/uploaded_files/EqualityAct/employercode.pdf

People 1st has a section of their website dedicated to addressing the under-representation of women in senior management positions in tourism and hospitality: http://www.people1st.co.uk/business-and-training-support/women-1st

Stonewall is an organization that supports gay people's right to equality: http://www.stonewall.org.uk/workplace. Among other things, Stonewall produces an annual Workplace Equality Index, which lists the top 100 gay-friendly employers.

Tourism for All's site can be found at http://www.tourismforall.org.uk

The Employers Forum on Age can be found at http://www.efa.org.uk

There's lots of useful material on managing an older workforce at http://www.businesslink.gov.uk/bdotg/action/layer?r.l1=1073858787&topicId=1082249786&r.lc=en&r.l2=1079568262&r.s=tl

The Apex Trust is a voluntary organization that helps ex-offenders get back into employment: http://www.apextrust.com/apextrust/exo_rehabact.shtm

For information on the various world religions, see http://www.bbc.co.uk/religion/religions/index.shtml

There are some interesting resources on diversity management at http://www.diversityworking.com/employerZone/diversityManagement/?id=13

## Additional material

Go to www.routledge.com/cw/nickson to find PowerPoint slides, chapter commentaries, test banks and additional case studies for each chapter.

# 7

# Human resource development

**This chapter considers the key role of human resource development in tourism and hospitality organizations. The chapter aims to:**

- Distinguish the different levels of analysis to understand approaches to human resource development.

- Appreciate the importance of government-level policy in establishing the context in which tourism and hospitality organizations develop their human resource development policies.

- Recognize debates surrounding terms such as education, training and development.

- Consider the range of training and development methods available to tourism and hospitality organizations.

It is increasingly recognized that human resource development (HRD) is crucial in ensuring effectiveness, quality and responsiveness in organizations to an ever-changing and complex environment. Heery and Noon (2008: 213) describe HRD as 'the process of encouraging employees to acquire new skills and knowledge through various training programmes, courses and learning packages'. Increasingly, HRD activities now seek to emphasize adaptability, flexibility and continuous development to ensure that organizations can survive and compete in an ever more competitive environment. However, the importance of HRD is not just apparent for organizations. As we are increasingly entreated to engage in lifelong learning, HRD becomes important for individuals. Moreover, there is now also recognition of the importance of national competitiveness, especially in an increasingly globalized world. HRD, therefore, becomes important from an individual, organizational and national perspective. We see more and more talk of the importance of HRD, which is likely to encompass notions of education, learning, training and development; the interchangeability or otherwise of these distinctions will also be something considered in the chapter. Before we begin to consider these issues in detail, though it is useful to delineate different levels of analysis in understanding HRD. Table 7.1 outlines the ways in which we can think of HRD.

| TABLE 7.1 Levels of analysis for understanding approaches to HRD | |
|---|---|
| Level | Main organizations involved/activities undertaken |
| National/ governmental level | • Government policy: for example, in recent years UK governments seeking a more proactive approach to encourage training and development in organizations<br>• Training initiatives: for example, in the UK Investors in People (IiP) and Apprenticeships |
| Industry level | • National training organizations (NTOs): for example, People 1st, the sector skills council (SSC) for hospitality, leisure, travel and tourism<br>• Industry-level initiatives: for example, WorldHost |
| Company level | • Creation of an overall view of a company's approach to training and development: for example, seeking IiP accreditation and being involved in WorldHost<br>• Ensuring 'fit' between what the company wants to achieve and how units can operationalize this |
| Unit level | • Ensuring on- and off-the-job training takes place<br>• Monitoring individuals' training and development plans<br>• Performance development and monitoring: for example, seeking to enhance quality service through training and development |
| Team level | • Motivation and performance<br>• Team building |
| Individual level | • Improvement in knowledge, skills and attitudes<br>• Sustaining employability<br>• Enhanced motivation and performance<br>• Improving aspects of discipline and behaviour<br>• Career progression |

Throughout this chapter we will consider various aspects of these levels and begin initially by considering the importance of how national government policy impacts on HRD.

## Setting the context: national-level response to HRD

It is often argued that a nation's competitive advantage depends on the skills and inventiveness of its people. Often the manner in which organizations seek to respond to this issue will be determined to a large extent by the views of the government. Increasingly in the UK from the 1980s onwards there was an emerging consensus from government, policy-makers and practitioners that HRD and the up-skilling of the workforce should be encouraged within organizations for the greater good of the economy. Despite the seeming acceptance by government and employers of the importance of training and development and the need to encourage it, there is a good deal of debate as to whether, in reality, there has been the revolution claimed with regard to the up-skilling of the UK workforce (see, for example, Keep and James, 2010). This point recognizes that the UK's record on developing people is poor compared to other nations such as Germany, Japan and Sweden, who are felt to invest heavily in a range of HRD activities. In this sense the UK has often been characterized as voluntaristic with regard to training and development, meaning that the state takes a hands-off view in terms of encouraging employers to train their employees (Grugulis, 2007). Instead, individual employers are largely left to their own devices with regard to how much, or indeed, how little training and development they provide. Consequently, there has been much debate about the levels of expenditure and commitment to training and development from employers. Hyman (1996: 306–7) exemplifies this scepticism in his recognition that 'what is more questionable . . . . concerns the extent to which the majority of British employers have taken responsibility for strategically training and developing their employees', with much activity simply being of the reactive 'fire-fighting' type. For many, then, there may be a gap between the perceived importance of HRD activities and the willingness to do something about it, with suspicions that in the UK too many organizations still see HRD activities as a cost and not an investment. Indeed, it could be argued that such a view may simply reflect the short-termism inherent in British business, where corporate objectives tend to be short term and defined by short-term profit and financial criteria.

### Review and reflect

Outline arguments for and against government intervention in support of training and education.

HRM in Practice 7.1 and 7.2 highlight the impact of the above discussion on the vocational education and training (VET) policies and practices in the UK and a number of other countries.

### HRM IN PRACTICE 7.1:
### An argument for greater government regulation in shaping national VET systems?

Grugulis (2007) notes the manner in which a number of European countries seek a more regulated approach to VET. For example, employers in France are required by the state to support training or pay a levy of 1.5 per cent of turnover plus an apprenticeship tax of 0.5 per cent. Countries such as Austria, Denmark, the Netherlands and Switzerland have extensive and rigorous apprenticeships, which are also supported by 'licences to practise' for particular occupations. Recognizing this situation, a recent report from Kelly *et al.* (2011) suggested that the UK government should seek to encourage greater levels of employer investment in skills by the use of occupational licensing, introducing industry levies and giving tax breaks for training. While recognizing that none of the systems operating in other countries would necessarily offer a 'magic bullet' solution to the problem of training investment in the UK, the report nevertheless argued that the evidence from other countries suggested that compulsory measures introduced by government can help to raise investment in training.

### HRM IN PRACTICE 7.2:
### National skill-creation systems and career paths in the tourism industry in the UK, Germany and the United States

Studies of the UK, Germany and the United States found that patterns of career development and commitment to working in the tourism industry are strongly influenced by the national VET system. Germany, which has a more structured approach compared to the UK and United States, encourages individuals to complete an apprenticeship prior to entering the tourism industry. Such an apprenticeship means that Germany's education and training system is geared to produce a much higher proportion of qualified staff for the tourism industry. As a result employees in Germany were able to secure relatively highly skilled and autonomous positions at an earlier age than their counterparts in the UK and the United States. There is also evidence which points to the greater productivity of German tourism employees over their British and American counterparts. One report concluded that Germany's high productivity and service levels are due to the wider use of qualified manpower trained through the partnership arrangements for the dual system. This study notes that craft qualifications were held by 2.5 times as many employees in Germany compared to the UK. A conclusion to be

drawn is that the dual system within which German employees for tourism are trained 'embeds' commitment to the sector to a much greater degree than elsewhere, and this, combined with high levels of reward, contributes to a greater sense of professionalism and productivity. Finally, German employees were also more likely to advance more rapidly within the industry due to the training and education they receive.

Derived from Finegold *et al.* (2000); Scottish Tourism Research Unit (1998)

Consequently, there has been much support for the notion that Britain needs to invest in training and development to ensure that it does not become a low-tech, low-wage, low-skill, cheap-labour economy wherein it seeks to compete on the basis of a low-skill, low-quality product market strategy relying on price-based competitiveness (Keep and James, 2010). What this has meant in practice is that in recent years the UK government has attempted to take a more active role by introducing a range of initiatives that aim to improve skill levels in the economy. Indeed, Keep (2005) considers the extent to which the UK may be entering a 'post-voluntarist' era, in which the government is seemingly increasingly prepared to take a more active role in encouraging learning and development. To an extent this change may be explicable by the sense that the UK is playing 'catch up' with a number of its international competitors. Resultantly, over the last 30 years or so, successive UK governments have, in the words of Grugulis (2007: 55), 'observed the ample evidence of market failure in VET and intervened'. These interventions have led to the introduction of a number of initiatives, such as National/Scottish Vocational Qualifications (N/SVQs), Investors in People (IiP) and Apprenticeships. It is important to reiterate that these initiatives remain voluntary in that employers do not have to engage with them, though clearly in introducing such initiatives UK governments have attempted to get employers to increase their investment in HRD. This is a point we consider in looking at these initiatives in more detail.

## National/Scottish Vocational Qualifications

The rationale for the introduction of N/SVQs in 1986 was to provide greater coherence in vocational qualifications; thus the existing vocational structure was rationalized into N/SVQs. N/SVQs are work-related, competence-based qualifications, which are appropriate to all industries and all levels of employment, from the shop floor to the boardroom. N/SVQs are statements confirming that the individual employee can perform to a specified standard and that they possess the skills, knowledge and understanding which makes possible such performance in the workplace. They provide a progressive route from Level 1, which is semi-skilled through to Level 5, which recognizes the skills needed to be an organizational leader. N/SVQs are important as they recognize achievements in the workplace and are based on assessing work experience and achievements. In terms of their broad equivalence to educational attainment, then Level 2, for example, is broadly similar to GCSEs, Level 3 is broadly equivalent to A/AS-levels or Scottish Highers, Level 4 is higher national diploma/degree-level, and Level 5 is degree/postgraduate-level (though within tourism and hospitality there are currently no options to seek Level 4 or 5 N/SVQs).

If the success of NVQs were to be measured simply by the number of people who had been awarded the certificate then it could be argued that the initiative has been successful. Between their introduction and the end of September 2010, 9.6 million N/SVQs have been achieved (Data Service, 2011). In the tourism and hospitality industry the largest number of registrations has tended to be at Levels 1 and 2, in areas such as food preparation and cooking and serving food and drink (Qualifications and Curriculum Authority, 2003). Hales (1996) suggests the case for developing and implementing N/SVQs is largely based on two reasons. First, their contribution in enhancing the competitiveness and performance of the UK economy by widening access to training and qualifications. Second, the benefits to participants, i.e. employees, in terms of increased recognition for workplace ability and competence, with the effect of increasing job satisfaction, motivation, a sense of achievement and standards of work. Hales reports on five case study organizations in the hotel sector. All of the case study organizations were small businesses employing 22–44 employees, and four of them had adopted and continued to use N/SVQs, with one adopting and then subsequently dropping them. Hales' research suggested that those hotels that had adopted and persevered with N/SVQs noted a pay-off in terms of better employee attitudes and behaviour, increased service quality and an overall improvement in business performance. However, he does remain sceptical about the extent to which N/SVQs may penetrate the small tourism and hospitality business sector generally, unless they are given active encouragement.

Others, such as Lucas (1995), have been rather more critical of the qualification. Lucas suggests that Levels 1 and 2 arguably do not fit the criteria of training as systematically developing knowledge, skills and abilities. Consequently, they represent 'qualifications without substance [and] lack any real sense of meaning or value' (Lucas, 1995: 60). Lucas' criticisms reflect more general critiques of N/SVQs with concerns about their skill levels and whether they are too narrowly defined and task-specific. There is also some disquiet about the overly bureaucratic nature of N/SVQs. The final criticism, which rather reflects all of the above, is the argument that there is little evidence that N/SVQs are able to cope with changing technologies, skill requirements and new methods of work (and for further discussion of the problematic aspects of N/SVQs – somewhat more cynically known as 'Not Very Qualified' or 'No Value or Quality' – see Cox (2007); Druce (2004); Grugulis (2003); James (2006)).

## Investors in People

IiP is a national-level initiative now overseen by the UK Commission for Employment and Skills. IiP is a key aspect of the UK skills policy landscape and is designed to be applicable to all organizations, whether large or small, public or private, manufacturing or service based. At its inception in 1991 IiP was concerned with attempts to link training and development to business strategy to improve business performance and secure competitive advantage for organizations. Since its introduction, IiP has undergone further revision, with the standard being revised and re-launched in 2004 and further modified in 2009 with the introduction of a number of award levels at Bronze, Silver and Gold. As a result of these revisions, the focus has moved beyond being solely on skills development to encompass broader aspects of management and leadership.

The standard has three core principles – plan, do and review – and these are underpinned by ten indicators of good practice, as indicated in Figure 7.1.

At the end of March 2010 around 6.3 million people (26 per cent of the workforce) were employed in an IiP-accredited organization covering around 25,000 organizations (Gloster *et al.*, 2010). It should also be noted that larger organizations are more likely than smaller organizations to commit to IiP. Generally, evidence from a range of studies suggests that the initiative has had a positive impact on those organizations gaining the accreditation (see, for

**FIGURE 7.1** The Principles of the Standard

Source: http://www.investorsinpeople.co.uk/Facts/Framework/Pages/PlanDoReview.aspx; reproduced with kind permission of Investors in People, © Investors in People – UK Commission for Employment and Skills, 2012.

example, Gloster *et al.*, 2010, 2011). Hoque (2003: 565), while offering some caveats as to the success of the standard, concludes that 'on average, training practice is better in IiP-accredited workplaces than in non-accredited work-places'. Equally, in relation to the tourism and hospitality industry, a number of case studies point to the manner in which IiP has improved organizational performance (see, for example, HRM in Practice 7.3).

## HRM IN PRACTICE 7.3:
## IiP a success at home and abroad

Café Spice Namasté is a small but expanding restaurant group based in London, which specializes in Indian and pan-Asian cuisine. First achieving the award in 1999, the company has been subsequently reassessed in 2002, 2005 and 2008 and was awarded IiP Champion status in 2005. Recognizing the manner in which the restaurant sector is notoriously bad for training, Café Spice Namasté have a strong commitment to training and developing their employees. The company has an extensive range of initiatives which recognize that around 70 per cent of employees have no formal education background and come from a variety of racial and cultural backgrounds. The company invests in their staff through things like NVQs, English-language lessons and a structured training programme encom-passing on- and off-the-job training. In addition, staff meetings, appraisals and coaching and mentoring sessions are used to encourage open dialogue between managers and employees. The success of the organization in committing to the IiP standard can be seen with regard to a number of industry awards and a labour turnover rate which is almost zero. IiP is also offered internationally, and the positive experience he had with the standard in the UK led to James Wilson, general manager of the Dusit Thani Hotel in Dubai, committing to gaining the standard. The hotel, which is part of the Thai-owned Dusit Hotel group, was initially assessed in 2010 and further visited in 2011. Assessors were particularly impressed with the manner in which the hotel had managed costs and kept employees informed in a difficult business environment. Allied to this, the hotel was praised for, among other things, its approach to multi-skilling and ensuring employees' development needs were identified in the performance review process. As James Wilson commented, 'although it is still early days after achieving recognition, we have a much more vibrant team, empowered and willing to engage. We can already see indications of improvements in both staff retention and the profitability of the hotel.'

Derived from http://www.investorsinpeople.co.uk/MediaResearch/CaseStudy/Pages/default.aspx

Supporters of IiP would therefore argue that the standard improves business performance, with increases in aspects such as turnover, efficiency, profitability, enhanced customer service and improvements in company

image; and HRM outcomes, such as increased productivity, lower labour turnover, better learning, training and development practices, management and leadership improvements, improved skills and competencies, improved communications and increased motivation. At the same time there are also some criticisms. For example, as already noted above, it is often larger organizations which have IiP. The level of engagement with IiP also differs across sectors, with greater take-up in the public and voluntary sectors compared to the private sector. It is also argued that many companies who have attained the IiP standard often already have good HR systems and procedures in place, so gaining the award may simply be nothing more than a 'badging' process.

Notwithstanding some of the criticisms, IiP seems to have established itself as a positive and important attempt to encourage employers to adopt more systematic approaches to training and development to improve organizational performance and competitiveness. Indeed, it could be argued that the success of the standard can be gauged by the fact stated on the IiP UK website that IiP has been adopted in over 20 countries as an example of attempting to encourage best-practice HRD and improve the competitiveness of the country.

## Apprenticeships

Government-subsidized apprenticeships were first introduced in 1995 as Modern Apprenticeships. Such apprenticeships aim to offer a career to those more motivated by workplace learning than pure academic study. The aim was to take the best aspects from traditional apprenticeship schemes, update them and extend them to the service and public sectors (Gospel and Fuller, 1998). The scheme was re-launched in May 2004 as Apprenticeships, though in Scotland they remain Modern Apprenticeships. Apprenticeships were originally aimed solely at 16–24-year-olds, though since 2007 there are now programmes available for those aged 25-plus. Indeed, Lanning (2011) notes that the number of people over 25 accessing apprenticeships has significantly increased in recent years. That said, Keep and James (2011) recognize that part of the reason for the significant rise in the number of apprenticeships for older people has largely been achieved by re-labelling existing training activity as an 'apprenticeship', with concerns about the length and quality of such training (see also HRM in Practice 7.4).

**HRM IN PRACTICE 7.4:**
**The long and short of apprenticeships**

Normally, apprenticeships in the UK would last 1–3 years, though apprenticeships in Europe last between 3–4 years. With some of the recent changes in the apprenticeship system in the UK there are now ever more ambitious targets to increase apprenticeship numbers, with the consequence that some 'apprentice-ships' in theory can be much shorter. One such example of the latter is the De Vere Academy of Hospitality, where people can train for just 12 weeks for a customer service role. There are suggestions that such courses should not be called apprenticeships as they may be confusing for potential employers. However, Kellie Rixon, the managing director of the De Vere Academy, rejects this criticism, noting that 72 per cent of their trainees, who often come from challenging backgrounds and are disengaged from education, have gone straight into full-time employment. This success rate is attributed to the intensive classroom-based and on-the-job training provided by the academy. In an attempt to address any concerns about the quality of apprenticeships, the National Apprenticeship Service in England has moved towards regulating them. For example, from August 2012 all apprenticeships which are publicly funded must last at least 12 months. Public money will also be withdrawn from training providers if training fails to meet the required quality standards.

Derived from Churchard (2012b); Chartered Institute of Personnel and Development (2012a); Keep and James (2011); Tickle (2011); see also http://www.deveregroup.co.uk/brands/de-vere-academy-of-hospitality.html

Apprenticeships are offered to people who want to obtain skills by combining a paid job with training. There are three levels: Intermediate Apprenticeship usually works towards a Level 2 NVQ; Advanced Apprenticeship usually works towards a Level 3 NVQ; and Higher Apprenticeships usually work towards a Level 4 NVQ. However, it should be noted that the vast majority of apprentice-ships are offered at the intermediate level. Apprenticeships alternate between productive employment with on- and off-the-job training to provide a mixture of occupationally specific training, as well as more generic key skills, such as communication, numeracy, literacy and team-working. Apprenticeships are a major publicly funded training route, attracting around £1.2 billion of government funding each year (National Audit Office, 2012). In 2009–10 around 280,000 people started an apprenticeship (Lanning, 2011). By 2010–11 this figure had risen to 442,700 (Tickle, 2011), largely because of the significant increase in adult learners mentioned above, who accounted for 71 per cent of the new apprentices (National Audit Office, 2012).

Accounts of the implementation of apprenticeships in tourism and hospitality offer guarded optimism with regard to their ability to attract young people, in particular, to work in the industry. For example, Lanning (2011) notes that hospitality and catering was third in the top ten list of sector frameworks, with 21,470 starting an apprenticeship in 2009–10, although only 13 per cent of these were at Level 3, with the remainder at Level 2. There have also been concerns expressed in the past at the high drop-out rate of those embarking on a hospitality apprenticeship (Anon, 2003a). More recent accounts, though,

suggest that this situation may be improving, and across the economy as a whole in 2009–10, three-quarters of all adult apprenticeships (i.e. those aged over 19) were successfully completed (National Audit Office, 2012; see also HRM in Practice 7.5).

## HRM IN PRACTICE 7.5:
## Apprenticeships in the travel sector

Travel companies Thomas Cook and TUI are both supportive in developing apprenticeships within their organizations. Thomas Cook have used apprenticeships as a means to attract fresh talent and to enable apprentices to gain the skills and knowledge to become excellent travel sales consultants. Apprentices complete the travel and tourism NVQ at Levels 2 and 3 and are supported with a number of innovative organizational approaches including: revising their apprentice website so potential applicants have an accurate and realistic view of the programme; developing a mentoring scheme for managers to ensure they manage and support apprentices appropriately; and a bespoke induction programme to ensure that new apprentices fully understand the company's vision and values. As a result, the company has seen successes improve significantly, and in 2009–10 91 per cent successfully completed their apprenticeship programme.

TUI had approximately 800 apprentices in 2008, with 450 undertaking the Level 2 apprenticeship in Travel and Tourism Services and the rest pursuing Level 3. The company is able to select from a large number of applicants, with around 15,000 applicants for the 450–500 positions that are available each year. Once through the rigorous recruitment and selection process, apprentices are supported by a two-day 'welcome event', have five hours each week study time, have access to the company's e-learning system and have six formal off-the-job training days to complete technical certificate training. Apprentices also have a workplace mentor, who is usually an ex-apprentice, and who provides support and inspiration to help them progress. Results from the company show improved staff retention rates and greater sales performance, with ex-apprentice travel advisors achieving over 16 per cent more sales than non-apprentices.

Derived from http://www.people1st.co.uk/apprenticeships/case-studies/employer-case-studies

## Industry level

The above discussion has considered the manner in which the VET infrastructure created by government will have a profound impact on HRD. Clearly, with the creation of initiatives such as N/SVQs, IiP and Apprenticeships, British governments over the last 30 years or so have attempted to encourage employers to offer more training. While all of these initiatives have had some impact in tourism and hospitality, they are not sector-specific, unlike another governmental initiative, the creation of sector skills councils (SSCs). Operating under licence to the UK government, SSCs are independent, employer-led, UK-wide organizations, who work in partnership with the UK Commission for Employment and Skills (UKCES). SSCs are primarily tasked with encouraging employers to take increasing ownership of the skills challenges facing their sector, support the development of smart solutions to their most pressing skills problems and stimulate greater and more effective employer investment in skills (UK Commission for Employment and Skills, 2011). In seeking to encourage collective employer ownership and investment to address the most critical skills needs of each sector of the economy, SSCs aim to support the UK Commission's four key priorities, to (UK Commission for Employment and Skills, 2011):

1   make and win the economic argument for greater investment in skills;
2   enhance the value and accessibility of vocational training, especially apprenticeships;
3   galvanize industries and sectors to improve the skills and productivity of their workforces;
4   work with sectors to ensure the creation of more and better jobs, maximizing opportunities for unemployed people.

As we noted in Chapter 1, the SSC for tourism and hospitality is People 1st, which came into existence in May 2004. Initially awarded a five-year licence, People 1st was relicensed in 2009. It is noteworthy that at the time it was relicensed by the government, People 1st was given a 'good' rating, though more recently this was upgraded to 'outstanding' (UK Commission for Employment and Skills, 2011). This identification of the excellent work by People 1st recognizes their strong engagement with the industry, something that was further recognized by the coalition government awarding them an additional £9 million to increase the profile of the hospitality, leisure, travel and tourism sector in terms of its importance to the UK economy. Thus, in positioning the sector as playing a key role in leading the UK out of its current economic difficulties, People 1st is aiming, over the period 2012–14 to (Wisdom, 2012):

•   help unemployed people into work, through, for example, pre-employment training programmes to make potential applicants job-ready;
•   accelerate social mobility, by, for example, reducing the churn of women, in particular, from the industry and encouraging them to progress into management;
•   professionalize the industry to address skills gaps and by encouraging organizations to train their staff to agreed standards through the

introduction of a licence to practise for a number of occupations. Smaller businesses will also be helped to take up the IiP standard;

- achieve economic growth by increasing levels of customer service skills of existing employees through increasing the number of providers who can deliver WorldHost (see HRM in Practice 7.6). Customer service training will also be at the heart of the pre-employment training and apprenticeship schemes;
- increase business investment in skills and reduce waste in public expenditure, for example by increasing completion rates for hospitality apprenticeships from 45 per cent to 70 per cent;
- align employers and stakeholders to deliver sustained growth through skills, for example through ensuring employer and stakeholder engagement to identify skills gaps and develop appropriate solutions.

In addition to governmental initiatives, there are also non-governmental initiatives that have attempted to improve training within tourism and hospitality, such as WorldHost, which is described in HRM in Practice 7.6.

## HRM IN PRACTICE 7.6:
## WorldHost: professionalizing the tourism industry

The WorldHost scheme is based on a Canadian hospitality programme called 'Superhost'. Introduced in British Columbia in 1986 to support the growth of tourism around the World Expo in Vancouver, the standard has become an international success story, with close to one million people trained around the world. Other franchises include 'Kiwi Host', 'Aussie Host', 'Alaska Host' and 'Super Host Japan'. Introduced initially in the UK in 1995 as Welcome Host, the scheme was 'an on-going, comprehensive, community-based programme designed to upgrade the standards of service and hospitality provided within the tourism industry' (Sweeney, 1995: 8). The scheme provided access to more formal training for smaller operators who would also be coming into contact with the visitor. The scheme seeks to instil a sense of professionalism and pride in tourism. Within the UK, the scheme was not just for tourism employees, such as travel agents and tour guides, but was also available to be taken by people like taxi drivers and traffic wardens and anybody else that tourists are likely to encounter within the destination. Welcome Host was re-branded to WorldHost in 2009 in preparation for the 2010 Olympic and Paralympic Winter Games in Vancouver. The Winter Games were labelled 'the friendliest games ever', with Vancouver and the host cities proving a strong commitment to customer service excellence. In a similar vein, WorldHost will also underpin customer service training for the 2012 London Olympic and Paralympic Games. People 1st secured the UK licence for the

WorldHost customer service training programme and was aiming to train at least 200,000 hospitality and tourism staff in the run up to the Games. In addition to WorldHost, there are also a number of other programmes such as Customers with Disabilities, which is a course designed to increase front-line employees' sensitivity towards people with disabilities, and to provide superior customer service skills that respect every visitor's unique needs; and Service Across Cultures, which is a training programme designed to give people working in the tourism industry greater confidence when meeting and greeting international visitors.

## Training and development: no longer a dichotomy?

Having outlined the broad context in which organizations are developing their overall approach to HRD and skills development and the importance of government policy within that process, we can now go on and look in greater detail at what exactly training and development are. Holden (2004: 313) recognizes how 'it is difficult to arrive at a consensus definition of terms such as "development", "education" and "training" because of the varied ways in which they are translated into work and life situations'. Many would argue that training and development have traditionally been seen as separate and a reflection of an organization's hierarchy. This point can be appreciated in acknowledging the manner in which training and development have been traditionally conceptualized as being distinctive activities.

On the one hand, training is usually characterized as having an immediate focus on employees enhancing their performance in their current job, by focusing on immediate improvements via the provision of certain skills. Thus, as Armstrong (2006: 535) notes, it is 'a planned and systematic modification of behaviour through learning events, programmes and instructions that enable individuals to achieve the levels of knowledge, skill and competence needed to carry out work effectively'. On the other hand, development has often been seen as being much more about the growth or realization of a person's ability and potential through conscious or unconscious learning (Armstrong, 2006). Development is often felt to have a longer-term focus, focusing on preparing individuals for further responsibilities. Development programmes also usually include elements of planned study and experience, and are frequently supported by a coaching or counselling facility. In that sense, at one time training was often perceived as being for non-managerial staff, while development was the preserve of managers, and this reflected the more nebulous concepts of reasoning, abstraction and personal growth (see Baum, 2006: 204–14 for further discussion of this issue). Now, though, it is increasingly recognized that within a HRM/D approach organizations will see the two aspects as being very much inter-connected, so training should be seen as part of and a precondition of development.

## Review and reflect

If you are currently undertaking a tourism or hospitality degree to what extent do you consider it to be training, education or development? What are some of the influences in making your decision?

Training and development can be seen as a key instrument in the implementation of HRM practices and policies, and there may be a number of benefits from undertaking training. For example, McKenna and Beech (2008) suggest a number of benefits generally stemming from training, including:

- helps employees learn jobs more quickly and effectively;
- improves work performance of existing employees and keeps them up to date in specialist skills;
- leads to a greater volume of work resulting from fewer mistakes and greater rapidity;
- frees management time, less of which is spent rectifying errors, and also reduces wastage;
- can help to reduce turnover among new and established staff;
- incorporating safety training can help reduce accidents;
- can help to attract good workers;
- is a precondition for flexible working;
- creates an attitude more receptive to coping with change;
- operationalizes certain management techniques, such as total quality management (TQM) and empowerment (see HRM in Practice 7.7).

**HRM IN PRACTICE 7.7:**
## Training and TQM in the restaurant industry in Canada

Salameh and Barrows (2001) recognize how a critical element of TQM is creating an organizational culture which is supportive of quality and customer satisfaction. TQM also requires that all members of an organization are involved in the process of quality improvement. Training therefore becomes crucial to the implementation of TQM. Research conducted by Salameh and Barrows in a coffee house restaurant and a casual dining restaurant in Canada demonstrated a number of similarities in the respective restaurants. Training programmes differed from job to job depending on the complexity of the job and associated tasks, and the length of time also varied. Both companies also used a range of training methods, such as on-the-job training, videos, seminars and extensive induction programmes. The case study organizations also recognized the challenges of training, including the time factor, keeping programmes simple, being proactive rather than reactive, and, in a mirror of the intent of TQM, seeing training as a process of continuous improvement. Managers suggested that there were a number of positive outcomes from training in support of TQM, including decreased labour turnover, greater employee commitment, increases in sales, greater customer responsiveness and enhanced quality service. In sum, the research suggested that training did result in a continuous performance improvement, a key goal in TQM.

On the point of the extent and success of training and development activities within the tourism and hospitality industry then the evidence is mixed. Wisdom (2010) reports on a 2010 survey of the travel industry conducted by People 1st on behalf of ABTA, which looked at 88 employers and nearly 500 employees. Key findings from the survey were that almost all (93 per cent) of respondents provided training for their staff, while 85 per cent of employees had undertaken some kind of training in the past year. A key reason for doing such training is the need to improve customer service, with 69 per cent of employees and 79 per cent of managers receiving training in this area in the past year. Similarly, data drawn from the UK-wide Employer Skills Survey and reported by People 1st (2011b) suggests that the hospitality, leisure, travel and tourism sector has the highest collective training expenditure of all sectors. The sector spends over £4 million annually on training, averaging out at £2,600 per employee.

However, this relatively positive picture needs to be tempered by recognizing that despite this training, more than one-quarter of establishments report skills gaps in their workforce and, importantly, the proportion of employers reporting such skills gaps has increased in recent years (People 1st, 2011b). Skills gaps mean that employers are reporting that some of their employees are not proficient in their jobs; the occupations least likely to be fully proficient are sales and customer service staff, and those in operational front-facing roles, such as waiting staff, bar staff and receptionists. Consequently, the skills employers say their staff lack are soft skills (customer handling, teamwork, oral communication and problem solving) and to a lesser extent technical, practical or job-specific skills (mainly chef skills). Moreover, the relatively high level of training expenditure is largely explained by two factors. First, within the industry there is a significant number of legislative requirements for certain parts of the sector, such as food safety, and health and safety, and this type of training is often regularly repeated. A second factor is the high labour turnover rates, which mean that organizations are continually training new and inexperienced staff. Furthermore, training spend is patchy across the sector, with larger organizations much more likely to train their staff. Lucas (2004), for example,

argues that access to training tends to be restricted to those in large multi-establishment organizations. Moreover, training incidence is at its lowest in non-standard forms of employment – for example, workers who are numerically flexible are likely to get little or no training. Ultimately, then, there may be those organizations who see training and development as an investment and those who pay lip service to the idea and in the good times spend money on HRD activities and in the bad times spend less or hardly anything on training and development (see HRM in Practice 7.8). Consequently, a lot of organizations will in times of skill or labour shortages recruit from other organizations rather than invest in their existing employees, something that has certainly been apparent in tourism and hospitality.

## HRM IN PRACTICE 7.8:
## The training Oscars

Set up in 1987 by the then Department for Education and Science, the National Training Awards are the UK's number-one accolade for businesses, organizations and individuals who have achieved lasting excellence and success through training and learning. In recent years there has been some success for the tourism and hospitality industry. In the 2010 awards, Center Parcs was recognized for its implementation of a unique customer service training programme for its 6,000 employees. The company, the largest provider of short-break holidays in the UK, operates four holiday villages which attract over 1.6 million guests each year. Prior to the training programme the company did not consistently encourage empowerment, and employees would often lack confidence in dealing with guests. To counteract this, the company developed a training programme, Making Memorable Moments. The programme was tailored to management and employees. The management training focused on behaviours to sustain excellent service, how to recruit and train the best staff and coaching and recognizing employees. Employees were taught about service recovery behaviours, how to listen and apologize and find solutions with the aim of surprising and delighting guests. Over the course of July to December 2009 virtually all of Center Parcs' employees went through the training, attending a four-hour programme which used high-energy activities and visuals such as giant jigsaws and posters. Participants were also in mixed groups to encourage inter-departmental working. Following the training there was a rise in guest satisfaction, occupancy increased to 97.4 per cent, repeat bookings increased by 45 per cent and labour turnover decreased by 6 per cent. This successful attempt to change employees' service behaviours was recognized by the CEO of the company, who noted how the 'Making Memorable Moments training has strengthened our corporate values and our commitment to offer the best short-break experience in the UK'.

Derived from http://nationaltrainingawards.apprenticeships.org.uk/databank

We have examined in some detail the wider picture of training and development and in this section of the chapter we can now move on to consider the manner in which training may be conducted and training methods used by organizations. To contextualize this discussion it is worth noting the three broad categories in which training is likely to be located. These are (Marchington and Wilkinson, 1996):

- *Socialization initiative*: particularly in terms of induction and becoming familiar with the prevailing organizational culture.
- *Development initiative*: this is more concerned with developing individuals, for example, preparing for promotion, coping with new technology or organizational change, such as attempting to become a more customer-focused organization.
- *Disciplinary initiative*: where some sort of training is offered to individuals who have fallen below the organization's acceptable level of quality, output or customer standards; this could be about rectifying deficiencies in technical skills or attitudinal training.

There is the potential for huge variations in how organizations go about devising and delivering training. Additionally, Marchington and Wilkinson (2005a) note that trainees themselves will bring significant 'baggage' to the learning event – for example, the mix of prior knowledge, skills, attitudes, motivations and expectations. Furthermore, trainees may also have very diverse reasons for being involved in the training – for example, some trainees may be there under duress. Consequently, we should be cautious in terms of being too prescriptive in describing how organizations should approach training. Nevertheless, there would seem to be a need to have some sort of systematic approach to developing training. For example, most textbooks on HRM acknowledge the idea of the 'systematic training cycle', and in the context of tourism and hospitality, Go *et al.* (1996) advocate the need for a nine-step approach to developing training within the organization.

## Step 1: assessing training needs

Analysing training needs is a crucial part of HRD as the identification of needed skills and active management of employee learning is integral to developing corporate and business strategies. Many would argue that for training to be effective it is necessary to discern not only the training needs of the individual and the group, but also how their needs fit the overall organizational objectives. Essentially, then, training-needs analysis allows for an appreciation of the need to ensure that there is a fit between training and the company culture, strategy and objectives. Equally, the training needs of the individual need to be reconciled with those of the organization. In terms of developing a training-needs analysis, aspects such as job descriptions, job analysis, person specifications or whether performance objectives agreed at appraisals have been met may all be potentially useful indicators.

## Step 2: preparing the training plan

The training plan is concerned with outlining what needs to be done based on the training needs of individuals, departments and the organization as a whole. In effect, the training plan provides an outline sketch of what the training should address, as well as considering practical aspects such as the method, time and location of the training.

## Step 3: specifying the training objectives

A key question to be asked before the training is operationalized is: what are the training objectives? It is important when employees are undertaking training that they understand what they should be able to accomplish when the training programme has been completed.

## Step 4: designing the training programme

Go *et al.* (1996) suggest a number of issues that need to be considered in designing the training programme, including:

- programme duration;
- programme structure;
- instructional methods;
- support resources (e.g. a training facility) and the selection of training materials (e.g. videos);
- training location or environment, which may also be determined by the task, for example, whether it involves practical skills;
- instructor and instructor's experience;
- origin of the training programme;
- criteria and methods for assessing participants' learning and achievement;
- criteria and methods for evaluating the programme.

## Step 5: selecting the instruction methods

There are a multitude of methods that organizations can use to train and develop staff. All of these various methods will have strengths and weaknesses, and in that sense there is no single 'best' training method. Rather, there is a need for organizations to adopt a contingent approach to training in developing training methods. Although there are a great variety of training methods, generally most writers broadly categorize them into three different types of training: in-company on-the-job; in-company off-the job; and external off-the-job. All of these are now briefly considered.

### In-company, on-the-job

This type of training is enduringly popular and accounts for about half of all the training delivered across all industries and sectors in the UK (Chartered Institute of Personnel and Development, 2005a). Often known colloquially as 'sitting next to Nellie', on-the-job training involves learning through watching and observing somebody with greater experience perform a task. On-the-job training is a very popular method of training when new skills and methods are being taught to employees. The advantages of on-the-job training are that it is cheap; the trainees get the opportunity to practise immediately; trainees get immediate feedback; and it can also help in integrating trainees into existing teams. There may be some drawbacks from this type of training. 'Nellie' may not be trained herself in skills and methods of training, which will often lead to training being rather piecemeal or not properly planned. Equally, Nellie may also pass on bad habits, although increasingly organizations may use the idea of training the trainer to ensure a more professional approach.

Another variant of on-the-job training is mentoring, wherein a senior, experienced member of staff takes responsibility for the development and progression of selected individuals. Ordinarily this process of mentoring would be for managerial staff and the selected individual will often be somebody who has aspirations to reach senior management levels. This type of relationship is more like father–son or mother–daughter than that of traditional master–apprentice. The trainee, or mentoree, will observe the skills displayed by the mentor and learn from their experience. Mentoring can also be a useful two-way process in terms of the mentor becoming more reflective about their own job and being forced to think about ways of improving their own performance. In a similar vein, shadowing allows employees the chance to see different parts of the organization in other departments. Finally, under the broader heading of on-the-job training is the idea of job rotation. In this approach those undergoing the training are placed into a job without any prior training; when they have learnt that job they move on to another job, and so on; this may also eventually lead to multi-skilling or functional flexibility, as discussed in Chapter 4.

### In-company, off-the-job

In contrast to on-the-job training, off-the-job training takes place outside of the employee's normal place of work. Off-the-job training will often involve a training intervention run by a specialized training department. This type of training could be relatively straightforward (see HRM in Practice 7.9) or be concerned with achieving proficiency in more advanced skills.

There is a wide array of other methods that come under the broad heading of off-the-job training. In a relatively passive sense, lectures can be good for the transmission of information to a relatively large number of trainees. Indeed, it is likely that most of us in our student, organizational or professional life will have sat through a lecture. Often the quality of a lecture will be dependent

## HRM IN PRACTICE 7.9:
### Heading off the induction crisis

Induction is often misunderstood as simply being about inducting people into the organization during the first day in a new job. However, induction will often extend beyond the first day and may involve events up to 12 months after the initial appointment. The need for a period of induction is increasingly seen as being important in socializing employees, especially in strong-culture organizations (an issue considered in Chapter 3). In addition, it may also be crucial to address the problem of the so-called 'induction crisis', where a new work environment can be perplexing and even frightening for new employees. As a result, employees may leave the organization during this period. Induction will not axiomatically always avert an induction crisis, but a well-designed induction programme can go some way to addressing this issue. Typically, in inducting new employees, tourism and hospitality organizations are likely to consider the following aspects:

- history of the organization
- consideration of the mission statement and organizational objectives
- outline of company ethics
- the structure of the organization
- appearance standards
- uniforms and dress codes
- pay systems and benefits
- holiday and sickness arrangements
- rules and regulations of the organization
- discipline and grievance procedures
- details of any trade unions or staff associations
- welfare policies and social facilities available in the organization
- health and safety measures
- introduction to immediate supervisor/line manager
- introduction to fellow workers

on the individual who is delivering it. Notwithstanding this point, it is generally recognized that the maximum concentration span of most individuals is typically less than 20 minutes. In a rather more active vein, there are a number of other methods which will involve greater interactivity. For example, case studies, role plays and simulations may all be usefully used by tourism and hospitality organizations, particularly in developing customer service skills. Lastly, there may also be opportunities for employees to learn via interactive computer learning packages, or what is often termed e-learning. The Chartered Institute of Personnel and Development (2009c: 1) defines e-learning as 'learning that is delivered, enabled or mediated using electronic technology for the explicit purposes of training in organizations'. Although there are debates about the effectiveness of e-learning, particularly when used on a standalone basis, it is becoming more commonplace. E-learning may work best as a complementary form of learning. Some of the potential benefits of e-learning include reductions in cost and time spent on delivery, flexibility in the 'where' and 'when' of access, the ability to reach large numbers of employees, the ability to personalize learning, the possibility of virtual collaboration among trainees and the ability to track learner activity remotely (see HRM in Practice 7.10).

## HRM IN PRACTICE 7.10:
## E-learning and 'virtual' role playing

The Travel Industry 2010 training survey found that 54 per cent of respondents had undertaken some form of e-learning in the past year – more than any other type of training. Two companies who have used e-learning are Thomas Cook and Hilton. Mari Harrison, head of learning and development at Thomas Cook, suggests that e-learning can be a cost-effective and flexible means of training. As she notes,

> our sales consultants have a bespoke e-learning systems programme that has achieved substantial costs savings. It used to be a two-day course and is now a four hour e-learning programme, broken down into sections so you don't have to go four hours in one go.

It is estimated by the company that the use of e-learning for its systems and product induction training saved over £35,000 in travel expenses for trainees, and £25,000 in improved efficiency by reducing the amount of time spent in the classroom. Importantly, e-learning has also been received very positively by employees. Having completed such training they ranked their knowledge of the key sales systems at 3.97 out of 5 (whereas previously the feedback following training had ranked it at 2.37) and the mainstream in-house products at 4.14 out of 5 (whereas previously the feedback following training had ranked it at 2.92).

Thomas Cook also benefits from the manner in which the online training allows for standardized training to be delivered quickly and easily across large numbers of employees – something that is especially useful in a multi-unit organization. The system also allows managers and employees to track their progress via a 'my development' page. The need to continually enhance customer service also lies at the heart of Hilton's use of virtual reality. Employees in the company's Garden Inn brand have the opportunity to use the virtual reality tool, Ultimate Team Play, which allows staff to play with a range of different hotel scenarios in four areas – front desk, housekeeping, engineering and food and beverage. The use of gaming allows the employees to emulate real-life scenarios. Ultimate Team Play

is not mandatory for the employees, who still undertake a conventional 30-day training programme. However, the game-playing nature of Ultimate Team Play has proved popular with employees in allowing them to enhance their training and guest interaction, as well as proving cost-effective for the company.

Derived from Moggridge (2009); Wisdom (2010)

## Review and reflect

Think of any on-the-job or off-the-job training you have undertaken in the workplace. Which was most useful and satisfying and why?

### External, off-the-job

The final aspect of training is that which again is undertaken off-the-job, though in this instance it is external to the organization. In an era of continuing professional development employees may be encouraged to undertake formal study to enhance their careers, for example taking courses such as the CIPD's courses for HR managers or in a more general sense a Master in Business Administration (MBA). A further aspect of external off-the-job training is what is termed outward-bound courses. Outdoor training ordinarily consists of a series of exercises which act as an opportunity for team-building, problem solving or leadership skills to be developed outside of an employee's or manager's 'comfort zone' (Trotter, 2005). In recent years such courses have grown enormously in popularity and there have been a number of hospitality and tourism organizations who have offered this kind of training, including Hilton and Thomas Cook. Some castigate this type of training as a fad or fashion with limited application to commercial situations or more seriously unsafe or downright dangerous, especially if there is too much emphasis on physical challenges or exercises. Some argue, however, that if this type of training is done properly and managed by experienced and qualified trainers, outdoor-based development can offer a highly effective tool for improving managerial performance in particular.

### Step 6: completing the training plan

With the establishment of the main design features and the methods which are to be used, the training plan can now be completed. Go *et al.* (1996) note that a complete training plan will have details about the target group (e.g. all service staff), the topic to be considered (e.g. customer handling), method(s) to be adopted (e.g. role play), time (e.g. two hours) and location (e.g. conference centre).

## Step 7: conducting the training

Go *et al.* (1996) suggest that if other aspects of the nine-step approach are adhered to, the training activity/programme should be effectively delivered. However, rather like Marchington and Wilkinson (2005a), they do also recognize a number of factors that might impact on the training, such as participant selection, ensuring the group feels comfortable physiologically and psychologically and ensuring the person delivering the training is properly prepared and has the right skills.

## Step 8: evaluating the training

The penultimate stage of the nine-step approach is to evaluate the training in order to glean feedback from the trainees. There are a number of methods of evaluating training, as identified by Holden (2004: 328):

- Questionnaires or so-called 'happiness sheets' are a useful way to elicit trainees' responses to courses and programmes.
- Tests or examinations are common in more formal training courses and are useful for checking the progress of trainees.
- Projects can be useful in providing useful information for instructors.
- Structured exercises and case studies allow for trainees to apply their learned skills and techniques under observation.
- Tutor reports allow for instructors to offer an assessment of the utility of the training.
- Interviews of trainees can be formal or informal, individual or group, or by telephone.
- Observation of courses by those responsible for devising training strategies can be very useful in the development of future training.
- Participation and discussion during the training is possible, though this requires a highly skilled facilitator.
- Appraisal allows for the line manager and trainee to consider the success or otherwise of training that has been undertaken during performance reviews.

Of course, a combination of these methods can be used in evaluating training and it is likely to be important to incorporate both trainee and trainer feedback in assessing the success or otherwise of training interventions.

## Step 9: planning further training

After the training and its evaluation, training has, in effect, come full circle and the planning process can begin again.

## Conclusion

HRD can be understood at a number of levels and it is particularly important to recognize the likely impact of government policy, in particular, in creating the VET infrastructure in which organizations will develop their policy and practice. Governments may either be relatively proactive in attempting to create an environment where training and development is seen as crucial, or much more voluntaristic in leaving such decisions to organizations. For a long time the UK government adopted a voluntaristic approach to training, but it has become increasingly involved in developing a range of initiatives in recent years to address perceived gaps in skills development in the UK, though employer engagement remains voluntary. In addition to the national-level infrastructure, we also recognize that the sectoral level is equally important, and as we noted, the picture is mixed in tourism and hospitality. Thus, although there is a relatively high spend on training and expenditure, there are skills gaps in areas such as customer service. Nevertheless, the chapter has also noted a number of good-practice examples of organizations that are seeking to address these concerns. Notwithstanding debates about the quality of provision of training and development in tourism and hospitality, when organizations *do* train they can draw upon a variety of differing methods, which are likely to vary in relation to different occupations and skills. In that sense there is no single best training and development method but, rather, different methods and techniques will be appropriate given the nature of the task and skills demanded, and, importantly, what is most cost-effective for organizations.

## Discussion questions

- What do you understand by the terms 'HRD', 'training', 'development' and 'education'?
- Assess the view that off-the-job training is always more likely to be more productive than on-the-job training.
- Consider the view that apprenticeships can only be meaningful if they last for at least one year.
- What are some of the strengths and weaknesses of e-learning?
- What are the key issues that need to be considered in designing training and development interventions?

## Further reading

Baum, T. (2006) *Human Resource Management for Tourism, Hospitality and Leisure: An International Perspective*, London: Thomson Learning.

Finegold, D., Wagner, K. and Mason, G. (2000) 'National skill-creation systems and career paths for service workers: hotels in the United States, Germany and the United Kingdom', *International Journal of International Human Resource Management*, 11, 3, 497–516.

Gloster, R., Sumption, F., Higgins, T., Cox, A. and Jones, R. (2010) *Perspectives and Performance of Investors in People: A Literature Review*, London: UKCES.

Grugulis, I. (2007) *Skills, Training and Human Resource Development*, Basingstoke: Palgrave Macmillan.

Keep, E. and James, S. (2010) *What Incentives to Learn at the Bottom End of the Labour Market?*, SKOPE Research Paper, No. 94, Universities of Cardiff and Oxford.

## Recommended websites

Details of the various programmes run by WorldHost can be found at: http://www.worldhosttraining.com/workshops/index.html

The American Society for Training and Development has some useful resources on workplace training and learning at http://www.astd.org/astd

Investors in People has a number of case studies, including several from the tourism and hospitality sector, at http://www.iipuk.co.uk/IIP/Web/Case+Studies/default.htm

Details of the work of the UK Commission for Employment and Skills, including a wide range of downloadable reports, can be found at http://www.ukces.org.uk

For more about apprenticeships see the National Apprenticeship Service's site at http://www.apprenticeships.org.uk/About-Us/National-Apprenticeship-Service.aspx; for apprenticeships specifically in tourism and hospitality, see http://www.people1st.co.uk/apprenticeships

## Additional material

Go to www.routledge.com/cw/nickson to find PowerPoint slides, chapter commentaries, test banks and additional case studies for each chapter.

## CHAPTER 8

# Performance management and performance appraisal

## CHAPTER OBJECTIVES

**This chapter discusses performance management and performance appraisal. Specifically, the aims of the chapter are:**

- To appreciate the difference between performance management and performance appraisal.

- To consider challenges facing tourism and hospitality managers in operationalizing performance appraisal schemes.

- To explore the differences between evaluative and developmental aspects of performance appraisal.

- To recognize the range of skills required by tourism and hospitality managers to successfully conduct performance appraisals.

## Introduction

In considering the nature of performance management and performance appraisal, we first need to appreciate how these two aspects are related, but equally should not be seen synonymously. In fairly simple terms performance management can be seen as a holistic process which aims to bring together a number of aspects, including appraisal (Chartered Institute of Personnel and Development, 2011b). Thus, performance management may be thought of as being more strategic in its intent to achieve high levels of organizational performance, with an emphasis on continuous improvement. By contrast, performance appraisal (or as it is sometimes known performance review) is best seen as being more operationally focused, with a focus on individual employees' short- to medium-term performance and development (Chartered

Institute of Personnel and Development, 2011c). Similarly, Latham *et al.* (2008: 365) suggest that 'a distinguishing feature of performance management relative to performance appraisal is that the former is an on-going process whereas the latter is done at discrete time intervals (e.g. annually)'.

Consequently, to fully contextualize the notion of performance appraisal it is important to locate it within wider issues concerned with performance management systems (PMS) which may have an organizational, team or individual focus. Armstrong (2009: 618) suggests that performance management has a number of aims:

> Performance management is a systematic process for improving organizational performance by developing the performance of individuals and teams. It is a means of getting better results by understanding and managing performance within an agreed framework of planned goals, standards and competency requirements.

Armstrong further identifies the main concerns of performance management as being concerned with aligning individual objectives to organizational objectives; making clear and enabling expectations to be agreed with regard to role responsibilities and accountabilities, skills and behaviours. Lastly, performance management should provide individuals with opportunities to identify their own goals and develop their skills and competencies. Clearly, then, organizations are always seeking improvements in their performance and these can be sustained by either development-type initiatives or more evaluative or even punitive measures, potentially encompassing aspects of discipline. In that sense, performance management and performance appraisal can arguably be seen to again reflect to some degree the notions of 'hard' and 'soft' HRM. For example, the harder approaches would point to the need for organizations and managers to seek control over their employees; on the other hand, softer approaches would point to the role of PMS in establishing greater commitment and developing careers. Recognizing the above discussion, this chapter will aim to consider the question of what options are open to an organization seeking to improve the performance of its employees.

## The nature of performance management and performance appraisal

A recent survey of over 500 HR professionals provides a snapshot of a number of features of performance management (Chartered Institute of Personnel and Development, 2009d). In answer to the question of what respondents understood by the term 'performance management', the top responses were that it allowed for a regular review meeting between a manager and employee, it allowed for objective or target setting and facilitated regular feedback to

individuals. Other aspects mentioned included performance appraisal, the assessment of development needs and career development. The responses to the question of what *actually happens* under the heading of performance management are outlined in Table 8.1.

Clearly, one of the most important aspects of enhancing performance is performance appraisal, which is a critical element of performance management and a key feature of organizational life. As Bach (2005: 289) notes, 'performance appraisals have become far more than just an annual ritual and are viewed as a key lever to enhance organizational performance'. Performance appraisal is defined by Heery and Noon (2008: 11) as 'the process of evaluating the performance and assessing the development/training needs of an employee'. The Labour Research Department (1997: 3) similarly notes how performance appraisal is 'A process of reviewing individual performances against pre-determined criteria or objectives, involving the gathering of information, one or more meetings and some form of report which may include a performance rating.' In sum, then, appraisal is a process that allows for an individual employee's overall capabilities and potential to be assessed, usually by their line manager, for the purposes of improving their performance.

The Industrial Relations Services (2005b) suggests that over 90 per cent of workplaces have some form of performance appraisal, usually a conventional top-down appraisal system. Moreover, there has been a shift in recent years which have seen more and more organizational members subject to such appraisal, which had traditionally been geared more to managerial staff. Clearly, given the skills mix that was discussed in Chapter 4, which points to a predominance of semi-skilled and unskilled workers in tourism and hospitality, there may well be a question of whether it is worthwhile appraising such workers, especially unskilled workers, as these jobs are likely to involve little technical expertise. For example, notwithstanding the earlier point about more organizational members being appraised, the Industrial Relations Services

| TABLE 8.1  Features of performance management | |
|---|---|
| Feature | % |
| Performance appraisal | 81 |
| Objective or target setting | 75 |
| Review meeting to assess progress | 62 |
| Development opportunities discussed | 52 |
| Performance-related pay | 31 |
| Career-development meetings | 24 |
| 360-degree feedback | 21 |
| Source: adapted from Chartered Institute of Personnel and Development (2009d) | |

(1999) suggested that less than one-quarter of organizations across the economy as a whole appraised semi-skilled or unskilled workers. If these employees are to be appraised some difficulties may be encountered in attempting to readily establish observable standards and criteria by which performance can be measured. There may also be the additional issue in tourism and hospitality of the predominance of small- and medium-sized enterprises. Boxall and Purcell (2008) recognize that performance appraisal is only likely to work well when it is well resourced and well led, leading them to suggest that small firms might be better advised to use informal methods instead. Indeed, within the context of tourism and hospitality, Goldsmith *et al.* (1997) note that appraisal is unlikely to be something that is realistic for a small family-concern-type business or a single-person operation. Consequently, they advocate that appraisal has certain minimum requisites or parameters, including (p. 165):

- the equivalent of at least 20 full-time, non-managerial employees;
- a minimum of one layer of professional management between the organization's proprietor and operative staff; and
- some evidence of departmentalization, where individual departments have their own heads or supervisors.

Given the above discussion it might seem reasonable to imagine that appraisal is less likely to be a part of a systematic approach to HRM in tourism and hospitality. However, the evidence seems to suggest that the opposite may in fact be true. For example, Lucas (2004), in her interrogation of the Workplace Employment Relations Survey (WERS) data found that 85 per cent of managers in the hospitality and tourism industry had responsibility for performance appraisal. Interestingly, Lucas also found that performance appraisal is more likely to be used in the hospitality industry compared to all private sector service organizations. Similarly, Hoque (1999) found that 89 per cent of the 232 hotels he surveyed regularly used appraisal, compared to 62 per cent of similar-sized establishments in manufacturing. Woods *et al.* (1998) also found a high incidence of appraisal in the United States. In a survey of 1,000 hotels covering all geographic areas, all types of market segment, ownership type, size and number of employees, Woods *et al.* found that two-thirds of his sample had an annual appraisal. Clearly, appraisal is a significant part of broader HRM concerns in hospitality and tourism and we can now go on to consider some of the challenges facing managers in operationalizing appraisal schemes.

## Performance appraisal in practice

To begin to assess the impact of performance appraisal we should start with a simple question: why should organizations appraise people at work? A range

of writers (see, for example, Bach, 2005; Industrial Relations Services, 2005a, 2005b) suggest a number of reasons, including:

- Appraisal can be an integral part of ensuring that organizational members are aware of what is expected of them and can thus play an important part in socializing organizational members to 'buy in' to the organizational culture. For example, Gröschl and Doherty (2002: 58) note how 'Its value as an organizational socialization process is closely associated with organizational attempts to manage "culture", another essential element of the HRM approach to the employment relationship.' Indeed, Bach (2005) notes that, increasingly, organizations are now using performance management as a means to introduce cultural changes in organizations.
- Clarifying performance expectations and standards.
- Improving current performance.
- Setting goals and targets.
- Providing feedback – we all seek approval and confirmation that we are doing the right thing, and we also like to advise or direct others on how they should do things.
- Increasing motivation.
- Identifying training and development needs.
- Identifying potential.
- Focusing on career development and succession planning.
- Awarding salary increases/performance-related pay.
- Evaluating the effectiveness of the selection process.
- Solving job problems.
- Setting objectives using the *SMART* mnemonic: **s**pecific or **s**tretching (define precisely what is required in clear language); **m**easurable (both quantitatively and qualitatively); **a**ccepted (objectives agreed and not imposed); **r**ealistic (achievable and fairly allocated); and **t**ime-bound (clear target dates). For example, in a tourism and hospitality context it might be things like servers trying to increase their sales per shift, chambermaids cleaning more rooms, receptionists attempting to become more skilled in information technology, improving communication skills or learning to speak a foreign language.

In reality, in most workplaces staff are being continually monitored and assessed by management in an informal manner. Indeed, it would seem prudent to encourage regular dialogue between managers and their staff about work performance. That said, the danger with such informality is that it is very much dependent on individual managers and whether they are giving regular feedback. Consequently, a more formal performance appraisal system can develop a greater degree of consistency by ensuring that managers and employees meet formally and regularly to discuss performance and potential. What we are concerned to examine in this chapter is the formalized manner by which staff are assessed during performance appraisals. That is, the process of reviewing individual performance against predetermined criteria or object-ives, involving the gathering of information and one or more meetings on a quarterly, six-monthly or annual basis, and producing some form of report which is likely to include a performance rating. As described above, per-formance appraisal can be seen in a fairly positive vein and useful in terms of things like raising morale, clarifying expectations, improving upward and downward communication and so on (see HRM in Practice 8.1).

## HRM IN PRACTICE 8.1:
## Appraisal: some good news

Research conducted by Armstrong and Baron (2005) found that employees and managers offered favourable rather than unfavourable views on appraisal. Some of the comments from the research included:

> You need appraisal to get the best out of people and develop them.

> In a one-to-one meeting, people can bring things out to their supervisors who say 'I've never been aware of that: why didn't you tell us before?' That's definitely an advantage.

> For me, the real strength of the process lies in the continuing dialogue and negotiation as the year goes on.

> You're one-to-one with your boss. You've chatted, and it wasn't as if it was your boss. It was more relaxed. He would listen and then you'd chat about it. I enjoyed it.

## Review and reflect

What are some of the likely difficulties in appraising employees in tourism and hospitality?

Despite the above discussion, which points to why performance appraisal might be thought of as a 'good' thing, in reality there is much debate and concern surrounding the notion of appraisal. For example, Torrington *et al.* (2011: 265) suggest that 'there are ... concerns that appraisal systems are treated as an administrative exercise, are ineffective and do little to improve performance of employees in the future'. W. Edwards Deming, a leading

advocate of total quality management (TQM), has suggested that appraisal is wrong in principle and an ineffective management philosophy, describing it as a 'deadly disease' (cited in Bach, 2005). Similarly, Stephen Covey, the well-known management guru, has described appraisal as a 'disgusting habit', outmoded and more suited for an industrial age that no longer exists (cited in Industrial Relations Services, 2005a). Indeed, as long ago as 1957 the famous management theorist Douglas McGregor, of Theory X and Y fame, was suggesting that appraisal is the most contentious and least popular part of a manager's job. Managers dislike the process as they do not like 'playing God', which leads to a judgemental and ultimately demotivating approach:

> The respect we hold for the inherent value of the individual leaves us distressed when we must take responsibility for judging the personal worth of a fellow man. Yet the conventional approach to performance appraisal forces us, not only to make such judgements and to see them acted upon, but also to communicate them to those we have judged. Small wonder we resist!
>
> (McGregor, 1957: 90)

Managers may also regard appraisal as a waste of time and overly bureaucratic, and may also see it as a process that involves relatively high costs in setting up the scheme and training employees in using the scheme. Indeed, Redman (2009: 186) suggests that 'performance appraisals appear to be one human resource activity that everyone loves to hate' (see HRM in Practice 8.2).

**HRM IN PRACTICE 8.2:**
**Appraisal – some common negative managerial thoughts about appraisal**

Well, here we go again, I'm sure you don't like this business any more than I do, so let's get on with it.

Now, there's nothing to worry about. It's quite painless and could be useful. So just relax and let me put a few questions to you.

I wonder if I will end up conning you more than you will succeed in conning me.

Right. Let the battle commence!

In part, some of the negative views of appraisal could potentially be addressed by training for managers to ensure that they are clear on the importance of appraisal. For example, Industrial Relations Services (2005b: 9) note that, 'if managers are not properly trained and committed to the appraisal system, the performance review can become just a paperwork exercise, at best, or – at worst – a harmful one'. This view points to the issue of whether appraisals *per se* are problematic or whether much of the problem lies in the carrying out of the appraisal – specifically whether appraisals are performed poorly by uninterested or badly trained managers. Training, then, may help managers to appreciate the importance of appraisal within a broader performance management approach, and also the need to develop coaching skills to facilitate a more developmental approach.

Such training may be appropriate in attempting to address some of the problems which may plague appraisal (Bach, 2005; Industrial Relations Services, 2005b; Redman, 2009; Torrington *et al.*, 2011) such as:

- prejudice – for example, sex or race discrimination;
- subjectivity and bias, especially with regard to rater bias;
- insufficient knowledge of the appraisee, meaning the appraiser's position is based on position in the hierarchy rather than any real knowledge of the appraisee's job;
- the 'halo' effect, which is where managers rate employees on the basis of their likeability and one positive criterion distorts the assessment of others. Similarly, the 'horns' effect is where a single negative aspect dominates the appraisal rating;
- the problem of context – the difficulty of distinguishing the work of appraisees from the context in which they work, especially when there is a degree of comparison with other appraisees;
- what might be termed the 'paradox of roles' in terms of the conflation of judge and counsellor (mentor) role can lead to confusion – for example, in the shift from an evaluative to a developmental approach managers have to manage such tensions;
- the paperwork – overly bureaucratic and simply about form filling;
- the formality – for both appraiser and appraisee it can be an uncomfortable experience;
- outcomes are ignored and follow-up actions agreed in the meeting often do not happen;
- everyone is 'average or just above average' – for example, managers may find it difficult to give an employee a bad rating as they would not want to justify the criticisms in the performance review interview;
- appraising the wrong features – too much stress on easily identifiable things like time-keeping, looking busy, being pleasant and so on.

- 'recency bias', leading to a tendency to base appraisals on the recent past, regardless of how representative it is of performance over the course of the previous year.

In many respects these issues reflect what Bach (2005) calls the 'orthodox critique', wherein many of the problems could potentially be addressed by seeking to remedy the imperfections in the design and implementation of the appraisal system or by improving managerial training in conducting appraisals. For some, though, there may well be much more fundamental criticisms to be made about the process of appraisal.

Bach (2005: 305) notes the emergence of more critical accounts of appraisal, in particular recognizing how:

> Unitary assumptions about the benevolent purposes of appraisal are replaced by a more radical ideology concerned to examine managerial objectives, especially tighter control over behaviour and performance, the potential to individualize the employment relationship and the scope for managers to use appraisal as a veneer to legitimate informal management.

For example, many of the criticisms, drawing on the work of Foucault, see appraisal as inherently sinister and about aiming to control all aspects of employee behaviour and eliminating scope for employee resistance. Appraisal becomes simply about bolstering managerial power and control, a point that is similar to some of the criticisms of organizational culture outlined in Chapter 3. In sum, Bach suggests that critical perspectives seek to highlight that it should not be assumed that clearer objectives and training of appraisers will necessarily yield satisfactory results. Consequently, it is important to recognize how 'the contested nature of appraisal, the specific managerial objectives sought, and the nature of the context in which it is applied, all have an important bearing on the impact of the appraisal process' (p. 306).

Thus, we can appreciate that appraisal is very much a contested issue, both conceptually and practically. Equally, though, as Holdsworth (1991: 65) rightly suggests,

> appraisal is a compulsively fascinating subject, full of paradoxes and love–hate relationships. And appraisal schemes are really controversial. . . . Some schemes are popular, with overtones of evangelical fervour, while others are at least equally detested and derided as the 'annual rain dance', 'the end of term report', etc.

See HRM in Practice 8.3 for how a number of the issues discussed above were played out within ANO, a French hotel chain, which introduced a new appraisal system.

## HRM IN PRACTICE 8.3:
## The rhetoric and reality of appraisal in ANO Hotels

Gröschl and Doherty (2002) report on the introduction of a new appraisal system in ANO, which is part of a French multinational travel and tourism group and operates at the three-star level. In 1998 a standardized appraisal system was developed for the company as a whole in order that it could be implemented in all their brands, including ANO. This attempt at standardizing appraisal was to ensure that all employees across the company's various brands would be appraised against the same criteria to ensure a consistent evaluation of employee performance.

The new appraisal system was developed at the corporate headquarters and the working group which developed the system initially evaluated the old system to identify weaknesses. Once this was done they developed suggestions and proposals for the new system, which were then sent to regional management teams for their comments and feedback. These exchanges continued for six months before there was finally agreement on the standardized criteria and a number of aims and objectives. A key aim of the new system was to ensure a basis for planning for action, particularly with regard to career progress. The new appraisal system was an example of a development-oriented appraisal system and the appraisal format was considered a formal and sophisticated document. Employees were assessed with ratings ranging from 'very good' to 'insufficient' on 13 standardized competencies, including aptitudes and skills. Although the process of introducing a new appraisal system seemed well planned and thought-out, there were still some issues. For example, some managers seemed unable to sufficiently differentiate between day-to-day feedback and the formal appraisal process. Appraisers would also often be inconsistent in their preparation for appraisal, failing to notify appraisees sufficiently in advance or not filling in the appraisal form correctly. Appraisers would often run appraisals in public spaces, such as bars and restaurants, which runs counter to the advice often offered in textbooks. Lastly, there was also significant variance in the appraisers' styles. Some appraisers recognized the developmental nature of the new system and developed an advisory/supportive role in the appraisal; others were much more judgemental and authoritarian. In sum, although ANO had clear objectives, documentation and guidelines, all of which reflected good-practice HRM, the implementation proved rather trickier. Closer monitoring of the process by the HR managers, or line managers with a strong interest/involvement in HRM, could have improved the situation. Equally, the case seems to point to the need to provide managers with the appropriate skills to allow them to take on more of a facilitator or coaching role in the appraisal process.

Ultimately, despite the debates surrounding its utility, appraisal is a fact of organizational life, and as Bratton and Gold (2007: 282) note, 'making judgements about an employee's contribution, value/worth, capability and potential has to be considered as a vital relationship with employees'. Moreover, as we noted above, there may be an argument, rather like employment interviewing, to say that the process itself is not necessarily flawed, but that the individuals operating it are insufficiently skilled.

---

### Review and reflect

What are some of the skills likely to be required by managers in order to conduct a good appraisal?

---

Given the reality of performance appraisal being an inevitable part of a manager's life, we can look at the practicalities of appraising employees. Regarding appraising employees, a number of writers have outlined two main perspectives: the evaluative and the developmental. In the former approach the main aim is to make a judgement about an appraisee's performance, with such a judgement being made against aspects such as the job description and established objectives, which may be linked to extrinsic rewards. Often this will also involve managers making rating or ranking decisions that differentiate between staff on the basis of their relative performance. On other hand, developmental approaches are likely to have a different premise, where the appraiser and appraisee aim to discuss the progress, hopes and fears of the appraisee in a mutually supportive atmosphere and where the ultimate aim is on developing performance by building on employees' strengths.

---

### Review and reflect

As we have already noted, there may be some debate as to whether performance reviews or appraisals should be evaluative or developmental. Consider how you would respond to the talking points that follow in assessing this conundrum.

*Talking point 1*

As part of an appraisal process you want to tell a member of staff in your travel agency that you feel as though they lack initiative and that this is severely hindering their performance in their front-line job. How do you approach this issue?

*Talking point 2*

Should appraisal be linked to pay?

*Talking point 3*

Should appraisal look forwards or backwards?

In reality, within any given organizational setting there may not be such an absolute and clear-cut distinction, and there may be elements of both evaluative and developmental approaches such that the purpose of performance appraisal has tended to oscillate between concerns about short-term performance to a more developmental orientation. Appraisal has also been used as a disciplinary tool by some organizations, with poor performance being something that appraisal systems have sought to address, a point to which we will return later. As we have already noted, the character and emphasis of appraisal has changed in recent years. Bach (2005: 291) notes how:

> During the 1990s there was a shift from almost exclusive emphasis on reward driven systems, based on individual performance related pay and quantifiable objectives, towards more rounded systems of performance management with a stronger developmental focus.

We will consider this point in due course. However, it is important to recognize that many appraisal systems will still retain attempts to measure performance, often using a variety of techniques. For example, Woods *et al.* (1998) found that hotels in their survey used one or more of four approaches: management by objective (MBO) (48 per cent); behaviourally anchored rating scales (BARS) (41 per cent); narrative essay (37 per cent); and graphic rating scale (28 per cent) (see also HRM in Practice 8.4).

## HRM IN PRACTICE 8.4:
## The use of BARS in the American hotel industry

BARS aims to evaluate managers' actions. Umbreit *et al.* (1986) developed a BARS format to evaluate what hotel managers do in their jobs by using seven rating scales for a number of key aspects of job performance. The aspects of job performance were: communication skills; handling guest complaints and promoting guest relations; developing marketing strategies and monitoring sales

programmes; motivating and modifying employee behaviour; implementing policy; making decisions and delegating responsibilities; monitoring operations and maintaining product quality; and handling personnel responsibilities. For example, with regard to communication skills, at the top of the scale at seven is a manager who communicates effectively by, for example, calling a meeting to explain why the hotel will be cutting staff. In the middle is a manager who communicates satisfactorily, at 4–5 on the scale, by meeting with several employees once per week for an informal talk about the hotel's activities. At the bottom is a manager who experiences difficulties in communicating with staff, sitting at 1–2 on the scale, for example, a manager who, during an executive meeting, dismisses a subordinate's comments as stupid.

Derived from Woods *et al.* (1998)

In a similar vein, behavioural observation scales allow raters to state the frequency with which they have observed specific job-related behaviours, such as whether an employee provides constructive feedback to a colleague, with such ratings usually on a 1–5 scale from 'never' to 'always'. Other methods which organizations may use include performance standards and matching performance against job descriptions, or rating an employee based on a scale ranging from 'outstanding' to 'unacceptable' (see the later discussion of 'forced ranking').

HRM in Practice 8.4 gives an indication of the types of activities that may be assessed in judging the performance of managers in the tourism and hospitality industry. In addition to these aspects there may be a range of other attributes that can be used to measure the individual performance of an employee. For example, the Chartered Institute of Personnel and Development (2005b), reporting on a survey of over 500 organizations across the economy, outline a number of criteria and their relative importance to how organizations measure individual performance; these are considered in Table 8.2.

Similarly, McKenna and Beech (2008) note a number of performance factors which are likely to be appraised, the most important being:

- knowledge, ability and skill on the job;
- attitude to work, expressed as enthusiasm, commitment and motivation;
- quality of work on a consistent basis with attention to detail;
- volume of productive output;
- interaction, as exemplified in communication skills and ability to relate to others in teams.

As we noted above, the focus of appraisal is increasingly argued to be shifting to a more developmental function. Given that much of the discussion above

**TABLE 8.2 Criteria used to measure individual performance**

| | Respondents (%) | | | |
|---|---|---|---|---|
| | Very important | Important | Not very important | Not used as a measure |
| Achievement of objectives | 52 | 42 | 3 | 1 |
| Competence | 53 | 40 | 3 | 2 |
| Contribution to team | 34 | 57 | 4 | 2 |
| Quality | 47 | 44 | 3 | 4 |
| Working relationships | 35 | 53 | 7 | 3 |
| Customer care | 45 | 40 | 7 | 5 |
| Productivity | 34 | 49 | 9 | 6 |
| Flexibility | 22 | 56 | 13 | 4 |
| Aligning personal objectives with organizational goals | 29 | 48 | 16 | 4 |
| Business awareness | 17 | 52 | 21 | 6 |
| Skills/learning targets | 18 | 57 | 16 | 4 |
| Financial awareness | 11 | 47 | 28 | 10 |

Source: adapted from Chartered Institute of Personnel and Development (2005a)

has outlined an approach to appraisal which is predominately top-down, there may be other approaches that may be seen as less biased and potentially offering greater scope for development. Some of these other approaches are now briefly discussed.

*Self-appraisal*. Bach (2005) notes the manner in which the appraisal process in a number of organizations increasingly expects employees to take greater ownership, 'with employees assigned greater responsibility for establishing their own performance goals and for obtaining feedback on their performance' (p. 293). With self-appraisal, then, instead of employees being passive recipients of their line manager's appraisal, they are increasingly involved via some form of self-assessment, often being more critical than if the manager conducted the appraisal (McKenna and Beech, 2008). In such an approach employees are increasingly expected to take the lead in the discussions – it should not just be a case of downwards feedback from the line manager. Indeed, in some instances employees may draft their own performance review, which then forms the basis for the discussion with their line manager (Income Data Services, 2005a).

*Peer appraisal.* Fellow team members, departmental colleagues or selected individuals with whom an individual has been working provide the assessment of performance.

*Upward appraisal.* Managers are appraised by their staff, usually via the use of an anonymous questionnaire. The process is anonymous to alleviate any worries that employees may have about providing honest but unfavourable feedback on managerial performance, thus lessening concerns about the potential for managerial retribution. Unsurprisingly, it has been reported that managers are not especially fond of upward appraisal systems, especially middle and junior managers (see the discussion of attitude surveys in Chapter 10).

*Customer appraisal.* Redman (2009) notes the increasing importance of customers in the appraisal process, which in part reflects the emergence and development of TQM and customer care programmes. As he recognizes, 'one impact of these initiatives is that organizations are now increasingly setting employee performance standards based upon customer care indicators and appraising staff against these' (p. 184). Redman notes that these can be in terms of 'hard' quantifiable measures, such as whether a drink is delivered in a certain amount of time in a restaurant, or 'soft' measures, which are more qualitative, such as whether a warm and friendly greeting is given by staff in giving the customer the drink. Moreover, Redman notes the use of service guarantees, 'which involve the payment of compensatory moneys to customers if the organizations do not reach the standards' (p. 184), which again also means a greater use of customer data in appraisal ratings.

In terms of the use of customer service data and how it may be used to appraise employees, Redman notes how it can be gathered by a variety of means:

- *Customer surveys*: organizations are now becoming increasingly sophisticated in the manner in which they gather customer feedback, which is gathered via a number of means such as the use of customer care cards, telephone surveys, interviews with customers and postal surveys.
- *Range of surveillance techniques*: managers may 'sample' the service encounter. For example, if a travel company had a call centre, managers could listen to some of the calls between customers and the call-centre operatives.
- *'Mystery' or 'phantom' shopper*: mystery shoppers observe and record their experience of the service encounter and report these findings back to the organization. Although this method may be seen as rather controversial – employees may view the mystery shoppers as 'spies' or 'snoopers' and indulge in 'shopper spotting' – it is widely used in the tourism and hospitality industry. Redman argues that the controversy surrounding mystery shoppers may be dissipated to an extent if they are used primarily for encouraging and rewarding good performance, rather than punishing staff

for performing poorly. Thus staff who receive good feedback from mystery shopper ratings should be rewarded, while those who receive poor ratings should use them as a source to identify potential training needs, as discussed in Chapter 7.

- *Multi-rater or 360-degree feedback.* Redman (2009) notes how 360-degree feedback has been increasingly used within UK organizations. In most organizations that use 360-degree feedback it is likely to be used as a management development tool. Performance data is generated from a variety of sources, which can include the person to whom the individual being assessed reports, people who report to them, peers (team colleagues or others in the organization), and internal and external customers. Positive accounts would suggest that 360-degree feedback is felt to provide a more rounded view of people, with less bias than if an assessment is conducted by one individual. However, it can be costly, produce a lot of information and 'simply replaces the subjectivity of a single appraiser with the subjectivity of multiple appraisers' (Redman, 2009: 182)

---

## Review and reflect

If you have been subject to any of the above aspects in your working life in tourism and hospitality, how did you feel about being assessed by these means? Did you feel that it gave a fair representation of your performance?

---

## The practicalities: the appraisal form and interview

Most PMS are likely to have a formal final performance review, where an individual employee is assessed against their objectives (inputs and outputs). This review is also likely to allow for a review of training and development needs. With regard to the practicalities of conducting the review, it is likely that most companies will use the appraisal form to structure the discussion. The Advisory, Conciliation and Arbitration Service (2010d) note how a typical performance review form is likely to contain provision for:

- Basic personal details, such as name and staff number.
- Job title.
- Whether the appraisee has any responsibility for managing staff and who they report to.
- A section for objectives to allow for objective-setting, which can be reviewed on an interim and final review basis.
- A section which allows the appraisee to comment on the extent to which they have achieved against various competencies, such as focusing on customers, learning new skills and communicating effectively.

- A section on personal development, which allows the appraisee to reflect on their current strengths, but also on future career plans and aspirations, including developing a personal development plan.
- A section which allows for a six-monthly interim review, including an indicative interim assessment of how the appraisee is performing against objectives and competencies.
- A summary section in which the appraiser and appraisee comment on the achievement of objectives, competencies and development.
- A final assessment of performance against objectives and competencies which would be assessed as being outstanding, standard, less than standard or unsatisfactory.
- Space for signing off the form, including a countersigning manager who would also be invited to comment if there was a dispute between the appraiser and appraisee.

The discussion so far gives a sense of some of the potential pitfalls that might befall a manager in conducting an appraisal interview. To an extent, the nature and tone of the appraisal interview will be dictated by whether a scheme is seeking a broadly evaluative or developmental approach. Torrington *et al.* (2011), in their review of appraisal interviewing, identify three broad styles of appraisal interview. The *problem-solving* approach involves the appraiser encouraging the appraisee to review their performance and identify any problems, but appraiser and appraisee then jointly seek to discuss joint solutions. The evaluation emerges from the discussion rather than being a unilateral judgement from the appraiser. As Torrington *et al.* note, 'this is certainly the most effective style provided that both the appraiser and appraisee have the skill and ability to handle it' (p. 723). In addition to the problem-solving approach, Torrington *et al.* also note the *tell and sell* style in which the appraiser acts more like a judge, telling the employee the results of the appraisal and how they might improve. Lastly, there is the *tell and listen*, where again the appraiser is the judge, but having passed on the outcome of the appraisal then listens to the appraisee's reaction. Although, as Torrington *et al.* note, the problem-solving approach might appear to be the 'best' as it 'appears to be the most civilized and searching' (p. 723), not all appraisal interviews will necessarily be conducted in this manner as appraisees might not be ready for such an approach or appraisers may not have the right skills to conduct an appraisal in this manner.

Much of the above discussion points to the need for managers to have the right skillset that allows them to appraise well, as well as understanding how appraisal fits into the wider issue of performance management and organizational strategy generally. Indeed, in much the same way that we described in Chapter 5 on how managers would often have an inflated view of their skills as interviewers, the same may be true for appraisal interviews. As Redman (2009: 187) notes, 'despite their widely held belief to the contrary, most managers are not naturally good at conducting performance appraisals'. Consequently, at the very least managers need to reflect on how they can potentially improve their skills, and in terms of practical skills there may be aspects such as asking the right questions, the ability to be a good listener and giving useful feedback. In sum, the Chartered Institute of Personnel and Development (2011c: 3) offers a view on what 'good' and 'bad' appraisals look like:

A 'good' and constructive appraisal meeting is one in which:

- appraisees do most of the talking;
- appraisers listen actively to what appraisees say;
- there is scope for reflection and analysis;
- performance is analysed, not personality;
- the whole period is reviewed and not just recent or isolated events;
- achievement is recognized and reinforced;
- the meeting ends positively with agreed action plans to improve and sustain performance in the future.

A 'bad' appraisal meeting:

- focuses on a catalogue of failures and omissions;
- is controlled by the appraiser;
- ends with disagreement between appraiser and appraisee;
- leaves the appraisee feeling disengaged or demotivated by the process.

## Managing poor performance

Of course, there is always the potential issue of how to manage poor performers and a clear rationale for the introduction of performance management systems is to seek to identify and address any instances of poor performance (see HRM in Practice 8.5).

Although HRM in Practice 8.5 describes a rather extreme way to address poor performance, the reality is that in most organizations if a PMS is underpinned by regular meetings, feedback and coaching then issues around poor performance should be picked up relatively quickly. Organizations can then attempt to address poor performance through some form of improvement development programme, which will often involve employees being given extensive help in the form of training and coaching. Armstrong (2009: 634–5) suggests that there are five basic steps in handling performance problems:

- Identify and agree the problem through analysing feedback and getting agreement from the employee of what the shortfall has been.
- Establish the reason(s) for the shortfall and avoid crudely attaching blame for problems in the job. Instead, the manager and employee should jointly

## HRM IN PRACTICE 8.5:
### 'Ranking and yanking': targeting poor performers

As we noted earlier in the chapter, managers often feel uncomfortable in giving poor ratings. Because of the level of discomfort this creates for them, managers will rate employees more leniently so everybody becomes 'average or just above average'. However, in recent years, in the United States in particular, there has been the rise of so-called 'ranking and yanking' or, more officially, 'forced ranking'. In such a system employees are ranked on a normal distribution such that 10 per cent typically receive a ranking which marks them out as superior performers, 80 per cent are graded as performing at a standard level and 10 per cent as underperformers. This use of forced ranking, in theory, allows organizations to identify underperformance and as such the role of the appraisal system is to weed out the underperformers. Having been identified, poor performers are initially given help and a period of time to improve. However, if they fail to rise in the ranking, they will find that their exit is 'encouraged' with a redundancy package. If the poor performer refuses to leave voluntarily, they will instead face the possibility of termination without compensation.

Unsurprisingly, there has been much debate about the effectiveness of such an approach. Proponents of such a tough approach believe the system forces managers to take unpleasant but tough decisions that, reflecting the point above, they would otherwise seek to avoid as being too fraught with conflict. It is also argued that this approach will increase productivity and motivation of those superior performers at the top. Critics question whether this approach motivates the 80 per cent who are labelled as standard performers. The system can also create a very difficult environment, discouraging teamwork and encouraging in-fighting and dysfunctional behaviour among employees. As well as these obvious problems with this approach demotivating lower-ranked employees, there are concerns about its legality – for example, whether it is discriminatory to older workers in particular. Thus, although it is claimed that this practice will improve the overall level of performance in the business, in reality there is very mixed evidence that this is the case.

Derived from Armstrong (2009); Brown and Lim (2010); Redman (2009)

identify what has contributed to the problem – for example, they may not have received appropriate support and guidance from their manager or did not have the appropriate skills.
- Decide and agree on the action required, whether it be things like the manager providing more support and guidance or the employee changing their attitude, behaviour or improvements in certain skills or abilities.

- Resource the action by providing coaching, training and guidance to ensure that changes can be made.
- Monitor and provide feedback, which involves both the manager and individual employee monitoring performance, ensuring appropriate feedback is provided and that any further action that may be necessary is agreed.

Thus, as the Income Data Services (2005a: 9) note, 'in this way, most poor performers will either improve to a satisfactory level within a given timescale or as a last resort would be liable for dismissal under capability procedures'. This issue is further discussed in Chapter 12.

## Conclusion

Despite concerns, performance appraisal remains a key part of organizational life. Often an integral part of a broader PMS, performance appraisals are a crucial, if rather unloved, part of a manager's job. We recognized in the chapter how debates about performance appraisal may not just reflect fundamental criticisms, but also more prosaic issues, such as managers not having the necessary skillset to conduct appraisals, especially those that are more developmentally oriented. Many of these issues are particularly pronounced in the tourism and hospitality sector, where the predominance of SMEs, the nature of the skills mix in the industry and difficulties in judging 'softer' and less quantifiable aspects of performance may all mean that the development of a systematic approach to appraisal remains problematic. Nevertheless, evidence suggests that the majority of larger tourism and hospitality organizations are seeking to appraise their employees. Given this reality, it is important for organizations and managers to recognize the challenges in conducting positive appraisals. Recognition of these challenges and the skills needed to address them means that 'playing God' may not be quite so painful for managers as has often been the case in the past.

## Discussion questions

- How can the terms 'performance management' and 'performance appraisal' be considered distinct?
- Why might it be difficult to measure the performance of a customer-facing tourism and hospitality employee?
- Argue for and against the use of forced rankings in appraisal.
- If you were appraising an employee, what are the key questions to create a positive discussion?

## Further reading

Armstrong, M. and Baron, A. (2005) *Managing Performance: Performance Management in Action*, London: CIPD.

Bach, S. (2005) 'New directions in performance management', in S. Bach (ed.) *Managing Human Resources: Personnel Management in Transition*, 4th edn, Oxford: Blackwell.

Brown, M. and Lim, V. (2010) 'Understanding performance management and appraisal: supervisory and employee perspectives', in A. Wilkinson, N. Bacon, T. Redman and S. Snell (eds), *The Sage Handbook of Human Resource Management*, London: Sage.

Gröschl, S. and Doherty, L. (2002) 'The appraisal process: beneath the surface', *Journal of Human Resources in Hospitality and Tourism*, 1, 3, 57–76.

Redman, T. (2009) 'Performance appraisal', in T. Redman and A. Wilkinson (eds), *Contemporary Human Resource Management: Texts and Cases*, 3rd edn, Harlow: Prentice Hall.

Woods, R., Sciarini, M. and Breiter, D. (1998) 'Performance appraisal in hotels', *Cornell Hotel and Restaurant Administration Quarterly*, 39, 2, 25–9.

## Recommended websites

Workforce Management has a description of a 360-degree appraisal process in Yum Brands Inc. (*Workforce Management*, April 2005, pp. 59–60). This article can be found at http://www.workforce.com. At the main site use the free registration facility then find the article via the search facility.

The CIPD Performance Management surveys can be found at http://www.cipd.co.uk/surveys

There are various resources on performance management on the ACAS website at http://www.acas.org.uk/index.aspx?articleid=2927

There is a guide to performance appraisal at http://www.doi.gov/hrm/guidance/370dm430hndbk.pdf

There are a number of helpful tips and tools to improve appraisal at http://www.businessballs.com/performanceappraisals.htm

A key part of the appraisal process is giving and receiving effective feedback; there are some handy tips at http://managementhelp.org/communicationsskills/feedback.htm

## Additional material

Go to www.routledge.com/cw/nickson to find PowerPoint slides, chapter commentaries, test banks and additional case studies for each chapter.

# Reward strategies in the tourism and hospitality industry

## CHAPTER OBJECTIVES

**This chapter considers reward strategies in the tourism and hospitality industry. Specifically, the chapter will:**

- Review differing employer and employee objectives with regard to pay.

- Consider debates about minimum and maximum wages and comparability of pay across tourism and hospitality sub-sectors and occupations.

- Recognize the importance of tipping as part of the reward package in tourism and hospitality.

- Discuss the variety of additional non-monetary rewards available to tourism and hospitality employers.

## Introduction

The first problem we face when thinking about the notion of reward strategies is a terminological one. When we talk about rewards we are likely to hear a variety of terms. For example, Foot and Hook (2008) note a number of terms commonly used to describe payment systems, including 'compensation', 'remuneration', 'reward', 'payment', 'wages' and 'salary'. Increasingly, in a prescriptive HRM sense there is much talk of 'total remuneration planning', 'reward management' or 'reward strategy' as denoting a more strategic and holistic approach to the rewarding of employees. Therefore, in this more prescriptive view it is argued that employees seek a range of monetary and non-monetary rewards – the so-called 'cafeteria approach' – from employment, of which money is only one aspect, even if it is often the primary consideration for employees. Thus, employees may seek both extrinsic and intrinsic and financial and non-financial rewards at work. That said, a more realistic assessment is that in reality the provision of extrinsic rewards is certainly the most substantive issue in the effort–reward bargain and often the most problematic aspect of employment. Therefore this chapter will focus on the notion of extrinsic rewards, especially pay as it will often be the main reason why people work. In considering pay and other aspects of remuneration the chapter will also recognize how the nature of tourism and hospitality as an employing sector will significantly impact on the development of reward strategies. For example, the existence of a relatively large number of unskilled and semi-skilled employees means low pay is endemic in many parts of the tourism and hospitality sector, particularly the sub-sectors of hotel and catering.

## Employee and employer views of pay

Torrington *et al.* (2011) recognize the manner in which the contract for payment will be satisfactory in so far as it meets the objectives of the respective parties in the employment relationship; that is, the employer and employee. In recognizing this point they further note how these objectives are likely to differ depending on whether it is that of the employee or employer, a point that is now discussed further.

## Employee objectives for the contract for payment

### Purchasing power

The absolute level of weekly or monthly earnings will determine the standard of living of individual employees, so they will aim to maximize their purchasing power. In simple terms, employees will ask themselves how much they can buy with their earnings. Torrington *et al.* (2011) suggest that employees will rarely be truly satisfied about their purchasing power. Indeed, it could be argued that purchasing power has become ever more resonant in an era of conspicuous consumption in which marketing and advertising portray a wide array of goods or services which people should be aspiring to consume (see HRM in Practice 9.1).

### Fairness

In many respects the notion of fairness is captured in the idiom of 'a fair day's pay for a fair day's work'. In this sense employees tend to have a strong sense of what they feel is an appropriate level of payment, which is fair to the job they are doing. As Torrington *et al.* note, employees who feel underpaid are likely to withdraw from the job and are more likely to be absent or late, for

## HRM IN PRACTICE 9.1:
## What is an appropriate minimum income?

Since 2008 the Joseph Rowntree Foundation (JRF) has published annual updates on a 'minimum income standard', based on what members of the public think people need to achieve a socially acceptable standard of living. In 2010 the JRF suggested that a single person in the UK needed to earn at least £14,400 per year, before tax, to afford a basic but acceptable standard of living. A couple with two children were suggested as needing £29,200. Members of the public who took part in the survey for the research suggested that as a minimum households need to have essential physical things to live and to be able to participate in society. For example, respondents thought that a certain basic budget for going out is required, that people need to be able to buy birthday presents and that everyone needs at least one week of holiday away each year, although not abroad. It is also suggested that items such as fridge-freezers, DVD players and mobile phones are such an integral part of modern life that everyone should be able to afford them. Lastly, it was felt that a computer and home internet access are now also essential for all working-age households to be able to engage in a meaningful way in society.

Derived from Davis *et al.* (2010)

example. This situation can be exacerbated if an employee has no real choice in terms of potentially moving elsewhere. Of course, employees may not simply feel underpaid; there may be some instances where employees actually feel they are overpaid. In such instances employees may feel guilty or attempt to look busy, which from an organizational point of view may not necessarily be particularly productive.

## Rights

Torrington *et al.* (2011) recognize the fundamental issue of the rights of employees to a particular share of a company's profit or the nation's wealth. Clearly, the manner in which wealth is currently shared out is one which engenders much debate, and many employees might feel that they are not getting a reasonable or fair share of the wealth that is created. This general sense of unease will often be expressed by trade unions in particular, who will seek to create a more fair division of wealth based often on notions of social and economic justice.

## Recognition

Torrington *et al.* (2011) note how most employees want to see their personal contribution recognized, either to be reassured of their worth or to facilitate career progression. Part of this recognition may well be financial recognition, though in reality there may be other aspects as well as the financial in recognizing and improving performance.

Notions of fairness, rights and recognition are particularly important and will often lie at the heart of much of the debate and controversy which is generated about pay, and especially whether people are being 'fairly' paid (see HRM in Practice 9.2).

## HRM IN PRACTICE 9.2:
## The disparities between those who have and those who do not have in tourism and hospitality

Much of the debate about disparities in pay focuses on notions of fairness and equity, and the difference between those at the top and bottom of the earnings ladder. Indeed, the issue of pay inequality has often been at the forefront of trade union campaigns to increase wages for those lower down the organizational hierarchy. For example, John Edmonds, then general secretary of the GMB union, once infamously railed against private sector bosses who awarded themselves inflated pay increases, describing them as 'greedy bastards' (Milne and White, 1998) who were indulging in the 'politics of the pig trough' (Milne, 1998a). Certainly this debate has some resonance with tourism and hospitality, and over the years there has been plenty of evidence to suggest that there is a significant pay gap between those who have and those who do not have in tourism and hospitality.

The Travel and Leisure Industry Salary Survey 1997 found that the highest paid directors at the UK's top 12 tourism and hospitality companies earned an average of £478,500, compared to a staff average of £11,360. Some of the so-called 'fat cats' were:

- Peter George – Ladbroke chief executive, at £1,280,000;
- Gerry Robinson – Granada chairman, at £728,000 (though in December 1999 by cashing in share options he made a pre-tax profit of £5.26 million);
- Sir Ian Prosser – Bass chairman, at £678,000

*Caterer and Hotelkeeper* (23 December 1999) reported that chief executives in the hospitality industry received an average pay increase of 20.8 per cent, compared to 3.5 per cent for employees.

*Caterer and Hotelkeeper* (18 May 2000) reported how David Thomas, Chief Executive of Whitbread, saw his total salary raised by 25.8 per cent, while group profits dropped by 14.8 per cent. His overall earnings were £593,103. The same article also reports how the average basic salary of 20 selected chief executives in the hospitality and leisure sectors was £330,835, which with bonuses and benefits rose to £370,293.

*Leisure and Hospitality Business* (25 July 2002) reported the highest paid chief executives packages for 2001–2. The highest earner was Tom Oliver, director of Six Continents Hotels and Resorts, who had a basic salary of £527,000, bonuses of £533,000 and benefits of £207,000, giving him an overall package of £1,267,000. The lowest paid director was Paul Dermody of the De Vere Group. His basic salary was £231,000, his bonus was £50,000 and his benefits £13,000, giving him a total salary of £294,000.

*IRS Employment Review* (19 May 2006) reported a survey of salaries in the leisure industry. Among other things, it notes that the average employee in the industry earned £18,602 per year, just 4.4 per cent of the average £501,613 paid to chief executives.

## Review and reflect

Are the chief executives in HRM in Practice 9.2 'greedy bastards', or are they fairly remunerated?

In the UK in recent years there has been much controversy over what many perceive as excessively high rewards for chief executives. For example, the High Pay Commission (2011) suggests that excessive top pay is deeply damaging to the UK as a whole, especially within the context of the economic downturn, which has seen large numbers of employees facing pay cuts, pay freezes and job losses. In particular, high levels of income inequality and the increasing gap this creates have had a number of economic and social consequences, such as exacerbating a 'take what you can get' culture. The report from the Commission found that there has been a public backlash against excessive rewards for executives. It cites a number of responses from the British Attitudes Survey, which suggest ordinary working people in Britain feel the imbalance between those at the top and bottom of the pay scale is increasingly damaging for society. For example, 73 per cent of people strongly agreed or agreed with the view that income differences in Britain are too large. Sixty per cent agreed or strongly agreed that ordinary working people do not get their fair share of the nation's wealth. Interestingly, nearly 60 per cent felt that the government had a responsibility to reduce the differences in income between people with the highest and lowest incomes.

### Composition

Torrington *et al.* (2011) note how the composition of a pay package can create questions about what is the best deal for employees. For example, they ask the question of whether £450 per week plus a pension is better than £500 per week without a pension. The answer to this and other questions with regard to the composition of pay packages will be dependent on the personal circumstances of individual employees. For example, younger employees may be much more concerned with high direct earnings at the expense of indirect benefits such as pensions, which are likely to be of more interest to older employees. Other issues surrounding the composition of pay packages include aspects such as overtime and incentives or performance-related pay.

## Employer objectives for the contract of payment

### Attracting staff

As Torrington *et al.* (2011) note, 'the reward package on offer must be sufficiently attractive vis-à-vis that of an organization's labour market competitors to ensure that it is able to secure the services of the staff it needs' (p. 520). As they further note, though, what is deemed to be attractive will obviously vary depending on the type of job and the labour market from which the organization is seeking to source employees. Clearly, an important part of attracting staff is the manner in which the organization is interacting with the external labour market and ensuring that they are getting the right kind of labour at the right kind of price (see HRM in Practice 9.3).

## HRM IN PRACTICE 9.3:
## Challenging perceptions of 'McJob'

As we noted in Chapter 1, McDonald's has often been at the forefront of arguments that suggest that work in tourism and hospitality is inherently low paid and with little meaning, as encapsulated by the notion of McJob. Recently the company has sought to address these issues with a sustained campaign to change perceptions about the McJob descriptor. A key part of this re-branding has been attempts to draw attention to fairness with regard to career opportunities and remuneration. For example, the company has suggested that the proportion of employees who regard their pay as 'fair' is 30 per cent higher than comparable companies. Part of the reason for this finding may be because McDonald's pay well above the lowest rate of the national minimum wage (NMW) for 16–17-year-olds. In 2010 the company's lowest rate for this group of employees was £4.35 per hour, which was well above the state's NMW rate for 16–17-year-olds, which stood at £3.57. Of course, McDonald's have a relatively large number of employees who will be in the 16–17 age bracket, and so arguably could be seen to be a 'good' employer to that particular segment of the labour market. Interestingly, this is in contrast to the rate for 18–21-year-olds and those aged 22, where the lowest rate was only slightly higher than the level of the NMW.

Derived from Income Data Services (2010a); Overell (2006)

## Retaining staff

Once employees are attracted into the organization there is also a need to ensure that effective performers are retained. Reward packages therefore have to be designed in such a way that prevents employees becoming dissatisfied and seeking opportunities elsewhere. This issue may be particularly challenging in terms of retaining employees who are highly skilled and are likely to have other opportunities in the labour market.

## Motivation and performance

Although there is much debate among occupational psychologists about the ability of monetary rewards to motivate people to work hard, Torrington *et al.* (2011) nevertheless make it clear that a poorly designed or implemented reward strategy is likely to lead to demotivated and unproductive employees. Consequently, 'the aim must be to reward people in such a way as to create the conditions in which they are prepared to work hard to help achieve their employer's objectives and, if possible, to demonstrate discretionary effort' (p. 521).

## Driving change

Pay may be used as part of a broader change management process. For example, there may be additional bonuses available for employees willing to develop new behaviour, attitudes or skills, which are required as part of a cultural change process.

## Corporate reputation

Increasingly, organizations are aiming to be seen as good employers in the labour market. In seeking this 'prestige', organizations need to ensure that their approaches to rewards are seen to encourage employees to aim to sustain high quality. In addition, it may also be argued that the maintenance of a reputation for being an ethical and socially responsible employer is important in sustaining a good corporate reputation.

## Affordability

Despite much of the above discussion, which points to the desirable aspects of creating an appropriate reward strategy, an unavoidable issue is that whatever approach organizations adopt it has to be affordable. In simple terms an organization has to ensure that it remains cost-effective. Consequently, organizations are unlikely to be able to develop a wholly 'ideal' reward package and choices have to be made. For example, as we discussed in HRM in Practice 9.2, there are often significant disparities between those at the top and bottom of the organization. Thus, although there may be a strong argument for paying all employees well, this aspiration may be somewhat compromised by the realities of ensuring affordability.

In sum, employers will be seeking an approach to reward management which is likely to have several principal objectives, including:

- attract and retain suitable employees;
- maintain or improve levels of employee performance;
- comply with employment legislation.

Clearly, the approach that an organization develops towards reward strategies does not exist in isolation, and there will be a number of other influences on pay determination that will affect such considerations, including:

- *Beliefs about the worth of the job*: for example, the size, responsibility, skill requirements and 'objectionableness' of duties.
- *Individual characteristics*: for example, age, experience, seniority, general qualifications, special skills, contribution, performance and potential.
- *Labour market*: the level and composition of any given reward package will be influenced by labour supply and demand at either national or local labour market level, and whether an organization is seeking to create a strong internal labour market.
- *Strength of bargaining groups*: for example, the potential for trade unions to influence pay determination. At any given time the relative strength of trade unions will be influenced by other external economic factors, such as the level of unemployment and feelings of job security.
- *Government intervention and regulatory pressures*: for example, public sector policy and other policy initiatives. Most obviously, the statutory national minimum wage, but also in terms of public policy towards aspects such as trade unions and collective bargaining.

There are a wide range of things which can conceivably influence and shape the rewards that employees may get and the 'market rate' for a particular sector or occupation. Let us now begin to develop this framework within the context of tourism and hospitality.

Generally when we are talking about remuneration in the tourism and hospitality industry, we can start with the fairly negative observation that relative to other industries the majority of jobs and occupations within the sector are poorly remunerated (Baum, 2006; Lucas, 2004). When we recognize that often there is low status ascribed to the industry, the perception held by a number of people is that for many tourism and hospitality is an employer of last resort, with mundane, degrading employment. The prevalence of low pay and perceptions about low status can be seen as being two key issues which continue to sustain the negative view many hold about tourism and hospitality

work (Lindsay and McQuaid, 2005). To begin to examine remuneration in tourism and hospitality in detail we should begin by recognizing the work of Mars and Mitchell (1976) and their notion of the 'total rewards system'. The 'total rewards system' has several aspects, which are: basic pay and subsidized food and lodging, which can be considered as the 'formalized' aspect of the wage–effort bargain; and other aspects which can be considered as more informal rewards, these being tips – which are semi-formalized – and 'fiddles and knock-offs', which are non-formalized. In reality, it is apparent that the notion of a 'total rewards system' is in fact a misnomer and there are a variety of other aspects in terms of a range of benefits that may be used by tourism and hospitality organizations to make up a reward package, a point which we will further consider later in the chapter. Nevertheless, at least initially the notion of the total rewards system provides a useful starting point to consider some fundamental issues and concerns in understanding reward practices in the tourism and hospitality industry, particularly with regard to basic pay and tipping.

## Basic or base pay

In a general sense, Torrington *et al.* (2011) note that there are a number of approaches to the setting of base pay rates. Here, of course, as we noted earlier in the chapter, managerial actions may be constrained by the manner in which the state influences pay determination, most obviously with the provision of minimum wage legislation. Employers also face limits in setting base pay with regard to the industry in which they operate, and especially with regard to how they remain competitive. Clearly, then, product and labour market characteristics will act to influence overall pay levels. In addition to these aspects, though, Torrington *et al.* also note the importance of external market comparisons and, for example, whether employers will pay at or above 'the going rate' for a particular job. There are also internal labour market mechanisms in which the skills and experience of employees will have a bearing on their pay. A further mechanism to determine pay is job evaluation, which is a systematic attempt to aid the establishment of differentials across jobs within a single employer. As a consequence, the organization's wage budget is divided among employees on the basis of assessing the nature and size of the job they do. The last mechanism identified by Torrington *et al.* is that of collective bargaining, where pay rates are determined through collective negotiations with trade unions or other employee representatives. As will be discussed in the following chapter, though, trade union representation has always been very low in the tourism and hospitality sector and collective bargaining has tended to have little influence on pay determination in the sector. Instead, determination of pay in tourism and hospitality has traditionally been a matter of managerial prerogative (Lucas, 2004).

In considering pay in tourism and hospitality the first point worth noting is the enduring and prevailing existence of low pay in the sector. For example, Wood (1997a: 69) notes how 'the majority of academic evidence concurs in suggesting both that basic rates of pay in hotels and catering are inadequate and employers are frequently ruthless in pursuing low-pay strategies'. Thus tourism and hospitality, and particularly the hotel and catering sub-sector, is low paid, both in absolute terms (i.e. purchasing power) and relative terms (compared to most other workers) (see HRM in Practice 9.4).

## HRM IN PRACTICE 9.4:
## Condemned to low pay? A history of low pay in the hospitality industry

*1975*: The Hotel and Catering Economic Committee suggested on the basis of low pay of 60p per hour for men and 55p per hour for women, 49 per cent of full-time men and 88 per cent of full-time women in hotels and catering were low paid, compared to 11 per cent and 53 per cent in 'all industries' across the economy.

*1989*: A British Hotels, Restaurants and Caterers Association survey revealed catering managers earned 27 per cent less than average non-manual workers and non-manual employees earned 28 per cent less than the average for manual workers.

*2003*: The Office of National Statistics' *New Earnings Survey 2003* found that hotel and restaurant employees were the lowest paid in the country. Average gross annual pay for full-time restaurant and hotel employees was just £16,533, compared to a UK average of £25,170.

*2010*: The Annual Survey of Hours and Earnings 2010 notes that the gross median full-time salary in the UK year ending April 2010 was £25,879. This figure can be compared to Accommodation and Food Service Activities, where the gross median full-time salary was £15,891. ASHE also notes that five of the 20 lowest gross full-time median salaries are in the hospitality industry, with the two lowest being waiter at £12,183 and bar staff at £12,228.

Derived from Annual Survey of Hours and Earnings (2010); Anon (2003b); Industrial Relations Services (2006b); Wood (1997a)

While the hotel and catering sub-sector is clearly low paid, the picture in other areas of the tourism sector may be more mixed. On the one hand, Baum (2006) notes how other sub-sectors such as travel agencies, airlines and tour operators, who are often staffed by young and female employees, also offer relatively poor remuneration. Often this will mean that for a number of front-line positions, such as travel advisors, the pay rate will also be at or near

the NMW. On the other hand, some positions in the broader tourism sector clearly pay higher wages. For example, travel agency, tour operator and other reservation service and related activities had a gross median full-time salary of £22,353 in 2010 (Annual Survey of Hours and Earnings, 2010). This latter figure is clearly significantly higher than the figures for the hotel and catering industry that we noted in HRM in Practice 9.4. Moreover, while relatively low pay may be true for a number of front-line positions in tourism and hospitality, it is a different picture for other occupational groups. For example, the gross median full-time salary in air transport was £32,757, though on average aircraft pilots earn £68,467 (Annual Survey of Hours and Earnings, 2010). Generally, though, as with the hospitality sub-sector, the bulk of employees within tourism-related occupations are likely to be relatively low paid (Baum, 2006). However, Baum also recognizes that, to an extent, within a number of tourism jobs aspects such as travel opportunities, uniforms and a generally pleasant working environment may encourage something of a trade-off between a desire for higher levels of pay and less acceptable conditions or other benefits (see HRM in Practice 9.5)

## HRM IN PRACTICE 9.5:
## Work as leisure

Guerrier and Adib (2004) conducted research by interviewing and observing 14 overseas tour reps in Mallorca. They found that for this group of employees there will often be a blurring between work and leisure, which may allow the worker to enjoy some of the benefits of leisure at work. As an example, overseas tour reps may not distinguish between their work and non-work lives. Customers may be their friends, their workplace is where they would 'hang out' anyway and their work does not demand a subordination of self but only a presentation of their authentic, fun-loving and sociable self.

## Wage regulation in tourism and hospitality

Although we noted above that pay determination has largely been dictated by the managerial prerogative, in more recent times the introduction of the NMW has introduced greater regulation by statutory means. The NMW marked a significant change in the British employment landscape and will be discussed in due course, especially as the greatest number of minimum-wage jobs are in hospitality (Low Pay Commission, 2011). To place the emergence of the NMW in context, it is worth briefly mentioning wages councils, which had previously played a role in setting a *de facto* minimum wage. For a large number of those working in tourism and hospitality, and particularly hotel and catering, the wages councils provided a minimum safety net with regard to wages for nearly 50 years. First introduced in 1909 as trade boards, and first covering the hospitality sector from the mid-1940s, wages councils peaked in the 1950s, covering over 3.5 million workers, providing surrogate collective bargaining for the low paid (Metcalf, 1999). At the time of their abolition in 1993 there were three wages councils that covered different sub-sectors of the commercial hospitality industry, and the mean hourly rate they set was £2.97 per hour, which was £115.96 for a 39-hour week or £6,029.92 per annum (Goldsmith *et al.*, 1997). From 1993 to the introduction of the NMW in 1999 there was no real protection for employees, and evidence suggests that a number of employers took advantage of this omission in an attempt to drive down wages (Lucas and Radiven, 1998).

The NMW is now a well-established aspect of the employment landscape in the UK, recently being described as 'one of the cornerstones of the UK labour market' (Low Pay Commission, 2011: vi), and is now endorsed by all major political parties. However, prior to its introduction there was vociferous debate about whether it should even be introduced. For example, the British Hospitality Association (BHA) was implacably opposed to the NMW. Much of the debate was centred on whether the argument was best understood from a moral or economic point of view (see Wood, 1997b for an overview of the debate). For example, in the interests of social justice, proponents of the NMW suggested that all employees should be 'decently' paid. On the other hand, opponents pointed to the likely rise in unemployment created by rising payroll costs stemming from the NMW. It was in this context that the NMW was introduced by the Labour government of Tony Blair. Once the NMW was accepted as a key policy plank of New Labour's notion of 'fairness at work', the main issues became practical ones, such as the level the wage was set at and the way it was implemented and enforced. To a large extent these issues were determined by the Low Pay Commission (LPC), which was established in July 1997 as a statutory body and has continued to play a key role even after the enactment of the minimum-wage legislation. The LPC consists of nine members who represent the interests of employers, unions and employees and 'objective' independent expert academics. Indeed, the LPC was able to largely agree on the terms of the implementation of the NMW and is suggested as providing an exemplar of a positive social partnership between employers and employees in particular (Metcalf, 1999; though see Thornley and Coffey 1999 for a more critical account) (see HRM in Practice 9.6).

The LPC reported in 1998, with the National Minimum Wage Act coming into being in the same year and the NMW actually starting on 1 April 1999, with the main rate set by the LPC at £3.60. In addition to the main rate there was also a development rate for 18–21-year-olds, which was initially set at £3 per hour, with 16–17-year-olds exempted. Two other key aspects which impacted on the tourism and hospitality industry were that tips and service charges distributed centrally via payroll could be counted against NMW, but cash tips paid by customers directly to staff would not be included (see HRM in Practice 9.7).

## HRM IN PRACTICE 9.6:
## The establishment of a High Pay Commission

In response to concerns about excessive pay and bonuses for those at the top of the organization, there were calls in 2009 for a High Pay Commission. Among other things, campaigners pointed out an employee working a 40-hour week earning the minimum wage would have to work around 226 years to receive the same remuneration as a FTSE 100 CEO earns in one year. Advocates of the High Pay Commission suggested that it should have the power to restrict excessive remuneration by, for example, introducing maximum wage ratios where the difference between the highest- and lowest-paid employee would be restricted, such as by a 20:1 ratio. It is estimated that top executives in FTSE 100 companies are paid an astonishing 145 times the average wage. The High Pay Commission was eventually established in November 2010 and developed an independent inquiry into high pay and boardroom pay across the public and private sectors in the UK. The Commission, which was established by the campaign organization Compass, with the support of the Joseph Rowntree Charitable Trust, produced its final report in 2011. The report had 12 recommendations, including calling for greater transparency in the calculation of executive pay, employee representation on remuneration committees, forcing companies to publish a pay ratio between the highest-paid executive and the company median and the establishment of a permanent body to monitor high pay, playing much the same role that the LPC plays at the lower end of the labour market.

Derived from High Pay Commission (2011); Labour Research Department (2011d); Stratton (2009)

## HRM IN PRACTICE 9.7:
## Ensuring tips are not part of the NMW?

From 2008 there was increasing recognition that the practice of using credit card tips via payroll to top up wages to the NMW was becoming increasingly contentious. In particular, the Unite trade union launched a campaign based on a Fair Tips Charter to ensure that both cash *and* credit card tips should go directly to staff. In response to the campaign the government agreed to end the practice of employers using tips to make up the minimum wage in October 2009. In response, voluntary codes of practice were drawn up by the government and the BHA. Despite these codes of practice, concerns still remain about the number of hospitality employers who are still not passing on credit card tips to staff. Indeed, the Unite union has suggested that the code of conduct is 'not worth the paper it is printed on'.

Derived from Druce (2010); Vaughan (2010)

Lastly, there was also an accommodation offset in which a maximum figure of £20 could be deducted by employers for the cost of employees' accommodation. The reaction to the NMW was mixed. On the one hand, employers views were generally favourable about what they felt was an acceptable rate. For example, the BHA applauded what they considered to be a 'realistic' wage, supported the 'sensible' level for 18–21-year-olds, but expressed regret that there were no regional variations (Clavey, 1998). There were also some concerns from some tourism employers that the accommodation offset would count towards payment of the NMW but only at the rate of £20 per week (at the time of writing this offset now stands at £32.27 per week). On the other hand, trade unions and the low pay campaigners were less sanguine at what they felt to be an overly prudent and overcautious rate. As Bill Morris, then general secretary of the TGWU, pithily put it, 'Thank you for the principle, shame about the rate' (cited in Metcalf, 1999: 193). Similarly, Rodney Bickerstaffe, then general secretary of Unison, applauded the implementation of the NMW while also suggesting that '£3.60 for an hour of anyone's life at the end of the 20th century in one of the richest countries on earth is not something to be proud of' (cited in Clavey, 1998: 10; also see HRM in Practice 9.8).

## HRM IN PRACTICE 9.8:
## A living wage?

Since the inception of the NMW, at what many trade unions felt to be an unnecessarily low level, there has been much discussion of what is an 'acceptable' level for the NMW. More recently, a campaign has emerged in support of a 'living wage'. Originating in America, the Living Wage campaign aims to address what it considers to be 'poverty wages'. At the time of writing it is suggested that the living wage for London should be £8.30 per hour and £7.20 per hour outside of London. With prime ministerial support (David Cameron has suggested that 'the living wage is an idea whose time has come'), mayoral support in London and a commitment from the London 2012 Olympic project team to the living wage, the campaign has enjoyed a good deal of success in raising the issue of low pay. Despite this success generally, campaigners have had less success in persuading tourism and hospitality employers that the living wage is appropriate, with the BHA recently suggesting that 'now is not the time to introduce a London Living Wage'.

Derived from Greater London Authority (2011); Sharkey (2009b); see also http://www.citizensuk.org/campaigns/living-wage-campaign

Despite the disappointment on the part of trade unions and other lobbying bodies at the rate at which the NMW was set, approximately two million workers did receive a wage increase as a result of the legislation, with many

of these workers being women, part-timers, youths, non-whites and single parents (Metcalf, 1999). Of course, many of these workers were to be found in tourism and hospitality with the LPC, estimating that around 800,000, or 42 per cent, were in the retail and hospitality sectors (Labour Research Department, 1998).

Although the tourism and hospitality industry was disproportionately affected in terms of the number of employees who benefited from the NMW, due to its low rate it has been suggested that in reality there has been 'minimum impact' and 'much ado about nothing', even in smaller businesses (Adam-Smith *et al.*, 2003; Rowson, 2000; Turnbull, 2000). Indeed, a survey undertaken of low-paying sectors by the IDS prior to the introduction of the NMW found that a number of larger tourism and hospitality companies, such as Center Parcs and Marriott, were already paying at or over the rate at the point of implementation (Income Data Services, 1999; though see HRM in Practice 9.9).

## HRM IN PRACTICE 9.9:
## Pizza Hut and Pizza Express: taking away from their employees?

Pizza giants Pizza Hut and Pizza Express found themselves at the centre of controversy when the NMW was implemented. Both companies responded to the implementation of the NMW by seeking to rein-in costs. Pizza Hut removed paid taxi fares home for their staff, claiming that they could no longer afford this benefit with the introduction of the NMW. Pizza Express initially retained a basic rate of pay of £3.10, with the expectation that tips would make up the shortfall, despite the law saying that tips could only be included if they were paid through the bill. As a result of this decision the company was ultimately forced to pay out £250,000 in backpay to waiting staff. More generally, concerns have been expressed about the extent of abuse of the NMW in hospitality. In particular, concerns have been expressed about the possible exploitation of migrant workers, who will often be afraid of speaking out for fear of losing their jobs. Indeed, hospitality businesses are much more likely to be probed by tax officials to ensure that they are paying the NMW.

Derived from Anon (1999a, 1999b); Harmer (2010b); Thomas (2009)

Employer concerns about issues such as loss of competitiveness and job losses have also proved to be wide of the mark (Low Pay Commission, 2011; Labour Research Department, 2008b), and in the period March 1999 to March 2006 total employment rose from 6.3 million to 6.7 million in the eight sectors most affected by the NMW, including hospitality (Metcalf, 2009).

As was noted earlier in the chapter, the LPC having initially recommended the rate for the NMW has had the responsibility of reviewing its operation. In the period since 1999 the LPC has recommended regular annual uprating, though this has reflected prevailing economic circumstances rather than any particular uprating formula. Interestingly, the minimum wage has increased by nearly 65 per cent between its inception in April 1999 to October 2010, an increase that was much higher than price inflation or average earnings growth (Low Pay Commission, 2011). However, in more recent reports the LPC has acknowledged that the phase in which they are committed to increasing the NMW above average earnings is now complete and in future will have no presumptions that increases above average earnings are required. Importantly, the LPC also recommended that 16–17-year-olds be brought under the umbrella of the NMW from October 2004 (see Table 9.1). Bringing 16–17-year-olds under the aegis of the NMW again disproportionately impacted on tourism and related industries, with retail and hospitality accounting for 45 per cent and 21 per cent, respectively, of the overall total brought under minimum wage protection (Low Pay Commission, 2006).

Although the NMW is a relatively recent phenomenon in the UK, nearly all OECD countries have minimum wage setting arrangements (Metcalf, 1999).

| TABLE 9.1 How the UK NMW has evolved since 1999 | | | |
|---|---|---|---|
| Date | Adult rate 21 and over | Development rate 18–20-year-olds | 16–17-year-olds rate |
| 1 April 1999 | £3.60 | £3.00 | – |
| 1 October 2000 | £3.70 | £3.20 | – |
| 1 October 2001 | £4.10 | £3.50 | – |
| 1 October 2002 | £4.20 | £3.60 | – |
| 1 October 2003 | £4.50 | £3.80 | – |
| 1 October 2004 | £4.85 | £4.10 | £3.00 |
| 1 October 2005 | £5.05 | £4.25 | £3.00 |
| 1 October 2006 | £5.35 | £4.45 | £3.30 |
| 1 October 2007 | £5.52 | £4.60 | £3.40 |
| 1 October 2008 | £5.73 | £4.77 | £3.53 |
| 1 October 2009 | £5.80 | £4.83 | £3.57 |
| 1 October 2010 | £5.93 | £4.92 | £3.64 |
| 1 October 2011 | £6.08 | £4.98 | £3.68 |
| 1 October 2012 | £6.19 | No change | No change |
| Source: adapted from http://www.lowpay.gov.uk | | | |

A number of Scandinavian countries, as well as countries such as Germany and Italy, rely on collective bargaining mechanisms to set minimum wages, ordinarily at a sectoral level. In a large number of countries there are statutory requirements and it is interesting to compare the UK with a number of other countries (Table 9.2).

| TABLE 9.2 Comparison of the level of the adult minimum wage across selected countries in 2010 | | | |
|---|---|---|---|
| Country (and year first introduced) | Minimum wage (£) | Age at which full rate usually applies | Adult rate as a percentage of full-time median earning |
| Australia (1996, some from since 1907) | 9.04 | 21 | 54.4/51.0* |
| Belgium (1975) | 6.86 | 21 | 50.8 |
| Canada (women 1918–30, men 1930–59) | 5.69 | 16 | 43.8 |
| France (1950, 1970 in current form) | 7.44 | 18 | 59.8 |
| Ireland (2000) | 7.27 | 20 | 51.1 |
| Japan (1959, 1968 in current form) | 5.55 | – | 36.2 |
| Netherlands (1968) | 6.86 | 23 | 43.5 |
| Portugal (1974) | 2.30 | 16 | 46.0 |
| Spain (1963, 1976 in current form) | 3.07 | 16 | 37.8 |
| United Kingdom (1999) | 5.93 | 22 | 52.2/46.1* |
| United States (1938) | 4.65 | 20 | 35.5 |

Note
* The figure depends on the earnings survey used.
Source: derived from Low Pay Commission (2011); Metcalf (1999)

## Review and reflect

In considering debates about the NMW and the issues outlined in HRM in practice 9.2 and 9.6, is there an argument for a *maximum* wage?

In addition to basic pay there are a number of other aspects which can be considered in reviewing payment issues in tourism and hospitality. The Income Data Services (2005b, 2005c) note a number of additional areas where employees could enhance basic pay in hotels, pubs and restaurants. Just over half of the 20 hotels they surveyed offered a premium for night work. This payment could be a flat rate, for example night porters in one hotel could earn £1,800 more per year than day porters; alternatively, some of the surveyed hotels paid a premium for those hours worked at night, with the IDS citing the example of food and beverage staff receiving an additional 30p an hour for every hour worked past midnight. With regard to the broader issue of bonus and incentive schemes, all but two of the surveyed hotels offered a bonus or incentive scheme. Many of these schemes attempt to incentivize front-line staff to offer good-quality service in showing appropriate behaviours and attitudes and may use some of the customer appraisal techniques discussed in the previous chapter, such as mystery guests. In over half of the schemes payments are related to sales, with profit- and performance-related payments being the next most common measure. The criteria differed across the hotels. The IDS cite the example of Hilton, where heads of division receive a bonus based on profit, service and people management, whereas staff received a bonus based on sales. In one of the surveyed hotels food and beverage staff received a bonus based on service charge. Only one of the surveyed hotels had a share option scheme and one also operated payments for guest mentions. A further issue is that of pay progression; the Income Data Services (2008a) note how a number of the fast-food companies that they surveyed linked pay to progression. For example, McDonald's links pay increases to performance appraisals, which are based on four performance ratings. Employees deemed as 'unsatisfactory' or 'needs improvement' do not receive any pay increase, those with a 'significant performer' get a 3 per cent rise, while those deemed 'exceptional' receive a 5 per cent increase. Pay progression may also be linked to the completion of training in Pret A Manger, where employees have to pass three assessments and written tests to progress. Similarly, within the travel industry a survey of salaries reported by the Industrial Relations Services (2006c) found that bonus payments were common at all levels of the industry. For example, half of the companies in the survey paid commission to employees, based on their sales.

## The practice of tipping

The notion of tipping is important in a number of ways, not least due to its economic importance. For example, Azar (2009) suggests that consumers tip over $40 billion per year in the United States. Tipping may allow some tourism and hospitality workers to significantly augment their income, though the potential impact with regards to issues such as job satisfaction and emotional

well-being equally need to be considered. Ogbonna and Harris (2002b) also note the possibility of tipping being used as a managerial mechanism to encourage individualization and subjugation of employees. Tipping in this latter view becomes an important managerial tool for the indirect control of employees in the employee–customer interaction, as well as potentially suppressing interest in more collective power, such as through trade union organization. Ogbonna and Harris (2002b) note how employees in the UK restaurant they studied resisted managerial attempts to resort to a system in which tips would be kept by the company in return for a 10 per cent increase in pay; in addition, in the same case study management threatened to abolish tipping if the employees became unionized.

## Review and reflect

What are likely to be some of the financial and emotional hazards for tourism and hospitality employees who are reliant on tips to sustain a reasonable wage?

It is important to note that tipping is very much culturally bound and, as Ogbonna and Harris (2002b: 726) recognize, 'although tipping is an internationally recognisable behaviour, the actual practice is heavily influenced by societal cultural considerations'. For example, tipping is widely practised within the United States, but is not as widespread in the UK and elsewhere (see HRM in Practice 9.10).

## HRM IN PRACTICE 9.10:
## Tipping in different countries

The United States is generally recognized as having the most highly developed approach to tipping. For example, it is not unusual for hotel guests to have to tip five people before they get to their room. In the United States, for many tipped positions the general expectation is that the customer should tip at least 15 per cent. Tipping is less prevalent in other countries such as Australia, New Zealand and Sweden. For example, in New Zealand tipping is not considered a normal cultural practice and movement to a US-type approach appears unlikely. Managers and employees in New Zealand saw the institutionalization of tipping in the United States as distasteful and were particularly unanimous in their denunciation of the US practice of using tips to boost poor wages. It was felt that employers should fairly remunerate employees and that this should not be left to customers. In many Southeast Asian countries it is not customary to tip and tipping can be a sensitive topic, especially if social conventions are breached and people 'lose face'. In contrast, research in France – where tipping is unusual – found that if a waitress touched customers she got more and better tips. This 'touch effect' is found in other countries, such as the United States, but seems particularly pronounced in France due to the tactile nature of social relations.

Derived from Callen and Tyson (2000); Casey (2001); Dewald (2001); Gueguen and Jacob (2005)

Tipping is largely driven by socio-cultural norms and/or individual conscience. In relation to tourism and hospitality we should recognize that some workers are in a position to enhance basic wages from tips, but this is only true for those in tipped positions. Even for those in tipped positions it should also be acknowledged that tips are notoriously unpredictable. Lynn (2001; and see also Lynn, 2003) conducted a meta-analysis of a number of studies that had examined the relationship between restaurant tipping and service quality and found a weak relationship. Consequently, for many front-line staff tipping may be more influenced by external factors such as the race and gender of the customer, prevailing weather conditions or even the result of football or rugby matches that are played near the restaurant (Ogbonna and Harris, 2002b).

The point is often made as well that tipping means losing sight of the fact that the vast majority of people in tipping positions are generally in low-wage, low-status occupations. Despite this point there is an argument, usually from employers, that tipping is a good motivator and that abolishing tips and paying higher wages is not the answer, while alternatively others argue that tips are an unwelcome part of the tourism and hospitality industry and a 'fair' fixed living wage would be more desirable (Wood, 1997a). Critics of tipping would also argue that the practice weakens social relationships as a number of inter-actions in tourism and hospitality become overtly economic exchanges. It is also argued that tipping increases power differences, as in menial low-status jobs it reinforces and makes salient the inferior status of workers. For example, Ogbonna and Harris (2002b) found that a number of waiters and waitresses they interviewed felt that they were often abused physically and mentally and had to accept subtle forms of sexual exploitation. Engaging in sexualized flirting with customers may be part of a process that degrades and debases front-line workers, often for comparatively little financial reward (see Chapter 11). There is also the final related point that tipping tends to encourage a very individualistic view of the workplace and does little to sustain harmonious workplace relationships and that tipping tends to weaken organizational commitment.

Clearly there is much debate about the efficacy and morality of tipping, though given the reality of this practice still being prevalent in a number of

tourism and hospitality environments it is worthwhile briefly considering the underlying motives for tipping and how servers may maximize their tips. With regard to motives underlying tipping, Lynn *et al.* (1993) suggest the following:

- desire for good service in the future;
- desire for social approval;
- to compensate servers equitably for their work – i.e. reward their effort;
- desire for status and power.

Furthermore, Lynn (1996, 2003; Lynn and McCall, 2009) reports on research which suggests a number of ways in which servers are likely to increase their tips, including:

- server introduction in a genuine and professional manner;
- squatting next to the table, though this is more likely to work in a casual dining environment, compared to fine-dining, where it may be considered inappropriate;
- smiling at customers;
- touching customers;
- credit card insignias on tip trays;
- writing 'thank you' on bills;
- drawing a 'happy face' on bills;
- the server wearing a flower in their hair and other means of personalizing their appearance;
- entertaining customers by, for example, telling a joke;
- forecasting good weather;
- calling the customer by name.

Of course, there are several obvious caveats to the above discussion. First, the research is based in the United States, where tipping is a culturally bound phenomenon. Second, not all of these tip-enhancing techniques will necessarily be appropriate for every type of restaurant or service setting, or indeed every server. Consequently, some of these aspects may work better than others and should be used carefully, both by individual employees and managers who encourage servers to use such techniques.

## Fiddles and knock-offs

While basic pay, accommodation and tipping represent the more formalized aspects of the reward package in tourism and hospitality, it is also briefly worth considering fiddles and knock-offs. Mars and Nicod (1984) found a large range of fiddles in their work and note how 'they are acts of dishonesty which the people involved do not consider dishonest' (p. 116). Fiddles generally involve pilferage from organizations, usually in a monetary sense. Knock-offs can also be considered a form of fiddle involving the purloining of (usually) small items such as soap, linen and towels. Generally these practices are institutionalized within the organization and may be dependent on a degree of management and supervisory collusion, although certain boundaries and parameters will be set to delineate what is 'acceptable'. Indeed, with regard to this notion of acceptability, organizations may tighten up on a 'blind eye' approach to fiddles and knock-offs when business slackens and the organization is looking to reduce labour costs (Lucas, 2004). A further important point noted by Wood (1997a) concerns the notion of individualism and the extent to which this is exacerbated by these practices. Thus,

> Whatever arrangements exist for the allocation of fiddles and knock-offs there are some grounds for believing that, as with tipping, these aspects of informal rewards militate against the development of a collective workplace or occupational ethic, fostering individualism and competitiveness.
>
> (p. 88)

## Other benefits

Although Mars and Mitchell (1976) characterized their model as a 'total rewards system', many critics have suggested that the use of 'total' in this instance is clearly a misnomer, and neglects a variety of other rewards which may be made available by the organization. For example, in their survey of a number of hotel companies, the Income Data Services (2009) found that larger or chain hotels are likely to provide free staff uniforms (and sometimes dry cleaning), free meals while on duty and discounts, including overnight stays. Additionally, other benefits provided by hotels include pension and sick-pay schemes, private medical insurance and discounts on gym membership. A similar survey conducted in the travel industry and reported by the Industrial Relations Services (2006c) also noted a range of benefits. Over 70 per cent of the 34 companies surveyed offered a company pension scheme, though only 11 per cent of companies offered a final salary pension scheme. Over half of the companies offered private health insurance, with 39 per cent offering life insurance (see HRM in Practice 9.11).

There may also be a degree of differentiation between different occupational groups in terms of the benefits available. For example, the Industrial Relations Services (2006d) report how First Choice Holidays reviewed the total reward package offered to pilots and as a consequence developed a 'Pilot Change Agenda'. The rigorous entry requirements and ongoing training and competency testing at least twice a year are indicative of the high level of responsibility associated with being a pilot. Consequently, a key part of the change agenda

**HRM IN PRACTICE 9.11:**
**Benefits in TUI UK and Ireland**

TUI UK and Ireland is part of TUI Travel Plc and has recently introduced a new benefits package. The package was developed over 2008 and introduced in 2009. Dione Matthews, reward manager at TUI, recognized how the company was seeking to develop a 'total reward approach' which aimed to communicate to employees how their basic pay was just one part of an overall reward package. The new benefits package was named 'Be Rewarded' and offered employees a range of new benefits. For example, employees in the company can now take advantage of a new holiday concession scheme which gives them discounts on package holidays and flights. In addition, the company also offers travel discounts, which increase with length of service. Employees can also pass on savings on the company's holidays to family and friends, such as £60 off the web price of a long-haul holiday. The company also seeks to reward long service with their long-service awards. On their tenth anniversary in the company employees receive £200 worth of TUI travel vouchers, and this rises to £400 for 15 years and £600 for 20 years. One long-serving employee who had worked for the company for 45 years received an award of £1,600 of vouchers.

Derived from Income Data Services (2010b)

was to ensure the pilots felt valued. Among other things this led to the company reviewing the pay and other rewards offered to pilots and the development of a new 'total reward' perspective. Traditionally, pilots already had a very good reward package including: competitive base pay; two final-salary pension schemes; a money purchase pension scheme; free medical checks; private medical insurance; concessions of £1,000 per year to spend on First Choice holidays, and the option to buy further holidays on a tax-efficient basis; free uniforms; duty and subsistence allowances; share plans; voluntary benefits such as childcare vouchers and other insurance; and generous annual leave entitlement. Under the new agenda additional aspects of the total reward system included a new bonus plan that linked payments to adherence to corporate values and desired behaviour or performance, a new share plan scheme, flexible working options and a new long-service award scheme. The nature of this package is very much driven by the highly competitive environment in which the company is operating and the unique nature of pilots as a group of employees in terms of their skills and qualities.

Although the above discussion illustrates the range of additional benefits that could potentially be made available to employees, in reality research suggests that a number of tourism and hospitality workers are less likely to enjoy such benefits. For example, Lucas (2004) cites figures from the Workplace

Employment Relations Survey (WERS) which compares the tourism and hospitality industry with all private sector services in terms of non-pay terms and conditions. With regard to employer pension scheme, company car/allowance, private health insurance and sick pay in excess of statutory requirements, tourism and hospitality employers were significantly lagging behind other employers in both private service sector and all industrial sectors. In that sense it seems likely that larger organizations are far more likely to be in a position to offer a more sophisticated reward package, compared to SMEs.

## Conclusion

We have examined a range of issues which cover rewards and payment, which demonstrate that arguably a fair and effective deal is still some way off for the bulk of the tourism and hospitality workforce, and especially those in the hotel and catering sub-sector. In an ideal world the effort–reward bargain would satisfy all parties, but the reality is different; for employers the strategy that is pursued seems to coincide with the controlling operations and cost aspects of Torrington *et al.*'s (2011) framework, and for the employees there is little choice and no real sense of aspiring to any of the loftier principles embodied in the Torrington *et al.* framework. Furthermore, prescriptive accounts of 'total reward' schemes that support the notion of employees picking and choosing from a range of options to tailor a pay and benefits package that meets their particular needs should be treated with some caution in tourism and hospitality, where the cafeteria approach remains rare. Of course, as we acknowledged, there are exceptions to low pay both sub-sectorally and occupationally, though for the majority of employees in tourism and hospitality notions of 'fair' remuneration remain somewhat elusive. Indeed, this may seem rather paradoxical, as often those entrusted with delivering high-quality service may be the lowest paid in the organization.

## Discussion questions

- What do you understand by the term 'total reward'?
- Why have employers and employees got differing objectives when it comes to pay?
- Should pay levels for chief executives be determined solely by what the market dictates?
- Outline arguments for and against the 'living wage'.
- Is it right that many tourism and hospitality employees rely on tips to make up their wages?

## Further reading

Adam-Smith, D., Norris, G. and Williams, S. (2003) 'Continuity or change? The implications of the National Minimum Wage for work and employment in the hospitality industry', *Work, Employment and Society*, 17, 1, 29–47.

High Pay Commission (2011) *Cheques with Balances: Why Tackling High Pay is in the National Interest – Final Report of the High Pay Commission*, available at http://highpaycommission.co.uk/wp-content/uploads/2011/11/HPC_final_report_WEB.pdf

Lynn, M. and McCall, M. (2009) 'Techniques for increasing servers' tips', *Cornell Hospitality Quarterly*, 50, 2, 198–208.

Metcalf, D. (2009) 'Why has the British National Minimum Wage had little or no impact on employment?', *Journal of Industrial Relations*, 50, 3, 489–512.

Ogbonna, E. and Harris, L. (2002) 'Institutionalization of tipping as a source of managerial control', *British Journal of Industrial Relations*, 40, 4, 725–52.

Wood, R.C. (1997) 'Rhetoric, reason and rationality: the national minimum wage debate and the UK hospitality industry', *International Journal of Hospitality Management*, 16, 4, 329–44.

## Recommended websites

There is an interesting report on the low pay endemic in the American restaurant industry which can be accessed at http://rocunited.org/tipped-over-the-edge-gender-inequity-in-the-restaurant-industry. Among other things, the report notes that the federal minimum wage for servers and other tipped workers has been frozen at only $2.13 per hour for the past 20 years.

For an interesting discussion of the campaign towards a 'living wage' see http://www.livingwage.org.uk. The US version of the campaign also has a website at http://www.letjusticeroll.org/index.html

The Low Pay Commission has lots of useful material on their site at http://www.lowpay.gov.uk

You can find details about the code of practice on tipping at: http://www.bis.gov.uk/files/file52948.pdf and http://www.bha.org.uk/wp-content/uploads/2010/10/BHA-Code-of-Practice-Service-Charges-2009.pdf

There is lots of interesting material on tipping at http://tippingresearch.com, http://www.tipping.org/index.shtml and http://www.bbc.co.uk/dna/h2g2/alabaster/A640018

## Additional material

Go to www.routledge.com/cw/nickson to find PowerPoint slides, chapter commentaries, test banks and additional case studies for each chapter.

# Employee relations, involvement and participation

## CHAPTER OBJECTIVES

**This chapter considers the notions of employee relations, employee involvement and employee participation to review the extent to which employees may influence managerial decision-making. In particular, the chapter aims to:**

- Recognize debates about employee/industrial relations.

- Assess the differing ways in which conflict may be conceptualized and resolved in the tourism and hospitality workplace.

- Consider the role, or lack of it, for trade unions in the tourism and hospitality industry.

- Appreciate how employee involvement and employee participation mechanisms can be used by tourism and hospitality organizations.

COMPANION @ WEBSITE

## Introduction

The idea of some kind of employee influence in organizational decision-making is one that seems to attract much support among all the parties who are involved in the employment relationship; that is, employers, employees, trade unions and the state. Indeed, as Blyton and Turnbull (2004) note, recent years have seen renewed interest in employee involvement and participation. This renewed interest is partly explicable by the attempts by the 'New' Labour governments (1997–2010) in particular to promote 'partnership' at work as well as the influence of the European social agenda, which has encouraged greater employee participation through a number of European Union (EU) directives. However, although there may be universal support in principle for the need for employee influence in decision-making, in reality there are likely to be sharply differing views on the degree (the extent to which employees are able to meaningfully influence managerial decisions), level (task, departmental, establishment or corporate), range (the range of subject matters likely to be discussed, from what might be trivial issues such as food in the staff canteen to fundamental strategic decisions) and form (either direct or indirect through representation) of such influence (Marchington and Wilkinson, 2005b).

Recognizing the above discussion, Blyton and Turnbull (2004) suggest a continuum from no involvement through to employee control, although in reality most organizations are likely to fit somewhere in between in the categories of receiving information, joint consultation and joint decision-making, which in a generic sense are likely to be characterized as being either employee involvement, participation or industrial democracy. Underpinning much of this discussion is a need to understand the nature of employee relations and the manner in which many argue that this notion marks a major shift from a more collective view of the employment relationship as embodied in the notion of industrial relations. Initially, then, the chapter will consider this debate about how best to conceptualize the contemporary employment landscape. Following this discussion we will move on and examine how these debates can be understood with regard to the 'frames of reference' (Fox, 1966) adopted by management in terms of dealing with potential conflict in the workplace. Conflict can be considered at a number of levels, one of which is the potential conflict of interests between trade unions and employers. However, the tourism and hospitality industry is often suggested as being one where trade unions have little or no influence. The veracity or otherwise of this view will be discussed, including the issue of why tourism and hospitality employees may or may not join trade unions. Having considered one mechanism for articulating an employee 'voice', that of trade unions, the chapter moves on to consider a range of other mechanisms which seek to involve employees in the decision-making process in organizations through the processes of employee involvement and participation.

## Employee or industrial relations?

In discussing the nature of employee relations in the UK economy, the Chartered Institute of Personnel and Development (CIPD) (2005c: 5) suggests that 'the term "industrial relations" summons up today a set of employment relationships that no longer widely exist, except in specific sectors, and even there, in modified form'. In this view industrial relations can be thought of as denoting formal arrangements between employers and trade unions, in which collective bargaining would provide the mechanism for joint regulation that would give trade unions a say in key management decisions. This view of industrial relations held by the CIPD is by no means universally held and, among others, Sisson (2005) responded with a wide-ranging rejoinder questioning

whether the description of industrial relations as being anachronistic is indeed true. While at one level this debate about the nature of 'industrial' or 'employee' relations might seem like a typical academic parlour game, it is nevertheless important to recognize that at the heart of this debate are a number of crucial concerns which are likely to significantly influence arguments about the nature of employee involvement and participation. To appreciate such debates it is worthwhile briefly considering how industrial and employee relations may be considered different.

Industrial relations has its roots very much in the social sciences and draws on a number of academic disciplines such as economics, law, sociology, psychology, history and politics. The scope of industrial relations has traditionally encompassed the study of social institutions, legislative controls and social mechanisms and the way they provided the framework for interactions between the key actors in the employment relationship: government, employers and their organizations and employees and their organizations. At the heart of industrial relations lies the notion of how these partners manage the employment relationship, which denotes an economic, social and political relationship for which employees provide manual, mental, emotional and aesthetic labour in exchange for rewards allocated by employers. Often, debates about the employment relationship centre on the notion of the effort–reward bargain. As we saw in the previous chapter, the effort–reward bargain refers to the manner in which employees are rewarded for the effort they expend on behalf of the organization. The potential conflict that would arise in the allocation of effort from employees and reward from employers would often be resolved through the use of, often adversarial, collective bargaining, where trade unions and employers would come together to seek a resolution based on their relative strengths. Industrial relations, then, is often thought of as denoting the formal arrangements to manage the employment relationship that existed in large manufacturing plants where the world of work largely consisted of full-time, unionized, male manual workers (Blyton and Turnbull, 2004).

By contrast, 'employee relations' emerged as a term in the 1980s in an attempt to capture the changing nature of the employment landscape. In particular, as the Chartered Institute of Personnel and Development (2005c: 3) argues, 'employee relations is now about managing in a more complex, fast-moving environment: the political, trade union and legislative climates are all shifting. In general, the agenda is no longer about trade unions.' Within this view of employee relations a key aspect of what is considered distinctive about the term is a lack of trade union influence. In addition, employee relations has also tended to be considered as denoting the changing nature of employment in terms of the shift from manufacturing to service employment and the feminization of the labour market. These shifts have had a significant impact on employment and work – for example, the increasing number of employees who work 'non-standard' hours or the much greater involvement of the customer as a third party in the employment relationship (Lucas, 2004).

As we acknowledged earlier, there are many who would argue that these are rather simplistic interpretations of the terms (Sisson, 2005, 2008). To an extent, though, the above discussion does have an element of truth and at the least it is useful in denoting key shifts in the nature of employment in recent years. In particular, the shift from manufacturing to service employment and reliance on collective institutions to a more individualized view of the employment relationship are clearly apparent (see Advisory, Conciliation and Arbitration Service, 2011a, for a recent review of the likely future of workplace relations).

## Frames of reference and the resolution of conflict

Notwithstanding the debate about the terms industrial and employee relations, a key point that remains is the likelihood of conflict or competing interests existing in the employment relationship. Of course, these aspects may also exist alongside more cooperative relationships, and this notion of how employers view both conflict and cooperation can be further appreciated by drawing upon the unitary and pluralist 'frames of reference' (Fox, 1966) through which the employment relationship can be viewed.

Within the unitary frame of reference, the metaphor of a football team is often used to illustrate this perspective on the employment relationship (Marchington and Wilkinson, 2005b). In this view organizations are conceptualized as a team in which all participants are aiming for the same goal, have similar objectives and are not in conflict with one another. The unitary perspective sees the organization as a cohesive and integrated team, where everybody shares common values, interests and objectives to achieve the goal of the efficient functioning of the enterprise. Within this approach a key element is the recognition of the managerial prerogative and the unrestrained 'right to manage'. Managers are the single source of authority and act in a benign and rational manner for the benefit of employees. Resultantly, a unitary view of the employment relationship would be framed and constrained by the idea that conflict and dissidence are unnecessary, undesirable, irrational and pathologically deviant behaviour. Any conflict that does arise will be rationalized as being a reflection of frictional rather than structural problems within the organization. Consequently, trade unions are viewed as being an unimportant and unnecessary intrusion into the organization. One final point about the unitary perspective is the need to recognize that there may be differing styles of management ranging from authoritarian to paternalistic, and the latter in particular may underpin a more sophisticated unitarism which finds organizational expression in talk of 'soft' human resource management (HRM) in particular. Although the unitary perspective may be easy to criticize for advocating an unrealistic view of the workplace, evidence suggests that many British managers still hold unitaristic views of the workplace. Indeed, Lucas (2004) suggests that unitaristic thinking is apparent in large parts of the

tourism and hospitality industry; and often this unitaristic thinking is the less sophisticated version premised on cost-minimization and 'unbridled' individualism, which creates a 'poor' employment experience for many in the industry.

The 'them and us' attitude which unitarism eschews is something that is accepted as being integral to the pluralist perspective on the employment relationship. Conflict is accepted as being inevitable and rational because of the plurality of interests in the organizational setting, though the resolution of such conflict may be through differing approaches. We can consider this in terms of both collective and individual approaches.

Collective approaches to conflict resolution will envisage a role for trade unions to represent the interests of employees, though there may be very different approaches adopted by trade unions depending on the institutional context in which bargaining with employers takes places. For example, in the UK the relationship has often been characterized as being reflective of a 'them and us' culture, where the relationship between employers and trade unions was antagonistic. In attempts to institutionalize conflict in such an environment the bargaining process would often be concerned with power bargaining or zero-sum 'winner takes all'-type bargaining. In such a process the relative economic strength of the employers and trade unions could determine the eventual resolution of any such dispute. By contrast, in a number of European countries the relationship between employers and trade unions has been rather more consensual and premised on notions such as 'social partnership' and 'social dialogue' (see HRM in Practice 10.1).

## HRM IN PRACTICE 10.1:
## Social partnership in Lufthansa

At a time when the airline industry faced huge challenges in the 1990s and the post-9/11 era, Lufthansa drew on the institutionally embedded social partnership approach common in Germany to stave off the worst effects of a downturn in the sector. At the heart of this social partnership is an understanding that the company will consult and negotiate with employees through works councils and trade unions. In particular, by considering the employee 'voice' the company chose to approach restructuring in a manner which did not lead to redundancies and a short-term response to the challenges in the industry. This approach was in contrast to a number of other airline companies who made large-scale job cuts in the wake of 9/11. By a process of consultation and negotiation Lufthansa was able to agree wage concessions and enhanced labour flexibility, through things like changes in working time and voluntary unpaid leave to avoid redundancies. Though these changes were made, overall there was no major deterioration in the terms and conditions of employees. Consequently, the trust and cooperation between the social partners was able to survive the immediate post-9/11 era and allowed the company to consider a brighter future without the latent mistrust stemming from widespread redundancies, a problem which faced other airlines.

Derived from Turnbull *et al.* (2004)

As we have already noted, many argue that British public policy in recent years, and especially in the New Labour years of 1997–2010, has attempted to foster a climate which is more concerned with partnership along European lines, a process that has also been driven to an extent by a number of EU directives encouraging greater consultation between employers and employees. As well as collective approaches to conflict, disagreement can also take place at a more individual level. Again, conflict is seen as inevitable but the resolution of such conflict does not take place within a collective framework or with the involvement of trade unions. Instead, the employment relationship is based on employment contracts determined by market forces and common law and 'freely' negotiated between employers and employees. Conflict may arise as employees seek the highest level of reward, best conditions and least exacting work, while employers seek the lowest level of payment, least costly conditions and most efficacious and flexible use of labour.

In addition, a final perspective initially developed by Fox (1974) and then refined by others, adopts a more radical view of the employment relationship. In this radical/Marxist approach the employment relationship is seen not so much in organizational terms, but in a much wider social, political and economic framework. In this broader analysis of capitalist society, capital and labour are conceptualized as being engaged in an antagonistic 'power struggle' that is waged very much on capital's terms. Marxists or neo-Marxists argue that trade union power is illusory and only maintains the delusion of a balance of power. In its purest form the Marxist perspective suggests that only by the working class gaining control will real equality be established. In contemporary market-driven economies moves to worker control are very unlikely. Nevertheless, it is important to recognize that the radical perspective provides the theoretical framework for more critical views of the employment relationship, such as labour process analysis.

## Review and reflect

Think of your current workplace or where you have previously spent time on work placement. Consider which frame of reference best describes how conflict is managed. Is this the best way to manage conflict?

There have been a number of significant changes in the employment relations landscape in recent years. The shift from industrial to employee relations and the decline of trade union power and influence has led to increasing talk of a more unitaristic and individualistic view of the employment relationship. As a consequence there is often increasingly talk of the 'death' of trade unions, a view which is now considered in more detail.

## Trade unions: in terminal decline?

A wide range of factors has contributed to a decline in trade union membership in the UK in recent years. In particular, the structural changes in the economy and the decline in so-called 'heavy' industries such as coal-mining, ship-building and steel has particularly impacted on the unions. Equally, as we noted in Chapter 4, the legislative programme enacted by the Thatcher and Major Conservative governments in the 1980s and 1990s can clearly be seen to be a significant influence. In addition to these aspects, the Chartered Institute of Personnel and Development (2005c) suggests that global competitive pressures and employee attitudes are equally important. In particular, younger people are unlikely to have ever belonged to a trade union. For example, the Labour Research Department (2012b) cites estimates published by the Department of Business, Innovation and Skills which put the number of union members aged 16–24 at fewer than 5 per cent. However, research suggests that young workers' reasons for not joining a union are often due to a lack of knowledge about trade unions rather than because they are intrinsically anti-union (Lucas, 2009; Tailby and Pollert, 2011). Clearly, though, trade unions face real challenges in seeking to target young workers to persuade them to become union members and will have to increase their visibility and accessibility to overcome the widespread ignorance about what they do (Labour Research Department, 2012b; Tailby and Pollert, 2011).

### Review and reflect

Trade unions are increasingly looking to recruit younger employees, and those in sectors where they have previously had few members, such as tourism and hospitality. Think about your own view of trade unions and consider why you think trade unions have had little success in the past in recruiting members in the tourism and hospitality industry.

The decline in trade union membership in the UK is within a context in which, in recent years, there has seemingly been greater state support for trade unions. This situation is a change from the past where historically there was little state support for trade union recognition in the UK; much of the twentieth century could be best characterized as being voluntaristic, with minimal intervention from the state in employment relations. More recently, though, there has been greater state intervention, including in the area of union recognition. In this sense the Employment Relations Act (ERA) (1999 and 2004) means that trade unions may gain recognition even where employers are implacably opposed to the idea (Labour Research Department, 2011e). Importantly, however, the legislation does not apply to small employers, defined as those with 20 or fewer workers, which of course is the majority of tourism and hospitality enterprises. However, even within the changing employment relations landscape described above, it is arguable the extent to which trade unions are likely to make a significant comeback. In part this reflects a wider sense of managerial resistance to trade unions. In attempting to understand the reasons for such resistance, Gall (2004) notes how the period 1979–1997 created what he terms a sense of 'managerial Thatcherism'. In essence, the legislative programme of primarily the Thatcher, but also the Major, governments sought to change the employment landscape by severely restricting the ability of trade unions to organize and take industrial action and thereby secure recognition and successfully pursue their members' interests in collective negotiations. For Gall, one of the obvious outcomes that this period engendered is a present-day situation of 'not insignificant employer opposition to granting recognition' (p. 36). Thus, despite the later attempts by the New Labour government of Tony Blair in particular to ostensibly create an employee relations public policy which foregrounded a stronger sense of partnership, it seems questionable, as Gennard (2002) argues, whether there really was a 'break with the past'. Thus, as Coats (2010: 7) notes, although New Labour did enact legislation such as the trade union recognition procedure, 'Labour did little to undo the Thatcher settlement'.

Regardless of debates concerning what is the most compelling explanation for declining trade union membership and activity, what is clear is the precipitous fall in trade union membership. In 1979 there were 13.289 million members, a density of over 50 per cent. By 2010 the figure had declined to approximately 6.5 million, a density of 26.6 per cent (Achur, 2011). More broadly, as Coats (2010: 4) notes, 'trade unions are struggling to maintain and rebuild their membership across the developed world' and low trade union membership is not confined to the UK, but is also seen in the United States, Australasia and large parts of Europe (Table 10.1).

While Table 10.1 outlines union density figures for the economy as a whole, often the figure will be lower again for the tourism and hospitality sector. For example, the International Labour Organization (ILO) (2001) has estimated that globally the average figure for the tourism and hospitality industry is 10 per cent. The European Foundation for the Improvement of Living and Working Conditions (EFILWC) (2012) notes that across the EU trade union density in hospitality is less than 15 per cent, lower than the overall European average

| TABLE 10.1 Union density in selected countries | |
| --- | --- |
| Country | Percentage union density (2010 unless stated) |
| United States | 11.4 |
| Australia | 18 |
| Japan | 18.4 |
| Germany | 18.6 |
| France | 7.6 (2008 figure) |
| Italy | 35.1 |
| Sweden | 68.4 |
| Netherlands | 19.4 (2009 figure) |
| Ireland | 33.7 (2009 figure) |
| New Zealand | 20.8 |
| Derived from OECD: http://www.oecd.org/document/34/0,3746,en_2649_33927_40917154_1_1_1_1,00.html#union | |

trade union density of 23 per cent. That said, we do have to exercise a degree of caution in recognizing this argument, not least because there may be significant differences between sub-sectors like hotel and catering, compared to the airline industry, for example. Even then there may be national differences in the relative strength of trade unions in certain sub-sectors. For example, within accommodation and food services in the UK the current trade union density is the lowest by some distance of all industries, at just 3.8 per cent (Achur, 2011) and trade unions have little real purchase or influence. A number of reasons have been forwarded for low levels of trade union density in the UK hotel and catering sub-sector (Aslan and Wood, 1993; Lucas, 2004; Macaulay and Wood, 1992; see also HRM in Practice 10.2):

- The ethos of hotel and catering: for example, the suggested conservatism and individualism of the workforce and reliance on informal rewards tends to create a workplace culture which is antipathetic to trade unions. The self-reliance that this individualism tends to breed means that employees prefer to represent themselves in negotiating with management.
- The predominance of small workplaces and their wide geographical dispersion pose considerable challenges to trade union recruitment and organizing strategies. The existence of a 'family culture' in many SMEs is also considered a significant barrier to organizing. For example, in her interrogation of the 1998 Workplace Employment Relations Survey (WERS) data, Lucas (2004) found that hospitality employees in very small workplaces demonstrated a much higher level of positive endorsement for their manager's style of management.

- Structure of the workforce: the workforce has high numbers of young workers, students, part-timers, women, employees from ethnic minorities and migrant workers, all groups who are not traditionally associated with trade union membership. This situation is also exacerbated by high labour turnover.
- Employer and management attitudes: as we have already noted, the industry is characterized by a unitary view of the employment relationship that sees no role for trade unions. Consequently, employers and managers are hostile towards trade unions and will often pursue an active non-union policy.
- Role of trade unions: notwithstanding recent attempts by the Transport and General Workers Union (TGWU) and the GMB to organize parts of the hospitality sector, it is generally acknowledged that for too long trade unions failed to develop effective strategies to organize the sector.

## HRM IN PRACTICE 10.2:
## Failing to organize the Dorchester Hotel

Wills (2005) reports how the TGWU targeted the world-famous Dorchester Hotel in 1999 in attempts to gain union recognition. The Dorchester was targeted as it was a stand-alone hotel which did not belong to a national or international chain, so for the purposes of the 1999 ERA would be counted as a single bargaining unit. Over 1999–2002 the TGWU sought to gain union recognition. Although some employees did join the union, high levels of labour turnover and the ethnic diversity of the staff made it difficult to sustain a common union identity. When the TGWU came to present its case to the Central Arbitration Committee in December 2002 the union was unable to present a sufficiently compelling case that a majority of workers constituting the bargaining unit would be likely to support recognition. In part this was due to the Dorchester claiming more workers worked in the hotel than the TGWU claimed – although the union also found that a number of their claimed members were either duplicate members or were no longer employed. The failure to organize the Dorchester seems to point to the need for British unions to change their tactics in seeking recognition and to develop a broader geographical, occupational and sectoral focus, rather than concentrating on the level of the individual workplace.

Although trade unions have failed to establish any real foothold within the UK hotel and catering industry, there is some evidence that they have had greater success elsewhere and in doing so improved the working lives of their members (see HRM in Practice 10.3 and 10.4).

## HRM IN PRACTICE 10.3:
## Unions making a difference in the United States

Research conducted by Bernhardt *et al.* (2003) in eight (half of which were unionized) high-end, full-service 'Class A' hotels in four US cities found that unions could make a difference to employees' lives. The research focused on room attendants and food and beverage staff and, among other things, found that in the unionized hotels wages were higher, work intensity was lower, contract provisions on workload were more constraining and innovative bargaining was more prevalent. Such outcomes involve a partnership of unions and management. These union–management partnerships, it was suggested, can help to tackle industry-wide problems and demonstrate that 'win–win' or 'mutual gains' solutions are possible in the hotel industry.

## HRM IN PRACTICE 10.4:
## Enhanced labour flexibility in Australian hotels

Research by Knox and Nickson (2007) suggests that within Australia some hotel employers engage in successful firm-level bargaining with trade unions, with unionization rates across the industry far higher than in the UK. Case studies of two hotels found that management at hotels with enterprise bargaining had decided to pursue both service excellence and cost minimization. This strategy focused on introducing employment practices that provided the dual benefits of quality enhancement and cost reduction in such a way that they were not in conflict with one another. This situation was achieved through partnerships and bargaining with the trade union. The employers believed that they could best achieve their aims by bargaining with the union rather than directly with employees because they were concerned with receiving the support and cooperation of the workforce. Sophisticated rostering systems were introduced in order to align the needs of employer and employee more effectively. The hotels also exhibited a strong commitment to enhanced functional flexibility, with initiatives directed towards improving multi-skilling, service quality, ongoing training and development and retention. In sum, the research highlighted Australia's unique institutional context and the potential benefits associated with regulation and union involvement.

The relative lack of trade union presence is not universal in the tourism and hospitality industry in terms of the relative strength of trade unions in different sub-sectors. For example, Baum (2006) recognizes that the airline industry has always had a stronger trade union presence when compared to the hotel and catering sub-sector, even in the UK (see HRM in Practice 10.5).

## HRM IN PRACTICE 10.5:
## Conflict in British Airways

British Airways (BA) has had something of a chequered history in recent years in its dealings with trade unions, with high-profile disputes in 2003, 2005, 2007 and most recently 2009–2011. Having narrowly averted a series of strikes in 2007, BA found itself enmeshed in a series of damaging disputes between 2009 and 2011. At the end of 2009 Bassa, the branch of the Unite trade union which represents 12,700 BA cabin crew, voted for a 12-day strike which was to take place over the Christmas and New Year period. The strike call was primarily in response to BA's intention to cut the number of cabin crew on long-haul flights from 15 to 14, to reduce the workforce by around 5,000 and, to a lesser extent, due to ongoing concerns about pay. The strike was averted at the last minute as BA won a court injunction against the strike due to some irregularities in the strike ballot. However, after the union re-balloted members in early 2010 there was a series of strikes over the course of that year.

The dispute became increasingly bitter and grew beyond the initial concerns about cuts in staff, now focusing more prominently on a variety of other issues. Among these other issues were pay, the withdrawal of travel concessions for staff who had previously taken strike action and, depending on your point of view, 'bully boy' tactics from the company or callousness on the part of the unions. Further ballots for strike action were conducted in 2011 while talks continued between the company and the union. Eventually, the dispute was settled in June 2011. Over the course of the dispute cabin crew were on strike for 22 days, which is estimated to have cost the company in excess of £150 million. In addition to the monetary loss the company had to contend with almost continuous bad publicity throughout the period, creating an ABBA – 'Anything But BA' – effect among passengers. The final deal saw: staff travel concessions returned to the BA crew who had the facility removed when they took strike action in 2010; agreements on safeguarding routes and working arrangements as BA introduces a new fleet of crew; and a pay deal. There was also an agreement that a third-party binding arbitration process be established to consider the cases of crew disciplined by the airline during the dispute. However, there was no reversal of the staff cuts from 2009 that had originally led to the dispute.

Derived from Davies (2009); Milmo (2007, 2009, 2010, 2011); Milmo and Webb (2009); Morgan (2003); Townsend (2005)

In sum, although there may be some pockets of trade union strength in the tourism and hospitality industry, generally trade unions remain a marginal presence. In a broader sense, any future for the trade union movement is contingent upon their ability to organize in the service sector. The evidence

to-date suggests that this may well be an uphill struggle for the trade union movement. As a consequence of this lack of collective 'voice' provided by the trade unions means that most tourism and hospitality employees are likely to sustain an influence in managerial decision-making through the processes of employee involvement and participation.

## Employee involvement and participation

As we have already noted, there is a definitional and terminological debate on the meanings of terms such as 'employee involvement', 'employee participation' and 'industrial democracy' (Blyton and Turnbull, 2004). Hyman and Mason (1995) suggest that, increasingly, talk of industrial democracy – which denotes a fundamental change in the balance of power in society generally and the workplace specifically, such as the establishment of employee self-management – has little currency in contemporary market-driven economies. Consequently, we are left with the notions of 'employee involvement' and 'employee participation', which represent the 'two principal and in many respects contradictory approaches to defining and operationalizing employee influence' (Hyman and Mason, 1995: 1).

## Employee involvement

Marchington and Wilkinson (2005b) recognize that there are a number of mechanisms that have been introduced under the broad heading of employee involvement, such as team-working and empowerment, to name just two. While there may be a number of differing initiatives, there is nonetheless common agreement on the intent of employee involvement. In that sense most writers recognize that employee involvement is concerned with measures that are introduced by management to optimize the utilization of labour while at the same time securing the employee's identification with the aims and needs of the organization. Employee involvement is seen as being very much a phenomenon of the 1980s and closely linked with 'soft' HRM and its emphasis on unitarism and the creation of common interests between employer and employee. Employee involvement is managerially initiated and characterized as direct, 'descending participation', which is task-centred as it attempts to involve all individuals in the workplace (Salamon, 2000). In this way it seeks to provide employees with opportunities to influence and take part in organizational decision-making, specifically within the context of their own workgroup or task. Therefore it is intended to motivate individual employees, increase job satisfaction and enhance the sense of identification with the aims, objectives and decisions of the organization. Organizations have a number of ways in which they can involve employees; Table 10.2 outlines the incidence of these aspects in British workplaces with ten or more employees, as found in the 2004 WERS.

| TABLE 10.2 Direct communication and information-sharing techniques | |
|---|---|
| Technique | Percentage of organizations using technique |
| Meetings between senior managers and the whole workforce | 79 |
| Noticeboards | 74 |
| Team briefings | 71 |
| Systematic use of management chain | 64 |
| Regular newsletter | 45 |
| Employee attitude surveys | 42 |
| E-mail | 38 |
| Intranet | 34 |
| Suggestion schemes | 30 |
| Source: adapted from Kersley et al. (2006) | |

Marchington and Wilkinson (2005b) note that these various techniques can be further broken down between those where the organization simply communicates downwards to employees and those more concerned with upward problem-solving. With regard to downward communication, it can be seen in Table 10.2 that this form of employee involvement is especially prevalent in organizations. Direct communication to the individual can take a variety of forms and involve a variety of media, both electronic and paper such as e-mail, intranet, company newsletters and noticeboards. The Industrial Relations Services (2005c) surveyed over 70 organizations across the economy and found that the most important aim of their communication strategy was to keep employees informed about changes in the organization, closely followed by improving employee engagement and improving employee performance. Though downward communications can be useful in attempting to achieve these aims, through informing and 'educating' employees about managerial actions and intentions, they are also passive and are characterized by Marchington and Wilkinson (2005b) as the most 'dilute' form of direct participation. Indeed, Hyman and Mason (1995) suggest downward communications mechanisms are ultimately rather superficial and question the extent to which they denote meaningful involvement (see HRM in Practice 10.6).

By contrast a number of upward problem-solving techniques are likely to denote more meaningful involvement for employees, usually involving two-way communication. These techniques may be directed at either individuals or workgroups. Suggestion schemes allow organizations to potentially tap into the creativity of their workforce to make significant improvements in just about

## HRM IN PRACTICE 10.6:
## Formal or informal involvement?

Recent work has recognized that within the hospitality industry, as well as formal means of employee involvement there are also informal means of involving employees. Marchington and Suter (2012) report on a non-union, UK-based restaurant company, RestaurantCo, which employs 7,000 staff in 300 branches. Similarly, Townsend *et al.* (2011) report the case of a luxury hotel operating in Australia, which is part of a larger international operation that employs over 100,000 people throughout the world. Across the two organizations there is evidence of formal involvement mechanisms such as newsletters, team briefings/meetings, notice-boards, employee opinion surveys and employee opinion focus groups. However, in RestaurantCo there were often constraints on formal mechanisms due to product and labour market constraints. For example, in terms of product market issues the nature of the restaurant industry, and its unpredictable customer demand, meant that team briefings would often be interrupted and terminated if there was a sudden influx of customers. Similarly, from a labour market point of view the extensive use of non-standard employment contracts meant the company employed a large number of part-time and temporary staff and they would often miss team briefings.

Townsend *et al.* also found that formal mechanisms were not necessarily the most appropriate means to provide the employees with the voice that both parties want. For example, there would often be a reticence among housekeeping staff to comment in a public forum, and some staff felt pressurized in the employee opinion survey as they had to complete it in the presence of their managers, and so would not offer an honest opinion. While the existence of these formal mechanisms across both cases had mixed success, there was much greater support for informal means. In RestaurantCo, both managers and employees were more positive about informal means. One branch manager suggested that 'about 70–80 per cent of what I learn about the restaurant, about the issues and what we can do to solve them are from informal chats. There is very little I can learn from a formal team meeting.'

Marchington and Suter (2012) report that employees were much more positive about informal communication and consultation, with 90 per cent agreeing or strongly agreeing that managers tried to seek consensus at work and about three-quarters felt that informal discussions took place before decisions were made and that staff had a say in these decisions. Within the hotel studied by Townsend *et al.*, employees would often have the opportunity beyond the formal avenues to communicate directly with managers, with one housekeeping employee noting that 'I just go straight to my manager, just straight to him. . . . If I've got anything at all to say, not in a harsh way, but anything about everything, I just say it straight away yeah.' In both cases features of the industry such as close team-working and interaction with customers created an environment where informal mechanisms were often experienced more positively than formal mechanisms.

every aspect of the business, such as improvements in customer service (Income Data Services, 2012). Such schemes can also improve levels of employee engagement and as a result they can improve the motivation and commitment of workers, as they see their voluntary activity as being integral to company success. Equally, there may also be more instrumental and tangible benefits both for the individual – whereby employees are rewarded for ideas – and for the organization, who may accrue significant cost savings from suggestions emanating from employees.

A second technique that aims to encourage more active employee involvement is an attitude survey. More often than not employee attitude surveys will be a census of all staff, usually yearly or bi-annually. Employees will usually be asked to give their views on a range of issues, including (Income Data Services, 2004a):

- the organization's strategic direction and leadership;
- organizational culture;
- the organization as an employer;
- pay and benefits;
- working environment and conditions;
- working relationships (i.e. with managers and colleagues);
- company image;
- overall satisfaction/commitment to the organization;
- reaction to the survey and previous follow-up action.

The last point is important in delineating the need for organizations to be transparent in both disseminating results and being seen to act on them. As was alluded to in Chapter 8, there may also be opportunities for employees to appraise their manager's performance. The suggested benefits of employees commenting on managerial performance through employee attitude surveys are that it makes for better management, although again this is contingent upon management accepting and acting upon the results of surveys.

---

### Review and reflect

Imagine you are a manager in a travel agency which is part of a large multinational company. As part of their involvement scheme the company runs an attitude survey which gives employees the opportunity to comment on your performance. In the last survey your employees have said that you are dictatorial and difficult to approach. How do you respond?

In a group sense, initiatives within tourism and hospitality which seek to encourage employees' involvement in upward communication are likely to be premised on the notion of improving quality within the organization and towards the customer, finding expression in techniques such as quality circles (QCs) and total quality management (TQM). Lashley (2001) notes how QCs are essentially concerned with consultation on the basis of management posing problems in the expectation of receiving suggestions from employees. Suggestions are likely to be directed towards improvements in service quality and productivity in particular. He also reports evidence from the Accor Group, where QCs have been used successfully. Although employees were expected to act as volunteers and are not paid for taking part in the QCs, there was still significant interest among employees. Among other things, the QCs in Accor were able to speed-up customers' breakfast service and guest check-out times on the basis of identifying problems, suggesting and testing solutions, measuring results and finally 'rolling out' the approved solution. A more all-embracing approach to quality is via the notion of TQM, which is more concerned with promulgating an integrated view of quality via company-wide improvements in quality both towards the internal customer (the employee) and the external customer. Baldachino (1995) reports a case study of a luxury hotel where the implementation of a TQM philosophy was beset by a number of problems including employee suspicion of the rhetoric of TQM, empowerment and involvement when faced with the realities of redundancy, industrial conflict and the more prosaic problem of a 'them and us' attitude emerging over the car parking situation for managers and employees at the hotel. More sanguine accounts of TQM claim several benefits from such a philosophy, including improved organizational efficiency, greater employee involvement, consistently 'delighting the customer' by exceeding their expectations and reduced labour turnover (Hope and Muhlemann, 1998). An integral part of a TQM framework is the role of empowerment, which is often seen as being synonymous with greater employee involvement.

Empowerment may actually encompass a variety of employee involvement techniques (Lashley, 2001; Wilkinson, 1998), though for clarity we will talk here of empowerment as being predominantly about encouraging front-line staff to solve customers' problems on the spot, without constant recourse to managerial approval. As was discussed in Chapter 3, tourism and hospitality organizations are increasingly attempting to develop an organizational culture which places high-quality service at its centre. With customer expectations becoming ever more dynamic, empowerment is increasingly sold as being the key to achieving not only high levels of service quality but also as a means to enhance the commitment and job satisfaction of employees. In principle, empowerment allows employees to exercise greater authority, discretion and autonomy in their dealings with guests. In reality, the latitude allowed to employees is often circumscribed. For example, Jones et al. (1997), in their study of the Americo hotel chain, found that the use of a 'compensation matrix' would dictate employee responses and allowed management to monitor and measure such responses, creating tightly constrained discretion (see also Hales and Klidas, 1998). Thus, although the rhetoric of empowerment is about attempting to move decisively from a control-oriented organization to a commitment-oriented organization, Riley (1996: 171) pragmatically recognizes that 'empowerment is giving the employees the right to "break the rules" to serve the customer' but it is also nonetheless important to recognize that 'rules are always necessary for an organization. It is a balance between organizational rules and discretion which must be available quickly.'

## Review and reflect

Can you really have empowerment which involves tightly constrained discretion?

As we recognized in Chapter 7, training and development of employees is also a crucial part in operationalizing empowerment strategies, with employees requiring training in areas like social skills, communication skills, decision-making skills, problem-solving skills, planning skills and team-working. Relatedly, there will also be a need to re-orient managerial thinking towards a more facilitative and coaching style, which should also attempt to impart a greater sense of trust and confidence in the ability of the front-line staff to make suitable decisions. This does not mean that management's role is completely emasculated or abrogated, but merely refined, although this may be particularly difficult for managers to accept (Wilkinson, 1998). Equally it is important to create a 'no blame' culture where 'well intentioned errors' are discussed in a supportive way in order that lessons can be learnt from any mistakes in decision taking by employees.

This latter point can be seen as one of the obvious benefits of empowerment and a review of several writers suggests several other benefits to be derived from empowerment (Baum, 2006; Lashley, 2001; Wilkinson, 1998):

- reduction in the so-called social distance between customers and employees, so service is not seen as servility;
- improved quality and guest satisfaction, as the removal of close supervision creates a more responsive service delivery system;
- enhanced motivation and job satisfaction for employees, leading to greater commitment and reduced labour turnover;
- more time for managers to engage in strategic planning and customer responsiveness;

- cost savings and improvements from ideas generated by employees;
- word-of-mouth advertising.

On the other hand, there may also be a number of potential problems in empowering employees. We have already noted how reality may not match the rhetoric of companies in relation to the tightly constrained discretion which characterizes many empowerment schemes. In addition, employees may also see empowerment as about increasing risks and responsibilities without any commensurate extra reward for the additional skills and discretion they are expected to demonstrate. A further issue is that of job security, as empower- ment may be used to justify delayering, which in turn leads to a drastic reduction in the number employed by the organization. There is also the vexed issue of the culturally bound nature of empowerment, which is often seen as a very Americanized approach to service (Nickson, 1999). Consequently, and as we noted in Chapter 2, it may be especially difficult to create an empowered culture in countries such as China and the post-communist Eastern European states, though even within parts of Western Europe there is also evidence of significant resistance to the precepts underlying empowerment (Klidas, 2002).

## Employee participation

Hyman and Mason (1995: 21) define participation as:

> state [or supra-state] initiatives which promote the collective rights of employees to be represented in organizational decision-making, or to the consequence of the efforts of employees themselves to establish collective representation in corporate decisions, possibly in the face of employer resistance.

Salamon (2000) characterizes participation as being pluralist, power-centred, indirect, representative and 'ascending' in its focus on the managerial preroga- tive and attempts to extend employees' collective interest into a variety of areas and decisions at higher levels of the organization. The expression of employee interests over company decisions may be via joint consultation, works councils and worker directors. With regard to joint consultative committees, Lucas (2004) notes how data from WERS 1998 suggests that management committees for joint consultation, rather than negotiation, are rare in the tourism and hospitality industry. Moreover, where such committees do exist they tend to have quite a narrow focus in terms of what they will allow consultation on. As Lucas notes, 'Where committees function in the HI [hospitality industry], health and safety is most likely to be discussed, followed by training, working practices and welfare services and facilities. Pay and government regulations are the least frequently discussed issues' (p. 161). Consequently, in this section the focus is mainly on works councils, both European and national.

## European and national works councils

Hyman and Mason (1995: 32) suggest works councils are 'a representative body composed of employees (and possibly containing employer representatives as well) which enjoy certain rights from the employer'. Works councils have two principal rights: first, the right to receive information on key aspects of company activity, such as restructuring, HRM/personnel issues, health and safety, etc.; and second, the right to consultation on such issues prior to their implementation by management. Works councils are common in Europe and often underpin approaches based on social partnership, but have been a relatively rare phenomenon in the UK, with only a small number of companies setting up voluntary agreements (see HRM in Practice 10.7).

## HRM IN PRACTICE 10.7:
## Pizza Express: spreading the word

As was noted in Chapter 9, Pizza Express' image was seriously damaged in 1999 following the revelation that they had been rather disingenuous in their interpretation of the minimum-wage legislation in the UK. Clearly, the company had to start improving internal communication to pinpoint and address sensitive issues that arose from this dispute. To tackle this problem, the HR department gave the job of communications manager to Steve Perkins, who was then a member of the restaurant staff. Perkins decided to set up a company-wide works council system similar to those running in EU nations. The first step was to look at other companies' practices, but Perkins was told to develop a system that best suited the company.

The new communication system took more than 18 months to become fully effective. The work councils are now run at local, regional and national levels, from individual restaurants to headquarters. They involve managers and staff representatives alike. At the restaurant level, forum discussions are held every two months and involve managers, staff representatives and staff themselves, who are encouraged to express their concerns. Problems can be settled at this stage, although unresolved issues can be taken to one of the seven regional councils held by regional managers and restaurant representatives. Again, issues can be brought to the national forum, which meets every six months and involves top executives and board members.

The new works council witnessed several breakthroughs. For instance, the system prevented massive complaints from employees about reduced wages when the company was only trying to take out an amount of the wages to adjust it tax-wise and give it back at a lower tax rate. Thanks to the forum, representatives were able to identify and calm their colleagues' fears. From a company point of view

the consultative process also has the advantage of avoiding negotiations with unions and resulting strike threats. Despite its successes, however, the communication system would not have worked without Pizza Express' commitment, which was fundamental in gaining staff commitment to the process. As James Sydmonds, the national forum representative for Café Pasta, said,

> When I started on the forum, I was very suspicious. . . . Every time I got to a different level and an issue was brought up, I'd think: 'What is actually going to happen at the next level?' But the company involvement has surprised me, and I have been so impressed that I have wanted to get more involved and spread the gospel.

Derived from Cooper (2001); Goymour (2000)

More recently, within the UK especially, the situation has changed regarding European-inspired regulation, which has established European works councils (EWCs) and national works councils. The directive establishing EWCs was adopted in September 1994. It was not till 2000 that the directive was finally implemented in the UK. The directive covers all companies with a presence in more than one EU member state and with at least 1,000 employees in total, of which at least 150 are located in each of two EU member states (Labour Research Department, 2011e). The EWCs are designed to provide a forum for informing and consulting with employees. Importantly, companies do not automatically have to establish an EWC, though both companies and employees (or their representatives) can trigger mechanisms to request an EWC (Labour Research Department, 2011e). More recently, in response to concerns that the original directive suffered from a number of shortcomings, the European Parliament approved a new, recast European Works Council Directive (2009/38/EC). Among other things, the new directive is seeking to increase the number of EWCs being established, offers a new definition of 'information', a clearer definition of 'consultation', a right to time off to undergo training to help members and those of special negotiating bodies undertake their duties and increases the maximum penalty for failure to comply with an EWC from £75,000 to £100,000. Transposed into the UK as the Transnational Information and Consultation of Employees (Amendment) Regulations 2010, the amended regulations came into force in June 2011 (see Department for Business, Innovation and Skills, 2010, for further details). It remains to be seen how the new regulations will impact on organizations and employees, though there are concerns about ambiguities existing in relation to the application of the new regulations and whether, from a trade union perspective, they adequately capture the spirit of the law (see, respectively, Eversheds, 2011; GMB, 2010).

The voluntary nature of EWCs means that of the more than 2,400 companies covered by the directive, less than half have established one (European Trade

Union Institute, 2011). Of the 965 currently active EWCs it is unclear how many cover tourism and hospitality organizations, as these organizations are subsumed under the broader sectoral heading of Food, Agriculture and Tourism (European Trade Union Institute, 2011). However, the International Labour Organization (ILO) (2010b) notes that as of April 2010 there were 15 EWCs established in hotel, restaurant and catering establishments, including: Accor, Aramark, Autogrill, Club Méditerranée, Compass Group, Elior, Hilton, InterContinental, LSG Skychefs, McDonald's, Rezidor, Scandic Hotels AB, Sodexo, SSP and Starwood/Sheraton (see HRM in Practice 10.8).

## HRM IN PRACTICE 10.8:
## Club Méditerranée

Club Méditerranée is a French company and one of the world leaders in holiday villages. The company operates in over 40 countries and has more than 20,000 employees. Club Med introduced its EWC in September 1996, though prior to this date the company had previously worked with unions to resolve issues such as re-employing seasonal staff and helping non-French nationals to settle into working in France. Initially the EWC agreement was signed for a period of three years; in 1999 the agreement was renewed indefinitely. Employee representatives are provided by the trade unions, both at a European level and for several individual countries in which Club Med operates. The EWC allows for the provision of information, reflection and consultation between the partners. Information provided through the EWC encompasses economic and financial matters, strategic perspectives, the employment situation, organizational changes and their consequences. In difficult times, such as the post-9/11 period, the process of consultation allowed the EWC to engender consensus on issues such as restructuring in what were difficult circumstances. In sum, the Club Med EWC is suggested as having several benefits, including: effective joint action during restructuring programmes with an impact on employment; production of ethics guidelines on sub-contracting to support local conflicts; and exchanges on strategic orientations or organizational changes within the group.

Derived from European Foundation for the Improvement of Living and Working Conditions (2005)

In addition to EWCs the EU parliament also adopted the information and consultation Directive in March 2002, which was implemented in the UK as the Information and Consultation of Employees Regulations 2004 (ICE Regulations). The directive requires member states to ensure that employers are under an obligation to consult with their workforce on an ongoing basis in order that employees have a better idea of potential changes in their employment. As

was noted earlier, these types of arrangements are common in many parts of Europe, though much less so in the UK context. For example, if we take joint consultative committees (JCCs) as a rough proxy for the sort of mechanisms required by the ICE Regulations, then WERS 2004 found that JCCs were present in 14 per cent of all UK workplaces, though this varied markedly with the size of the workplace, with the figures being 26 per cent in workplaces with 50–99 employees and 47 per cent in those with 100–199 employees (Kersley *et al.*, 2006). Employers covered by the ICE Regulations do not automatically have to inform and consult with employees, and indeed some employers may have pre-existing arrangements that are considered acceptable. If such arrangements do not exist, under the terms of the ICE Regulations UK employers have to establish consultation bodies for the information and consultation of employees if 10 per cent of the workforce requests it (Labour Research Department, 2011e). The ICE Regulations were initially introduced from April 2005 and only applied to companies with more than 150 employees. This situation has changed over time and the regulations covered companies with at least 100 employees from April 2007, and those with at least 50 from April 2008. Under the terms of the ICE Regulations employees have the right to be (Labour Research Department, 2004):

- informed about the organization's economic situation;
- informed and consulted about its current employment situation and employment prospects;
- informed and consulted about decisions likely to lead to major changes in contractual decisions or work organization. This could cover a range of topics including working time and practices, training, equal opportunities and pensions.

Despite noting some evidence generally that the ICE Regulations promoted an initial increase in the incidence of information and consultation arrangements, in reporting a four year investigation of the impact of the regulations Hall *et al.* (2010) found no evidence of employees triggering the setting up of a works council. Instead, management were more likely to influence the form of information and consultation arrangements, though this was not usually to comply with the regulations. Overall, Hall *et al.* (2010) suggest that the majority of enterprises covered by the regulations have largely ignored them. Similarly, Gumbrell-McCormack and Hyman (2010) recognize the serious limitations of European-type work councils in the UK, not least the opposition from both employers and trade unions, with the former seeking to retain their managerial prerogative and the latter their 'single channel' of representation. In sum, as the Chartered Institute of Personnel and Development (2011d: 4) notes, 'there is no evidence that the [regulations] have led to any reversal of the trend for employers to rely more heavily on direct and less on indirect (representative) forms of employee voice'.

## Conclusion

In this chapter we recognized that while there may be broad agreement on the principle of ensuring that employees have a voice in managerial decision-making, the form of influence will vary enormously. In some institutional contexts the voice may be provided by trade unions. This is especially true for a number of European countries where the principle of social partnership ensures that unions play an active part in organizational decision-making. In the UK it is more likely within the tourism and hospitality sector that employee influence will be sustained through a variety of formal and informal involvement and participation mechanisms. There is much debate as to the efficacy – in relation to issues like improving employee morale and raising productivity – and democratic intent of employee involvement, and particularly the extent to which the various initiatives represent 'pseudo-participation' in their lack of a challenge to the managerial prerogative. On the other hand it remains questionable whether the representative approaches which are now increasingly encouraged through a number of European directives will provide the meaningful participation that is intended. Ultimately, approaches to employee involvement and participation should aim to promote improved dialogue in the workplace. Workplaces that involve and engage their employees in matters that affect their employment experience are likely to benefit through increased commitment and motivation, something that social partnership seems to have achieved in a number of European contexts and from which lessons can seemingly be drawn by UK companies.

## Discussion questions

- How useful are the concepts of unitarism, pluralism and Marxism in explaining the management of conflict in tourism and hospitality workplaces?
- What do we mean by the idea of employee 'voice'?
- Why have trade unions declined so much since the 1970s?
- Will unions ever have a meaningful role to play in tourism and hospitality workplaces?
- Drawing on your own workplace experience, what do you consider is the best way to communicate with employees in tourism and hospitality?
- Assess the extent to which formal or informal employee involvement mechanisms are more effective in tourism and hospitality workplaces.
- Consider arguments for and against the creation of European works councils and national works councils.

## Further reading

Bernhardt, A., Dresser, L. and Hatton, E. (2003) 'The coffee pot wars: unions and firm restructuring in the hotel industry', in E. Appelbaum, A. Bernhardt and R.J. Murnane (eds), *Low Wage America*, New York, NY: Russell Sage Foundation.

Gumbrell-McCormick, R. and Hyman, R. (2010) 'Work councils: the European model of industrial democracy', in A. Wilkinson, P. Gollan, M. Marchington and D. Lewin (eds), *The Oxford Handbook of Participation in Organizations*, Oxford: Oxford University Press.

Hales, C. and Klidas, A. (1998) 'Empowerment in five star hotels: choice, voice or rhetoric?', *International Journal of Contemporary Hospitality Management*, 10, 3, 88–95.

Kersley, B., Alpin, C., Forth, J., Bryson, A., Bewley, H., Gix, G. and Oxenbridge, S. (2006) *Inside the Workplace: Findings from the 2004 Workplace Employment Relations Survey*, London: Routledge.

Lashley, C. (2001) *Empowerment HR Strategies for Service Excellence*, Oxford: Butterworth-Heinemann.

Lucas, R. (2004) *Employment Relations in the Hospitality and Tourism Industries*, London: Routledge.

Lucas, R. (2009) 'Is low unionization in the British hospitality industry due to industry characteristics?', *International Journal of Hospitality Management*, 28, 1, 42–52.

Marchington, M. and Wilkinson, A. (2005) 'Direct participation and involvement', in S. Bach (ed.), *Managing Human Resources: Personnel Management in Transition*, 4th edn, Oxford: Blackwell.

Turnbull, P., Blyton, P. and Harvey, G. (2004) 'Cleared for take-off? Management–labour partnership in the European civil aviation industry', *European Journal of Industrial Relations*, 10, 3, 287–307.

## Recommended websites

The Trades Union Congress website gives a sense of their views on a range of employment and political issues at www.tuc.org.uk

There are a number of case studies concerning employee participation in European companies at http://www.eurofound.europa.eu/areas/participationatwork/index.htm

The Hospitality, Leisure, Sport and Tourism Network has a useful guide to empowerment, involvement and participation at http://www.heacademy.ac.uk/assets/hlst/documents/resource_guides/employee_empowerment_perception_and_involvement.pdf

Details of a number of hospitality and tourism organizations' European works councils agreements can be found at http://www.ewcdb.eu/ewc.php

## Additional material

Go to www.routledge.com/cw/nickson to find PowerPoint slides, chapter commentaries, test banks and additional case studies for each chapter.

# Employee well-being, welfare, health and safety in the workplace

COMPANION @ WEBSITE

## CHAPTER OBJECTIVES

**This chapter considers the range of issues concerned with the development of welfare policies in tourism and hospitality. Recognizing the ethical, legal and business aspects of welfare, the chapter aims to:**

- Appreciate the differing rationales for developing welfare policy.

- Consider the balance between the public and private life of organizational members.

- Recognize the increasing business emphasis in the development of welfare policies.

- Assess the extent to which welfare issues are particularly resonant within the tourism and hospitality industry.

## Introduction

Every year thousands of people suffer serious injury or even death in the workplace. Many more suffer from work-related illnesses or are absent from work due to work-related stress. In order to alleviate dangers in the workplace and ensure that employees are working in a healthy or happy environment, it is essential that tourism and hospitality organizations consider the development of appropriate welfare policies. Goss (1994: 122) recognizes how, 'Welfare provision generally refers to those policies which are directed at some aspect of employee wellbeing, both in a physical and emotional sense.' Torrington *et al.* (2011) suggest that the physical aspects of a broader welfare policy stem from measures to improve health and safety in the workplace, as well as issues such as the provision of paid holidays and reduced working hours. From an emotional/psychological perspective, organizations are likely to be concerned with the mental well-being of their employees, or more broadly anything involving the 'human relations' needs of people at work. Of course, in reality there is a degree of interconnectedness between physical and mental aspects of welfare, though it is also important to consider the potential distinctions that may be made between them.

From the above discussion we might ask ourselves why organizations should have a welfare policy and indeed whether the subject of the more sensitive aspects of welfare-related issues should remain personal and private. To answer these questions we should recognize various reasons for the existence of welfare policies. Goss (1994) suggests that organizations have usually developed welfare provision within the paradigm of three common 'welfare rationales', these being: legal-reactive, corporate conscience and company paternalism. These are now briefly discussed.

- *Legalistic-reactive*: in this approach an organization's approach to welfare policy is primarily driven by legislative requirements, such as responding to health and safety legislation. With such an approach the organization does not see developing welfare policy as an important part of its core objectives, but rather something that has to be complied with.
- *Corporate conscience*: Goss notes how historically the role of personnel had a strong welfare orientation and, arguably, how over time this welfarist approach became increasingly seen as 'soft' and 'indulgent', especially within a more competitive business environment.
- *Company paternalism*: This approach is concerned with the 'fatherly' manner in which organizations seek to look after all aspects of their employees' lives. By taking an 'encompassing' approach, companies that practised company paternalism would be concerned not only with the immediate work environment, but the manner in which employees lived their lives outside of work. Underpinning company paternalism is a strong sense of religious and moral commitment, and employees would be expected to lead a life that fitted with this ethos (see Nickson (1997) for a description of company paternalism in the Marriott, Hilton, Holiday Inn and Forte organizations).

In many respects the above description of differing welfare rationales has a clear overlap with some of the discussion in Chapter 6 on equal opportunities. In Chapter 6 the question was considered as to whether organizations should develop policies due to legal, ethical or business aspects, and the same arguments can be made with regard to the welfare of employees. Clearly, within this discussion the legal dimension is one that cannot be ignored and this aspect will be a concern throughout the chapter. To an extent, the notion of corporate conscience and company paternalism would seem to rest more on

an ethical view of welfare. Increasingly, though, it is argued that the main argument for developing welfare policies that enhance employee well-being is from the point of view of the HRM business case/efficiency argument. Much of this discussion about adopting a more efficient approach to welfare is generally seen through the lens of cost savings by reducing absence and improving the performance of employees in the workplace by addressing any problems or concerns that they might have. Clearly, then, welfare is an important topic, which may conceivably cover a variety of different issues. In this sense we can think of a welfare 'alphabet', encompassing a range of issues such as: absence management, AIDS/HIV, alcohol/drug misuse, sexual harassment, stress, working time and workplace violence. These aspects are now considered.

## Absence management

Increasingly, organizations are attempting to take a more proactive approach to the management of absence, recognizing both its direct and indirect costs. With regard to direct costs, absence can be a significant drain for organizations in terms of the cost of occupational sick pay, lost production or the need to bring in replacement staff. Overall, it is estimated that there were 190 million working days lost in 2010 in the UK, which cost the UK economy around £17 billion, at an average cost for each absent employee of £760 per year (Confederation of British Industry/Pfizer, 2011; see HRM in Practice 11.1).

### HRM IN PRACTICE 11.1:
### The UK: the sick man of Europe?

There has been much debate over whether the UK is the 'sick man of Europe'. For example, the Industrial Relations Services (2004) reported research by the European Union (EU) which suggests that the UK has a particularly poor health record, with more than one in four working-age adults having a long-term health problem. This figure was second only to Finland (32.2 per cent) and higher than direct competitors such as Germany (11.2 per cent), France (24.6 per cent) and Holland (25.4 per cent). The lowest figures in the survey were Romania (5.8 per cent) and Italy (6.6 per cent). For those actually in employment, the UK again had one of the highest rates of employees suffering long-term health problems at 20.4 per cent (surpassing only Finland and France), compared to the EU average of 12.7 per cent. However, others are critical of this characterization of 'sick note Britain', and Taylor et al. (2010) provide an interesting counter argument suggesting that British workers' sickness absence remains relatively low by international standards and the 'problem' of sickness absence has been overstated. Indeed, evidence suggests that 'presenteeism' is equally problematic as people struggle into work when they are unwell. A survey of 1,600 employees by the healthcare charity Nuffield Health (2012) found that 30 per cent of workers are now more inclined to go to work sick as a result of the current economic climate, with half of these workers suffering from a contagious illness such as flu or a cold.

More indirectly, and less easy to quantify, absences may place burdens on other organizational members, leading to poor morale, lower productivity, reduced customer retention and profitability (Income Data Services, 2005d; Industrial Relations Services, 2001).

The Chartered Institute of Personnel and Development (2011e) notes that in broad terms there are two types of absence, short term and long term. Short-term sickness absence will usually be self-certificated, although after seven days will be covered by a doctor's fit note, which indicates whether an employee is 'unfit for work' or 'may be fit for work'. For longer-term absence there may be a need to involve occupational health professionals or utilize rehabilitation programmes in order to get the employee back to work (Chartered Institute of Personnel and Development, 2011e), though this may be more likely in larger organizations. There are a number of causes of absence, though the most prevalent is usually minor illness, such as colds or flu. Other reasons for absence include aspects such as back pain, musculoskeletal injuries and other recurring medical conditions, though increasingly the primary cause for absence after minor illnesses is stress, which is further considered later in this chapter (Chartered Institute of Personnel and Development, 2011e).

Regardless of the nature of the absence and whether it is short or long term, it is increasingly suggested that there is a need for organizations to adopt a more proactive approach, especially if the costs described previously and so-called 'non-genuine illness' are taken into account. For example, it is suggested that organizations are making progress in measuring absence and taking specific steps to address the most obvious causes, though it is also important that such an approach is seen as part of a broader, integrated approach to create a healthy, high-quality workplace, where the link between employer performance and employee satisfaction is clearly understood. At the least, the organization should have a basic sickness absence policy, which should aim to (Chartered Institute of Personnel and Development, 2011e: 3):

- provide details of contractual sick pay terms and its relationship with statutory sick pay;
- outline the process employees must follow if taking time off sick – covering when and whom employees should notify if they are not able to attend work;

- include when (after how many days) employees need a self-certificate form;
- contain details of when they require a 'fit note' from their doctor;
- mention that the organization reserves the right to require employees to attend an examination by a company doctor and (with the employee's consent) to request a report from the employee's doctor;
- include the provision for return-to-work interviews as these have been identified as the most effective intervention to manage short-term absence;
- give guidance on absence during major or adverse events (for example: snow, pandemics or popular events such as the Olympic Games or World Cup).

HRM in Practice 11.2 notes an attempt by British Airways (BA) to take a more proactive approach to managing absence which, among other things, demonstrates the importance of training line managers to become involved in the process of managing absence.

## HRM IN PRACTICE 11.2:
## Tackling absence at British Airways

BA previously had real problems with levels of absence in the company. In 2002 the company acknowledged the scale of the problem by choosing to go 'loud, proud and wide' on the issue. By October 2004 the average absence per employee was 16.7 days per year, well above the sectoral average. Around 90 per cent of this absence was short term, and the overall cost to the company was put at £70 million. It was at this time that BA introduced a new absence-management policy, which developed a single set of clear absence policies and procedures for all staff. The aim of the new approach was to reduce absence by March 2006 to an average of ten days per employee, thus saving the company an estimated £30 million annually. As Peter Holloway, head of people and organizational development at BA, recognizes, 'absence management is not fun, sexy or exciting; it is about day to day following through of simple management practices'. Recognizing this point, among other things the new policy sought to encourage regular attendance at work, promote early intervention from line managers and HR managers and provide support for those with legitimate reasons for absence, with the intent of assisting their return to work at the earliest opportunity. Resultant policy interventions included employees having to have a conversation with their line manager as soon as possible regarding the nature of their absence and a standard informal return-to-work discussion after every occasion of absence. There was also a tightening of absence-recording mechanisms, which are now done electronically. Line managers were also tasked with taking a more active role in absence management and 'triggering' an 'absence review interview', a more formal version of the return-to-work interview. The absence review interviews are triggered if an employee is absent more than twice in three months or takes more than ten consecutive days off. When conducting the absence review interviews managers have a degree of discretion in considering the personal circumstances then of the employee and aspects such as the then Disability Discrimination Act. Although there were some teething problems with the new policy, especially in terms of the manner in which line managers applied discretion and some inconsistencies in interpretation of the new rules, the policy appears to have been very successful, with the company suggesting that employee absences are now around eight days per employee.

Derived from Income Data Services (2005d); Simms (2005)

In an even more proactive vein, some organizations are investing in a wide range of measures to tackle the underlying causes of sickness absence, taking the view that prevention is better than cure. The Income Data Services (2011c) note how a growing number of employers are seeking to cut absence by investing in employee well-being and health-promotion initiatives, including aspects such as having an on-site gym or subsidized gym membership, health checks, walking and running clubs and support for those who wish to stop smoking or lose weight via the provision of expert advice in areas such as nutrition. Other aspects include physiotherapy, stress counselling and complementary therapies, such as reflexology. This proactive approach to creating a healthy organization aims to help employees to look and feel better and to be physically healthy or fit. The emphasis is less on managing employees when they get sick, but instead seeks to manage healthy employees so they do not get sick. Such initiatives are likely to be part of a broader package of HRM policies which aim to create a great place to work. Organizations may also encourage employees by rewarding good attendance by, for example, offering an annual reward scheme for employees who have not been absent in the previous 12 months.

In sum, organizations are increasingly seeking to adopt more proactive approaches to absenteeism. In part, this approach can be achieved by integrated absence management approaches which look to address short- and long-term absences, and importantly also recognizes the potential for underlying causes for absence that may be explicable by broader HRM failings.

## AIDS/HIV

AIDS, or acquired immune deficiency syndrome, was first diagnosed in 1981. It is caused by the human immunodeficiency virus (HIV), which attacks the body's natural defence system and leaves it open to various infections and

cancers. Worldwide there are 33.3 million people with HIV, with nearly 70 per cent of them in sub-Saharan Africa (Chartered Institute of Personnel and Development, 2011f; UNAIDS, 2010). Within North America, Western Europe and Central Europe the figure stands at approximately 3.5 million (MacAskill, 2006). Currently, approximately 10 per cent of known HIV-positive individuals have developed AIDS. Importantly, many people who are HIV-positive are well most of the time, but develop some minor symptoms such as swollen lymph glands. In this sense HIV infection alone does not affect a person's ability to do his or her job, at least until employees develop illnesses that may make them unfit for work. Till that point there is no reason why someone who is HIV-positive cannot continue to work normally, as long as they are fit to do so. Moreover, a person who is HIV-positive is no real danger to others at work, in that transmission during normal working activities is virtually impossible (Radcliffe, 2009).

The International Labour Organization (ILO) (2011) finds that 90 per cent of working-age people living with HIV are engaged in some sort of employment. Ladki (1994) notes that 96 per cent of those diagnosed with AIDS in the United States were in their prime employment years (20–64 years old). Similarly, Breuer (1995), again writing in the US context, suggests that 1 in 300 employees may be HIV-positive or have AIDS, and that 90 per cent of HIV-infected Americans are in the workplace. Clearly, then, AIDS/HIV is something that organizations have to respond to as a major environmental feature – for example, with regard to aspects such as employee education and understanding the legal implications of how best to respond to employees who are HIV-positive. AIDS presents a major managerial challenge encompassing moral, social and medical issues resulting from health, safety, legal and humanitarian problems (Arkin, 2005b). Consequently, as Bratton and Gold (2007: 502) note, 'a textbook on human resource management for this new millennium would be incomplete if no reference were made to society's most recent menace'.

Indeed, it may well be that these sentiments have a particular resonance within the tourism and hospitality industry, which is one of the largest employers of people living with HIV (Radcliffe, 2009). This higher incidence of employees with HIV in tourism and hospitality is explicable by a number of reasons, including (Adam-Smith and Goss, 1993):

- Age composition and accommodation arrangements. Many organizations within the sector rely to a great extent on young workers. This is the group in society perceived to be at the most risk of infection through high-risk behaviour, whether that be drug abuse or unprotected sex. For example, most of those infected with HIV are in the age groups that have the highest level of economic activity, thus half of all known infections are in those aged 15–24 (Goss, 1997). It is also possible that there is a greater concentration of high-risk behaviour when many young workers are living together in shared accommodation, or working in a potentially sexually charged environment (see HRM in Practice 11.3).

- Perceived high concentration of homosexual males working in the industry. Despite research suggesting that this group has now changed its sexual practices, there may be a number who were affected before the risks became apparent.

- The nature of the work in certain sub-sectors, such as working in kitchens and restaurants. Here, there may be a very slightly greater risk of infection than in other workplaces. For example, blood being transmitted through accidents in the kitchen or hypodermic needles being found in hotel bedrooms or clubs/discos and the risk of blood contact through violent encounters.

- Sensitivity to public fears. Despite medical advice to the contrary, the public may feel that there is a significant risk of HIV being transmitted through food. In the 1990s employers in the American restaurant industry saw AIDS as the number-one long-term issue facing the industry (Ladki, 1994).

## HRM IN PRACTICE 11.3:
## Sexual activity in the tourism industry

Guerrier and Adib (2004), in their study of tour reps in Mallorca, found that male reps in particular were much more likely to instigate sexual relations with customers. Often these approaches and liaisons would take place after organized nights out, where male reps were also more likely than female reps to drink with customers. Guerrier and Adib recognize that for the male tour reps engaging in this type of behaviour was an attempt to reinforce their masculine identity, which they suggest is especially important in feminized environments when it may be in doubt.

Much of the above discussion points to the need for a considered managerial response. Before we move on to discuss this point further, first of all consider the following issues:

## Review and reflect

Read the following scenarios.

A member of staff in your travel agency comes to you and informs you that they are HIV-positive. How do you react?

A male cook who works in your restaurant kitchen is quite open about the fact that he lives in a homosexual relationship. Most of the other people in the kitchen are aware of this. One day a rumour is started that he is HIV-positive. Despite this rumour being *untrue*, very quickly a number of his colleagues have been to see you to ask for him to be dismissed. How do you handle this situation?

How, as a manager, would you respond to these scenarios?

Having considered your response to these scenarios, consider HRM in Practice 11.4, which outlines how one organization dealt with a very similar problem.

## HRM IN PRACTICE 11.4:
## Public misperceptions about AIDS

Barrows *et al.* (1996) report how a well-known Californian restaurant, Bon Appetit, found that its business was seriously affected when news emerged that a former employee had died of AIDS. Customer counts declined significantly when the media released a story that an executive chef who had previously worked in the restaurant had died of AIDS. The owner of the restaurant, Ralph Granthem, showed a proactive response to the situation by holding a press conference, where he recognized the overwhelming medical evidence that suggests that AIDS is not transmitted by food handling. Greater clarity was also offered by a well-publicized visit from the director of the California Department of Health Services. Along with his wife, the director ate in the restaurant and also produced a statement declaring that people do not get AIDS from restaurants. By taking a proactive approach the restaurant was able to reverse the decline in business, but the case illustrates the risk of uninformed public responses to AIDS.

HRM in Practice 11.4 illustrates the need for a clear and sensible approach to managing AIDS/HIV, though some of the difficulties in developing such an approach are encapsulated in the view of one manager quoted in Bratton and Gold (2007: 502), who recognizes that 'I was not trained to manage fear, discrimination, and dying in the workplace.' Much of the discussion above stems from potential misinformation about the nature of AIDS/HIV, and in particular the notion of perceived risk of infection. Adam-Smith and Goss (1993) identify three potential responses to the perceived risk of infection in the workplace.

- *Rational response*: individuals fully understand the probability of risk and on this basis make an informed choice about the acceptability of working with somebody who is HIV-positive. As we have already noted, the risk of transmission in a normal workplace situation is minimal and as long as employees are aware of this point then their rational response is such that they would have little or no fear of contracting the disease or working with somebody who is HIV-positive.
- *Bounded rationality response*: individuals are likely to view the issue on the basis of factually incomplete or incorrect information, often leading to a misunderstanding of the degree of risk. Consequently, employees may overemphasize the perceived hazard of AIDS/HIV and, for example, refuse to work with a fellow employee who is HIV-positive because of an inflated sense of risk.
- *Subjective response*: moral or subjective beliefs will determine the level of acceptability of working with somebody who is HIV-positive. For example, somebody who is homophobic may see AIDS/HIV as being a disease that is 'self-inflicted' and refuse to work with a homosexual colleague who is HIV-positive.

Adam-Smith and Goss recognize that, in reality, 'individuals are likely to use a complex mix of these decision-making processes in their assessment of risk' (p. 28). Furthermore, the organizational context will also be important in determining employees' assessment of risk, a point we touched on earlier.

## Policy responses to AIDS/HIV

To a large extent the discussion above also points to the manner in which organizations can develop a response to the issue of AIDS/HIV, which can take one of several forms:

- total denial that AIDS/HIV is a workplace issue;
- wait-and-see approach;
- deliberate no-policy decision and reliance on existing arrangements;
- AIDS/HIV to be treated as any other life-threatening disease;
- introduce a specific policy.

Given much of the discussion above, a more proactive response seems appropriate. In this way the reasons for having a policy include things like countering misunderstanding, lack of knowledge, fear and prejudice. Although ostensibly there is no statutory obligation for such a policy, the designation of HIV under the Equality Act (2010), wherein someone with HIV is deemed to have a disability, means that organizations should be proactive, particularly with regard to the notion of making 'reasonable adjustments' to address progressively disabling conditions. In developing a policy there are a number

of aspects organizations can consider as being integral to a successful policy, including (see, for example, Industrial Relations Services, 1997):

- a general statement of the company's commitment to non-discrimination;
- affirmation of usual hiring procedures so there is no discrimination in recruitment against applicants on the grounds that they are HIV-positive or have AIDS;
- assurance of continued employment;
- employees who are HIV-positive will be redeployed to alternative employment at their own request and will not be prevented from continuing work, except where they are deemed 'medically unfit' through the standard procedures;
- equitable benefits;
- guarantee of medical confidentiality;
- access to employee assistance programmes, such as counselling services;
- a statement that individuals who refuse to work normally with people with AIDS or who are HIV-positive will be interviewed to find out the circumstances of their refusal and if appropriate dealt with under the organization's disciplinary procedure;
- arrangements for staff who travel overseas.

A policy such as that suggested above may also be developed in conjunction with an education programme to ensure that all employees are fully aware of AIDS/HIV and particularly the lack of any real risk in normal workplace situations (Radcliffe, 2009).

## Alcohol/drug misuse

Drink- and drug-related problems are one of the most common causes of sickness absence in the workplace (Chartered Institute of Personnel and Development, 2007c). Figures suggest that in the UK over seven million people are considered to be 'hazardous and harmful drinkers' (Boseley, 2007), with 1 in 13 Britons said to be dependent on alcohol (BBC, 2003). The result is that those drinking over the recommended number of units (21–28 per week for men; 14–21 for women) are twice as likely to take sick leave (Income Data Services, 2005e). It is estimated that alcohol-related sickness or illness costs UK employers around £6.4 billion, with up to 17.4 million working days lost (Institute of Alcohol Studies, 2009). Moreover, research from Alcohol Concern suggests that one in four accidents at work are due to alcohol misuse (Trades Union Congress, 2003). Across the EU it is estimated that the cost of lost productivity through absenteeism, unemployment and lost working years through premature deaths resulting from alcohol abuse is €59 billion per year (Institute of Alcohol Studies, 2006). Similarly, research in the United States has suggested that workplace alcohol use and impairment affects approximately 15 per cent of the workforce (Alcohol Concern, 2006). Problem drinkers are also absent from work in the United States, on average, 22 days per year and are twice as likely as non-alcohol drinkers to have accidents at work (Corsun and Young, 1998). While problem drinking is a significant workplace concern, the same is also true for drug misuse. More than one in four British workers under the age of 30 took illegal drugs in the previous year, with 13 per cent of all workers reporting drug use (Income Data Services, 2008b). Drug abuse costs British industry around £800 million each year (Hilpern, 2001). In the United States one in four workers either has used or knows someone who uses illegal drugs and it is suggested that drug abuse costs US business $60 billion annually (Eade, 1993).

Therefore, the direct and indirect consequences of alcohol and drug abuse can be seen in a number of ways, such as costs of accidents, lower productivity, poor-quality work, bad decisions, damage to the organization's reputation, absenteeism and unreliability, managers losing time in dealing with problems and increased labour turnover. Many argue that alcohol and drug misuse has a particular resonance in the tourism and hospitality sector. For example, the industry is often suggested as being fast paced and having a 'work hard, play hard' culture where employees may unwind with alcohol or drugs. In addition, other factors that create an environment which arguably encourages alcohol and drug abuse include:

- long working hours;
- sociability of the workplace;
- availability of alcohol in the workplace, and often the expectation that employees will drink as part of their employment;
- stress, such as employees having to sustain emotional labour so that even during stress-inducing encounters with customers, employees are expected to be positive, friendly, cheerful and helpful.

Reflecting the above discussion it is unsurprising to find that hospitality and tourism workers have been identified as particularly at risk with regard to alcohol and drug abuse. For example, Thomas (2007) reports a survey of 300 hospitality professionals which found that 89 per cent of respondents felt that alcohol and drug misuse was a problem for the industry. Over 70 per cent had seen colleagues misusing alcohol or drugs at work or immediately before work. Although cannabis usage was the most frequently reported, 65 per cent of the respondents also reported seeing colleagues using cocaine (see also Belhassen and Shani, 2012). Similarly, publicans, managers of licensed premises, bar and waiting staff are the occupations most likely to consume alcohol at high-risk levels. For example, research conducted in Canada found that food and beverage employees were twice as likely to have a high-risk level of alcohol consumption when compared to the general population (Pizam, 2010).

Similarly, within the UK context both male and female bar staff are twice as likely as average to die of alcohol-related problems; waiters/waitresses and chefs also showed up as having an above-average death rate from alcohol-related problems (Kirby, 2007).

## Developing policy on alcohol and drugs

On the question of a policy covering alcohol and drugs, it is worthwhile initially considering the extent to which employers can seek to intervene in something that may be taking place outside the workplace. In developing welfare policies there may be times when employers are intervening in an employee's private life outside the organization. Proponents of the business case for welfare would argue that if an employee attends work while still impaired through the use of alcohol or drugs, then it is likely to significantly affect their performance. Consequently, they would dismiss concerns as to the appropriateness of an employer taking an active interest in an employee's life outside of work.

Of course, within the workplace the issue is less ambiguous and employers have a legitimate right to develop policies for alcohol and drug misuse. A further issue that impacts on the development of such a policy is the difference between alcohol and drugs in that rules on drugs at work are inevitably more stringent because drugs are illegal (Income Data Services, 2011d). In terms of developing policy it is useful to acknowledge the view of the Income Data Services (2004b: 10), who recognize that 'there is an increasing trend towards treating long-term alcoholism and, to a lesser extent, dependence on illegal drugs as serious illnesses'. When viewing alcohol and drug misuse in this light the organization is likely to be supportive rather than punitive and will encourage an employee who has a drink or drug problem to seek voluntary help, although this may be facilitated by establishing links with outside organizations, such as those providing employee assistance programmes (EAPs), who can provide expert advice and support. That said, even supportive policies will also usually contain provision for a more punitive approach if there is no improvement in the employee, with around eight in ten employers managing alcohol and drug problems as a combined disciplinary and health issue (Chartered Institute of Personnel and Development, 2007c). For example, an employee may face disciplinary action and ultimately dismissal on the grounds of capability if they are unable to address their misuse. Furthermore, the Income Data Services (2004b) also note that there may be circumstances in which an employee recklessly or even deliberately disregards company rules or acceptable standards of conduct on alcohol and drugs, in which case dismissal on the grounds of misconduct may be acceptable. Within this context an organization's alcohol and drug policy may contain the following (Income Data Services, 2004b):

- a general statement covering the background to the policy, including any legal obligations;

- a clear outline of the aims and purposes of the policy, including the balance between the discipline and support for employees;
- details of the responsibilities of different staff and the training and guidance available;
- who is covered by the policy and if there are tighter restrictions for any particular groups;
- rules and procedures around drug use, including definitions of what constitutes alcohol and drug misuse and rules regarding prescription medicine;
- the disciplinary action that will be invoked following a policy breach, and what the company's stance is in regards to misconduct relating to alcohol or drugs, but not dependency;
- information for employees on safe drinking limits, classes of drugs, the effects of alcohol and drugs and where to receive help;
- details of how an employee can refer themselves for treatment, the support the company will offer and what action the company will take if treatment is declined, not completed or the employee relapses;
- an overview of any testing process, including an explanation of why tests are carried out and when, who administers the tests and what happens if a test is positive or an employee admits to a dependency during the testing process (see HRM in Practice 11.5).

## HRM IN PRACTICE 11.5:
## Drug and alcohol testing: an ethical or legal issue?

There are debates about the usefulness of drug and alcohol testing in the workplace, with concerns being expressed about the moral, ethical and legal aspects of testing; and particularly whether testing is the best way to address the problem of misuse. For example, within the European context some argue that under the Human Rights Act 1998, random testing impinges on an individual's right to privacy. Where testing does take place there are significant differences on who is likely to be tested, depending on aspects such as the country and sectoral context. In the United States it is suggested that around 70 per cent of companies across all industries screen employees for illegal substances. More specifically, research conducted in the 1990s in the hotel sector found that nearly 50 per cent of a sample of 110 hotels conducted drug testing both for applicants for jobs and existing employees. In the UK the figure is much lower, with some estimates suggesting it is as low as 4 per cent. As well as the national differences, there may also be differences in terms of occupations. For example, jobs in industries which are considered 'safety critical' are much more likely to have testing on the job; this would include some parts of the tourism industry, such as the airline industry. The British Airline Pilots Association (BALPA), a trade union

representing over 10,000 pilots, have voiced concerns about random testing of pilots, suggesting that this approach merely drives the problem underground. Instead, their solution to alcohol and drug misuse is support via a 'peer intervention programme'. In this approach flight crew are encouraged to confront a colleague with a problem and urge them to seek help. Evidence seems to suggest that this approach is more successful in detecting the problem and helping individuals deal with it and has recently been endorsed by the International Federation of Airline Pilots Association, which represents pilots worldwide. The ferry and cruise ship industries also tend to operate a strict 'no-alcohol at work' policy for both sea- and shore-based employees, and will often randomly test on-board employees for alcohol or drugs.

Derived from Casado (1997); Income Data Services (2011d); Labour Research Department (2008c); Trades Union Congress (2010)

## Review and reflect

To what extent do you agree that peer pressure is likely to have more impact on changing behaviour with regards to alcohol or drugs than organizationally directed interventions?

## Sexual harassment

While definitions of sexual harassment across organizations are generally similar, there may still be different perceptions as to what constitutes sexual harassment (see, for example, the International Labour Organization (1999) for a review of practices across a number of companies and countries). Before we move on to consider the substance of this statement, consider the scenarios below:

## Review and reflect

Consider the following scenarios and make a note of what you would consider sexual harassment and why:

- patting, hugging or touching a co-worker
- comments about the way a woman looks
- lewd remarks or glances directed towards a male employee from a female employee

- questions about an employee's sex life
- requests for sexual favours
- allowing suggestive posters of either sex in the workplace
- intimate physical contact within the workplace
- a manager beginning a sexual relationship with one of his/her subordinates.

In 2002 the Council of Ministers and European Parliament agreed the text on a new directive on the equal treatment of women and men, which included a new definition of sexual harassment. As of 1 October 2005 this new European-wide definition was introduced into law and suggests that sexual harassment is 'any form of unwanted verbal, non-verbal or physical conduct of a sexual nature [which] occurs with the purpose of violating the dignity of a person, in particular when creating an intimidating, hostile, degrading, humiliating or offensive environment' (cited in Labour Research Department, 2005: 21). Sexual harassment therefore is unwanted behaviour which a person finds intimidating, upsetting, embarrassing, humiliating or offensive; in that sense it is unique to the individual.

The individual nature of sexual harassment means that, at certain times, it may be rather subjective and behaviour that one person may consider as acceptable could be seen as harassment by another. For example, you may have felt that all of the actions in the previous review and reflect section denoted sexual harassment, yet the next person might have indicated something different. There is also the added complication that many of us now meet our partners in the workplace, which means that romantic conduct or romantic liaisons are increasingly evident in the workplace. For example, according to the Industrial Relations Services (2000b), while the majority of UK employees disapproved of overt sexual activity in the workplace, the majority of survey respondents were comfortable with flirting and almost 40 per cent were or had been involved in workplace romantic or sexual relationships. This estimate is cautious given that such relationships are often deliberately covert, but is also confirmed by Kakabadse and Kakabadse's (2004) recent international study of romance in the workplace. With the workplace 'becoming a common meeting ground for romantic liaisons' (Kakabadse and Kakabadse, 2004: 42) there is a need to recognize the line between legitimate and accepted behaviour and that considered sexually harassing.

Where behaviour does err on the side of unacceptable it is usually women who are the worst affected by sexual harassment, although men can suffer as well. Equally, there may be occasional cases of same-sex harassment (Sherwyn et al., 2000). Generally, though, it is women who experience sexual harassment by men. For example, the Industrial Society (now the Work Foundation) produced a report in the mid-1990s which suggested that 93 per cent of

sufferers of sexual harassment were women (Coupe and Johnson, 1999). Often it is a male superior who is the harasser. Gilbert *et al.* (1998) note how two-thirds of sexual harassment complaints in the largest companies in the United States were made against immediate supervisors and upper management. Moreover, the extent to which sexual harassment is experienced is widespread. The Industrial Relations Services (1996), for example, reporting their own and other survey data suggests that well over 50 per cent of women have suffered harassment at work.

Despite the fact that it is often viewed as a 'joke', 'just a bit of fun' or 'a bit of harmless flirting', sexual harassment is, in reality, usually about the misuse of power as well as being humiliating and degrading for the recipient and therefore likely to affect confidence and job performance. It can also have a serious impact on physical and mental health and lead to absenteeism. Clearly, then, there are several reasons why employers should take action to prevent sexual harassment. Some of these may be pragmatic, such as protecting the company image and avoiding litigation as the courts increasingly view the prevention of harassment as the responsibility of the employer; some may be concerned with business aspects such as reducing absenteeism. Arguably, though, the strongest argument lies in our earlier identification of the ethical dimension of broader welfare policies. No employee should have to suffer sexual harassment and the workplace should be a place where every employee has the right to be treated with dignity and not suffer from harassing behaviour (International Labour Organization, 1999).

## Tourism and hospitality: a breeding ground for sexual harassment?

It is important to realize that sexual harassment may be particularly prevalent in the tourism and hospitality industry (Poulston, 2008). Coupe and Johnson (1999: 37) note that 'Female employees within traditional service spheres of employment, such as operative employees in the hospitality industry, will be extremely vulnerable to sexual harassment.' Research has confirmed that high incidences of sexual harassment in tourism and hospitality are common throughout the world (Poulston, 2008). For example, the UK Worsfold and McCann (2000), reporting on the experiences of 274 students on supervised work experience in the hospitality industry, found that 156 (57 per cent) had experienced instances of sexual harassment. Similarly, Lin's (2006) survey of 301 students in Taiwan found both male and female students had experienced harassment, with 97 per cent of the sample reporting at least one incident of such harassment, such as sexual remarks. The female students in Lin's sample were also more likely to have been subject to sexually harassing behaviour. Lastly, Mkono (2010) found that 78 per cent of 77 female hospitality management students undertaking a placement in Zimbabwe had been victims of sexual harassment. Why is this the case? First, within the hospitality sub-sector in particular there is the notion of many departments often being dominated by a single gender, such as men in the kitchen (see HRM in Practice 11.6).

## HRM IN PRACTICE 11.6:
## If you can't stand the heat . . .

The kitchen is often felt to be a very masculine environment with a very macho culture, which may lead to sexist attitudes being prevalent. It is suggested that to fit in employees may have to swear, ogle pornography and generally 'act like men'. Such an environment can create attitudes where sexually harassing behaviour could be construed as just a 'bit of a laugh'. One female chef reporting on her experiences working in a kitchen notes several incidences of sexual harassment, including a colleague having her trousers pulled down in front of an all-male kitchen. She also notes the experiences of female chefs in the United States, where sexism seems equally prevalent, with one noting how she was routinely groped.

Derived from Packer (1998); Roche (2004)

A further issue is the extent to which tourism and hospitality organizations may either tacitly or even deliberately exploit women's sexuality. As Gilbert *et al.* (1998: 49) note, 'the inherent characteristics of service organizations create a prime breeding ground for sexual harassment'. Within tourism and hospitality many accounts (for example: Adkins, 1995; Hall, 1993; Tyler and Abbott, 1998) recognize the manner in which some organizations may sanction sexuality as part of the performative aspects of their front-line employees. In this way tourism and hospitality workplaces may be, in Mano and Gabriel's (2006) view, 'hot' climates. Workplaces which are considered 'hot' climates often have a high degree of aestheticization of the workplace that emphasizes the importance of appearance, style and sensuousness, which in turn creates what Mano and Gabriel term a 'sexual simmer'. Workplaces which have this sexual simmer are also likely to encourage flirtation, sexualized language, innuendo and an emphasis on appearance and image. This notion of certain service workplaces being inherently sexualized is supported by Guerrier and Adib (2000). In their study of sexual harassment of hotel workers they suggest a contributing factor is that hotels often suggest the promise of sexual activity:

> The space of the hotel is laden with sexuality. In particular, the hotel's function is sexualized. Hotel bedrooms provide a space for guests to engage in sexual activity. The sexualization of the hotel space is reflected in the sexualization of hotel workers. In many of the incidents of harassment

in this study, assumptions were made about the hotel workers and their roles as service providers within a sexualized setting

(p. 720)

Beyond the hotel sub-sector, Guerrier and Adib (2000, 2004) also note how other tourism- and hospitality-related settings such as restaurants, airlines and working in a resort as a tour rep are also inherently sexualized environments (see HRM in Practice 11.7).

### HRM IN PRACTICE 11.7:
### Skilled professional or 'trolley dolly'?

Historically, the process of sexualization of airline cabin crew has been one which has changed over time. At the outset of the airline industry flying was an all-male preserve, including the job of air steward. Though there was limited experimentation with the recruitment of female air stewards in the 1930s, it was not until the mid-1940s that the job was really feminized. In the 1950s and 1960s airlines began to sexualize their stewardesses, mainly through their advertising and marketing by portraying the 'sexy' image of female cabin crew. Sexually suggestive advertising slogans used in the past have included Delta's 'Ready when you are', National's 'I'm Anne, fly me' and Continental's 'We really move our tail for you'. This portrayal of what have often been described as 'trolley dollies' was one which seemingly became increasingly anachronistic as airlines were accused of sex discrimination and sexism, especially by the trade unions representing stewardesses. By the mid-to-late 1970s the selling of overt sexuality seemed to wane. However, a recent review of aesthetic labour in the airline industry offers evidence as to how some airlines still seem to mobilize their employees' physical disposition to move beyond an aesthetic appeal to one where the appeal seems to be to the sexual desires of customers. The examples cited are Virgin Blue and Air Asia, two new airlines operating in the low-cost carrier market. An examination of the advertising and marketing of these two airlines points to the manner in which female employees are sexualized, particularly in Virgin Blue, which was described in one newspaper as the world's sexiest airline. For example, one advert produced by the company featured smiling, attractive and youthful flight attendants and was captioned 'Plane Fares, Beautiful Service'.

Derived from Mills (1996); Spiess and Waring (2005)

As can be seen from the above discussion, it is women who are more likely to face sexualization and potentially sexual harassment. Adkins (1995) is one of several authors who recognize how female employees experience greater pressure from tourism and hospitality organizations to sustain an 'attractive' or alluring appearance. She reports how managers in the leisure organization she studied would enforce uniform requirements that required that women would have their dresses pulled down off the shoulder. Indeed, she even notes how male managers would often physically pull down employees' dresses into that position. In this way potentially neutral dress and appearance standards are sexualized by managerial action. Organizations may also encourage a degree of flirting in the interaction with customers. Crucially, alcohol consumption – indeed, often excessive consumption – is an integral part of many tourism and hospitality workplaces, frequently loosening the tongues and morals of customers, in particular.

Hall (1993) notes the importance of 'job flirt' to the waiting staff she studied. Taking part in such activities could potentially be gender neutral in that both men and women might conceivably engage in this type of behaviour in the work setting. Guerrier and Adib (2000) note how the restaurant chain TGI Friday's encourages both male and female waiting staff to flirt with customers to increase customer spend and their own tips. Nevertheless, Hall (1993: 465) notes how, 'although playing the flirting game is an accepted part of interacting with customers, waitresses are more likely than waiters to be the subject of sexual approaches' (see HRM in Practice 11.8).

## HRM IN PRACTICE 11.8:
## Hooters: an acceptable form of sexualization?

Although selling itself as a 'family restaurant' (though 70 per cent of customers are men aged 25–54), the Hooters company uniform of short shorts and a choice of either a tight tank top, crop or tight T-shirt suggests that the intent of the company is to project an image of sexy, eager waitresses. Golding (1998: 7) notes how the company 'unashamedly uses nubile young waitresses dressed in skimpy tops to attract customers' – the so-called 'Hooters Girls'. The success of the company is such that they now have over 400 restaurants in the United States, as well as a presence in 19 other countries. Additionally, until recently the company also had an airline, Hooters Air, which in addition to the airline crew also featured two Hooters Girls on each flight. A recent case study of Hooters in *Fortune* recognizes the extent to which Hooters is considered a mainstream business success (Helyar, 2003). Indeed, the company's marketing and branding strategy has survived a challenge in the American courts on the basis that the company brand is 'female sex appeal'. It is also interesting to note the reaction of the then editor of *Caterer and Hotelkeeper* to the arrival of the first Hooters restaurant in the UK. In an opinion piece the editor saw little to worry about in the emergence of Hooters. In answer to his own question of whether 'the moralists and protectors of women's rights [are] being distracted by a bit of harmless fun?', he goes on to suggest that:

Blatant titillation has become widely accepted in the selling of countless commodities, from fast cars to chocolate bars, from drinks to holidays. . . . If we are not offended by this, then we shouldn't get upset about Hooters, because the principle is much the same.

(Mutch, 1998: 23)

## Review and reflect

To what extent do you agree with Mutch's sentiment?

What the above discussion points to is that within tourism and hospitality there is not only the potential for sexual harassment in terms of the superior–subordinate relationship, but also via potentially pernicious customer interactions, though changes to UK law in 2008 now mean that employers have to protect their staff from sexual harassment by customers. Indeed, at the time of the introduction of the new legislation it was suggested that it would have the biggest impact in the hospitality industry (Dyer, 2008). That said, there has been little evidence of many employees seeking damages from employers and some argue that in reality the protection afforded to employees from third-party harassment is limited (Labour Research Department, 2011f). Indeed, there is also evidence that often some tourism and hospitality organizations may allow a certain amount of ambiguity to creep in with regard to what is deemed acceptable behaviour on the part of customers. For example, in Loe's (1996) thinly disguised ethnographic study of 'Bazooms', she notes how new employees had to sign the official Bazooms sexual harassment policy, which states that 'In a work atmosphere based upon sex appeal, joking and innuendo are commonplace' (p. 400). Of course, there is potentially a thin line between innuendo and what may be thought of as harassing behaviour. Such an issue seemed less of a concern for the company, and the Bazooms employee handbook described sexual harassment in the following manner:

Sexual harassment does not refer to occasional compliments of a socially acceptable nature. It does not refer to mutually acceptable joking or teasing. It refers to behaviour which is unwelcome, that is personally offensive, that debilitates morale, and that, therefore, interferes with work effectiveness.

(Quoted in Loe, 1996: 412)

While ultimately the manner in which some tourism and hospitality organizations portray a certain 'style' may be one which is debated in terms of the extent to which it encourages customers to engage in unacceptable behaviour, the key point remains that sexually harassing behaviour can have a significantly harmful impact on employees. Consequently, it is important that the organization develops a suitable policy response.

## Developing policy for sexual harassment

Therefore, as a way of preventing sexual harassment, organizations should implement an effective policy, which should aim to:

- set out what is considered to be inappropriate behaviour, as well as defining positive and supporting behaviours;
- explain the damaging effects and why it will not be tolerated;
- affirm that sexual harassment will be treated as a disciplinary offence with appropriate penalties attached;
- explain complaints procedure, including how to get help and make a complaint, formally and informally;
- affirm that the complaint will be treated seriously, speedily and con-fidentially, and that there will be no victimization for making a complaint;
- make it a duty for supervisors/managers to implement policy and ensure it is understood.

By offering a clear policy, employees who are being sexually harassed can feel confident that the issue will be taken seriously. This point is important as in bringing forward a complaint of sexual harassment the employee should not have to fear reprisals or continued harassment, or be worried about things like risking future promotion opportunities. Once a complaint is made the investigation should begin as soon as possible and provide:

- a prompt, thorough and impartial response;
- independent, skilled and objective investigators;
- representation for both parties;
- complaint details, the right to respond and adequate time to respond;
- a time scale for resolving the problem;
- confidentiality for all parties.

Investigations of sexual harassment may either be by formal or informal means, though often the preference will be for an informal resolution (Income Data Services, 2003). If there is a more formal investigation, depending on the outcome of any investigation, there may be a range of potential decisions. For example, if the harassment is sufficiently serious it could lead to the dismissal of the perpetrator. Alternatively, there may be disciplinary action short of dismissal, counselling for the person whose behaviour is unacceptable and often the perpetrator may be transferred. There may be occasions where individuals are unclear on how their behaviour may be seen as harassing and

ensuring that they are aware of acceptable and unacceptable behaviour at work will prevent ambiguity and stop harassment reoccurring.

## Stress

Stress has increasingly become a major issue in the workplace, with a seemingly ever larger part of the workforce suffering from work-related stress. Indeed, the UK's Health and Safety Executive (HSE) indicate that stress is one of the most dangerous risks to businesses in the twenty-first century. For example, the Chartered Institute of Personnel and Development (2011e) has recognized how stress has become the most common cause of long-term sickness absence for both manual and non-manual employees. In simple terms stress is the adverse reaction people have to excessive demands or pressure when trying to cope with tasks and responsibilities in the workplace (Labour Research Department, 2011g). At one level stress is a normal part of everyday life, and within the workplace many writers talk about so-called 'good' stress or 'eustress'. This optimum level of stress is felt to be important to sustain high performance and will of course vary with individuals. Once an employee feels unable to cope or control the pressure then they will experience stress as 'distress', which will lead to declining performance. The HSE indicates that in 2010 over 400,000 workers in the UK were suffering from work-related stress, depression or anxiety caused or made worse by their current or past work. It is estimated that there were 10.8 million lost working days due to work-related stress in 2010–11 (Labour Research Department, 2011g). Europe-wide research has suggested that over 40 million EU workers are affected by work-related stress, with the European Commission suggesting that the 'conservative' estimate of the cost of this stress is €20 billion (£16 billion) (Labour Research Department, 2002).

---

### Review and reflect

Think about what makes you stressed at work and how you can address this. To what extent is your stress at work alleviated by the organization and its work processes, and to what extent by your own initiative? Where should the responsibility lie, with the organization or the individual?

---

As with a number of other aspects discussed in this chapter, organizational responses to stress are likely to reflect both legal and business arguments. From a legal point of view employers have a general duty of care under section 2 of the Health and Safety at Work Act (HASWA) 1974 to ensure the health, safety and welfare at work of all employees, including their mental health. In addition, there is also European-inspired regulation and Regulation 3 of the Management of Health and Safety at Work Regulations 1999 requires employers to undertake risk assessment in order to minimize the hazards facing staff, including ensuring that employees' health is not placed at risk by excessive and sustained levels of stress. Failure to comply with the duties contained in the HASWA and the Management of Health and Safety at Work Regulations may result in significant compensation being paid by employers. For example, a number of recent court and out-of-court settlements in the UK have seen figures of up to £830,000 paid by employers (Chartered Institute of Personnel and Development, 2010d). From a business point of view Table 11.1 outlines a number of possible negative effects of stress, which will have a deleterious impact physiologically and psychologically on individuals, which in turn is likely to significantly hamper organizational performance.

As we noted above, there is a need for organizations to be proactive in recognizing and responding to potential stressors in the workplace. The HSE has sought to develop a management standard which classifies some of the key areas which, if mismanaged, can become workplace stressors, these are (HSE, 2009):

- *Demands*: including issues like workload, work patterns, and the work environment. The standard expects that employees are able to cope with

| TABLE 11.1 Some negative effects of stress for the individual and organization | |
|---|---|
| Individual | Organizational |
| Anxiety | Impaired job performance |
| Alcohol abuse | Increased absenteeism |
| Drug abuse | Decreased commitment and motivation |
| Job dissatisfaction | Higher turnover rates |
| Depression | Higher accident rates |
| Panic attacks | Lower productivity |
| Irritability | Lower morale |
| Low self-esteem | Damaged reputation |
| Disturbed sleeping patterns | Recruitment problems |
| Poor concentration | |
| Frequent headaches | |
| Gastric and intestinal problems | |
| High blood pressure | |
| Heart disease | |
| Source: adapted from Income Data Services (2004d) | |

the demands of their jobs. To achieve the standard the organization should provide employees with adequate and achievable demands in relation to the agreed hours of work; ensure that people's skills and abilities are matched to the job demands; that jobs are designed to be within the capabilities of employees; and that any employee concerns about their work environment are addressed.

- *Control*: this is primarily concerned with how much say the person has in the way they do their work. The standard suggests that employees are able to have a say about the way they do their work. To achieve the standard the organization should aim, where possible, to ensure that employees have control over their pace of work; that employees are encouraged to use their skills and initiative to do their work; that employees are encouraged to develop new skills to help them undertake new and challenging pieces of work; the organization encourages employees to develop their skills; employees have a say over when breaks can be taken; and employees are consulted over their work patterns.

- *Support*: this includes the encouragement, sponsorship and resources provided by the organization, line management and colleagues. The standard suggests that employees should receive adequate information and support from their colleagues and superiors. To achieve the standard: the organization should have policies and procedures to adequately support employees; systems should be in place to enable and encourage managers to support their staff; systems should be in place to enable and encourage employees to support their colleagues; employees should know what support is available and how and when to access it; employees should know how to access the required resources to do their job; and employees should receive regular and constructive feedback.

- *Relationships*: this includes promoting positive working to avoid conflict, as well as dealing with unacceptable behaviour. The standard expects that employees should not be subjected to unacceptable behaviours such as bullying and harassment at work. To achieve the standard the organization should promote positive behaviours at work to avoid conflict and ensure fairness; employees should share information relevant to their work; the organization needs agreed-upon policies and procedures to prevent or resolve unacceptable behaviour; systems should be in place to enable and encourage managers to deal with unacceptable behaviour; and systems should be in place to enable and encourage employees to report unacceptable behaviour.

- *Role*: this includes whether people understand their role within the organization and whether the organization ensures that the person does not have conflicting roles. The standard expects that employees understand their role and responsibilities. To achieve the standard the organization should ensure that, as far as possible: the different requirements it places upon employees are compatible; the organization provides information to enable employees to understand their role and responsibilities; the organization ensures that, as far as possible, the requirements it places upon employees are clear; and systems are in place to enable employees to raise concerns about any uncertainties or conflicts they have in their role and responsibilities.

- *Change*: this includes how organizational change (large or small) is managed and communicated in the organization. The standard expects that the organization will frequently engage with employees when under-going an organizational change. To achieve the standard the organization should: provide employees with timely information to enable them to understand the reasons for proposed changes; ensure adequate employee consultation on changes and provides opportunities for employees to influence proposals; and make sure employees are aware of the prob-able impact of any changes to their jobs. If necessary, employees should: be given training to support any changes in their jobs; are aware of timetables for changes; have access to relevant support during changes.

A number of the above aspects can be seen in research examining stress in the tourism and hospitality sector, with a recent Institute for Hospitality survey finding that the primary cause of stress was an excessive workload, closely followed by difficulties with colleagues and customers (Walker, 2010). In a similar vein, Ineson *et al.* (2001) conducted in-depth interviews with ten UK tour managers and identified 117 critical incidents that induced stress. These aspects were grouped into four categories relating to colleagues, clients, nature of the job and poor management. For example, with regard to the nature of the job, the particular work environment of tour managers means that they may face situations such as medical emergencies or logistical problems such as breakdowns and getting stuck in traffic jams. Similarly, a number of the tour managers recalled instances where clients had questioned and contradicted their commentaries, which had undermined their professional authority as they appeared to be incompetent. Interestingly, though, the most common source of stress was employer/management-induced. Examples of such stress included lack of training from the employer and a lack of management com-munication and support. Similar results were also apparent in Law *et al.*'s (1995) study of 102 front-line staff from 14 Australian tourist attractions. Again, poor management was the reason mentioned most often by respondents as a source of stress. A number of the other stressors tended to revolve around the inter-actions with customers, such as difficulties in controlling crowds. While it might seem self-evident that difficult customers are an occupational hazard for tourism and hospitality employees, there is a need to ensure that they are properly trained to deal with such situations. This and other aspects are clearly reliant on proactive management, and in considering workplace stressors it is clear that there is significant responsibility on employers and managers to address these issues in a proactive manner, including developing a stress policy.

## Developing policy

The Income Data Services (2004c) recognize the importance of having a stress policy in bringing the subject out into the open, ensuring that stress is not seen as a taboo subject and employees do not feel stigmatized for feeling 'stressed'. They also recognize that a standard stress policy is likely to have the following aspects:

- a definition of stress;
- a description of the symptoms of stress and stress-related illnesses;
- an outline of the organization's responsibilities for managing stress;
- an outline of managers' and employees' responsibilities for managing stress;
- a list of both internal and external sources of help for stress-related issues (see HRM in Practice 11.9).

### HRM IN PRACTICE 11.9:
### Employee assistance programmes (EAPs): helping employees in the workplace

EAPs are external help services provided by employers which aim to assist in the identification and resolution of employee concerns that affect performance. EAPs originated in the United States and remain popular there, with over 85 per cent of the largest *Fortune* 500 companies using their services. Outside the United States the uptake is rather patchier. In Europe EAPs are rarely used, though there is evidence that more UK employers are using their services, with the Employee Assistance Professionals Association (EAPA) suggesting that over 8.2 million employees in over 5,000 UK organizations currently have access to support, advice and counselling from an EAP. EAPs typically provide a 24-hour, 365-days-a-year telephone counselling service for employees on issues such as stress, bullying, violence, and drug and alcohol misuse. A key decision in the Court of Appeal on work-related stress has given EAPs a significant boost. The ruling from the Court of Appeal suggested that EAP provision to address stress pointed to a proactive employer response and consequently employers who use such services are less likely to be found to be in breach of the duty of care expected in health and safety legislation.

Derived from Labour Research Department (2003c); http://www.eapa.org.uk

## Working time

Excessive working time has often been linked to stress (Labour Research Department, 2011g) and clearly is deleterious to a healthy work–life balance.

Estimates suggest that around 20 per cent of UK employees currently work more than 45 hours per week, creating concerns about 'burn out' (Chartered Institute of Personnel and Development, 2012b). Thus UK workers work some of the longest hours in Europe, with full-time workers working on average 42.7 hours, compared to an EU average of 41.6 hours (BBC, 2011). Interestingly, though, compared to non-EU countries, the UK has shorter working hours than Australia, Japan and the United States (Chartered Institute of Personnel and Development, 2012b). Many would argue that debates about long working hours are particularly pertinent to tourism and hospitality. The long-hours culture in the industry means that many employees work excessive hours, which is likely to have a harmful impact on their health. A survey of nearly 700 hotel, restaurant and bar employees reported in *Caterer and Hotelkeeper* (9 June 2005, 'Long working hours the norm') found that 93 per cent worked more than 40 hours, with nearly one-fifth (17 per cent) working more than 60 hours per week. The same is also very much true for managers and operators of small business, with a survey of 1,400 small hospitality businesses finding that 46 per cent of publicans, 43 per cent of hoteliers and 13 per cent of restaurateurs worked more than 70 hours each week (Cushing, 2004).

The continuing prevalence of excessive working time for many tourism and hospitality employees may seem surprising, given the introduction of the Working Time Regulations (WTR) in 1998. The introduction of the WTR in the UK was not without controversy. The WTR were initially introduced as a health and safety measure. Despite this, the then UK government sought to challenge the legality of the measure via the European Court of Justice (ECJ), but eventually lost the case in November 1996, as the ECJ ruled that working hours were a health and safety issue as opposed to a more general social issue. As a result, the UK government eventually introduced the WTR into law in October 1998 and the main provisions are (Chartered Institute of Personnel and Development, 2012b):

- a limit of an average of 48 hours per week over a 17-week period that a worker can be required to work;
- a limit of an average of eight hours work in 24 hours, which night workers can work;
- a right to 11 hours of rest per day;
- a right to a day off each week;
- a right to an in-work rest break if the working day is longer than six hours;
- a right to 28 days paid leave per year for full-time workers.

When they were first introduced it was felt that the WTR would have a significant impact on UK organizations. In particular, the extension of paid annual leave to the UK, the only EU country not to previously have a legal right to paid holidays, affected around 2.5 million workers, mostly part-time and female workers. Moreover, just over four million workers had less than three

weeks' leave and six million less than four weeks' leave (Milne, 1998b). In reality the impact of the WTR has proved to be less than thought, in part because of a series of derogations which the UK government negotiated (Hurrell, 2005). Chief among these is the ability of companies to offer an 'opt-out' where employees sign away their right to a 48-hour limit on their working week. This measure is one which has been adopted by a large number of tourism and hospitality employers. Although the European Commission has sought to restrict the UK's right to offer an opt-out clause, at the time of writing the UK government seems determined to retain the opt-out (Anon, 2011).

## Workplace violence

Tourism and hospitality establishments rank high on the list of workplaces with high incidences of violence. For example, the Labour Research Department (2003d) reports evidence from the British Crime Survey on the number of workers reporting assaults or threats which occurred while the victim was working and were perpetrated by a member of the public. Across all occupations the percentage of workers who faced violence was just 1.2 per cent. However, for leisure service providers the figure rises to 3.7 per cent and for publicans and bar staff it rises significantly to 11.5 per cent. Boyd (2002), in a survey of nearly 1,200 employees in the airline and railway industries, also found that 70 per cent of her respondents reported an increase in the number of abusive passengers over the previous year. Such abuse was both verbal and physical, with 74 per cent of respondents experiencing verbal abuse from passengers at least once a month. Even more worrying were the nearly 40 per cent of her respondents who had experienced at least two types of physical abuse and 26 per cent who had experienced at least three types of physical abuse. Instances of such abuse included being pushed, punched, kicked, slapped, struck with an object and spat at.

These relatively high figures reflect the fact that many employees in the tourism and hospitality sector have to deal with members of the public, exchange or collect money, work at night and work alone or in small numbers. Added to these aspects many workplaces in tourism and hospitality involve the consumption of alcohol, often to excess. Certainly alcohol seems to have a catalytic effect in many instances of workplace violence in tourism and hospitality. Morgan and Nickson (2001), in a review of 'air rage' in the airline industry, found that excessive alcohol consumption was by far the most commonly cited contributory factor to passenger violence or aggression. Other reasons included being deprived of nicotine and the inherently stressful nature of flying.

Workplace violence is undoubtedly a complex issue, though again there is a need for organizations to be proactive. Certainly an argument could be made that the Management of Health and Safety at Work Regulations would encourage organizations to assess and act upon any potential risks of violence. Among other things, organizations could consider issues such as the underlying cause of the violence, working practices and the provision of suitable training and support needs (see HRM in Practice 11.10).

## HRM IN PRACTICE 11.10:
## A proactive response to 'air rage'

The Income Data Services (2000) report on how Virgin Atlantic have sought to address violence at work, specifically air rage, by improving their human resource approaches. Within the recruitment and selection process, for instance, Virgin look for key skills in relation to communication skills, assertiveness and customer service orientation. Although not a primary consideration in the selection process, there is an assessment of how potential employees may respond to difficult scenarios involving aggressive customers. Employees also receive training in observation skills to help them identify potentially disruptive passengers at an early stage. Staff are taught how to recognize potential precursors of an air rage incident, such as the tapping of fingers or the reddening of a passengers face, and in response to these use calming techniques – such as friendly gentle tones and body language – to defuse the situation. As a result of these approaches the need to have recourse to actual physical restraint has significantly decreased for Virgin Atlantic. If a major incident does occur the company also looks to provide a supportive response. There is an automatic debriefing to the whole flight crew, even those employees not directly affected by the incident. Attendance at such debriefings is mandatory and this recognizes that there may be a delayed response from employees to what is a potentially very stressful experience. Further to this, Virgin Atlantic also provide follow-up counselling, if necessary, through their occupational health department. Finally, the company also offers legal and financial support to employees who wish to pursue legal action against assailants.

## Conclusion

Welfare, health and safety issues have become increasingly important to tourism and hospitality organizations as the business case for proactive responses has become recognized. In considering the 'alphabet' of welfare issues, a number of these issues seem to have a particular resonance within the tourism and hospitality sector. The presence of demanding customers, the blurring of work and leisure and often catalytic effect of alcohol create particular circumstances where the duty of care of employers seems particularly pronounced. That said, it was also recognized that in seeking to intervene in often sensitive issues that the balance between an organizational member's

public and private life is far from clear-cut. Undoubtedly managers in modern organizations require an awareness of these issues and how best to intervene for the benefit of both the organization and individual; a task that is far from easy in dealing with potentially sensitive issues.

## Discussion questions

- Why should tourism and hospitality organizations take an interest in their employees' well-being?
- What are some of the consequences of the 'work hard, play hard' mentality for tourism and hospitality employees?
- How can tourism and hospitality organizations best address the issue of sexual harassment?
- Imagine you have been asked to put on a workshop in the hotel where you work, which is concerned with educating the workforce about HIV/AIDS. How would you approach this?
- Is working in tourism and hospitality more stressful than other industries? Justify your answer.

## Further reading

Adam-Smith, D. and Goss, D. (1993) 'HIV/AIDS and hotel and catering employment: some implications of perceived risk', *Employee Relations*, 15, 2, 25–32.

Guerrier, Y. and Adib, A. (2000) ' "No we don't provide that service": the harassment of hotel employees by customers', *Work, Employment and Society*, 14, 4, 689–705.

Law, J., Pearce, P. and Woods, B. (1995) 'Stress and coping in tourist attraction employees', *Tourism Management*, 16, 4, 277–84.

Morgan, M. and Nickson, D. (2001) 'Uncivil aviation: a review of the air rage phenomenon', *International Journal of Tourism Research*, 3, 6, 443–57.

Poulston, J. (2008) 'Metamorphosis in hospitality: a tradition of sexual harassment', *International Journal of Hospitality Management*, 27, 2, 232–40.

Taylor, P., Cunningham, I., Newsome, K. and Scholarios, D. (2010) ' "Too scared to go sick": reformulating the research agenda on sickness absence', *Industrial Relations Journal*, 41, 4, 270–88.

## Recommended websites

Lots of organizations now use the so-called Bradford Index for accurately calculating sickness absence. See http://www.simplypersonnel.co.uk/MB/RecordReduce Absences.html; http://www.simplypersonnel.co.uk/gettingstarted/bradfordfactor. pdf; http://www.simplypersonnel.co.uk/downloads/2010/Bradford%20Factor% 20Overview.pdf and consider arguments for and against the use of this measure.

ACAS has very helpful guidance on health, work and well-being at http://www.acas. org.uk/media/pdf/d/a/Acas_Health_Work___Wellbeing_(August_2011).pdf

Two charitable organizations that campaign on issues related to AIDS/HIV are the Terence Higgins Trust and the National Aids Trust: http://www.tht.org.uk; http://www.nat.org.uk/

The Ark Foundation is a service offered by Hospitality Action, set up for the purpose of educating hospitality industry students, employees and management as to the dangers of alcohol dependency and other drug misuse: http://www.theark foundation.co.uk

DrugScope offers some interesting views on policy issues surrounding drugs and can be found at http://www.drugscope.org.uk

Women Against Sexual Harassment is a global organization that campaigns against sexual harassment: http://washrag.org/WASH

The HSE's stress at work page can be found at http://www.hse.gov.uk/stress/index.htm

The HSE's violence at work page can be found at http://www.hse.gov.uk/violence/index.htm

The Department for Business, Innovation and Skills has details of the Working Time Regulations and other case studies on how to reduce long hours http://www.bis.gov.uk/policies/employment-matters/rights/working-time

## Additional material

Go to www.routledge.com/cw/nickson to find PowerPoint slides, chapter commentaries, test banks and additional case studies for each chapter.

## CHAPTER 12

# Grievance and disciplinary procedures

## CHAPTER OBJECTIVES

**This chapter examines the importance of rules and regulations in the employment relationship, focusing on grievance and disciplinary procedures. Specifically, the chapter aims to:**

- Consider the complementary nature of grievance and disciplinary procedures.

- Identify sources of employee grievances.

- Assess the differing severity of organizational responses to breaches of discipline.

- Recognize the need for fairness in dismissing employees.

## Introduction

It is generally accepted that there is a need for procedures in the employment relationship to ensure that both managers and employees are aware of the expectations of the organization. In this sense managers need a framework within which to direct and guide behaviour of employees in the workplace. Similarly, employees need to understand their place in the organization and its expectations. Thus, there is a need for some articulated order which is likely to be important to sustain organizational effectiveness. Consequently, rules are needed which cover the whole range of human resourcing, such as what work is done, how jobs are constituted, training and promotion, hours of work, health and safety and standards of behaviour and performance. Equally, there is a need for procedures to provide a framework which allows for notions of organizational justice and reciprocity. This point is particularly true when we think of grievance and disciplinary procedures. We can conceptualize grievance and disciplinary procedures as being complementary, but also distinct. In this way the former is a mechanism whereby employees can challenge management's power, either collectively or individually, and the latter is a way of establishing and maintaining standards which are acceptable to management. While much of this discussion may seem rather prosaic, it is important to recognize that all managers should have at least a working knowledge of grievance and disciplinary procedures, particularly with regard to the ultimate sanction of dismissal. Edwards (2005) notes how dismissal represents the 'dark' or 'murky' side of human resource management (HRM) and is often omitted in many discussions of the subject. It is, however, a fact of organizational life, in much the same way as employees choosing voluntarily to leave the organization. Ultimately, then, as Torrington *et al.* (2011: 490) rather neatly express it, 'The two complementary processes are intended to find ways of avoiding the ultimate sanction of the employee quitting or being dismissed, but at the same time preparing the ground for those sanctions if all else fails.'

## Setting the scene on grievance and disciplinary procedures

Salamon (1992: 568) defines grievance as 'a formal expression of individual or collective employee dissatisfaction primarily, but not exclusively, in respect of the application or non-application of collective agreements, managerial policies and actions or customs and practice'. In recognizing the distinction between individual and collective aspects of dissatisfaction many writers suggest that grievances are usually about individual concerns, while collective dissatisfaction is likely to become a dispute, especially if a trade union is involved. On the other hand, discipline is defined by Salamon (2000) as 'formal action taken by management against an individual or group who have failed to conform to the rules established by management within the organization' (p. 565). Often, grievance and disciplinary procedures will be conceptualized in quasi-judicial terms wherein a body of recognized rules is administered under a judicial-type procedure.

Although the argument in support of the establishment of clear rules and regulations in an organizational setting seems compelling, research undertaken in the tourism and hospitality industry suggests that in the past some organizations have been slow to develop policy. For example, Price (1994) found that only 24 per cent of 241 organizations she surveyed had a well-developed disciplinary procedure. The need to develop clear procedures is important and, as the Chartered Institute of Personnel and Development (2011g) notes, disciplinary and grievance procedures should provide a clear and transparent framework for resolving conflict in the employment relationship. As they suggest, such procedures 'are necessary to ensure that everybody is

treated in the same way in similar circumstances, to ensure issues are dealt with fairly and reasonably, and that employers are compliant with current legislation' (p. 1). In developing a policy an obvious starting point is the Advisory, Conciliation and Arbitration Service's (ACAS) Code of Practice on disciplinary and grievance procedures. Originally produced in 1977 and most recently revised in 2009, the Code of Practice provides clear guidelines on how best to approach grievance and disciplinary procedures, setting out the 'standard of reasonable behaviour' (Advisory, Conciliation and Arbitration Service, 2009: 2). As the Code of Practice notes, 'whenever a disciplinary or grievance process is being followed it is important to deal with issues fairly' (p 3). Thus ACAS recommends that within any grievance or disciplinary process, in order to ensure that they are dealt with fairly (p. 4):

- employers and employees should raise and deal with issues promptly and should not unreasonably delay meetings, decisions or confirmation of those decisions;
- employers and employees should act consistently;
- employers should carry out any necessary investigations, to establish the facts of the case;
- employers should inform employees of the basis of the problem and give them an opportunity to put their case in response before any decisions are made;
- employers should allow employees to be accompanied at any formal disciplinary or grievance meeting;
- employers should allow an employee to appeal against any formal decisions made.

Indeed, adherence to the Code is particularly apposite for tourism and hospitality managers, as evidence suggests that they may be more likely to find themselves enmeshed in either a grievance or disciplinary situation, including potentially finding themselves in an employment tribunal (ET). For example, the Chartered Institute of Personnel and Development (2004), in a survey of nearly 1,200 UK and Irish companies (including 142 tourism and retail employers), found that private sector service employers had twice as many grievance and disciplinary cases compared to the manufacturing, public and voluntary sectors. Similarly, Thomas (2007) recognizes that hospitality staff are among the most likely to consider making ET claims. The relatively large number of tribunal claims emanating from hospitality is arguably a reflection of a number of features, such as high labour turnover, lack of trade union representation and a lack of procedure or good HR practices in the sector. Indeed, it is suggested that many employers are small- and medium-sized enterprises (SMEs) which, as we noted in Chapter 1, predominate in the tourism and hospitality sector and often have under-developed HR practices. This point is felt to be especially true for those employers who employ less than ten people.

That said, it is also important to note that as of March 2012 the UK government has issued a 'call for evidence' which queries whether the ACAS Code in its present form is appropriate for smaller employers and it remains to be seen whether smaller businesses may come under a different regime with regards to grievance and disciplinary procedures (Department for Business Innovation and Skills, 2012b; see also HRM in Practice 12.1).

## Grievance procedures

What is a grievance? Generally, as we have noted, a grievance is the right of employees to express and attempt to resolve dissatisfaction that they might have in the work situation. Torrington *et al.* (2011: 495) outline degrees of discontent that employees may have in the workplace:

- *Dissatisfaction*: anything that disturbs an employee, whether or not the unrest is expressed in words.
- *Complaint*: a spoken or written dissatisfaction brought to the attention of the supervisor and/or other responsible person.
- *Grievance*: a complaint that has been formally presented to an appropriate management representative or to a union official.

---

### Review and reflect

What makes you unhappy at work? Would you be willing to articulate this dissatisfaction as a grievance? If not, why not?

---

Grievances can take a number of forms; Salipante and Bouwen (1990) have provided a widely used schema to categorize sources of conflict and grievance. They suggest that conflict can be distinguished in three ways:

1  *Environmental conflict* is primarily concerned with working conditions and the nature of the work. These problems will encompass the economic terms and conditions of the job, the physical job conditions and job demands either being too great or too little for the individual's skills and abilities.
2  *Social substantive* grievances stem from perceived inequalities in treatment or disagreements over goals or means. Conflict of this nature may be precipitated by organizational policy or management action, which creates a perception of inequity arising from how decisions are taken.
3  *Social relational* grievances arise from the relationships between individuals and groups within the organization – for example, personality conflicts, racism and sexism.

The findings of the Workplace Employment Relations Survey (WERS) (2004) echo the above categorization, while also suggesting that the bulk of grievances raised are more likely to be in relation to Salipante and Bouwen's environmental and social substantive aspects. In that sense pay and conditions, relations with supervisors/line managers and work practices, work allocation and the pace of work were the most common grievances raised by employees (Kersley *et al.*, 2006). Similarly, *Personnel Today* (2010) cite figures from an Industrial Relations Services (IRS) survey of 197 employers across the economy as whole on individual dispute resolution. The survey found that poor working relationships between line managers and employees accounted for 77 per cent of workplace disputes. In addition, 40 per cent of employers saw grievances about pay at least occasionally, with 32 per cent experiencing issues related to working hours and 30 per cent of grievances relating to non-pay terms and conditions. Worryingly, the survey also noted that instances of grievances about race (30 per cent), sex (27 per cent) and disability (27 per cent) were relatively common.

As suggested earlier, all of us at some point in our organizational lives will have a degree of dissatisfaction with our work situation, though the extent to which we will be willing to formally articulate this will vary. Ordinarily, it is unlikely that we will choose to formally register our dissatisfaction as a grievance. Instead, employees may express their dissatisfaction in a number of ways short of formally registering a grievance. For example, employees may simply impose their own unilateral solution through things like increased absenteeism, withdrawing their goodwill or in a reduction in morale/motivation. Ultimately, the dissatisfaction may be such that the employee chooses to leave; the high rate of labour turnover in hospitality and tourism suggests that many employees take such a course of action. If, however, an individual chooses to stay in the organization and decides to formally present a grievance, it is important that it is properly considered and addressed. The ACAS Code of Practice offers a clear procedure for addressing grievances, with several steps (Advisory, Conciliation and Arbitration Service, 2009):

- The employee should let the employer know in writing the nature of the grievance.
- The employer should hold a meeting with the employee to discuss the grievance. This meeting should be organized without delay after a grievance is received.
- The employer should allow the employee to be accompanied at the meeting. Employees now have the statutory right to be accompanied to the meeting by a fellow worker, a trade union representative or an official employed by a trade union.
- Following the meeting, the employer should decide on appropriate action. Decisions should be communicated to the employee and, where appropriate, should set out what action they intend to take to resolve the grievance.

- The employer should allow the employee to take the grievance further if not resolved.

Ordinarily, employees would initially raise the grievance with their line manager, unless somebody else is specified in the organization's procedure. Once received, a grievance will then lead to a meeting between the employee and manager where the grievance will be discussed (see Torrington *et al.* (2011) for details of how to approach grievance and disciplinary interviewing). Finally, the decision will be communicated in writing to the employee, who, if they are still unhappy, will then have the right to appeal, which ordinarily would be dealt with by a more senior manager, who again will write to the employee with the final decision. Failure to raise a grievance formally is not in itself a formal bar to later bringing an ET claim, though if an employee unreasonably fails to raise a grievance through the organization's grievance procedure any subsequent ET award could be reduced by up to 25 per cent (Labour Research Department, 2009).

## Disciplinary procedures

Having examined grievance procedures we can now consider discipline in the organization. In discussing discipline in the organization it is interesting to note the extent to which we are likely to be predisposed to obey rules and authority.

### Review and reflect

What might explain our predisposition to respect rules and authority?

Torrington *et al.* (2011: 491–2) draw on the work of the famous social psychologist Stanley Milgram to suggest a number of features which explain our propensity to be obedient towards authority and how this is likely to shape workplace behaviour, including:

- *Family*: the inculcation of respect for adult and parental authority encourages us to generally respect authority.
- *Institutional setting*: in school, university and work we learn how to function in an organization, often accepting our subordinate position.
- *Rewards*: compliance brings rewards, disobedience brings punishment.
- *Perception of authority*: authority is normatively supported, so we are generally predisposed to follow organizational and managerial rules, but where this does not happen the organization may have to take disciplinary action.

Again, for developing a disciplinary procedure, the Advisory, Conciliation and Arbitration Service (2011b) provide a template in their accompanying guide to the Code of Practice, suggesting that good disciplinary procedures should (pp. 13–14):

- be in writing;
- be non-discriminatory;
- provide for matters to be dealt with speedily;
- allow for information to be kept confidential;
- state the disciplinary actions which may be taken;
- tell employees what disciplinary action might be taken;
- say what levels of management have the authority to take the various forms of disciplinary action;
- require employees to be informed of the complaints against them and supporting evidence, before a disciplinary meeting;
- give employees a chance to have their say before management reaches a decision;
- provide employees with the right to be accompanied at a disciplinary meeting;
- provide that no employee is dismissed for a first breach of discipline, except in cases of gross misconduct;
- require management to investigate fully before any disciplinary action is taken;
- ensure that employees are given an explanation for any sanction and allow employees to appeal against a decision;
- apply to all employees, irrespective of their length of service and status, and should state if there are different rules for different groups.

Implicit in the guidelines is recognition of the differing severity of organizational responses in terms of misconduct; ordinarily the distinction is made between minor misconduct, serious misconduct and gross misconduct. For many instances of minor misconduct or unsatisfactory performance a quiet word from a manager may be all that is needed to improve an employee's performance and resolve the issue. However, if this informal action does not bring the desired improvement, then an employer may take a more formal approach. In essence, there are five key stages: investigation, letter, meeting, action and appeal. In a more detailed sense, the ACAS Code of Practice outlines how employers should (Advisory, Conciliation and Arbitration Service, 2009: 5–8):

- establish the facts of the case, for example collating the evidence which will be used at the disciplinary hearing;
- inform the employee in writing of the problem, ensuring that this notification contains sufficient information about the alleged misconduct or poor performance and possible consequences to enable employees to properly prepare for the meeting;

- hold a meeting with the employee to discuss the problem. In this meeting the employer should clearly explain the complaint against the employee and outline the evidence. The employee should be given the opportunity to set out their case and address any allegations by, for example, presenting evidence or calling witnesses;
- allow the employee to be accompanied at the meeting – employees now have the statutory right to be accompanied to the meeting by a fellow worker, a trade union representative or an official employed by a trade union;
- decide on appropriate action and whether or not any disciplinary or other action is justified and inform the employee accordingly in writing;
- provide employees with an opportunity to appeal if they feel that the disciplinary action taken against them is wrong or unjust.

The decision on disciplinary action will clearly be influenced by the nature of misconduct; in that sense, Table 12.1 outlines a typical disciplinary procedure with commensurate organizational responses.

Examples of minor/serious misconduct could include things such as persistent absenteeism, poor timekeeping, failure to adhere to dress codes or appearance standards, or unacceptable performance; if employees do receive oral or written warnings they are likely to have a specified 'life', after which they are disregarded. For example, for an oral warning the period is likely to be six months, for a written warning it will be one year, and a final written warning will be two years (Income Data Services, 2009). For gross misconduct the Advisory, Conciliation and Arbitration Service (2011b) notes how instances of such misconduct are likely to be decided by the organization depending on their own particular circumstances, while still noting some typical examples, including:

- theft or fraud;
- physical violence or bullying;
- deliberate and serious damage to property;

**TABLE 12.1  Typical disciplinary procedure**

| Nature of the disciplinary matter | Management response and action |
| --- | --- |
| Minor misconduct | Recorded oral warning |
| Serious misconduct or repeated minor misconduct for which a written or oral warning has been received | Written warning followed by final written warning |
| Gross misconduct or further misconduct for which a final written warning has been received | Action short of dismissal:<br>– transfer<br>– demotion<br>– reward deferment<br>– suspension<br>Dismissal |

- serious misuse of an organization's property or name;
- deliberately accessing internet sites containing pornographic, offensive or obscene material;
- serious insubordination;
- unlawful discrimination or harassment;
- bringing the organization into serious disrepute;
- serious incapability at work brought on by alcohol or illegal drugs;
- causing loss, damage or injury through serious negligence;
- a serious breach of health and safety rules;
- a serious breach of confidence.

---

### Review and reflect

Taking into account the discussion in Chapter 11 of alcohol and drug misuse in the hospitality and tourism industries, consider whether the example described below is gross misconduct and whether you are likely to dismiss the employee.

You are the owner of a relatively new and popular restaurant in London. Recently, you have become increasingly concerned about the behaviour of your head chef. The head chef joined the restaurant about two years ago and has for the most part been a great asset, proving very popular with customers and colleagues. However, more recently you have noticed that the head chef's timekeeping is poor and absences have increased dramatically. You have also noticed that the head chef has often looked unwell and appears tired and drawn and can be very irritable. There have also been a few complaints about behaviour from other staff. You have spoken informally to the head chef about this disruptive behaviour on a couple of occasions, and the reasons given for the poor timekeeping and mood swings were very vague. On this particular day the head chef was late for work again and when, later in the day, you went into the kitchen to discuss the late start you found the head chef at the back of the kitchen finishing off a bottle of wine.

What do you decide to do and why?

---

Research undertaken by the Industrial Relations Services (2005d) is useful in pointing to the reasons for disciplinary action. In a survey of over 100 employers in all sectors of the economy they found that the most likely issues for disciplinary action were attendance, performance and capability, timekeeping and general behaviour and conduct. Clearly, most of these aspects are likely to fall into the minor/serious misconduct category, so it is likely to be rare for employees to be dismissed for gross misconduct. Regardless of whether an employee is dismissed for gross misconduct or repeated minor or serious misconduct, a key point is that any dismissal should follow due procedure, something that we now consider.

Employers need to ensure that disciplinary procedures are fully utilized to ensure that any dismissal is considered fair and reasonable, both in a legal and moral sense. For example, an organization might consider that it has acted ethically in dismissing an employee, but even if an organization or individual acting on behalf of the organization has acted in good faith, an ET may decide the dismissal was unfair if the correct procedure was not followed. Moreover, although procedurally incorrect dismissals are no longer automatically unfair, tribunals may take employers' adherence to the ACAS Code into account when considering cases, and if an employer loses a case the award given to the employee can be increased by up to 25 per cent for an 'unreasonable failure' to comply (Evans, 2009). Clearly, then, a key point in any dismissal is the notion of whether the organization has acted in a reasonable, equitable and procedurally fair manner. If not, then the organization could be faced with a claim for unfair dismissal (see HRM in Practice 12.1).

In considering whether a dismissal is fair or unfair we should first look at acceptable reasons for dismissal. There are five potentially fair reasons for

## HRM IN PRACTICE 12.1:
## The changing nature of unfair dismissal protection

As we noted in Chapter 4, governments face a choice as to how much they seek to regulate the labour market and the employment relationship. One of the key aspects to this debate is the qualifying period for bringing an unfair dismissal claim. In line with changing governments this has been something of a political football since the early 1970s. First introduced by the Conservative government's Industrial Relations Act in 1971, the qualifying period for employees to raise an unfair dismissal claim was two years. This was amended in 1974 by the Labour government to just six months. In 1980 Margaret Thatcher's Conservative government increased the amount of continuous service from six months to one year for businesses with over 20 employees, and to two years for businesses with 20 employees or fewer. Five years later, the Conservative government made the qualifying period two years for all employees. With the election of Tony Blair's Labour government in 1997 the qualifying period was again cut to one year in 1999. The Conservative–Liberal Democrat coalition government elected in 2010 has again opted to raise the qualifying period for unfair dismissal from one to two years with effect from 6 April 2012. However, it should be recognized that the increase applies only to employees whose employment with their employer began on or after 6 April 2012. The one-year qualifying period will continue to apply to employees who started with their employer prior to that date.

At the time of writing the government has launched proposals which are seeking to make it easier for small businesses to dismiss staff, despite concerns from organizations such as the CIPD that there is 'no economic case' to make such a

change and concerns about creating a demotivated and disengaged workforce. These proposed changes would enable employers with less than ten workers to sack an employee without reason via a 'no-fault' dismissal, on the understanding that the employee would be paid compensation.

Derived from Churchard (2012c); Labour Research Department (2012c)

dismissal (Chartered Institute of Personnel and Development, 2011h; also see HRM in Practice 12.2):

- Lack of capability or qualifications: this may refer to when employees encounter difficulties in their performance and struggle to fulfil their responsibilities; alternatively, there may also be situations where an employee is unable to do their job due to ill-health.
- Misconduct: as we noted above, this can range from minor to gross misconduct, with differing sanctions.
- Illegality or contravention of a statutory duty
- Redundancy: the law regarding redundancy is quite complex, though in simple terms a redundancy will arise when a business is closing, a workplace is closing or there is a diminishing need for employees to do particular kinds of work in an organization.
- Some other substantial reason: this category is deliberately vague as it is intended to give employers scope to dismiss employees in circumstances that were not envisaged when the legislation was drawn up.

## HRM IN PRACTICE 12.2:
## Prime candidates for dismissal?

Rayner (1998) reports on the controversy created in the late 1990s when it emerged that some local authorities were sending managers on a course to learn how to sack troublesome employees. The course was run by an American company, Padgett-Thompson. Among other things, the course offered participants advice on how to 'deal with employees who drive you crazy' or good performers who had 'know-it-all attitudes'. The course also offered 'a tried and tested technique for silencing employees who want to argue about being dismissed'. In addition, the course identified four employee types who managers are likely to want to dismiss. These types were: the chatterbox (who keeps everyone away from work by constantly talking with colleagues); the plot-ician (who collects the dirt on colleagues and enjoys manipulating those around them); the shark (who enjoys making people squirm and chews up anyone who gets in their way); and the snoop (who delves into other people's personal things and private lives).

> ## Review and reflect
>
> To what extent is a course of the nature described in HRM in Practice 12.2 ethical?

In further considering the notion of whether a dismissal is fair, it is important to recognize that there are a number of things which would be considered automatically unfair regardless of the qualifying period, including (Labour Research Department, 2011d):

- dismissal on grounds of pregnancy or assertion of parental paternity or adoption leave rights;
- dismissal on grounds of trade union membership or stating an intention to join a trade union;
- dismissal for refusing to work on a Sunday (in the case of retail workers);
- dismissal on grounds of actual or proposed trade union activity undertaken at an appropriate time;
- dismissal of an employee without going through the required disciplinary procedure;
- dismissal connected with the transfer in the organization's ownership – Transfer of Undertaking Regulations 2006 (TUPE);
- dismissal where no reason is given;
- dismissal where the employee has been unfairly selected for redundancy;
- dismissal on the basis of a past criminal offence which is spent;
- dismissal on the basis of sex, race, disability, sexual orientation or religion/ beliefs;
- during the first 12 weeks of official industrial action (i.e. action sanctioned by a trade union executive body);
- dismissal for asserting a statutory right, for example the national minimum wage;
- dismissal for 'blowing the whistle' on malpractice in the workplace;
- dismissal for refusal to do something on health and safety grounds.

In 2010–11 there were 47,900 claims for unfair dismissal submitted to the Employment Tribunal Service, down from 57,400 in 2009–10 (Ministry of Justice, 2011). Of these, the vast majority were withdrawn or settled with the intervention of ACAS. Ultimately, nearly 10,500 cases reached a formal ET hearing. Of those cases that were heard by the tribunal service, 4,200 were successful, just 8 per cent of the overall figure for unfair dismissal claims submitted to the Employment Tribunal System (Ministry of Justice, 2011).

The success rate for employees in ETs is not very high, but if they win their case then there are several options open to the ET. The first is the basic award,

which depends on length of service and age and is based on the same rate as statutory redundancy pay (Labour Research Department, 2011d):

- Aged under 22: half a week's pay for each complete year worked under this age.
- Aged 22–40: one week's pay for each complete year worked between these ages.
- Aged 41–65: 1.5 weeks' pay for each complete year worked between these ages.

In addition, there is also a compensatory award, which considers aspects such as loss of earnings, loss of pension rights and the cost to an employee of time and effort in seeking new work. In awarding a compensatory award the ET can also award an amount that it considers 'just and equitable' given the circumstances (Labour Research Department, 2011d). There is no upper limit for cases where dismissal was based on discrimination, for health and safety or whistle-blowing reasons. For other cases the maximum compensatory award is £72,300 (Chartered Institute of Personnel and Development, 2012c). In 2010–11 the highest award was £181,754 (this award was before a maximum award for compensation was introduced in February 2011), though the median award was £4,591 and average award £8,924 (Ministry of Justice, 2011). The final option is either reinstatement (where the employee gets their old job back) or re-engagement (where they are given a different but comparable job). In reality, very few people take this option and in 2010–11 just eight successful claimants chose this course of action (Ministry of Justice, 2011).

## Conclusion

This chapter has considered the need for a clearly articulated order in the organization, particularly with regard to grievance and disciplinary procedures. Evidence suggests that these issues may have a particular resonance within tourism and hospitality; yet at the same time tourism and hospitality organizations often seem to lack the formal policies that sustain a sound approach towards these issues. Although the predominance of SMEs may go some way to explain this lack of formal policies and procedures, clear guidelines from ACAS means that all organizations should now have well-established grievance and disciplinary procedures. Establishment of such procedures means that employees have a channel in which to express their dissatisfaction and employers a means by which to articulate concerns about employee performance or behaviour. Though characterized as the 'murky' or 'dark' side of HRM, dismissal is an organizational reality and all managers should be aware of what constitutes a fair or unfair dismissal. Although a relatively small number of cases end up at an ET, those that do may lead to an organization facing significant costs for a badly handled dismissal. In this way it is clear that rules and procedures in the employment relationship are integral to ensuring that decisions taken by organizations are both ethically and procedurally fair and a sense of natural justice prevails in the organizational setting.

## Discussion questions

- What is the difference between discipline and grievance?
- Why is there a need for clear rules and regulations when it comes to grievance and disciplinary procedures?
- What issues should a company consider to ensure it is handling disciplinary matters, up to and including the dismissal of an employee, in a fair manner?
- Outline arguments for and against either a six-month qualifying period or a two-year qualifying period to bring an unfair dismissal claim.

## Further reading

Advisory, Conciliation and Arbitration Service (2009) *Disciplinary and Grievance Procedures Code of Practice*, London: ACAS.

Advisory, Conciliation and Arbitration Service (2011) *Discipline and Grievance at Work: The Acas Guide*, London: ACAS.

Edwards, P. (2005) 'Discipline and attendance', in S. Bach (ed.) *Managing Human Resources: Personnel Management in Transition*, 4th edn, Oxford: Blackwell.

Salipante, P. and Bouwen, R. (1990) 'Behavioural analysis of grievances: conflict, sources, complexity and transformation', *Employee Relations*, 12, 3, 17–22.

Torrington, D., Hall, L., Taylor, S. and Atkinson, C. (2011) *Human Resource Management*, 8th edn, London: Prentice Hall.

## Recommended websites

ACAS has a number of useful resources at http://www.acas.org.uk/index.aspx?articleid=360&detailid=548

The Directgov website has a range of information on resolving workplace disputes and dismissal; these can be found at http://www.direct.gov.uk/en/Employment/ResolvingWorkplaceDisputes/index.htm; http://www.direct.gov.uk/en/Employment/RedundancyAndLeavingYourJob/Dismissal/index.htm

## Additional material

Go to www.routledge.com/cw/nickson to find PowerPoint slides, chapter commentaries, test banks and additional case studies for each chapter.

# Human resource management in the events industry

COMPANION @ WEBSITE

## CHAPTER OBJECTIVES

**This chapter is concerned with the events industry as a related, but distinct, part of the tourism and hospitality industry. It considers the nature of the events industry and in particular recognizes the significant challenges of managing volunteers, who supply a major part of the events industry workforce. Therefore, the aims of this chapter are:**

- To recognize the events industry as a distinct part of the tourism and hospitality industry.

- To fully understand the heterogeneous nature of the events industry.

- To consider the particular challenges of managing a volunteer workforce.

## Introduction

In many respects, any discussion of human resource management (HRM) in the events sector is no different from much of the discussion that has preceded this chapter. For example, a recent textbook covering HRM in the events industry covered aspects such as organizational culture, recruitment and selection, training and development and grievance and disciplinary procedures (van der Wagen, 2007). Similarly, Deery (2009), in her discussion of employee recruitment and retention strategies for event management frames her discussion by drawing lessons from the literature on these issues from the tourism and hospitality industries. However, while a number of the functional aspects of HRM will not differ, there are a number of significant differences which make a separate chapter on the events industry a necessity. Thus, as a recent edited collection on human resource (HR) issues in the events industry noted:

> we have witnessed in recent decades the emergence of events as an experience phenomenon that is clearly differentiated from tourism and hospitality while having close links, both conceptually and organizationally, to these areas. It is a sector that is emerging as a separate domain to study, with a growing education and research agenda.
>
> (Baum *et al.*, 2009b: 217)

To consider this notion of difference the chapter will consider the different types of events, including recognizing the key concept of the 'pulsating organization' (Hanlon and Jago, 2009). This notion of the pulsating organization draws on the work of Alvin Toffler (1990) and refers to an organization which has a small number of core personnel for much of the year but as the event gets nearer and takes places significantly increases the number of staff. Of course, within the events industry a large number of these new staff are volunteers and it is this notion of the events industry employing a range of different types of employees – permanent paid staff, paid seasonal staff and volunteers – which is another obvious source of difference between 'normal', commercially operating tourism and hospitality organizations (Deery, 2009). For example, van der Wagen (2007) notes that for the Sydney 2000 and Athens 2004 Olympic Games paid staff made up less than 5 per cent of the workforce and instead the majority of staff was provided by contractors and volunteers. Similarly, Elstad (2003) recognizes that over three-quarters of festivals within the UK use volunteers. Indeed, many existing tourism and hospitality employees may well be potential volunteers. It is suggested that tourism and hospitality organizations should encourage staff if they wish to volunteer as it is likely to positively affect their morale and also potentially lead to them developing skills which they can take back to their workplaces (Blackhurst, 2011).

Though it is important to recognize how the events industry might be considered distinct, it is also appropriate to recognize that event organizations, like other tourism and hospitality organizations, are seeking to ensure that people attending the event experience high levels of service and a good customer experience (Drummond and Anderson, 2004), so the role of event staff is equally important as other front-line tourism and hospitality employees. Clearly, then, event organizations have to manage all of their staff, paid and volunteer, in a manner that encourages them to offer a good customer experience. In that sense, often people attending an event will not be aware of whether the employees they are interacting with are paid staff or volunteer staff. That said, given our earlier recognition of the importance of volunteers, and the distinctiveness that this creates in the events industry, this chapter will pay particular attention to the management of this unique group of

employees. The chapter initially discusses the nature of the events industry, recognizing the range of different types of events. This section of the chapter will also briefly consider the extent and nature of paid employment in the events industry. Following this discussion, the chapter moves on to consider the importance of volunteering and the manner in which the motivation of volunteers may vary. Having considered the broader aspects of the events industry and, in particular, the key role of volunteers, the chapter then examines key challenges facing organizations, first in recruiting and selecting, then training and finally rewarding and retaining volunteers.

## A brief word on the nature of the events industry

There have been numerous attempts to categorize the nature of events. While there is no universally accepted typology it is common for writers to talk about sporting events, business events, music and entertainment events and arts and cultural events. Sporting events can be so-called mega-events such as the Olympic Games and FIFA World Cup, which are global in scope and 'permeate into almost every aspect of life at the destination during the event' (Mair, 2009: 5) and are capable of attracting significant visitor numbers and related employment benefits (see HRM in Practice 13.1). The same is also true for other major sporting events such as the Open Golf Championship, F1 Grand Prix, Grand Slam tennis tournaments and the FA Cup Final.

### HRM IN PRACTICE 13.1:
### Britain's monumental sporting decade

Throughout the period 2012–19 Britain has a series of major sporting events which will be expected to create plentiful paid employment opportunities both during the events and subsequently. This 'golden decade of sporting events' includes the 2012 Olympics in London, the 2013 Rugby League World Cup, the 2014 Commonwealth Games in Glasgow, the 2015 Rugby Union World Cup and the 2017 World Athletics Championship. For example, the London Organising Committee of the Olympic Games estimates that around 30,000 paid jobs will be generated by the actual staging of the 2012 Games. Subsequent to this it further estimates that five years after the Olympic Games the hospitality workforce in London will have grown by 10 per cent, with the creation of an additional 37,000 jobs.

Derived from Experian (2006); Gerrard (2010); Gibson (2009, 2011a)

Indeed, Baum *et al.* (2009b), in summarizing the range of research undertaken on HR issues in the events industry, recognize that often there is a dominance of work focusing on sporting and mega-events. Part of the explanation for this dominance perhaps lies in Mair's point above about the manner in which the event becomes all-pervasive, and consequently the event will often be perceived as a catalyst to address broader employment and skills issues. HRM in Practice 13.2 outlines how the London Olympic Games have been seen as a catalyst to address and improve levels of customer service across the whole of the UK hospitality, leisure, travel and tourism industry (see also http://www.people1st.co.uk/preparing-for-2012).

## HRM IN PRACTICE 13.2:
## The 2012 London Olympic Games as a catalyst to improve customer skills in the UK

A report written in 2008 by Skills for Business recognizes the major opportunity that the London 2012 Olympic Games and Paralympic Games will provide to showcase the UK visitor economy. The report recognizes how the Games provide a chance for the UK to shine on the world stage, recognizing that key to the success of the Games and UK Plc will be the people who visitors interact with. It is also noteworthy how the report notes that the success of the Games will be dependent on not just the obvious key visitor economy areas of hospitality, leisure, travel and tourism, but that visitors to the Games will also potentially find themselves interacting with the creative and cultural industries, passenger transport, active leisure activities, retail and justice and security, reinforcing Mair's point above about the all-encompassing nature of a sporting mega-event. Though the report recognizes the enormous potential of the Games to showcase the UK visitor economy, it also notes concerns about poor levels of customer service within the UK. In addressing this point the report offers a series of recommendations which encompass the creation of a high-profile customer service campaign led by VisitBritain, providing branding to recognize excellence in customer service and developing specific interventions to improve the customer experience for 2012 (see the discussion in Chapter 7 related to People 1st and WorldHost).

Derived from Skills for Business (2008)

Business events encompass conferences, meetings and exhibitions, incentive travel, corporate events and corporate hospitality. Music and entertainment events encompass a range of musical and performing tastes from Glastonbury through to Celtic music events such as Celtic Connections in Scotland. Finally, arts and cultural events are often closely linked to festivals,

such as the Edinburgh International Festival and Edinburgh Fringe Festival. Although this chapter draws examples from a number of these different types of events, inevitably it cannot cover all of these sub-sectors in detail and indeed, reiterating our earlier point, much of the reported research and examples are often drawn from the sporting world. Readers are directed elsewhere for a fuller discussion of HRM issues in the full range of events organizations (see, for example, Baum *et al.*, 2009a; Bowdin *et al.*, 2010; van der Wagen, 2007).

In recognizing this range of different types of events, it is also worth noting that several writers make a distinction between business and other types of events. More specifically, it is suggested that business events will often provide greater stability in employment opportunities, and in that sense are similar to 'normal' commercially operating tourism and hospitality organizations, with the provision of permanent, full-time ongoing employment (Deery, 2009). This situation can be compared to the temporal nature of a major sporting or cultural event, for example. A further distinction can also be made between recurring and one-off events. Recurring events, such as the Australian Open Tennis tournament, are those that take place on an annual basis, whereas one-off mega-events, such as the Olympic Games, take place at set intervals, but in a different location on each occasion. In a pragmatic sense, then, there may be different approaches taken, for example, with regard to retention strategies whereby the recurring event aims to create a sense of loyalty and commitment from its volunteers so they will return or 'bounce back' year-on-year (Smith and Lockstone, 2009).

## Paid employment in the events industry

Although the focus of this chapter is predominately on the challenges of managing a volunteer workforce, it is important not to give the impression that the events industry only generates volunteer employment. For example, there has been a major growth in event-management companies in recent years, focusing on a range of event types as described above. It should be noted that, in much the same way that we recognized the diversity of employment in the tourism and hospitality industry in Chapter 1, there are a wide variety of jobs available in the events industry from skilled management jobs through to relatively unskilled jobs, many of which will have the same characteristics of a number of the tourism and hospitality jobs that we have been discussing throughout the book. All major events provide a wide range of long-term and short-term paid employment opportunities in specialist events areas. These employment opportunities may demand a range of managerial or technical skills, or be in more mundane areas such as stewarding, catering, cleaning and so on (see HRM in Practice 13.3).

Event halls and conference centres regularly host a wide array of face-to-face meetings, trade shows, conferences and so on, all of which, as noted above, need to be staffed on a more permanent basis.

## HRM IN PRACTICE 13.3:
## Staffing a literary festival

The Hay Festival of Literature and Arts is an annual ten-day gathering held at Hay-on-Wye in Wales. The festival, which in 2012 celebrates its twenty-fifth anniversary, brings together writers from around the world with the aim of celebrating great writing and is, in Bill Clinton's words, 'The Woodstock of the mind'. The festival is a good indication of the range of jobs, both paid and volunteer, that are available during a large international festival, and also the extent to which these jobs overlap with the hospitality sector. For example, site crew are required to assist with the construction and deconstruction of the festival site in the weeks running up to and following the festival. Prior to the festival starting the Box Office employs an extra ten paid staff. Interested applicants for the Box Office are expected to work very long hours, though the festival suggests that they will receive fair pay in return. Applicants are expected to be calm, good on the telephone, familiar with computers, to enjoy working with the public, have retail experience and, as the festival's website notes, 'a sense of humour and rhino-hide help'. Indirectly, there are paid jobs available within a newly opened restaurant which is run by an organization called Capital Cuisines, which provides high-class event catering. Contracted solely for the length of the festival, jobs are available for waiters and waitresses, chefs, kitchen assistants and kitchen porters, with uniforms and meals on duty provided. In addition, there are a range of paid opportunities for bar and catering staff offered by concession-holders (e.g. food and drink stands) on the festival site. There are volunteer opportunities as well, as all the festival events are stewarded by teams of between four and ten stewards. The main job of these volunteer stewards is to make sure the audiences are safe and happy before, during and after each event. Internships are also offered at the festival. As the festival organizers suggest, the work is very demanding, but the atmosphere is 'great' and enduring friendships are formed through people's experiences as both paid and volunteer employees.

Derived from http://www.hayfestival.com/

There is no definitive view as to the size of the paid workforce, as the industry is extremely diverse and difficult to define, as well as potentially overlapping with other elements of the tourism and hospitality sector, as we noted above. As Mair (2009: 12) notes, 'it is difficult to ascertain the size of the industry simply because events form a part of so many other sectors and people working on events may not even consider themselves to be part of the events industry'. That said, People 1st (2010c) estimate employment within the UK events industry using three different elements of the events industry. It is suggested that the whole events industry (including suppliers) generates total employment

of 530,000. In addition, the number of those working in convention and trade show organizer establishments is 23,200 and there are estimated to be 15,500 people working in conference, event and exhibition manager roles. Paid staff in the events industry, and particularly those in front-line positions, are expected to give good service, even though, along with many other tourism and hospitality employees, many of them may receive poor pay, indifferent working conditions and bad management (Tum *et al.*, 2006). Clearly, then, in many respects the challenges of managing paid front-line staff in the events industry are similar to a number of those challenges facing tourism and hospitality organizations, as outlined in Chapter 1 and considered throughout the book. This point is particularly true of the business events sub-sector due to the more permanent nature of employment (Deery, 2009).

Although there are a considerable number of paid employment opportunities in the events sector, one, if not the key, distinctive feature of the events sector is the role of volunteers. Before the chapter begins to consider how event organizations go about recruiting and selecting, training and rewarding their volunteer workforce, it is worthwhile considering the importance of volunteering, volunteers and their motivations.

## The importance of volunteering, volunteers and volunteer motivation

Consideration of the importance of volunteers allows us to identify a number of benefits of volunteering from an individual, organizational and societal point of view. Thus, van der Wagen (2007) notes a number of reasons why an event would seek to recruit volunteers as a component of the workforce, or in some cases the complete workforce. These are (p. 65):

- *Establishing the event*: for example, many music festivals often start from small beginnings and grow over time, with volunteers often playing a significant part in this growth.
- *Expanding the workforce*: commonly, volunteers will be utilized as a cost-effective way to expand the workforce. Indeed, 'without the contribution of volunteers many mega-events and hallmark events would not be able to run in their present format as the contribution of volunteers is so significant in terms of the total hours contributed' (p. 65). For example, van der Wagen notes how volunteers at the 2002 Manchester Commonwealth Games contributed 1,260,000 hours.
- *Expanding the level of customer service*: as volunteers usually take on a customer service role this can significantly contribute to the ambience of the event.
- *Contributing to community spirit*: volunteering can develop and enhance community spirit.

- *Creating a social impact*: the use of volunteers can be linked to broader societal aspirations to create useful and productive citizens. In this way volunteering can potentially improve people's qualifications and employment prospects (see also HRM in Practice 13.4).
- *Contribution to diversity*: it is noted that event volunteers come from a very varied range of backgrounds, thus providing representative languages and cultures to events.
- *Expanding the network*: volunteers may have been co-opted by family or friends and they in turn may co-opt other family and friends, thus extending the volunteering network.
- *Belief in the ethos of volunteerism*: some organizations have a strong ethos of volunteerism.

### HRM IN PRACTICE 13.4:
### Creating a legacy: the example of the Manchester Commonwealth Games 2002

A report written by the North West Development Agency (NWDA) which sought to assess the direct economic, social and regeneration impacts of the 2002 Manchester Commonwealth Games noted the particular success of the volunteer programme that supported the Games. Initially there were around 17,000 applicants to be volunteers at the Games, with around 10,000 of these being appointed. For the volunteers themselves research undertaken by UK Sport into the Games volunteer programme found that:

- 18 per cent of volunteers agreed that being a Games volunteer had improved their chances of employment;
- 50 per cent of volunteers agreed that the fact of being a Games volunteer looked good on their CV;
- 47 per cent of volunteers agreed that they had learned new skills and capabilities from being a Games volunteer;
- 46 per cent of volunteers agreed that being a Games volunteer had enhanced their personal development;
- 69 per cent of volunteers said that the Games had made them feel much more part of the wider community.

In part, some of the findings above might reflect the fact that the Games were the first to offer a nationally accredited qualification programme to volunteers. A pre-volunteer programme was run to promote personal development, raising self-esteem, motivation to participate socially, interest in participation in sport, health, conflict management and community involvement. Arguably reflecting these findings, the Games also seemed to create a positive attitude towards volun-

teering, and a pool of volunteers who might be utilized for other events and activities. Indeed, following the Games a Post Games Volunteer Project (PGVP) was set up. The PGVP had two broad aims. First, it provided a link between organizations and event organizers trying to recruit volunteers and those on the database looking for volunteering opportunities. Second, it sought to use volunteering as a method of engaging those outside the labour market in order to (re)connect them to employment and training opportunities. The report notes how Games volunteers responded positively to requests for support for other activities and successfully carried out a number of roles at major events such as the UEFA Champions League Final at Old Trafford in 2003 and the Europride event, also in 2003.

Derived from North West Development Agency (2004)

## Volunteer motivation

In a recent comparison of volunteering at events in Australia and the United States it was recognized that the motives of volunteers will often be linked to the cultural and social mores of a nation (Goldblatt and Matheson, 2009). For example, within high-context cultures, such as North America and Western Europe, volunteers are more engaged, while in lower-context cultures, such as Asia, South and Central America, volunteer engagement was much lower. Thus volunteer motivations may well be strongly linked to the socio-cultural context in which an event is taking place, which in turn affects their motivations and engagement. As well as these differences at a broad national cultural level, there are likely to be significant differences as to why individuals volunteer and what they are seeking from the experience.

### Review and reflect

What would be the main reasons for you to volunteer for an event? To what extent are these reasons dictated by the nature of the event?

Hoye and Cuskelly (2009) note how there are likely to be a variety of motives held by event volunteers and that they should not be treated as a homogenous group, but rather as a collection of individuals each with different motives for engaging in volunteering. For example, Ralston et al. (2004) note that men generally have to be asked to volunteer and do so primarily in response to their own needs and interests, or due to the social benefits. Women are more likely to offer help, often in response to the needs of family and friends. Age is also another important variable; Hoye and Cuskelly (2009) note how volunteer motives may change over time. For example, Ralston et al. (2004) and Tum et al. (2006) recognize that younger volunteers will often be aiming to learn new skills while others, possibly in an older age group, will volunteer for personal enrichment and to help others. Clearly, then, volunteer motivations may be complex and can encompass an array of reasons – for example, career development, personal rewards or the need for a fulfilling experience, or a combination of all of these and lots of other factors. Hanlon and Jago (2009) found that this sense of personal enrichment and enjoyment was often found in terms of volunteer motivation to participate in major sports events. Related to this point is the need to try and ensure a fit between what volunteers are seeking when they engage in volunteering that reflects congruence between their role and their own personal motivations, meaning there is greater scope for a win–win situation. For example, Ralston et al. (2004) found that for the Manchester Commonwealth Games the main reason for volunteering was to be part of the whole experience and not necessarily to use any skills or experience which volunteers might have. Consequently, volunteers were happy to take on a range of tasks. As a result of this congruence between the volunteers' motivations and what the event could provide, the roles allocated to volunteers met and, in some cases, exceeded their motivations and expectations. Clearly, then, it is important to recognize the potential for heterogeneity in volunteers, both in terms of their motivations and what they are seeking from the experience of volunteering for an event. That said, there may be a number of common issues which events organizations should be aware of in terms of some of the HR challenges arising from the management of volunteers.

In considering the particular issue of managing volunteers as a unique aspect of the events industry, it is important to consider some of the HR challenges. In that regard Elstad (2003: 106) found from studying volunteers at a Norwegian jazz festival that the main reasons for them to quit were (in order):

1  their overall workload;
2  a lack of appreciation of their contribution;
3  problems with how the festival was organized;
4  disagreement with changing goals or ideology;
5  wanting more free time for other activities;
6  a lack of a 'sense of community' among volunteers;
7  family responsibilities;
8  the festival becoming too large;
9  the inability to make decisions regarding their own position;
10  a dislike of some of their responsibilities;
11  lack of remuneration;
12  moving out of the festival's geographic area.

Similarly, Ralston *et al.* (2004: 16) found a number of things which caused potential burnout in volunteers, including:

- an intense time and energy commitment;
- over-demanding workloads;
- insufficient number of volunteers;
- tensions between volunteers, staff and others;
- open public scrutiny;
- lack of effective leadership;
- absence of tangible rewards;
- insecurity over one's appointment or volunteer role;
- boring or unfulfilling labour.

In response to some of the issues of managing volunteers, van der Wagen (2007) recognizes that most professional event organizations are likely to have a code of conduct for managing volunteers. Thus an event organization which has such a code of conduct for managing volunteers will aim to (p. 67):

- meet all legal obligations such as anti-discrimination legislation;
- provide a healthy and safe working environment;
- plan and document safe working practices;
- provide insurance cover for volunteers;
- provide clear and accurate information about how volunteer expectations will be met;
- provide orientation and training;
- avoid placing volunteers in positions more suitable for paid staff;
- treat volunteers as an integral part of the team;
- avoid placing volunteers in situations that are difficult or dangerous;
- provide meals, drinks and breaks as required;
- provide protection from the sun and elements;
- define jobs and issue job descriptions or checklists;
- develop HR policies and make these available to volunteers, including procedures for grievance resolution;
- acknowledge the rights of volunteers;
- offer opportunities for learning and development where possible;
- meet out-of-pocket expenses such as transportation;
- keep volunteers up-to-date with important information;
- constantly acknowledge the contribution of volunteers on both and individual and group basis.

Clearly, then, event organizers need to understand volunteer motivations and what is likely to lessen dissatisfaction and the likelihood of volunteers leaving, and aim to increase their satisfaction with the volunteering experience. The fact that there may be a variety of reasons underlying why people volunteer, depending on factors like the nature of the event or the individuals themselves, should be taken into account as the event organization begins to develop its approach to key HR aspects such as recruitment and selection, training and development and reward and retention.

## Recruitment and selection

As we noted earlier in the chapter, the nature of the event is likely to significantly impact on the approaches taken to recruitment and selection, as the type of event will often determine the type of staff the events organization seeks.

---

### Review and reflect

What are the likely challenges in recruiting for a mega-event such as the Olympic Games and for a small-scale local festival?

---

Van der Wagen (2007) notes how the Chelsea Flower Show, the UK's most prominent horticultural event, will have an expectation that volunteers working on the front-line with exhibitors and visitors would have horticultural expertise and a passion for the industry. Indeed, it is also worth reiterating the point about the type of event having a major impact in terms of its potential attractiveness to volunteers. There will often be a major difference between a mega-event, such as a major sporting occasion, and a smaller, recurring event, such as a local festival. For the former there is often a massive oversupply of potential volunteers, but smaller, recurring events will often have much less choice in filling roles (Smith and Lockstone, 2009) and, as we will discuss later, often for recurring events HR initiatives are more likely to be geared towards retention issues.

While for smaller, recurring events the challenge is often finding a supply of sufficient volunteers, for larger events, particularly sporting mega-events, the recruitment challenge lies in the fact that they will often be massively over-subscribed. Thus, rather than attracting applicants, the challenge becomes one of filtering from such a large group of applicants. For example, the London 2012 Olympic Games organizing committee had to whittle down 250,000 applicants to the 70,000 volunteers required for the event (Churchard, 2011). The recruitment process, which was described as 'the UK's largest peace-time recruitment event' (Stevens, 2011: 7), began in July 2010 with the initial attraction phase. Even through some of the successful applicants began training from October 2011 at the McDonald's University in London, selection events were taking place till March 2012 (Blackhurst, 2011). In a similar vein,

van der Wagen (2007) notes that attracting potential volunteers would also be relatively straightforward for a major rock concert as she suggests that one phone call would ensure that word would soon spread, thus ensuring that advertising would not be necessary (see HRM in Practice 13.5).

## HRM IN PRACTICE 13.5:
## Oxfam 'win–win' stewarding for music festivals

Each summer Oxfam provides a professional stewarding service to some of the UK's biggest music festivals. In return the organization receives a donation from the festival organizers. In 2010, Oxfam provided 5,000 stewards to 14 major festivals and raised £1 million. Stewarding roles include manning gates, such as entrance gates, being responsible for fire towers, monitoring appropriate accreditation for accessible viewing platforms, monitoring crowd levels around the stage, chaperoning vehicles and finally being a response team steward whereby volunteers are on standby at the start of their shift to fill any gaps there may be around the site and also to respond to help with unplanned situations that may arise around the site. This initiative is very popular and the volunteer places quickly fill up, leading to waiting lists if any volunteers drop out for any reason. As one volunteer steward noted, 'stewarding is the way forward. Free festival tickets and fab friends; fun in the sun and raves in the rain – summer will never be the same again.'

Derived from http://www.oxfam.org.uk/Stewarding

Smith and Lockstone (2009) note that there is a need to create a delicate balance in the recruitment and selection period with regard to seeking to inspire volunteers, while at the same time 'creating realistic expectations regarding workload commitments, responsibilities, organizational support and the overall volunteer experience' (p. 155). A good example of this need to create realistic expectations can be seen in the recent public pronouncements of Lord Coe, chairman of the 2012 London Organising Committee of the Olympic Games. In recognizing that potential volunteers may often have a misperception of their likely role during the course of the Games, Lord Coe was at pains to present a realistic picture of what volunteers are likely to be doing:

> I've been very upfront on this for a long time because I wanted people to be excited by it but not deluded into thinking they would be sitting with Usain Bolt for two hours. Even if they are in the stadium the chances are they will be in the bowels of it. They may never see a track event.
>
> (Cited in Gibson, 2011b: 9)

Event organizations will use a number of similar recruitment mechanisms as those we discussed in Chapter 5, depending on the resources available to them. Thus recruitment methods used by events organizations include: word-of-mouth/referrals from other employees; internet advertising both by the event organization and via general volunteering websites; employment agencies; newspaper advertising; using stakeholders such as local councils, community groups, sponsors and event suppliers to communicate the events staffing needs to respective networks; utilizing existing programmes for the unemployed, colleges and universities and, particularly for larger sporting events, associations and sports clubs, who often provide qualified umpires and officials (Bowdin *et al.*, 2010; van der Wagen, 2007).

As well as seeking new volunteers, if it is a recurring event the organizers may seek to bring back volunteers from previous years. For example, Smith and Lockstone (2009) in their study of 12 annual cultural festivals in Australia covering events in the arts, music, food, wine and annual celebrations (Christmas, Easter, etc.) found that the vast majority of these events were reliant on large numbers of returning or 'bounce back' volunteers. Indeed, the same authors note how volunteers often return to the same role, which means they need less training and development to be competent in that role. Of course, the event also has to show a degree of proactivity in ensuring this high rate of return for volunteers. For example, the study found how past volunteers are initially approached to see if they want to return, and once this is done then other recruitment methods can be considered, depending on the answers. In general, returning volunteers did not have to re-apply, and if there had been any concerns about their performance they could still be asked back, but in a new role.

A similar proactive approach to recruiting volunteers is seen at the Australian Open, though here recruitment begins almost as soon as the previous event has finished (Deery, 2009; Hanlon and Jago, 2009). For a tournament of this type there are a wide range of positions, such as court services staff, ball kids, courtesy car drivers, corporate hospitality assistants and media workroom staff; in order to fill all of these positions recruitment begins ten months before the event. Indeed, it is important to recognize the significant diversity in the type of jobs or volunteer positions that are available in the events industry. Some of these may be highly specialized and have significant skill require-ments, such as medical and technical skills, while some will be simply about general volunteers helping people who are attending the event. For example, volunteers to the Harrogate International Festival, a summer international arts festival encompassing music and storytelling, are expected to have a strong commitment to the aims and objectives of the festival, as well as to be knowledgeable and enthusiastic about the arts. However, for other events the personal characteristics which are sought in volunteers are rather more generic and include being reliable, enthusiastic, hard-working and flexible (Bowdin *et al.*, 2010; see HRM in Practice 13.6).

With selection, event organizations' approaches are likely to differ depending on the nature of the event and the resources at their disposal. Bowdin *et al.*

## HRM IN PRACTICE 13.6:
## Supporting an international boat show

Sanctuary Cove International Boat Show is a leading marine event in the Asia Pacific region. Held in Australia, this annual event has been running over 20 years and in 2011 attracted nearly 400 exhibitors from Australia, China, Taiwan, South Africa, Singapore, Sri Lanka, New Zealand, South Korea and the United States. The four-day event draws buyers and delegates from around the world, as well as lots of visitors who go to see super yachts, power and sail boats, trailerable boats, marine accessories, engines, electronics and marine business-to-business services. In support of the event there are a number of volunteer positions. Prior to the event starting there are opportunities for event set-up assistants, who among other things must be physically fit. Once the event is running, roles include volunteers required to assist pedestrians crossing the road to get to the event and also main entry, taxi shuttles and exit positions to ensure the public are directed to the appropriate entrances to enter the event, provide advice to people catching shuttle services and ensure people exit the event appropriately. For these latter positions the event is seeking people who are team players, with a good personality, well presented, mature and healthy individuals, who have extremely good communications skills and are able to follow orders.

Derived from http://www.sanctuarycoveboatshow.com.au/pages/volunteers.php

(2010) note that often selection for volunteers may be based solely on the information supplied on their application/registration form, with successful applicants being contacted and asked to attend a briefing session. Where, however, event organizations use more systematic approaches these will often be the same approaches as those discussed in Chapter 5. For example, Deery (2009) notes how the Australian Open holds lengthy interviews, which are conducted by a recruitment company and which explore candidates' work experience and customer service skills and attitudes and why they wish to work at the tournament. Interviews also include briefings on the requirements with regard to uniforms and grooming standards so that volunteers are clear about what is required of them. Similarly for London 2012, of the initial 250,000 applicants around 100,000 people had to be interviewed for the final figure of 70,000 volunteers, with around 300 interviews a day taking place six days per week over several months (Churchard, 2011).

## Training

As with the range of training interventions discussed in Chapter 7, event organizations are likely to offer induction training to properly induct volunteers, venue training to ensure they are fully aware of the venue and finally job-specific training. We will now briefly consider each of these aspects.

## Event induction training

As we discussed in Chapter 7, induction is an important activity in socializing employees so that they fully understand the nature of the event and how they are likely to fit within the event. Within the events context there may be particular challenges facing larger events in inducting a large number of volunteers. For example, Hanlon and Jago (2009) note the obvious difference between a conventional organization and a major sporting event with regard to the number of staff to be inducted. Thus, while induction would normally encompass a relatively small number of new organizational members in a conventional organization, the numbers are often very large for a major sporting event. While larger numbers allow for 'economies of scale' in the actual induction, there may be difficulties thereafter as there are not enough permanent staff within the organization to provide further guidance or a reference point for new staff beyond the induction process. Technology can potentially play a key role in this process, with Hanlon and Jago noting the importance of things like an intranet site which facilitates induction via an e-learning system, something that is successfully used by the Australian Open.

More generally, with regard to the likely topics to be covered in induction, van der Wagen (2007: 145) provides an indication of what will be covered:

- event overview
- event history
- event aims
- symbols
- organization
- sponsors
- event programme
- event venues
- performers or athletes
- previous shows/events
- workforce roles
- what to expect
- commitment and expectations
- customer service.

## Venue-specific training

In addition to a general induction, there may also be a need for venue-specific training to ensure that all staff are fully conversant with their working environment. Van der Wagen (2007) notes how a treasure hunt is often a good

and fun way to help people fully familiarize themselves with the venue. In addition, the same author notes a range of topics likely to be discussed in venue training:

- the event precinct (general area of operations)
- the event venue (performance location)
- locations within the venue (e.g. stair lifts, exits, communications control)
- functional areas represented at the venue (e.g. medical, accreditation, security)
- accreditation zones (who can go where)
- safety of staff and visitors
- emergency procedures
- incident reporting
- crowd control
- recycling and waste management
- staff procedures, check-in, meals, etc.
- communicating in the team
- staff rules
- common questions customers will ask
- venue management team and their support.

## Job-specific training

As we noted in Chapter 7, approaches to training are likely to work best when there is a clear and systematic approach. The discussion in Chapter 7 outlined a nine-step approach; van der Wagen (2007) reflects this systematic approach in noting how training for the events industry should also follow the formula of plan, deliver, assess and evaluate. In adopting such an approach, van der Wagen outlines a number of different approaches to training, which reflect our earlier noted approaches to on- and off-the-job training, encompassing activities such as demonstrations, mentoring, brainstorming, lectures, role plays and presentations. As well as ensuring that volunteers have the right kind of training to, for example, improve their customer responsiveness, learn how to use two-way radios, correctly set up athletic equipment and interact appropriately with VIPs, van der Wagen also makes the point that training should seek to impress upon volunteers that the manner in which they represent the event is of absolute importance. For example, she relays the story of how one event organization used a role play very effectively for this purpose. The role play was developed with the idea of a 'good' and 'bad' volunteer and was acted out by the event manager and assistant manager and powerfully communicated to the volunteers that their behaviour was a significant reflection on the event. In the role play:

> The bad guy got waylaid on the way home from his first shift, went drinking in his volunteer uniform, forgot his accreditation pass in the morning and

missed the train. . . . Of course the 'good volunteer' laid out her clothes for the next morning (not forgetting her accreditation pass), was polite to people on the train, arrived on time as bright as a button and so on.

(p. 159)

In sum, training for the event should ensure that volunteers are fully aware of the history, mission and purpose of the event. In addition, there is a need to ensure that venue training and job-specific training allows volunteers to do their job competently in ensuring that people attending the event have a quality experience.

## Retention and rewards

As we have noted throughout the book, the nature of tourism and hospitality creates major challenges for organizations in managing people. This has often been exacerbated by 'poor' HR practices. Consequently, within the tourism and hospitality industry rewarding and retaining employees remains challenging; this point is equally true within the events industry (Deery, 2009). For example, van der Wagen (2007) notes how, unlike paid staff in 'normal' organizations, volunteers can, if they wish, simply walk off the job with no real repercussions. At a practical level there are a number of immediate issues that have to be addressed to ensure that both paid staff and volunteers feel they are being appropriately treated. For example, paid staff and volunteers need their rosters to be sorted out, they require appropriate uniforms both stylistically and practically (for example, at winter events they will need warm uniforms), they need food and they need somewhere to sit during their breaks. As van der Wagen (2007: 173) notes, 'amongst the most common complaints from volunteers are those concerning the most elementary of needs, for example, being left on a gate collecting tickets for too long without being "relieved" or given a drink'. Similarly, Elstad (2003) notes that volunteers' satisfaction with the food provided at the event has a significant effect on their continuing commitment. Therefore, as well as getting the right people in the event organization through appropriate recruitment and selection and ensuring that employees are fully aware of what is expected of them through training, there is also a need to ensure that they are looked after physically and emotionally.

Smith and Lockstone (2009) note that during the event, event organizers should try to make volunteers feel welcome and involved and ensure that they get thanked in person. This sense of making volunteers feel valued is a common theme in discussions around how to retain employees. For example, Elstad (2003) and Hoye and Cuskelly (2009) note that volunteers' satisfaction levels were increased as a result of event managers giving regular feedback on performance and recognition of their efforts. Bowdin et al. (2010) and

Goldblatt and Matheson (2009) also recognize a range of additional things that are likely to increase the satisfaction of volunteers, including:

- training in new skills;
- free merchandise (e.g. clothing, badges, event posters);
- thank them in person, early and often;
- thank them publicly, early and often, through group meetings and publications (online and in print);
- hospitality in the form of opening and closing parties;
- gifts of sponsor products;
- opportunities to meet with celebrities, sporting stars and other VIPs;
- promotion to more interesting volunteer positions with each year of service;
- free tickets to the event;
- provide rewards such as a certificate of achievement, emblematic jewellery such as a lapel pin, a thank-you letter to the volunteer's employer or family, and a social event to honour them.

In sum, Goldblatt and Matheson (2009) offer a number of dos and don'ts for retaining volunteers. The dos are concerned with appointing the right volunteer to perform the right task, providing orientation and training, assigning a mentor and/or coach, promoting continuous communication and rewarding and recognizing volunteers' contribution in order to promote retention. The don'ts caution against appointing volunteers without thorough screenings and assessment to ensure goodness of fit, under-utilizing a volunteer's skill, talent and experience, promoting miscommunication through delays, barriers, cumbersome filters, providing the wrong rewards and failing to recognize early and often the contribution of volunteers.

As we noted earlier in the chapter, ensuring that volunteers, in particular, have a good experience may be essential to encourage them to 'bounce back' to recurring events. More generally, in examining the notion of retention it is also worth noting the recent work of Hanlon and Jago (2009), which focuses on paid employees. They note that retaining paid staff is often particularly challenging as an event winds down. In that sense staff may find the lead-up to an event an exciting time due to the anticipation, and this anticipation is often matched by the staff passion and commitment during the event. However, 'as events wind up . . . HR managers need to employ motivational strategies to stop staff "going flat" or losing a sense of connection with the event and the organization' (p. 101). Thus, for non-permanent staff the organization can consider a number of approaches to enhance the chances of staff being retained for the following year. Such approaches could include aspects such as staggering pay over the cycle of the event and using performance-based remuneration based on agreed targets. Even for full-time permanent staff it can be difficult to retain staff as there is often a trough after the event when such staff can feel bored. A key issue as well is the ability of events organizations to retain seasonal staff from year to year. Although not ongoing employees of the organization, such staff are highly valued due to their familiarity with the organization and the event itself. For example, Hanlon and Jago suggest that the organization should seek to develop a sense of belonging among personnel for major sporting events, something which can be facilitated by strong communication channels during the event. Seasonal staff can be encouraged to return if there are possibilities to progress through different roles. Recognizing this latter point, Hanlon and Jago note that

> some major sporting events have introduced what is akin to career structures within their different categories of personnel so that there is a sense of achievement derived by staff within these different categories as they move up the structure in terms of positions occupied over the years.
>
> (p. 102)

In addition to this developing internal labour market within some major sporting event organizations, Jago and Mair (2009) also discuss the emergence of a *sectoral* internal labour market in the events industry more generally. Unlike the internal labour market discussed in Chapter 4, which is within the organization, the sectoral internal labour market described by Jago and Mair sees key paid staff rotate between different major event organizations in order to secure year-round employment. In recognizing this emergent sectoral internal labour market, the same authors caution that the full potential of an internal labour market will only be realized when the major event sector become less fragmented and adopts this sectoral approach to staff development.

## Conclusion

This chapter has considered the events industry as a related but distinct part of the tourism and hospitality sector. Although the chapter sought to recognize how the events industry might be considered distinct, it nevertheless recognized that event organizations, like other tourism and hospitality organizations, are seeking to ensure that people attending the event receive a high level of service and have a generally good experience of the event. Consequently the chapter recognized the key role of event staff in creating this high-quality experience. The chapter also recognized the heterogeneous nature of events, which can range from a large mega-event to a small, local festival. The nature of the event will also impact on the type of people who will be working at the event. While recognizing that the industry employs a large number of paid employees, the chapter particularly focused on the unique challenges of managing a volunteer workforce. Having initially recognized the importance of volunteering and the manner in which the motivation of volunteers may vary, the chapter considered three key HR practices – recruitment and selection,

training, and retention – which sought to exemplify some of the challenges and possible organizational responses in managing volunteers.

## Discussion questions

- What are the main HR challenges in the events industry?
- What are likely to be the key similarities or differences in managing paid staff and volunteers?
- Is it more challenging to manage employees at a 'pulsating event' compared to managing employees in a conference and exhibition centre?

## Further reading

Elstad, B. (2003) 'Continuance commitment and reasons to quit: a study of volunteers at a jazz festival', *Event Management*, 8, 2, 99–108.

Hanlon, C. and Jago, L. (2009) 'Managing pulsating major sporting event organisations', in T. Baum, M. Deery, C. Hanlon, L. Lockstone and K. Smith (eds), *People and Work in Events and Conventions: A Research Perspective*, Wallingford: CABI.

Jago, L. and Mair, J. (2009) 'Career theory and major event employment', in T. Baum, M. Deery, C. Hanlon, L. Lockstone and K. Smith (eds), *People and Work in Events and Conventions: A Research Perspective*, Wallingford: CABI.

Mair, J. (2009) 'The events industry: the employment context', in T. Baum, M. Deery, C. Hanlon, L. Lockstone and K. Smith (eds), *People and Work in Events and Conventions: A Research Perspective*, Wallingford: CABI.

Ralston, R., Downward, P. and Lumsden, L. (2004) 'The expectations of volunteers prior to the XVII Commonwealth Games, 2002: a qualitative study', *Event Management*, 9, 1–2, 13–26.

Smith, K. and Lockstone, L. (2009) 'Involving and keeping event volunteers: management insights from cultural festivals', in T. Baum, M. Deery, C. Hanlon, L. Lockstone and K. Smith (eds), *People and Work in Events and Conventions: A Research Perspective*, Wallingford: CABI.

van der Wagen, L. (2007) *Human Resource Management for Events: Managing the Event Workforce*, Oxford: Butterworth-Heinemann.

## Recommended websites

To get an insight into some of the key issues facing HR managers in events, have a look at a course which is specifically geared to considering HRM and events, at http://www.courses.napier.ac.uk/courses.aspx?ID=%2fU34306.htm

The International Festivals and Events Association has a code of professional responsibility, including a standard specifically concerned with HRM, which can be seen at http://www.ifea.com/pdf/IFEA%20Industry%20Code%20of%20 Professional%20Conduct%20and%20Ethics.pdf

For an example of paid and volunteer jobs at the Edinburgh International Film Festival, go to http://www.edfilmfest.org.uk/jobs

Volunteering England have an array of services designed to help and support everyone who works with and manages volunteers; these can be accessed at http://www.volunteering.org.uk/resources

## Additional material

Go to www.routledge.com/cw/nickson to find PowerPoint slides, chapter commentaries, test banks and additional case studies for each chapter.

# References

Achur, J. (2011) *Trade Union Membership 2010*, London: Department for Business Innovation and Skills.

Adam-Smith, D. and Goss, D. (1993) 'HIV/AIDS and hotel and catering employment: some implications of perceived risk', *Employee Relations*, 15, 2, 25–32.

Adam-Smith, D., Norris, G. and Williams, S. (2003) 'Continuity or change? The implications of the National Minimum Wage for work and employment in the hospitality industry', *Work, Employment and Society*, 17, 1, 29–47.

Adkins, L. (1995) *Gendered Work: Sexuality, Family and the Labour Market*, Buckingham: Open University Press.

Adler, P. and Adler, P. (2004) *Paradise Laborers: Hotel Work in the Global Economy*, Ithaca, NY: Cornell University Press.

Advisory, Conciliation and Arbitration Service (2009) *Disciplinary and Grievance Procedures Code of Practice*, London: Acas.

Advisory, Conciliation and Arbitration Service (2010a) *The Equality Act: What's New For Employers?*, London: Acas.

Advisory, Conciliation and Arbitration Service (2010b) *Annual Report and Accounts 2009/10*, London: Acas.

Advisory, Conciliation and Arbitration Service (2010c) *Religion or Belief and the Workplace*, London: Acas.

Advisory, Conciliation and Arbitration Service (2010d) *How to Manage Performance*, London: Acas.

Advisory, Conciliation and Arbitration Service (2011a) *The Future of Workplace Relations: An Acas View*, London: Acas.

Advisory, Conciliation and Arbitration Service (2011b) *Discipline and Grievance at Work: The Acas Guide*, London: Acas.

Alcohol Concern (2006) 'Impact of alcohol problems on the workplace', *Acquire: Alcohol Concern's Quarterly Information and Research Bulletin,* winter, i–viii.

Allcock, S. (2008) 'Road to redemption', *Hospitality*, 10, 26–9.

Allen, K. (2009) 'Union fears BA job losses could lead to strike action', *Guardian*, 8 October, 28.

Alvesson, M. (2002) *Understanding Organizational Culture*, London: Sage.

*Annual Survey of Hours and Earnings 2010* (2010), available at http://www.statistics. gov.uk/statbase/Product.asp?vlnk=1951 (accessed 11 April 2011).

Anon (1999a) 'Restaurant chains make staff pay for the minimum wage', *Caterer and Hotelkeeper*, 22 April, 4.

Anon (1999b) 'Pizza Express hits out at MP's slur on pay', *Caterer and Hotelkeeper*, 15 July, 10.

Anon (2001) 'Strange interview techniques', *Glasgow Chamber of Commerce Journal*, November/December, 15.

Anon (2002) 'So what was the interviewer like?', *Metro*, 26 February, 3.

Anon (2003a) 'Staying the course', *Hospitality*, March, 16–17.

Anon (2003b) 'Hospitality is lowest-paying industry', *Caterer and Hotelkeeper*, 23 October, 6.

Anon (2011) 'Working Time Directive to be re-examined in Euro talks', *People Management Online*, 22 November.

Arkin, A. (2005a) 'Chip off the old block', *People Management*, 21 April, 32–4.

Arkin, A. (2005b) 'Out of the shadows', *People Management*, 24 November, 24–8.

Armstrong, M. (2006) *A Handbook of Human Resource Management Practice*, 10th edn, London: Kogan Page.

Armstrong, M. (2009) *A Handbook of Human Resource Management Practice*, 11th edn, London: Kogan Page.

Armstrong, M. and Baron, A. (2005) *Managing Performance: Performance Management in Action*, London: CIPD.

Aslan, A. and Wood, R. (1993) 'Trade unions in the hotel and catering industry: the views of hotel managers', *Employee Relations*, 15, 2, 61–70.

Atkinson, J. (1984) 'Manpower strategies for flexible organizations', *Personnel Management*, 16, 8, 28–31.

Australian Government (2009) 'Australia's paid parental leave scheme: supporting working Australian families', available at http://www.deewr.gov.au/Department/ Publications/Documents/PPLBooklet.pdf (accessed 1 November 2011).

Azar, O. (2009) 'Incentives and service quality in the restaurant industry: the tipping service puzzle', *Applied Economics*, 41, 15, 1917–27.

Bach, S. (2005) 'New directions in performance management', in S. Bach (ed.), *Managing Human Resources: Personnel Management in Transition*, 4th edn, Oxford: Blackwell.

Baker, J. (1999) 'Friday's people', *Caterer and Hotelkeeper*, 28 January, 30–1.

Bald, S. (1997) 'No excuse for patronising language', *People Management*, 3 April, 19.

Baldachino, G. (1995) 'Total quality management in a luxury hotel: a critique of practice', *International Journal of Hospitality Management*, 14, 1, 67–78.

Barrows, C., Gallo, M. and Mulleady, T. (1996) 'AIDS in the hospitality industry: recommendations for education and policy formulations', *International Journal of Contemporary Hospitality Management*, 8, 1, 5–9.

Bate, P. (1995) *Strategies for Cultural Change*, Oxford: Butterworth-Heinemann.

Baum, T. (1995) *Managing Human Resources in the European Hospitality and Tourism Industry: A Strategic Approach*, London: Chapman and Hall.

Baum, T. (1996) 'Managing cultural diversity in tourism', *Toursim Insights*, November, A77–A84.

Baum, T. (1997) 'Making or breaking the tourist experience: the role of human resource management', in C. Ryan (ed.), *The Tourist Experience: A New Introduction*, London: Cassell.

Baum, T. (2002) 'Skills and training for the hospitality sector: a review of issues', *Journal of Vocational Education and Training*, 54, 3, 343–63.

Baum, T. (2006) *Human Resource Management for Tourism, Hospitality and Leisure: An International Perspective*, London: Thomson Learning.

Baum, T. (2007) 'Human resources in tourism: still waiting for change', *Tourism Management*, 28, 6, 1383–99.

Baum, T. (2008) 'Implications of hospitality and tourism labour markets for talent management', *International Journal of Contemporary Hospitality Management*, 20, 7, 720–9.

Baum, T. (2012) *Migrant Workers in the International Hotel Industry*, Geneva: ILO.

Baum, T., Deery, M., Hanlon, C., Lockstone, L. and Smith, K. (2009a) *People and Work in Events and Conventions: A Research Perspective*, Wallingford: CABI.

Baum, T., Deery, M., Hanlon, C., Lockstone, L. and Smith, K. (2009b) 'Conclusion', in T. Baum, M. Deery, C. Hanlon, L. Lockstone and K. Smith (eds), *People and Work in Events and Conventions: A Research Perspective*, Wallingford: CABI.

BBC (2003) 'Millions hooked on alcohol', available at http://news.bbc.co.uk/1/hi/health/2817781.stm (accessed 1 June 2006).

BBC (2011) 'UK employees work longer hours than most EU neighbours', available at http://www.bbc.co.uk/news/business-16082186 (accessed 28 January 2012).

Beal, B. (2004) 'Psychological search for Hilton hotel managers', *Human Resource Management International Digest*, 12, 1, 30–2.

Bearden, T. (2001) 'High flyer', *PBS News*, 28 November, available at http://www.pbs.org/newshour/bb/transportation/july-dec01/southwest_11–28.html (accessed 8 August 2005).

Belhassen, Y. and Shani, Y. (2012) 'Hotels workers' substance use and abuse', *International Journal of Hospitality Management*, 31, 4, 1292–302.

Bernhardt, A., Dresser, L. and Hatton, E. (2003) 'The coffee pot wars: unions and firm restructuring in the hotel industry', in E. Appelbaum, A. Bernhardt and R.J. Murnane (eds), *Low Wage America*, New York, NY: Russell Sage Foundation.

Black, K. (2007) 'Religious festivals', *Caterer and Hotelkeeper*, 18 October, 74.

Blackhurst, A. (2011) 'Managing the 2012 Olympics', *Hospitality*, 23, 42–5.

Blyton, P. and Turnbull, P. (2004) *Dynamics of Employee Relations*, 3rd edn, Basingstoke: Palgrave Macmillan.

Boseley, S. (2007) 'Doctors call for higher taxes to deter UK's 7m harmful drinkers', *Guardian*, 6 June, 15.

Boston Consulting Group (2011) 'Creating people advantage 2011: HR certainties in uncertain times', available at http://www.bcg.com/documents/file87639.pdf (accessed 12 January 2012).

Bowdin, G., Allen, J., O'Toole, W., Harris, R. and McDonnell, I. (2010) *Events Management*, 3rd edn, Oxford: Butterworth-Heinemann.

Boxall, P. (1995) 'Building the theory of comparative HRM', *Human Resource Management Journal*, 5, 5, 5–17.

Boxall, P. and Purcell, J. (2000) 'Strategic human resource management: where have we come from and where should we be going?', *International Journal of Management Reviews*, 2, 2, 183–203.

Boxall, P. and Purcell, J. (2003) *Strategy and Human Resource Management*, Basingstoke: Palgrave Macmillan.

Boxall, P. and Purcell, J. (2008) *Strategy and Human Resource Management*, 2nd edn, Basingstoke: Palgrave Macmillan.

Boyd, C. (2002) 'Customer violence and employee health and safety', *Work, Employment and Society*, 16, 1, 151–69.

Branine, M. (1994) 'The cultural imperative of human resource management: a reconsideration of convergence and divergence factors', paper presented at *The Strategic Direction of Human Resource Management: Empowerment, Diversity and Control*, Nottingham Trent University, December.

Bratton, J. and Gold, J. (2007) *Human Resource Management: Theory and Practice*, 4th edn, Basingstoke: Palgrave Macmillan.

Breuer, N. (1995) 'Emerging trends for managing AIDS in the workplace', *Personnel Journal*, June, 125–34.

Brewster, C. (1995) 'National culture and international management', in S. Tyson (ed.), *Strategic Prospects for Human Resource Management*, London: IPD.

Brockett, J. (2012) 'Employers use exclusions to get round agency regulations', *People Management Online*, available at http://www.peoplemanagement.co.uk/pm/articles/2012/04/employers-use-exclusions-to-get-round-agency-regulations.htm (accessed 6 May 2012).

Brown, A. (1998) *Organizational Culture*, 2nd edn, London: Pitman.

Brown, M. and Lim, V. (2010) 'Understanding performance management and appraisal: supervisory and employee perspectives', in A. Wilkinson, N. Bacon, T. Redman and S. Snell (eds), *The Sage Handbook of Human Resource Management*, London: Sage.

Bryman, A. (2004) *The Disneyization of Society*, London: Sage.

Burns, P. (1997) 'Hard-skills, soft-skills: undervaluing hospitality's "service with a smile"', *Progress in Tourism and Hospitality Research*, 3, 239–48.

Cahalane, C. (2010) 'Is it safe to come out yet?' *Guardian Work*, 13 November, 1–2.

Caligiuri, P. and Stroh, L. (1995) 'Multinational corporation management strategies and international human resources practices: bringing IHRM to the bottom line', *International Journal of Human Resource Management*, 6, 3, 494–507.

Callen, R. and Tyson, K. (2000) 'Tipping behaviour in hospitality embodying a comparative prolegomenon of English and Italian customers', *Tourism and Hospitality Research*, 2, 3, 242–61.

Canny, A. (2002) 'Flexible labour? The growth of student employment in the UK', *Journal of Education and Work*, 15, 3, 277–301.

Carlzon, J. (1987) *Moments of Truth*, New York, NY: Ballinger.

Casado, M. (1997) 'Drug-testing practices in US hotels', *International Journal of Hospitality Management*, 16, 4, 393–401.

Casey, B. (2001) 'Tipping in New Zealand's restaurants', *Cornell Hotel and Restaurant Administration Quarterly*, February, 21–5.

Chan, B. and Coleman, M. (2004) 'Skills and competencies needed for the Hong Kong hotel industry: the perspective of the hotel human resources manager', *Journal of Human Resources in Hospitality and Tourism*, 3, 1, 3–18.

Chand, M. and Katou, A. (2007) 'The impact of HRM practices on organizational performance in the Indian hotel industry', *Employee Relations*, 29, 6, 576–94.

Chartered Institute of Personnel and Development (2004) *Managing Conflict at Work: A Survey of the UK and Ireland*, London: CIPD.

Chartered Institute of Personnel and Development (2005a) *On-the-Job Training Factsheet*, London: CIPD.

Chartered Institute of Personnel and Development (2005b) *Performance Management Survey Report*, London: CIPD.

Chartered Institute of Personnel and Development (2005c) *What is Employee Relations?*, London: CIPD.

Chartered Institute of Personnel and Development (2006) *The Guide To Recruitment Marketing*, London: CIPD.

Chartered Institute of Personnel and Development (2007a) *Employing People with Criminal Records Factsheet*, London: CIPD.

Chartered Institute of Personnel and Development (2007b) *Employing Ex-Offenders to Capture Talent*, London: CIPD.

Chartered Institute of Personnel and Development (2007c) *The CIPD Drug and Alcohol Misuse at Work Survey*, London: CIPD.

Chartered Institute of Personnel and Development (2009a) *E-Recruitment Factsheet*, London: CIPD.

Chartered Institute of Personnel and Development (2009b) *Employers' Experiences in Addressing Sexual Orientation, Religion and Belief at Work*, London: CIPD.

Chartered Institute of Personnel and Development (2009c) *E-Learning: Progress and Prospects Factsheet*, London: CIPD.

Chartered Institute of Personnel and Development (2009d) *Performance Management in Action: Current Trends and Practice*, London: CIPD.

Chartered Institute of Personnel and Development (2010a) 'Talent development in the BRIC countries', available at http://www.cipd.co.uk/NR/rdonlyres/EB69B9A5-BAC0–4D67–94EA-C65B5601A0AA/0/Talent_development_BRIC_countries.pdf (accessed 30 April 2012).

Chartered Institute of Personnel and Development (2010b) *Resourcing and Talent Planning: Annual Survey Report*, London: CIPD.

Chartered Institute of Personnel and Development (2010c) *Selection Methods Factsheet*, London: CIPD.

Chartered Institute of Personnel and Development (2010d) *Work Related Stress: What the Law Says*, London: CIPD.

Chartered Institute of Personnel and Development (2011a) 'The economic rights and wrongs of employment regulation', available at http://www.cipd.co.uk/NR/rdonlyres/0EBF0ADF-A0E1–4FB3-BF69-92A2F939271D/0/5547_Work_Horizons.pdf (accessed 3 November 2011).

Chartered Institute of Personnel and Development (2011b) *Performance Management Factsheet*, London: CIPD.

Chartered Institute of Personnel and Development (2011c) *Performance Appraisal Factsheet*, London: CIPD.

Chartered Institute of Personnel and Development (2011d) *Employee Voice Factsheet*, London: CIPD.

Chartered Institute of Personnel and Development (2011e) *Absence Measurement and Management Factsheet*, London: CIPD.

Chartered Institute of Personnel and Development (2011f) *HIV and AIDS in the Workplace: A Global Perspective*, London: CIPD.

Chartered Institute of Personnel and Development (2011g) *Discipline and Grievances at Work Factsheet*, London: CIPD.

Chartered Institute of Personnel and Development (2011h) *Dismissal Factsheet*, London: CIPD.

Chartered Institute of Personnel and Development (2012a) *Managing a Healthy Ageing Workforce: A National Business Imperative*, London: CIPD.

Chartered Institute of Personnel and Development (2012b) *Working Hours and Time-Off Work Factsheet*, London: CIPD.

Chartered Institute of Personnel and Development (2012c) 'Employment law at work data', available at http://www.cipd.co.uk/hr-resources/employment-law-work-data.aspx (accessed 20 April 2012).

Churchard, C. (2011) 'Olympic volunteer recruitment gathers pace', *People Management Online*, available at: http://www.peoplemanagement.co.uk/pm/articles/2011/07/olympic-volunteer-recruitment-gathers-pace.htm (accessed 12 March 2012).

Churchard, C. (2012a) 'Restaurants serving Asian and Oriental food are being forced to seek UK chefs as migrant limits and visa costs bite', *People Management*, March, 10–11.

Churchard, C. (2012b) 'Government imposes minimum length of a year for apprentice schemes', *People Management Online*, available at http://www.peoplemanage ment.co.uk/pm/articles/2012/04/government-imposes-minimum-length-of-a-year-for-apprentice-schemes.htm (accessed 7 May 2012).

Churchard, C. (2012c) '"No economic case" for fire-at-will change', *People Management Online*, available at http://www.peoplemanagement.co.uk/pm/articles/2012/03/no-economic-case-for-fire-at-will-change-says-cipd.htm (accessed 17 April 2012).

Chynoweth, C. (2009) 'Time is of the essence', *People Management Guide to Assessment*, 8 October, 4–5.

Clark, N. and Hardy, J. (2011) *Free Movement in the EU: The Case of Great Britain*, Berlin: Friedrich Ebert Stiftung.

Clavey, J. (1998) 'Unions slam level of minimum wage', *Caterer and Hotelkeeper*, 4 June, 10.

Coats, D. (2010) 'Time to cut the Gordian Knot: the case for consensus and reform of the UK's employment relations system', available at http://www.smith-institute.org.uk/file/time%20to%20cut%20the%20Gordian%20Knot.pdf (accessed 18 April 2012).

Collings, D. and Scullion, H. (2006) 'Approaches to international staffing', in H. Scullion and D. Collings (eds), *Global Staffing*, London: Routledge.

Confederation of British Industry (2011) 'Thinking positively: the 21st century employment relationship', available at http://www.cbi.org.uk/business-issues/employment/news/ (accessed 3 November 2011).

Confederation of British Industry/Pfizer (2011) *Health Returns? Absence and Workplace Health Survey 2011*, London: CBI.

Cooper, C. (2001) 'Talking Italian', *People Management*, 14 June, 38–41.

Cooper, C. (2003) 'Minority support', *People Management*, 4 December, 24–7.

Corsun, D. and Young, C. (1998) 'An occupational hazard: alcohol consumption among hospitality managers', *Marriage and Family Review*, 28, 1–2, 187–211.

Coupe, V. and Johnson, K. (1999) 'Sexual harassment: "That'll do nicely sir"', *Hospitality Review*, April, 36–41.

Coupland, D. (1993) *Generation X: Tales for an Accelerated Culture*, London: Abacus.

Cox, A. (2007) *Re-visiting the NVQ debate: 'Bad' Qualifications, Expansive Learning Environments and Prospects for Upskilling Workers*, SKOPE Research Paper, No. 71, Universities of Cardiff and Oxford.

Curtis, S. and Lucas, R. (2001) 'A coincidence of needs? Employers and full-time students', *Employee Relations*, 23, 1, 38–54.

Cushing, K. (2004) 'Concerns raised over UK long-hours culture', *Caterer and Hotelkeeper*, 11 June, 9.

D'Annunzio-Green, N. (1997) 'Developing international managers in the hospitality industry', *International Journal of Contemporary Hospitality Management*, 9, 5–6, 199–208.

D'Annunzio-Green, N. (2002) 'An examination of the organizational and cross-cultural challenges facing international hotel managers in Russia', *International Journal of Contemporary Hospitality Management*, 14, 6, 266–73.

D'Annunzio-Green, N., Maxwell, G. and Watson, S. (2002) *Human Resource Management: International Perspectives in Hospitality and Tourism*, London: Continuum.

Data Service (2011) 'Vocational qualifications in the UK: 2009/10', available at: http://www.thedataservice.org.uk/NR/rdonlyres/AA0BA84A-7ACF-4280–8180-CEA7565A98A9/0/VQ200910Commentary.pdf (accessed 9 March 2012).

Davies, C. (2009) 'Passengers buy "anything but BA"', *Guardian*, 15 December, 12.

Davies Report (2011) 'Women on boards', available at http://www.bis.gov.uk/assets/biscore/business-law/docs/w/11–745-women-on-boards.pdf (accessed 13 November 2011).

Davis, A., Hirsch, D. and Smith, N. (2010) 'A minimum income standard for the UK in 2010', Joseph Rowntree Foundation, available at http://www.jrf.org.uk/sites/files/jrf/MIS-2010-report_0.pdf (accessed 13 August 2011).

Deal, T. and Kennedy, A. (1988) *Corporate Cultures: The Rites and Rituals of Corporate Culture*, Harmondsworth: Penguin.

Deal, T. and Kennedy, A. (1999) *The New Corporate Cultures: Revitalizing the Workplace after Downsizing, Mergers, and Reengineering*, Cambridge, MA: Perseus.

Deery, M. (2009) 'Employee retention strategies for event management', in T. Baum, M. Deery, C. Hanlon, L. Lockstone and K. Smith (eds), *People and Work in Events and Conventions: A Research Perspective*, Wallingford: CABI.

Deery, M. and Jago, L. (2002) 'The core and periphery: an examination of the flexible workforce model in the hotel industry', *International Journal of Hospitality Management*, 21, 4, 339–51.

Department for Business, Innovation and Skills (2010) 'Guidance to the Transnational Information and Consultation of Employees (Amendment) Regulations 2010', available at http://www.bis.gov.uk/assets/biscore/employment-matters/docs/10-888-transnational-information-consultation-regulations-2010-guidance (accessed 24 April 2012).

Department for Business, Innovation and Skills (2011) 'Flexible, effective, fair: promoting economic growth through a strong and efficient labour market', available at http://www.bis.gov.uk/assets/biscore/employment-matters/docs/F/11-1308-flexible-effective-fair-labour-market (accessed 14 January 2012).

Department for Business, Innovation and Skills (2012a) 'Employment law review: annual update 2012', available at http://www.bis.gov.uk/assets/biscore/employment-matters/docs/e/12-p136-employment-law-review-2012.pdf (accessed 6 May 2012).

Department for Business, Innovation and Skills (2012b) 'Dealing with dismissal and "compensated no fault dismissal" for micro business', available at http://www.bis.gov.uk/assets/biscore/employment-matters/docs/d/12-626-dismissal-for-micro-businesses-call (accessed 18 April 2012).

Department for Education and Employment (2000) *Employers Skill Survey: Case Study Hospitality Sector*, London: DfEE.

Dewald, B. (2001) 'Restaurant tipping by tourists in Hong Kong', *Anatolia: An International Journal of Tourism and Hospitality Research*, 12, 2, 139–51.

Dewald, B. and Self, J. (2008) 'Cross-cultural training for expatriate hotel managers: an exploratory study', *International Journal of Hospitality and Tourism Administration*, 9, 4, 352–64.

Doherty, L. (2008) 'Mind the gender gap', *Hospitality*, 10, 36–9.

Druce, C. (2004) 'NVQs fail to meet the industry needs, agree colleges and employers', *Caterer and Hotelkeeper*, 21 October, 9.

Druce, C. (2010) 'Time to move on from tips?', *Caterer and Hotelkeeper*, 8 October, 10.

Drummond, S. and Anderson, H. (2004) 'Service quality and managing your people', in I. Yeoman, M. Robertson, J. Ali-Knight, S. Drummond and U. McMahon-Beattie (eds), *Festival and Events Management: An International Arts and Culture Perspective*, Oxford: Butterworth-Heinemann.

Dyer, C. (2008) 'New sexual harassment law to protect staff from customers', *Guardian*, 31 March, 14.

Eade, L. (2009) 'Supporting the female leaders of tomorrow', *En Passant*, December, 26–7.

Eade, V. (1993) 'Drug abuse in the hospitality industry', *Florida International University Hospitality Review*, 11, 2, 81–6.

Eaton, J. (2001) *Globalization and Human Resource Management in the Airline Industry*, Aldershot: Ashgate.

Edwards, P. (2005) 'Discipline and attendance', in S. Bach (ed.), *Managing Human Resources: Personnel Management in Transition*, 4th edn, Oxford: Blackwell.

Ellis, C. and Sonnenfield, J. (1994) 'Diverse approaches to managing diversity', *Human Resource Management*, 33, 1, 79–109.

Elstad, B. (2003) 'Continuance commitment and reasons to quit: a study of volunteers at a jazz festival', *Event Management*, 8, 2, 99–108

Enz, C. (2009) 'Human resource management: a troubling issue for the global hospitality industry', *Cornell Hospitality Quarterly*, 50, 4, 578–83.

Equality and Human Rights Commission (2010) 'How fair is Britain? Equality, human rights and good relations in 2010', available at http://www.equalityhumanrights. com/uploaded_files/triennial_review/how_fair_is_britain_-_complete_report.pdf (accessed 15 November 2011).

Equality and Human Rights Commission (2011) *Equality Act 2010: Employment Statutory Code of Practice*, Norwich: The Stationery Office.

European Foundation for the Improvement of Living and Working Conditions (2005) 'EWC case studies: Club Med', at http://www.eurofound.europa.eu/pubdocs/ 2005/7140/en/1/ef057140en.pdf (accessed 12 July 2006).

European Foundation for the Improvement of Living and Working Conditions (2012) 'Employment and industrial relations in the hotels and restaurant sector', available at http://www.eurofound.europa.eu/docs/eiro/tn1109011s/tn1109011s. pdf (accessed 3 May 2012).

European Parliament (2012) 'Gender quotas in management boards', available at http://www.europarl.europa.eu/committees/fr/studiesdownload.html?language Document=EN&file=66951 (accessed 1 May 2012).

European Professional Women's Network (2006) 'Second bi-annual EuropeanPWN BoardWomen Monitor 2006', press release, available at http://www.europeanpwn. net/files/boardwomen_press_release120606_1.pdf (accessed 14 January 2006).

European Professional Women's Network (2010) 'EPWN board women monitor, 4th edn', available at http://www.europeanpwn.net/files/europeanpwn_boardmonitor_ 2010.pdf (accessed 13 April 2012).

European Trade Union Institute (2011) 'EWC database', available at http://www. worker-participation.eu/Media/Files/2011_11_EN (accessed 24 April 2012).

Evans, J. (2009) 'Shape up or pay up', *People Management*, 9 April, 28–30.

Eversheds (2011) 'HR e-briefing 508: significant change for European Works Councils from 5 June 2011', available at https://www.eversheds.com/uk/home/articles/ index1.page?ArticleID=templatedata/Eversheds/articles/data/en/Employment_and _labour_law/Eversheds_HR_e-briefing_508_Significant_change_for_European_ Works_Councils&SIDpassed=templatedataEvershedsServiceListdataenEmploy ment_and_labour_law (accessed 24 April 2012).

Experian (2006) 'Employment and skills for the 2012 Games: research and evidence', report for the Learning and Skills Council and London Development Agency.

Ferner, A. (1994) 'Multinational companies and human resource management: an overview of research issues', *Human Resource Management Journal*, 4, 2, 79–102.

Ferner, A. (1997) 'Country-of-origin effect and HRM in multinational companies', *Human Resource Management Journal*, 7, 1, 19–37.

Ferner, A. (2010) 'HRM in multinational companies', in A. Wilkinson, N. Bacon, T. Redman and S. Snell (eds), *The Sage Handbook of Human Resource Management*, London: Sage.

Finegold, D., Wagner, K. and Mason, G. (2000) 'National skill-creation systems and career paths for service workers: hotels in the United States, Germany and the United Kingdom', *International Journal of International Human Resource Management*, 11, 3, 497–516.

Foot, M. and Hook, C. (2008) *Introducing Human Resource Management*, 5th edn, London: Financial Times/Prentice Hall.

Fouche, G. (2008) 'The rise of the Valkyries: Norwegian women take their place at the top', *Guardian*, available at http://www.guardian.co.uk/world/2008/nov/17/norway-gender-executive-salaries (accessed 14 November 2011).

Fox, A. (1966) 'Industrial sociology and industrial relations', *Royal Commission Research Paper No. 3*, HMSO.

Fox, A. (1974) *Beyond Contract: Work, Power and Trust Relations*, London: Faber.

Fraser, M. (1966) *Employment Interviewing*, London: McDonald and Evans.

Gall, G. (2004) 'British employer resistance to trade union recognition', *Human Resource Management Journal*, 14, 2, 36–53.

Gennard, J. (2002) 'Employee relations public policy developments, 1997–2001: a break from the past?', *Employee Relations*, 24, 6, 581–94.

Gerrard, N. (2010) 'Clearing the Olympic hurdle', *Caterer and Hotelkeeper*, 30 July, 22–3.

Gibson, O. (2009) 'Britain lands rugby World Cup double', *Guardian*, 28 July, available at http://www.guardian.co.uk/sport/2009/jul/28/rugby-union-league-world-cup (accessed 17 July 2011).

Gibson, O. (2011a) 'London wins bid to host 2017 World Athletics Championships', *Guardian*, 11 November, available at http://www.guardian.co.uk/sport/2011/nov/11/london-2017-world-athletics-championships (accessed 15 February 2012).

Gibson, O. (2011b) 'London 2012 volunteers face the toughest hurdle to "be the best"', *Guardian*, 1 February, 9.

Gilbert, D., Guerrier, Y. and Guy, J. (1998) 'Sexual harassment issues in the hospitality industry', *International Journal of Contemporary Hospitality Management,* 10, 2, 48–53.

Gilbert, H. (2007) 'Hospitality failing to embrace ethnic diversity at the top', *Caterer and Hotelkeeper*, 15 November, 7.

Gilbert, H. (2008) 'Travelodge recruits two thirds from LEP programme', *Caterer and Hotelkeeper*, 5 September, available at http://www.caterersearch.com/Articles/2008/09/05/323279/travelodge-recruits-two-thirds-from-lep-programme.htm (accessed 13 August 2011).

Gittell, J. and Bamber, G. (2010) 'High- and low-road strategies for competing on costs and their implications for employment relations: international studies in the airline industry', *International Journal of Human Resource Management*, 21, 2, 165–79.

Glasgow City Council (2011) 'Glasgow economic review', November, available at http://www.glasgow.gov.uk/NR/rdonlyres/2B99981D-83ED-40AE-BD13-2D5516433548/0/Economicreview121011.pdf (accessed 14 January 2012).

Gledhill, B. (2002) 'Releasing potential', *Caterer and Hotelkeeper*, 10 October, 32–4.

Gliatis, N. and Guerrier, Y. (1994) 'Managing international career moves in international hotel companies', in C. Cooper and A. Lockwood (eds), *Progress in Tourism, Recreation and Hospitality Management*, Vol. 5, Chichester: John Wiley.

Gloster, R., Sumption, F., Higgins, T., Cox, A. and Jones, R. (2010) *Perspectives and Performance of Investors in People: A Literature Review*, London: UKCES.

Gloster, R., Higgins, T., Cox, A. and Jones, R. (2011) *Exploring Employer Behaviour in Relation to Investors in People*, London: UKCES.

GMB (2010) 'GMB response to BIS consultation: implementation of the European Works Council Directive 2009/38/EC', available at http://www.gmb.org.uk/pdf/

GMB%20response%20to%20BIS%20consultation%20on%20recast%20EWC% 20final.pdf (accessed 24 April 2012).

Go, F., Monachello, M. and Baum, T. (1996) *Human Resource Management for the Hospitality Industry*, New York, NY: Wiley.

Goldblatt, J. and Matheson, C. (2009) 'Volunteer recruitment and retention: an Australian–USA comparison', in T. Baum, M. Deery, C. Hanlon, L. Lockstone and K. Smith (eds), *People and Work in Events and Conventions: A Research Perspective*, Wallingford: CABI.

Golding, C. (1998) 'Britain gets first look at Hooters', *Caterer and Hotelkeeper*, 30 April, 7.

Goldsmith, A., Nickson, D., Sloan, D. and Wood, R. (1997) *Human Resources Management for Hospitality Services*, London: International Thomson Business Press.

Gospel, H. and Fuller, A. (1998) 'The modern apprenticeship: new wine in old bottles?', *Human Resource Management Journal*, 8, 1, 5–22.

Goss, D. (1994) *Principles of Human Resource Management*, London: Routledge.

Goss, D. (1997) *Human Resource Management: The Basics*, London: International Thomson Business Press.

Gottleib, M. (1992) 'Letter to the editor' in *Caterer and Hotelkeeper*, 25 June, 20.

Goymour, D. (2000) 'Let's talk', *Hospitality*, May, 28.

Greater London Authority (2011) *A Fairer London: The Living Wage in London 2011*, London: GLA.

Gröschl, S. (2007) 'An exploration of HR policies and practices affecting the integration of persons with disabilities in the hotel industry in major Canadian tourism destinations', *International Journal of Hospitality Management*, 26, 666–86.

Gröschl, S. (2011) 'Diversity management strategies of global hotel groups: a corporate web sited based exploration', *International Journal of Contemporary Hospitality Management*, 23, 2, 224–40.

Gröschl, S. and Doherty, L. (1999) 'Diversity management in practice', *International Journal of Contemporary Hospitality Management*, 11, 6, 262–8.

Gröschl, S. and Doherty, L. (2002) 'The appraisal process: beneath the surface', *Journal of Human Resources in Hospitality and Tourism*, 1, 3, 57–76.

Groskop, V. (2006) 'Mamafesto', *New Statesman*, 17 July, 26–8.

Grugulis, I. (2003) 'The contribution of NVQs to the growth of skills in the UK', *British Journal of Industrial Relations*, 41, 3, 457–75.

Grugulis, I. (2007) *Skills, Training and Human Resource Development*, Basingstoke: Palgrave Macmillan.

Grugulis, I. and Wilkinson, A. (2002) 'Managing culture at British Airways: hype, hope and reality', *Long Range Planning*, 35, 2, 179–94.

Gueguen, N. and Jacob, C. (2005) 'The effect of touch in tipping: an evaluation in a French bar', *International Journal of Hospitality Management*, 24, 2, 295–9.

Guerrier, Y. and Adib, A. (2000) '"No we don't provide that service": the harassment of hotel employees by customers', *Work, Employment and Society*, 14, 4, 689–705.

Guerrier, Y. and Adib, A. (2004) 'Gendered identities in the work of overseas tour reps', *Gender, Work and Organizations*, 11, 3, 334–50.

Guest, D. (1990) 'Human resource management and the American Dream', *Journal of Management Studies*, 27, 4, 378–97.

Guild, S. (2002) 'Willing and able', *Caterer and Hotelkeeper*, 17 January, 29.

Gumbrell-McCormick, R. and Hyman, R. (2010) 'Work councils: the European model of industrial democracy', in A. Wilkinson, P. Gollan, M. Marchington and D. Lewin (eds), *The Oxford Handbook of Participation in Organizations*, Oxford: Oxford University Press.

Hales, C. (1996) 'Factors influencing the adoption of NVQs in small hospitality businesses', *International Journal of Contemporary Hospitality Management*, 8, 5, 5–9.

Hales, C. and Klidas, A. (1998) 'Empowerment in five star hotels: choice, voice or rhetoric?', *International Journal of Contemporary Hospitality Management*, 10, 3, 88–95.

Hall, E. (1993) 'Smiling, deferring and flirting: doing gender and giving "good service"', *Work and Occupations*, 20, 4, 452–71.

Hall, M., Hutchinson, S., Purcell, J., Terry, M. and Parker, J. (2010) 'Information and consultation under the ICE Regulations: evidence from longitudinal case studies', available at http://www.bis.gov.uk/assets/biscore/employment-matters/docs/I/10-1380-information-consultation-ice-regulations (accessed 24 April 2012).

Hanlon, C. and Jago, L. (2009) 'Managing pulsating major sporting event organisations', in T. Baum, M. Deery, C. Hanlon, L. Lockstone and K. Smith (eds), *People and Work in Events and Conventions: A Research Perspective*, Wallingford: CABI.

Harmer, J. (2010a) 'New immigration policy could damage industry', *Caterer and Hotelkeeper*, 2 July, 6.

Harmer, J. (2010b) 'Revenue launches more investigations on minimum wage', *Caterer and Hotelkeeper*, 28 May, 5.

Harzing, A.W. (2004a) 'Strategy and structure of multinational companies', in A.W. Harzing and J. Van Ruysseveldt (eds), *International Human Resource Management*, 2nd edn, London: Sage.

Harzing, A.W. (2004b) 'Composing an International Staff', in A.W. Harzing and J. Van Ruysseveldt (eds), *International Human Resource Management*, 2nd edn, London: Sage.

Health and Safety Executive (2009) '*How to* tackle work-related stress: a guide for employers making the management standards work', at http://www.hse.gov.uk/pubns/indg430.pdf (accessed 28 January 2012).

Heenan, D. and Perlmutter, H. (1979) *Multinational Organizational Development: A Social Architecture Perspective*, Reading, MA: Addison Wesley.

Heery, E. and Noon, M. (2008) *A Dictionary of Human Resource Management*, 2nd edn, Oxford: Oxford University Press.

Helyar, J. (2003) 'Hooters: a case study', *Fortune*, 1 September, 140–6.

Henkoff, R. (1994) 'Finding and keeping the best service workers', *Fortune*, 3 October, 52–8.

Heyes, J. (2011) 'Flexicurity, employment protection and the jobs crisis', *Work, Employment and Society*, 25, 4, 642–57.

High Pay Commission (2011) 'Cheques with balances: why tackling high pay is in the national interest – final report of the High Pay Commission', available at

http://highpaycommission.co.uk/wp-content/uploads/2011/11/HPC_final_report_ WEB.pdf (accessed 10 January 2012).

Hills, R. (2004) 'Who would you most like to be stuck in a lift with?', *Sunday Herald*, 23 May, 12.

Hilpern, K. (2001) 'What's your poison', *Guardian*, 19 January, Office Hours section, 2.

Hilton, C.N. (1957) *Be My Guest*, Englewood Cliffs, NJ: Prentice-Hall.

Hinkin, T. and Tracey, B. (2010) 'What makes it so great? An analysis of human resources practices among *Fortune*'s Best Companies to Work For', *Cornell Hospitality Quarterly*, 51, 2, 158–70.

Hochschild, A. (1983) *The Managed Heart*, Berkeley, CA: University of California Press.

Hofstede, G. (1980) *Culture's Consequences: International Differences in Work Related Values*, London: Sage.

Hofstede, G. (2001) *Culture's Consequences: International Differences in Work Related Values*, 2nd edn, London: Sage.

Hofstede, G. (2002) 'Dimensions do not exist: a reply to Brendan McSweeney', *Human Relations*, 55, 11, 1355–61.

Holden, L. (2004) 'Human resource development: the organization and the national framework', in I. Beardwell, L. Holden and T. Claydon (eds), *Human Resource Management: A Contemporary Approach*, 4th edn, London: Financial Times/ Prentice Hall.

Holdsworth, R. (1991) 'Appraisal', in F. Neale (ed.), *The Handbook of Performance Management*, London: IPM.

Hope, C. and Muhlemann, A. (1998) 'Total quality, human resource management and tourism', *Tourism Economics*, 4, 4, 367–86.

Hope, K. (2005) 'Holding back the years', *People Management*, 21 April, 24–30.

Hoque, K. (1999) 'New approaches to HRM in the UK hotel industry', *Human Resource Management Journal*, 9, 2, 64–76.

Hoque, K. (2000) *Human Resource Management in the Hotel Industry*, London: Routledge.

Hoque, K. (2003) 'All in all, it's just another plaque on the wall: the incidence and impact of the Investors in People standard', *Journal of Management Studies*, 40, 2, 543–71.

Hotel and Catering International Management Association (1999) *Managing Diversity: Women at Work*, London: HCIMA.

Houtenville, A. and Kalargyrou, V. (2012) 'People with disabilities: employers' perspectives on recruitment practices, strategies, and challenges in leisure and hospitality', *Cornell Hospitality Quarterly*, 53, 1, 40–52.

Hoye, R. and Cuskelly, G. (2009) 'The psychology of sport event volunteerism: a review of volunteer motives, involvement and behaviour', in T. Baum, M. Deery, C. Hanlon, L. Lockstone and K. Smith (eds), *People and Work in Events and Conventions: A Research Perspective*, Wallingford: CABI.

Hu, Y. (1992) 'Global or stateless corporations are national firms with international operations', *California Management Review*, Winter, 107–26.

*Human Resource Management International Digest* (2007) 'Age discrimination: don't let the joke be on you', *Human Resource Management International Digest*, 15, 3, 21–3.

Hurrell, S. (2005) 'Dilute to taste? The impact of the Working Time Regulations in the hospitality industry', *Employee Relations*, 27, 5, 523–46.

Hyman, J. (1996) 'Training and development: the employer's responsibility?', in B. Towers (ed.), *The Handbook of Human Resource Management*, 2nd edn, Oxford: Blackwell.

Hyman, J. and Mason, B. (1995) *Managing Employee Involvement and Participation*, London: Sage.

Income Data Services (1999) 'Implementing the National Minimum Wage', IDS Report No. 783, April, 8–13.

Income Data Services (2000) 'Violence at work', IDS Studies No. 683, February.

Income Data Services (2001) 'Promoting racial equality', IDS HR Studies No. 719, September.

Income Data Services (2003) 'Opportunity now', IDS HR Studies No. 758, September.

Income Data Services (2004a) 'Employee attitude surveys', IDS HR Studies No. 777, July.

Income Data Services (2004b) 'Alcohol and drug policies', IDS HR Studies No. 771, April.

Income Data Services (2004c) 'Stress management', IDS HR Studies No. 775, June.

Income Data Services (2005a) 'Performance management', IDS HR Studies No. 796, April.

Income Data Services (2005b) 'Pay in hotels', IDS Pay Report No. 943, December, 11–15.

Income Data Services (2005c) 'Pay in pubs and restaurants 2004/5', IDS Pay Report No. 931, June, 11–15.

Income Data Services (2005d) 'Absence management', IDS HR Studies No. 810, November.

Income Data Services (2005e) 'Alcohol, drugs and employment law', IDS Brief No. 779, April, 10–17.

Income Data Services (2008a) 'Pay in fast food, pubs and restaurants', IDS Pay Report No. 1014, 11–15.

Income Data Services (2008b) 'Alcohol and drug policies', IDS HR Studies No. 884, December.

Income Data Services (2009) 'Pay in hotels 2009', IDS Pay Report No. 1035, 7–10.

Income Data Services (2010a) 'McDonalds', IDS Pay Report No. 1060, 22.

Income Data Services (2010b) 'Employee benefits', IDS HR Studies No. 915, April.

Income Data Services (2011a) *Maternity and Paternity Leave*, London: IDS.

Income Data Services (2011b) 'Age and the workforce', IDS HR Studies No. 948, August.

Income Data Services (2011c) 'Absence management', IDS HR Studies No. 936, February.

Income Data Services (2011d) 'Alcohol and drug policies', IDS HR Studies No. 943, June.

Income Data Services (2012) 'Suggestion schemes', IDS HR Studies No. 960, February.

Industrial Relations Services (1996) 'Sexual harassment at work (1): incidence and outcomes', *IRS Employment Trends*, 615, September, 4–10.

Industrial Relations Services (1997) 'HIV and AIDS: a workplace issue', *IRS Employment Trends*, 633, June, 8–16.

Industrial Relations Services (1999) 'New ways to perform appraisals', *IRS Employment Review*, 676, March, 7–16.

Industrial Relations Services (2000a) 'The interview: its role in effective selection', *Employee Development Bulletin*, 122, February, 12–16.

Industrial Relations Services (2000b) 'Sex at work: everything that you wanted to know but were afraid to ask', *IRS Employment Trends*, 713, October, 5–10.

Industrial Relations Services (2001) 'Counting the cost of absence', *IRS Employment Review*, 739, 1 November, 46–7.

Industrial Relations Services (2002) 'Psychometrics: the next generation', *IRS Employment Review*, 744, 28 January, 36–40.

Industrial Relations Services (2003a) 'The mouse trap: company culture at Disney World', *IRS Employment Review*, 783, 3 October, 21–3.

Industrial Relations Services (2003b) 'Managing disability 2003: a progress report', *IRS Employment Review*, 785, 3 October, 11–17.

Industrial Relations Services (2004) 'UK has the second-worst health rate', *IRS Employment Review*, 792, 23 January, 17.

Industrial Relations Services (2005a) 'Centre of attention', *IRS Employment Review*, 816, 28 January, 42–8.

Industrial Relations Services (2005b) 'Appraisals (1): not living up to expectations', *IRS Employment Review*, 828, 29 July, 9–15.

Industrial Relations Services (2005c) 'Dialogue or monologue: is the message getting through', *IRS Employment Review*, 834, 28 October, 8–16.

Industrial Relations Services (2005d) 'Disciplinary and grievance policies at work', *IRS Employment Review*, 825, 10 June, 9–18.

Industrial Relations Services (2006a) 'In the hiring line: boosting managers' recruitment skills', *IRS Employment Review*, 846, 5 May, 42–8.

Industrial Relations Services (2006b) 'ASHE 2005: earnings growth fails to keep pace with inflation', *IRS Employment Review*, 840, 3 February, 31–5.

Industrial Relations Services (2006c) '£21,753 a year for travel industry employees', *IRS Employment Review*, 843, 24 March, 28.

Industrial Relations Services (2006d) 'Smooth take-off for First Choice Airways' new reward strategy', *IRS Employment Review*, 843, 24 March, 29–32.

Ineson, L., Batty, L. and Wynne, J. (2001) 'Tour management and occupational stress', paper presented at the *2001 EuroChrie Conference*, Switzerland.

Institute of Alcohol Studies (2006) 'Alcohol in Europe: a public health perspective', available at http://ec.europa.eu/health-eu/news_alcoholineurope_en.htm (accessed 1 June 2006).

Institute of Alcohol Studies (2009) 'Alcohol and the workplace', available at http://www.ias.org.uk/resources/factsheets/workplace.pdf (accessed 16 January 2012).

International Labour Organization (1999) *Sexual Harassment: An ILO Survey of Company Practice*, Geneva: ILO.

International Labour Organization (2001) *Human Resource Development, Employment and Globalization in the Hotel Catering and Tourism Sector*, Geneva: ILO.

International Labour Organization (2010a) 'Employment in tourism to grow significantly over the coming decade, say ILO report', available at http://www.ilocarib.org.tt/portal/index.php?option=com_content&task=view&id=1440&Itemid=368 (accessed 13 October 2011).

International Labour Organization (2010b) *Developments and Challenges in the Hospitality and Tourism Sector*, Geneva: ILO.

International Labour Organization (2011) *Equality at Work: The Continuing Challenge*, Geneva: ILO.

International Transport Workers Federation (2004) 'The cuts don't work', available at http://www.itfglobal.org/transport-international/ti10cuts.cfm (accessed 2 July 2006).

Jackson, M., Goldthorpe, J. and Mills, C. (2005) 'Education, employers and class mobility', *Research in Social Stratification and Mobility*, 23, 1–30.

Jago, L. and Mair, J. (2009) 'Career theory and major event employment', in T. Baum, M. Deery, C. Hanlon, L. Lockstone and K. Smith (eds), *People and Work in Events and Conventions: A Research Perspective*, Wallingford: CABI.

James, S. (2006) 'Adding new ingredients to an old recipe: NVQs and the influence of CATERBASE', SKOPE Issue Paper 13, Universities of Cardiff and Oxford.

Jameson, S. (2000) 'Recruitment and training in small firms', *Journal of European Industrial Training*, 24, 1, 43–9.

Jansen-Verbeke, M. (1996) 'Cross-cultural differences in the practices of hotel managers: a study of Dutch and Belgian hotel managers', *Tourism Management*, 17, 7, 544–8.

Janta, H., Ladkin, A., Brown, L. and Lugosi, P. (2011) 'Employment experiences of Polish migrant workers in the UK hospitality sector', *Tourism Management*, 32, 1006–19.

Jones, C., Nickson, D. and Taylor, G. (1997) 'Whatever it takes? Managing "empowered" employees and the service encounter in the international hotel industry', *Work, Employment and Society*, 11, 3, 541–54.

Jones, R. and Vasagar, J. (2006) 'Budget airline launches bid to employ some of its passengers', *Guardian*, 1 July, available at http://www.guardian.co.uk/business/2006/jul/01/theairlineindustry.uknews (accessed 13 August 2011).

Joppe, M. (2012) 'Migrant workers: challenges and opportunities in addressing tourism labour shortages', *Tourism Management*, 33, 3, 662–71.

Kakabadse, A. and Kakabadse, N. (2004) *Intimacy: International Survey of the Sex Lives of People at Work*, Basingstoke: Palgrave.

Kandola, R. and Fullerton, J. (1998) *Diversity in Action: Managing the Mosaic*, 2nd edn, London: CIPD.

Keep, E. (2005) 'Skills, training and the quest for the holy grail of influence', in S. Bach (ed.), *Managing Human Resources: Personnel Management in Transition*, 4th edn, Oxford: Blackwell.

Keep, E. and James, S. (2010) 'What incentives to learn at the bottom end of the labour market?', SKOPE Research Paper, No. 94, Universities of Cardiff and Oxford.

Keep, E. and James, S. (2011) 'Employer demand for apprenticeships', in T. Dolphin and T. Lanning (eds), *Rethinking Apprenticeships*, London: Institute of Public Policy Research.

Keep, E. and Mayhew, K. (1999) *The Leisure Sector (Skills Task Force Research Paper 6)*, London: DfEE.

Kelliher, C. and Johnson, K. (1997) 'Personnel management in hotels: an update – a move to human resource management?', *Progress in Tourism and Hospitality Research*, 3, 321–31.

Kelliher, C. and Perrett, G. (2001) 'Business strategy and approaches to HRM: a case study of new developments in the United Kingdom restaurant industry', *Personnel Review*, 30, 4, 421–37.

Kelliher, C. and Riley, M. (2003) 'Beyond flexibility: some by-products of functional flexibility', *Service Industries Journal*, 23, 4, 98–113.

Kelly, S., Patel, R., Patel, D., Pullen, C., Balfour, J. and Ashmead, B. (2011) *Business as Usual? Increasing Employer Investment in Skills*, London: LSN.

Kemp, S. and Dwyer, L. (2001) 'An examination of organizational culture: the Regent Hotel, Sydney', *International Journal of Hospitality Management*, 20, 1, 77–93.

Kersley, B., Alpin, C., Forth, J., Bryson, A., Bewley, H., Gix, G. and Oxenbridge, S. (2006) *Inside the Workplace: Findings from the 2004 Workplace Employment Relations Survey*, London: Routledge.

Kirby, J. (2007) 'Bar staff most at risk of drink-related death', *Guardian*, 24 August, 7.

Klidas, A. (2002) 'Employee empowerment in the European cultural context: findings from the hotel industry', Paper presented at the *CRANET 2nd International Conference on Human Resource Management in Europe: Trends and Challenges*, Athens.

Know, A. and Walsh, J. (2005) 'Organizational flexibility and HRM in the hotel industry: evidence from Australia', *Human Resource Management Journal*, 15, 1, 57–75.

Knox, A. and Nickson, D. (2007) 'Regulation in Australian hotels: is there a lesson for the UK?', *Employee Relations*, 29, 1, 50–67.

Kumra, S. and Manfredi, S. (2012) *Managing Equality and Diversity: Theory and Practice*, Oxford: Oxford University Press.

Kusluvan, S., Kusluvan, Z., Ilhan, I. and Buyruk, L. (2010) 'The human dimension: a review of human resource management issues in the tourism and hospitality industry', *Cornell Hospitality Quarterly*, 51, 2, 171–214.

Labour Research Department (1997) *Performance Appraisal*, London: LRD.

Labour Research Department (1998) 'Short changing young workers', *Labour Research*, December, 11–13.

Labour Research Department (2000a) *Tackling Disability Discrimination*, London: LRD.

Labour Research Department (2000b) 'UK soft on homophobia', *Labour Research*, July, 10–12.

Labour Research Department (2002) 'Europe "must address stress"', *Labour Research*, October, 20–2.

Labour Research Department (2003a) 'Employers warned over bias in aptitude tests', *Labour Research*, December, 25.

Labour Research Department (2003b) 'Two cheers for gay-bias rules', *Labour Research*, July, 11–13.

Labour Research Department (2003c) 'Can "help firms" really stop staff stress?', *Labour Research*, August, 9–11.

Labour Research Department (2003d) 'Can "zero tolerance" deliver?', *Labour Research*, May, 12–15.

Labour Research Department (2004) 'Be organized, be consulted', *Labour Research*, November, 17–19.

Labour Research Department (2005) 'Legal changes define sexual harassment', *Labour Research*, November, 21.

Labour Research Department (2007) 'Disability audits offer a route to equality in the workplace', *Workplace Report*, January, 15–16.

Labour Research Department (2008a) 'Study claims being out at work boosts performance', *Workplace Report*, July, 6.

Labour Research Department (2008b) 'Labour gets tougher on minimum wage evasion', *Labour Research*, November, 25.

Labour Research Department (2008c) *Drug and Alcohol Policies at Work*, London: LRD.

Labour Research Department (2009) *Disciplinary and Grievance Procedures*, London: LRD.

Labour Research Department (2010) *Discrimination at Work: A Guide to the Equality Act 2010*, London: LRD.

Labour Research Department (2011a) *The Agency Worker Regulation*, London: LRD.

Labour Research Department (2011b) 'Women's presence in UK workforce gets bigger', *Labour Research*, March, 28.

Labour Research Department (2011c) 'Age bias "most common form of discrimination"', *Workplace Report*, June, 6.

Labour Research Department (2011d) 'Big-company chief paid 145 times average', *Workplace Report*, May, 3.

Labour Research Department (2011e) *Law at Work*, London: LRD.

Labour Research Department (2011f) 'Equality further changes', *Labour Research*, May, 27.

Labour Research Department (2011g) *Stress and Mental Health at Work*, London: LRD.

Labour Research Department (2012a) 'Workers' rights come under siege', *Labour Research*, January, 16–18.

Labour Research Department (2012b) 'Do unions have youth appeal?', *Labour Research*, April, 16–18.

Labour Research Department (2012c) 'Qualifying period for dismissal claims rises', *Labour Research*, March, 23.

Ladki, S. (1994) 'Strategies for combating fear of AIDS in the hospitality industry', *Hospitality and Tourism Educator*, 6, 1, 75–7.

Lai, P. and Baum, T. (2005) 'Just-in-time labour supply in the hotel sector: the role of agencies', *Employee Relations*, 27, 1, 86–102.

Lanning, T. (2011) 'Why rethink apprenticeships?', in T. Dolphin and T. Lanning (eds), *Rethinking Apprenticeships*, London: Institute of Public Policy Research.

Lashley, C. (2001) *Empowerment HR Strategies for Service Excellence*, Oxford: Butterworth-Heinemann.

Lashley, C. and Lee-Ross, D. (2003) *Organization Behaviour for Leisure Services*, Oxford: Butterworth-Heinemann.

Lashley, C. and Taylor, S. (1998) 'Hospitality retail operations types and styles in the management of human resources', *Journal of Retailing and Consumer Services*, 5, 3, 153–65.

Latham, G., Sulsky, L. and MacDonald, H. (2008) 'Performance management', in P. Boxall, J. Purcell and P. Wright (eds), *The Oxford Handbook of Human Resource Management*, Oxford: Oxford University Press.

Law, J., Pearce, P. and Woods, B. (1995) 'Stress and coping in tourist attraction employees', *Tourism Management*, 16, 4, 277–84.

Legge, K. (1994) 'Managing culture: fact or fiction', in K. Sisson (ed.), *Personnel Management: A Comprehensive Guide to Theory and Practice in Britain*, Oxford: Blackwell.

Lin, Y. (2006) 'The incidence of sexual harassment of students while undergoing practicum training experience in the Taiwanese hospitality industry: individual reactions and relationships to perpetrators', *Tourism Management*, 27, 1, 51–68.

Lindsay, C. and McQuaid, R.W. (2004) 'Avoiding the "McJobs": unemployed job seekers and attitudes to service work', *Work, Employment and Society*, 18, 2, 297–319.

Lloyd, C. and Payne, J. (2012) 'Flat whites: who gets progression in the UK café sector?', *Industrial Relations*, 43, 1, 38–52.

Lockyer, C. and Scholarios, D. (2004) 'Selecting hotel staff: why best practice does not always work', *International Journal of Contemporary Hospitality Management*, 16, 2, 121–35.

Loe, M. (1996) 'Working for men at the intersection of power, gender and sexuality', *Sociological Enquiry*, 66, 4, 399–421.

Low Pay Commission (2006) *National Minimum Wage Low Pay Commission Report 2006*, Norwich: The Stationery Office.

Low Pay Commission (2011) *National Minimum Wage Low Pay Commission Report 2011*, Norwich: The Stationery Office.

Lowe, C. (2002) 'Marriott's cross-training', *Leisure and Hospitality Business*, 29 November, 14.

Lucas, R. (1995) *Managing Employee Relations in the Hotel and Catering Industry*, London: Cassell.

Lucas, R. (2004) *Employment Relations in the Hospitality and Tourism Industries*, London: Routledge.

Lucas, R. (2009) 'Is low unionization in the British hospitality industry due to industry characteristics?', *International Journal of Hospitality Management*, 28, 1, 42–52.

Lucas, R. and Mansfield, S. (2010) 'The use of migrant labour in the hospitality sector: current and future implications', in M. Ruhs and B. Anderson (eds), *Who Needs Migrant Workers: Labour Shortages, Immigration and Public Policy*, Oxford: Oxford University Press.

Lucas, R. and Radiven, N. (1998) 'After wages councils: minimum pay and practice', *Human Resource Management Journal*, 8, 4, 5–19.

Lucas, R., Marinova, M., Kucerova, J. and Vetrokova, M. (2004) 'HRM practices in emerging economies: a long way to go in the Slovak hotel industry?', *International Journal of Human Resource Management*, 15, 7, 1262–79.

Lynn, M. (1996) 'Seven ways to increase servers' tips', *Cornell Hotel and Restaurant Administration Quarterly*, 37, 24–9.

Lynn, M. (2001) 'Restaurant tipping and service quality', *Cornell Hotel and Restaurant Administration Quarterly*, 42, 14–20.

Lynn, M. (2003) 'Tip levels and service: an update, extension, and reconciliation', *Cornell Hotel and Restaurant Administration Quarterly*, 44, 5–6, 139–48.

Lynn, M. and McCall, M. (2009) 'Techniques for increasing servers' tips', *Cornell Hospitality Quarterly*, 50, 2, 198–208.

Lynn, M., Zinkhan, G. and Harris, J. (1993) 'Consumer tipping: a cross-country study', *Journal of Consumer Research*, 20, 478–88.

MacAskill, E. (2006) 'US blocking international deal on fighting Aids', *Guardian*, 2 June, 18.

Macaulay, I. and Wood, R. (1992) 'Hotel and catering industry employees' attitudes towards trade unions', *Employee Relations*, 14, 2, 20–8.

McCollum, D. and Findlay, A. (2011) 'Employer and labour provider perspectives on Eastern European migration to the UK', ESRC Centre for Population Change Working Paper No. 14.

MacDonald, C. and Sirianni, C. (1996) *Working in the Service Society*, Philadelphia, PA: Temple University Press.

McGregor, D. (1957) 'An uneasy look at performance appraisal', *Harvard Business Review*, 35, 3, 89–94.

McGunnigle, P. and Jameson, S. (2000) 'HRM in UK hotels: a focus on commitment', *Employee Relations*, 22, 4, 403–22.

McKenna, E. and Beech, N. (2008) *Human Resource Management: A Concise Analysis*, 2nd edn, Harlow: Pearson Education Limited.

McSweeney, B. (2002a) 'Hofstede's model of national cultural differences and their consequences: a triumph of faith – a failure of analysis', *Human Relations*, 55, 1, 89–118.

McSweeney, B. (2002b) 'The essentials of scholarship: a reply to Geert Hofstede', *Human Relations*, 55, 11, 1363–72.

Magd, H. (2003) 'Management attitudes and perceptions of older employees in hospitality management', *International Journal of Hospitality Management*, 15, 7, 393–401.

Mair, J. (2009) 'The events industry: the employment context', in T. Baum, M. Deery, C. Hanlon, L. Lockstone and K. Smith (eds), *People and Work in Events and Conventions: A Research Perspective*, Wallingford: CABI.

Mano, R. and Gabriel, Y. (2006) 'Workplace romances in cold and hot organizational climates: the experiences of Israel and Taiwan', *Human Relations*, 59, 1, 7–35.

Marchington, M. and Suter, J. (2012) 'Where informality really matters: patterns of employee involvement and participation in a non-union firm', *Industrial Relations*.

Marchington, M. and Wilkinson, A. (1996) *Core Personnel and Development*, London: CIPD.

Marchington, M. and Wilkinson, A. (2005a) *Human Resource Management at Work: People Management and Development*, 3rd edn, London: CIPD.

Marchington, M. and Wilkinson, A. (2005b) 'Direct participation and involvement', in S. Bach (ed.), *Managing Human Resources: Personnel Management in Transition*, 4th edn, Oxford: Blackwell.

Marchington, M. and Wilkinson, A. (2008) *Human Resource Management at Work: People Management and Development*, 4th edn, London: CIPD.

Mars, G. and Mitchell, P. (1976) *Room for Reform? A Case Study of Industrial Relations in the Hotel Industry*, Milton Keynes: Open University Press.

Mars, G. and Nicod, M. (1984) *The World of Waiters*, London: George Allen and Unwin.

Mayrhofer, W. and Brewster, C. (1996) 'In praise of ethnocentricity: expatriate policies in European multinationals', *The International Executive*, 38, 6, 749–78.

Metcalf, D. (1999) 'The British National Minimum Wage', *British Journal of Industrial Relations*, 37, 2, 171–201.

Metcalf, D. (2009) 'Why has the British National Minimum Wage had little or no impact on employment?', *Journal of Industrial Relations*, 50, 3, 489–512.

Metcalf, H. and Meadows, P. (2010) *Second Survey of Employers' Policies, Practices and Preferences Relating to Age, 2010*, London: Department for Business, Innovation and Skills and the Department for Work and Pensions.

Miao, L., Alder, H. and Xu, X. (2011) 'A stakeholder approach to expatriate management: perceptions of expatriate managers in China', *International Journal of Hospitality Management*, 30, 3, 530–41.

Migration Advisory Committee (2011) 'Skilled shortage sensible: full review of the recommended shortage occupation lists for the UK and Scotland', available at http://www.ukba.homeoffice.gov.uk/sitecontent/documents/aboutus/working withus/mac/skilled-shortage-sensible/skilled-report.pdf?view=Binary (accessed 5 November 2011).

Mills, A. (1996) 'Strategy, sexuality and the stratosphere: airlines and the gendering of organizations', in L. Morris and E. Stina Lyon (eds), *Gender Relations in Public and Private: New Research Perspectives*, Basingstoke: Macmillan.

Milmo, D. (2007) 'BA loses £80m over cabin crew strike threat', *Guardian*, 3 February, 34.

Milmo, D. (2009) 'United or divided? Union tensions that lay behind BA cabin crew strike plan', *Observer*, 20 December, Business Section, 3.

Milmo, D. (2010) 'Chaos looms for BA passengers as Unite calls 20 days of strikes', *Guardian*, 18 May, 14.

Milmo, D. (2011) 'British Airways settles cabin crew dispute', *Guardian*, 22 June, 3.

Milmo, D. and Webb, T. (2009) 'Talks to avert strike action deadlocked as Brown turns on the heat', *Guardian*, 17 December, 4.

Milne, S. (1998a) 'Politics of the pig trough', *Guardian*, 15 September, 10.

Milne, S. (1998b) 'Holiday rules will aid 4m', *Guardian*, 6 April, 9.

Milne, S. and White, M. (1998) 'Read my lips "you greedy bastards"', *Guardian*, 15 September, 7.

Ministry of Justice (2011) 'Employment tribunal and EAT statistics, 2010–11', available at http://www.justice.gov.uk/downloads/statistics/mojstats/employment-trib-stats-april-march-2010–11.pdf (accessed 17 April 2012).

Mkono, M. (2010) 'Zimbabwean hospitality students' experience of sexual harassment in the hotel industry', *Tourism Management*, 29, 4, 729–35.

Moggridge, M. (2009) 'Let the games begin', *Hospitality*, 15, 26–30.

Morgan, M. and Nickson, D. (2001) 'Uncivil aviation: a review of the air rage phenomenon', *International Journal of Tourism Research*, 3, 6, 443–57.

Morgan, O. (2003) 'Swipe strike costs BA £50m', *Observer Business Section*, 27 July, 1.

Mutch, F. (1998) 'Sex sells: so why not in restaurants?', *Caterer and Hotelkeeper*, 30 April, 23.

Mwaura, G., Sutton, J. and Roberts, D. (1998) 'Corporate and national culture: an irreconcilable dilemma for the hospitality manager?', *International Journal of Contemporary Hospitality Management*, 10, 6, 212–20.

Nankevis, A. and Debrah, Y. (1995) 'Human resource management in hotels: a comparative study', *Tourism Management*, 16, 7, 507–13.

National Audit Office (2012) *Adult Apprenticeships*, London: The Stationery Office.

Nickson, D. (1997) '"Colorful stories"' or historical insight? A review of the auto/biographies of Charles Forte, Conrad Hilton, J.W. Marriott and Kemmons Wilson', *Journal of Hospitality and Tourism Research*, 21, 1, 179–92.

Nickson, D. (1999) 'A review of the internationalization strategies of three hotel companies with a particular focus on human resource management', unpublished PhD Thesis, University of Strathclyde.

Nickson, D. and Warhurst, C. (2001) 'From globalization to internationalization to Americanization: the example of "Little Americas" in the hotel sector', in M. Hughes and J. Taggart (eds), *Multinationals in a New Era: International Strategy and Management*, Basingstoke: Palgrave.

Nickson, D. and Wood, R.C. (2000) 'HRM in the hotel industry: a comment and response', *Human Resource Management Journal*, 10, 4, 88–90.

Nickson, D., Warhurst, C., Witz, A. and Cullen, A.M. (2001) 'The importance of being aesthetic: work, employment and service organization', in A. Sturdy, I. Grugulis and H. Wilmott (eds) *Customer Service: Empowerment and Entrapment*, Basingstoke: Palgrave.

Nickson, D., Warhurst, C., Cullen, A.M. and Watt, A. (2003) 'Bringing in the excluded? Aesthetic labour, skills and training in the new economy', *Journal of Education and Work*, 16, 2, 185–203.

Nickson, D., Warhurst, C. and Dutton, E. (2005) 'The importance of attitude and appearance in the service encounter in retail and hospitality', *Managing Service Quality*, 15, 2, 195–208.

Noon, M. (2010a) 'Managing equality and diversity', in J. Beardwell and T. Claydon (eds), *Human Resource Management: A Contemporary Approach*, 6th edn, London: Financial Times/Prentice Hall.

Noon, M. (2010b) 'The shackled runner: time to rethink positive discrimination?', *Work, Employment and Society*, 24, 4, 728–39.

North West Development Agency (2004) *Commonwealth Games Benefit Study: Final Report*, Manchester: NWDA.

Nuffield Health (2012) 'Economic fears forcing one third of staff into work when sick', available at http://www.nuffieldhealth.com/about-us/news/one-third-of-staff-into-work-when-sick-17–01–12 (accessed 17 January 2012).

O'Brien, R. (1977) *Marriott: The J Willard Marriott Story*, Salt Lake City, UT: Desert Book Company.

Ogbonna, E. (1992) 'Organizational culture and human resource management', in P. Blyton and P. Turnbull (eds), *Reassessing Human Resource Management*, London: Sage.

Ogbonna, E. and Harris, L. (2002a) 'Managing organizational culture: insights from the hospitality industry', *Human Resource Management Journal*, 12, 1, 33–53.

Ogbonna, E. and Harris, L. (2002b) 'Institutionalization of tipping as a source of managerial control', *British Journal of Industrial Relations*, 40, 4, 725–52.

Ogbonna, E. and Wilkinson, B. (1990) 'Corporate strategy and corporate culture: the view from the checkout', *Personnel Review*, 19, 4, 9–15.

O'Hara, M. (2007) 'Living with a label', *Guardian Society*, 24 January, 3.

Olie, R. (1995) 'The "culture" factor in personnel and organization policies', in A. Harzing and J. van Ruysseveldt (eds), *International Human Resource Management*, London: Sage.

Olins, W. (1991) *Corporate Identity*, London: Thames and Hudson.

Opportunity Now (2005) *Review 05:06: All About Opportunity Now and Its Future Plans*, London: Opportunity Now.

Overell, S. (2006) 'Fast forward', *People Management*, 9 February, 26–31.

Packer, N. (1998) 'Women driven away by kitchen culture', *Caterer and Hotelkeeper*, 21 May, 5.

Parry, E. and Tyson, S. (2008) 'An analysis of the use and success of online recruitment methods in the UK', *Human Resource Management Journal*, 18, 3, 257–74.

Paton, N. (2010) 'Preparing for the upturn', *UK's Best Workplaces: Special Report*, London: Great Places to Work Institute.

Pauuwe, J. and Dewe, P. (1995) 'Organizational structure of multinational corporations', in A.W. Harzing and J. van Ruysseveldt (eds), *International Human Resource Management*, London: Sage.

People 1st (2010a) *Sector Skills Assessment for the UK's Hospitality, Leisure, Travel and Tourism Sector*, London: People 1st.

People 1st (2010b) *The Case for Change: Women Working in the Hospitality, Leisure, Travel and Tourism Sector*, London: People 1st.

People 1st (2010c) *Labour Market Review of the Events Industry*, London: People 1st.

People 1st (2011a) *Communication 1st 2011*, London: People 1st.

People 1st (2011b) *State of the Nation Report 2011*, London: People 1st.

Perlmutter, H. (1969) 'The torturous evolution of the multinational corporation', *Columbia Journal of World Business*, 4, 1, 9–18.

*Personnel Today* (2010) 'Grievances: what employers need to know to avoid or deal with them', available at http://www.personneltoday.com/articles/2010/04/22/55312/grievances-what-employers-need-to-know-to-avoid-or-deal-with-them.html (accessed 17 April 2012).

Peters, T. and Waterman, R. (1982) *In Search of Excellence: Lessons from America's Best-run Companies*, London: Harper and Row.

Pizam, A. (2010) 'Alcoholism among hospitality employees', *International Journal of Hospitality Management*, 29, 4, 547–8.

Poulston, J. (2008) 'Metamorphosis in hospitality: a tradition of sexual harassment', *International Journal of Hospitality Management*, 27, 2, 232–40.

Poulston, J. (2009) 'Working conditions in hospitality: employees' views of the dissatisfactory hygiene factors', *Journal of Quality Assurance in Hospitality and Tourism*, 10, 1, 23–43.

Price, L. (1994) 'Poor personnel practice in the hotel and catering industry: does it matter?', *Human Resource Management Journal*, 4, 4, 44–62.

Qu, H. and Cheng, S.Y. (1996) 'Attitudes towards utilising older workers in the Hong Kong hotel industry', *International Journal of Hospitality Management*, 15, 3, 245–54.

Qualifications and Curriculum Authority (2003) *Establishing Qualification Requirements: Hospitality and Catering Industry*, London: QCA.

Race for Opportunity (2004) *RFO Newsletter*, Summer, 16.

Race for Opportunity (2009a) *Race to the Top: The Place of Ethnic Minority Groups Within the UK Workforce*, London: Race for Opportunity.

Race for Opportunity (2009b) *RfO Benchmarking Report 2009: Transparency at the Heart of Diversity*, London: Race for Opportunity.

Race for Opportunity (2010) *Race to the Future: The Challenges and Opportunities for Ethnic Minorities in the UK Workforce in 2025*, London: Race for Opportunity.

Radcliffe, S. (2009) 'Working with HIV: tips for employers and managers', *Hospitality*, 16, 50–1.

Rafaeli, A. (1993) 'Dress and behaviour of customer contact employees: a framework for analysis', *Services Marketing and Management*, 2, 175–211.

Ralston, R., Downward, P. and Lumsden, L. (2004) 'The expectations of volunteers prior to the XVII Commonwealth Games, 2002: a qualitative study', *Event Management*, 9, 1–2, 13–26.

Raub, S. and Streit, E. (2006) 'Realistic recruitment: an empirical study of the cruise industry', *International Journal of Contemporary Hospitality Management*, 18, 4, 278–89.

Rayner, J. (1998) 'Bolshie staff? We have ways of purging them', *Observer*, 13 December, 6.

Recruitment and Employment Confederation (2010) *Recruitment Industry Trends 2009/10*, London: REC.

Redman, T. (2009) 'Performance appraisal', in T. Redman and A. Wilkinson (eds), *Contemporary Human Resource Management: Texts and Cases*, 3rd edn, Harlow: Prentice Hall.

Redman, T. and Matthews, B. (1998) 'Service quality and human resource management: a review and research agenda', *Personnel Review*, 27, 1, 57–77.

Riddell, S., Edward, S., Weedon, E. and Ahlgren, L. (2010) *Disability, Skills and Employment: A Review of Recent Statistics and Literature on Policy and Initiatives*, London: Equality and Human Rights Commission.

Riley, M. (1992) 'Functional flexibility in hotels: is it feasible?', *Tourism Management*, 13, 4, 363–67.

Riley, M. (1996) *Human Resource Management in the Hospitality and Tourism Industry*, 2nd edn, Oxford: Butterworth-Heinemann.

Riley, M. and Szivas, E. (2009) 'The valuation of skill and the configuration of HRM', *Tourism Economics*, 15, 1, 105–20.

Riley, M., Gore, J. and Kelliher, C. (2000) 'Economic determinism and human resource management practice in the hospitality and tourism industry', *Tourism and Hospitality Research*, 2, 2, 118–28.

Ritzer, G. (2004) *The McDonaldization of Society, Revised New Century Edition*, Thousand Oaks, CA: Pine Forge Press.

Roche, E. (2004) 'If you can't stand the heat ... get some balls', *Guardian: G2*, 28 January, available at http://www.guardian.co.uk/g2/story/0,03604,1132605,00. html (accessed 12 June 2006).

Rodger, A. (1952) *The Seven Point Plan*, London: National Institute for Industrial Psychology.

Roper, A., Brookes, M., Price, L. and Hampton, A. (1997) 'Towards an understanding of centricity: profiling international hotel groups', in N. Hemmington (ed.), *Proceedings of the Sixth Annual Council for Hospitality Management Education (CHME) Research Conference*, Oxford: Oxford Brookes University.

Roper, A., Doherty, L., Brookes, M. and Hampton, A. (1998) '"Company Man" meets international hotel customer', in D. Littlejohn (ed.), *Proceedings of the Seventh Annual Council for Hospitality Management Education (CHME) Annual Conference*, Glasgow: Glasgow Caledonian University.

Rowson, B. (2000) 'Much ado about nothing: the impact on small hotels of the national minimum wage', *The Hospitality Review*, January, 15–17.

Royle, T. (2002) 'Just say no! Union busting in the European fast food industry: the case of McDonalds', *Industrial Relations Journal*, 33, 3, 262–78.

Royle, T. and Towers, B. (2002) *Labour Relations in the Global Fast Food Industry*, London: Routledge.

Salameh, M. and Barrows, C. (2001) 'The role of training in achieving TQM in restaurants', *Journal of Quality Assurance in Hospitality and Tourism*, 1, 4, 73–95.

Salamon, M. (1992) *Industrial Relations: Theory and Practice*, Harlow: Prentice Hall.

Salamon, M. (2000) *Industrial Relations: Theory and Practice*, 4th edn, Harlow: Prentice Hall.

Salipante, P. and Bouwen, R. (1990) 'Behavioural analysis of grievances: conflict, sources, complexity and transformation', *Employee Relations*, 12, 3, 17–22.

Sappal, S. (2005) 'Top scorers', *People Management*, 13 January, 38–40.

Schein, E. (1985) *Organizational Culture and Leadership*, San Francisco, CA: Jossey-Bass Publishers.

Schuler, R. and Jackson, S. (1987) 'Linking competitive strategy with human resource management', *The Academy of Management Executive*, 1, 3, 207–19.

Schuler, R., Dowling, P. and De Ceiri, H. (1993) 'An integrative framework of strategic international human resource management', *International Journal of Human Resource Management*, 4, 4, 717–65.

Scottish Tourism Research Unit (1998) *International Benchmarking and Best Practice Study of Training and Education for Tourism*, Glasgow: STRU.

Scullion, H., Collings, D. and Gunnigle, P. (2007) 'International human resource management in the 21st century: emerging themes and contemporary debates', *Human Resource Management Journal*, 17, 4, 309–19.

Sealy, R. and Vinnicombe, S. (2012) *The Female FTSE Board Report 2012: Milestone or Millstone?*, Cranfield: Cranfield University School of Management.

Sharkey, G. (2009a) 'Hundreds of jobs go at Accor and Hilton', *Caterer and Hotelkeeper*, 10 July, 6.

Sharkey, G. (2009b) 'Campaigners hit out at hospitality over Living Wage', *Caterer and Hotelkeeper*, 3 April, 7.

Sherwyn, D., Kaufman, E. and Klausner, A. (2000) 'Same-sex sexual harassment: how the "equal opportunity harasser" became a legitimate defence', *Cornell Hotel and Restaurant Administration Quarterly*, 41, 6, 75–80.

Sheth, J. (2011) *Chindia Rising: Implications for Global Competitiveness*, Decatur, GA: Incore Publishing.

Siedsma, A. (2011) 'Marriott hopes to win with Facebook game', *Workforce Management Online*, available at http://www.workforce.com (accessed 15 January 2012).

Simms, S. (2005) 'Better by design', *People Management*, 29 September, 24–9.

Sisson, K. (2005) 'Responding to Mike Emmott: what "industrial relations" suggests should be at the heart of "employee relations"', available at http://buira.org.uk/component/option,com_docman/Itemid,/task,doc_download/gid,2 (accessed 5 July 2006).

Sisson, K. (2008) 'Putting the record straight: industrial relations and the employment relationship', available at http://www2.warwick.ac.uk/fac/soc/wbs/research/irru/wpir/wpir_88.pdf (accessed 24 April 2012).

Skills for Business (2008) 'World class service . . . for 2012 and beyond', available at http://www.podium.ac.uk/resources/download/76/world-class-customer-service-for-2012-and-beyond.pdf (accessed 13 March 2012).

Smedley, T. (2011) 'Cap in hand', *People Management*, May, 22–5.

Smethhurst, S. (2004a) 'Ageism rife in UK workplace', *People Management*, 15 January, 10.

Smith, C. and Meiksins, P. (1995) 'Systems, society and dominance effects in cross-national organizational analysis', *Work, Employment and Society*, 9, 2, 241–67.

Smith, K. and Lockstone, L. (2009) 'Involving and keeping event volunteers: management insights from cultural festivals', in T. Baum, M. Deery, C. Hanlon, L. Lockstone and K. Smith (eds), *People and Work in Events and Conventions: A Research Perspective*, Wallingford: CABI.

Smith, P. (2002) '*Culture's Consequences*: something old and something new', *Human Relations*, 55, 1, 119–35.

Somner, T. (2006) 'Is the 21st century going to be the Asian century?', available at http://www.asienkunde.de/content/zeitschrift_asien/archiv/pdf/A100_070_078.pdf (accessed 30 April 2012).

Speizer, I. (2004) 'Diversity on the menu', *Workforce Management*, November, 41–5.

Spiess, L. and Waring, P. (2005) 'Emotional and aesthetic labour: cost minimization and the labour process in the Asia Pacific airline industry', *Employee Relations*, 27, 2, 193–207.

Stevens, M. (2009) 'McDonald's relishes the benefits of older workers', *People Management*, 27 August, 7.

Stevens, M. (2011) 'Olympic targets make diversity the real winner', *People Management*, 10 February, 7.

Storey, J. (1987) 'Developments in the management of human resources: an interim report', Warwick Papers in Industrial Relations No. 17, IRRU.

Storey, J. (1995) 'Human resource management: still marching on, or marching out?', in J. Storey (ed.), *Human Resource Management: A Critical Text*, London: Routledge.

Stratton, A. (2009) 'Coalition calls on government to regulate high pay', *Guardian*, 17 August, 4.

Sufi, T. and Lyons, H. (2003) 'Mission statements exposed', *International Journal of Contemporary Hospitality Management*, 15, 5, 255–62.

Sunoo, B. (1995) 'How fun flies at Southwest Airlines', *Personnel Journal*, 74, 6, 62–71.

Sweeney, A. (1995) 'Improving interpersonal relationships between staff and visitors with the "Welcome Host" scheme', *Proceedings of the Fourth Annual Council for Hospitality Management Education (CHME) Research Conference*, Brighton: University of Brighton.

Tailby, S. and Pollert, A. (2011) 'Non-unionized young workers and organizing the unorganized', *Economic and Industrial Democracy*, 32, 3, 499–522.

Tayeb, M. (1994) 'Organizations and national culture: methodology considered', *Organization Studies*, 15, 3, 429–46.

Taylor, P., Cunningham, I., Newsome, K. and Scholarios, D. (2010) '"Too scared to go sick": reformulating the research agenda on sickness absence', *Industrial Relations Journal*, 41, 4, 270–88.

Taylor, S. (1998) *Employee Resourcing*, London: IPM.

Taylor, S., Beechler, S. and Napier, N. (1996) 'Toward an integrative model of strategic international human resource management', *Academy of Management Review*, 21, 4, 959–85.

Thite, M., Wilkinson, A. and Shah, D. (2012) 'Internationalization and HRM strategies across subsidiaries in multinational corporations from emerging economies: a conceptual framework', *Journal of World Business*, 47, 2, 251–8.

Thomas, D. (2007) 'Hospitality staff are among the most likely to use Employment Tribunals', available at http://www.caterersearch.com/Articles/30/10/2007/316 978/hospitality-staff-are-among-most-likely-to-use-employment-tribunals.htm (accessed 16 April 2012).

Thomas, D. (2008) 'Marriott signs deal with Jobcentre Plus', *Caterer and Hotelkeeper*, 3 March, available at: http://www.caterersearch.com/Articles/2008/03/03/319369/ Marriott-signs-deal-with-JobCentre-Plus.htm (accessed 13 August 2011).

Thomas, D. (2009) 'Rogue hoteliers are paying staff below the minimum wage', *Caterer and Hotelkeeper*, 19 June, 7.

Thomas, D. (2010) 'A clear path to success', *Caterer and Hotelkeeper*, 8 January, 40–1.

Thompson, P. and McHugh, D. (2001) *Work Organizations: A Critical Introduction*, 3rd edn, Basingstoke: Macmillan Press.

Thornley, C. and Coffey, D. (1999) 'The Low Pay Commission in context', *Work, Employment and Society*, 13, 3, 525–38.

Tickle, L. (2011) 'Long and short apprenticeships', *Guardian Work*, 10 December, 1–2.

Toffler, A. (1990) *Power Shift*, New York, NY: Bantam.

Torrington, D. (1994) *International Human Resource Management: Think Globally, Act Locally*, London: Prentice Hall.

Torrington, D., Hall, L., Taylor, S. and Atkinson, C. (2011) *Human Resource Management*, 8th edn, London: Prentice Hall.

Townsend, K., Wilkinson, A. and Burgess, J. (2011) '*Filling the* gaps: patterns of formal and informal voice', available at http://www.griffith.edu.au/__data/assets/pdf_file/0006/293856/FILLING-THE-GAPS-7-3-11.pdf (accessed 24 April 2012).

Townsend, M. (2005) 'BA makes a meal of sari strike', *The Observer*, 14 August, 15.

Trades Union Congress (2003) *Alcohol and Work: A Potent Cocktail*, London: TUC.

Trades Union Congress (2010) 'Drug testing at work', available at http://www.tuc.org.uk/workplace/tuc-18000-f0.pdf (accessed 11 November 2011).

Trotter, A. (2005) 'Smells like team spirit', *Guardian Office Hours*, 21 March, 2–3.

Tum, J., Norton, P. and Wright, J. (2006) *Management of Event Operations*, Oxford: Butterworth-Heinemann.

Turnbull, D. (2000) 'Minimum impact', *The Hospitality Review*, January, 12–14.

Turnbull, P., Blyton, P. and Harvey, G. (2004) 'Cleared for take-off? Management–labour partnership in the European civil aviation industry', *European Journal of Industrial Relations*, 10, 3, 287–307.

Tyler, M. and Abbott, P. (1998) 'Chocs away: weighting watching in the contemporary airline industry', *Sociology*, 32, 3, 433–50.

Umbreit, T., Eder, R. and McConnell, J. (1986) 'Performance appraisals: making them fair and making them work', *Cornell Hotel and Restaurant Administration Quarterly*, 26, 4, 59–69.

UK Commission for Employment and Skills (2011) *UK Sector Skills Councils Annual Performance Report*, London: UKCES.

UNAIDS (2010) 'Global report: Sub-Saharan Africa', available at http://www.unaids.org/documents/20101123_FS_SSA_em_en.pdf (accessed 14 November 2011).

van der Wagen, L. (2007) *Human Resource Management for Events: Managing the Event Workforce*, Oxford: Butterworth-Heinemann.

van Maanen, J. (1991) 'The smile factory: work at Disneyland', in P. Frost, L. Moore, M. Louis, C. Lundberg and J. Martin (eds), *Reframing Organizational Culture*, London: Sage.

van Maanen, J. and Laurent, A. (1993) 'The flow of culture: some notes on globalization and the multinational corporation', in S. Ghoshal and D. Westney (eds), *Organization Theory and the Multinational Corporation*, New York, NY: St Martin's Press.

Vaughan, T. (2010) 'Tipping points', *Caterer and Hotelkeeper*, 7 May, 34.

Walker, B. (2010) 'Stress! Who needs it!', *Hospitality*, 17, 22–3.

Walker, B. (2011) 'What is the point of talking about older workers?', *Hospitality*, 21, 33–5.

Walsh, T. (1990) 'Flexible employment in the retail and hotel trades', in A. Pollert (ed.), *Farewell to Flexibility*, Oxford: Blackwell.

Ward, J. (2003) 'How to address sexual orientation', *People Management*, 23 October, 62–3.

Warhurst, C. and Nickson, D. (2001) *Looking Good, Sounding Right*, London: Industrial Society.

Watson, T. (1994) 'Recruitment and selection', in K. Sisson (ed.), *Personnel Management: A Comprehensive Guide to Theory and Practice in Britain*, Oxford: Blackwell.

Wearden, G. (2009) 'Aer Lingus to cut 670 jobs and slash pay', *Guardian*, 8 October, 28.

Wilborn, L. and Weaver, P. (2002) 'Diversity management training initiatives: a profile of current practices within the lodging industry', *Journal of Human Resources in Hospitality and Tourism*, 1, 4, 79–96.

Wilkinson, A. (1998) 'Empowerment: theory and practice', *Personnel Review*, 27, 1, 40–56.

Wills, J. (2005) 'The geography of union organizing in the low-paid service industries in the UK: lessons from the T&G's campaign to unionize the Dorchester in London', *Antipode*, 37, 1, 139–59.

Wilmott, H. (1993) 'Strength is ignorance; slavery is freedom: managing culture in modern organizations', *Journal of Management Studies*, 30, 4, 515–52.

Wisdom, B. (2012) 'A unique opportunity', *En Passant*, 41, 10–11.

Wisdom, L. (2010) 'Travel industry finds value in training', *En Passant*, 35, 48–9.

Witz, A., Warhurst, C. and Nickson, D. (2003) 'The labour of aesthetics and the aesthetics of organization', *Organization*, 10, 1, 33–54.

Wood, R.C. (1997a) *Working in Hotels and Catering*, 2nd edn, London: International Thomson Press.

Wood, R.C (1997b) 'Rhetoric, reason and rationality: the national minimum wage debate and the UK hospitality industry', *International Journal of Hospitality Management*, 16, 4, 329–44.

Woods, R., Sciarini, M. and Breiter, D. (1998) 'Performance appraisal in hotels', *Cornell Hotel and Restaurant Administration Quarterly*, 39, 2, 25–9.

World Travel and Tourism Council (2012) 'Benchmarking travel and tourism: global summary', available at http://www.wttc.org/site_media/uploads/downloads/WTTC_Sectors_Summary_Global.pdf (accessed 30 April 2012).

Worsfold, P. and McCann, C. (2000) 'Supervised work experience and sexual harassment', *International Journal of Contemporary Hospitality Management*, 12, 4, 249–55.

Zhang, H. and Wu, E. (2004) 'Human resource issues facing the hotel and travel industry in China', *International Journal of Contemporary Hospitality Management*, 16, 7, 424–8.

# Index

Page number in **bold** refer to figures, page numbers in *italic* refer to tables.

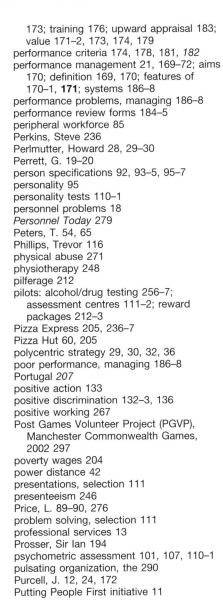